Whistleblower
Soldier
Spy

First published in 2013 by
Liberties Press
140 Terenure Road North | Terenure | Dublin 6W
Tel: +353 (1) 405 5701
www.libertiespress.com | info@libertiespress.com

Trade enquiries to Gill & Macmillan Distribution
Hume Avenue | Park West | Dublin 12
T: +353 (1) 500 9534 | F: +353 (1) 500 9595 | E: sales@gillmacmillan.ie

Distributed in the UK by
Turnaround Publisher Services
Unit 3 | Olympia Trading Estate | Coburg Road | London N22 6TZ
T: +44 (0) 20 8829 3000 | E: orders@turnaround-uk.com

Distributed in the United States by
IPM | 22841 Quicksilver Dr | Dulles, VA 20166

ISBN: 978-1-907593-96-3
2 4 6 8 10 9 7 5 3 1

A CIP record for this title is available from the British Library.

Cover design by Nina Lyons
Internal design by Liberties Press

Whistleblower
Soldier
Spy

A Journey into the Dark Heart of the
Global War on Terror

Tom Clonan

LIB
ERT
IES

Contents

Acknowledgements   9

Foreword   11

Prologue   15

Chapter 1   Welcome to Bosnia   19

Chapter 2   Breakfast in Bosnia   24

Chapter 3   After Dark   32

Chapter 4   Schweinfest   38

Chapter 5   Omarska   48

Chapter 6   Feminist Theory   55

Chapter 7   Sisters in Arms   65

Chapter 8   DFHQ   72

Chapter 9   Didn't I tell you not to fuck up?   81

Chapter 10   Girl Talk   92

Chapter 11   Sexual Harassment   98

Chapter 12   Farewell to Lebanon   106

Chapter 13   Farewell to Arms   116

Chapter 14   Ivory Tower   126

Chapter 15   Breaking News   131

Chapter 16   Iodine Tablets   141

Chapter 17   The Doyle Report   151

Chapter 18	We Break Things and Kill People	157
Chapter 19	Grey Lady	163
Chapter 20	Mission Accomplished	173
Chapter 21	Neuromuscular Disorder	179
Chapter 22	Investigations	187
Chapter 23	White Lady	195
Chapter 24	Beslan	205
Chapter 25	Court Case	213
Chapter 26	GTMO	221
Chapter 27	Cuba	231
Chapter 28	Camp Delta	241
Chapter 29	Camp Echo	250
Chapter 30	Landstuhl	260
Chapter 31	Polytrauma	269
Chapter 32	Bessbrook Mill	278
Chapter 33	Pauline	284
Chapter 34	Shannon	293
Chapter 35	Thunderbirds Are Go	304
Chapter 36	Missile Shield	313
Chapter 37	Syria	325
Chapter 38	Death	337
Chapter 39	Postscript	343

For Aideen,
Darach, Eoghan, Ailbhe, Rossa
&
our precious angel, Liadain

Acknowledgements

I wish to thank Aideen, Theo Dorgan, Denis O'Brien, Una Murray, Benji Bennett and Rosie Head for their mentoring, invaluable advice and sharp editorial skills. I am also very grateful to Seán O'Keeffe and the team at Liberties Press for their support and friendship.

I would like to thank the men and women of the Irish Defence Forces, with whom I am proud to have served at home and abroad. The Irish armed forces mentored me, educated me and above all, taught me to fight. I am grateful for these gifts – they have proved to be essential life skills. I wish to thank those journalists who allowed me to tell my story as a whistleblower. A big thank you also to my many colleagues at the Dublin Institute of Technology and the *Irish Times* for their collegiality and kindness. As a researcher and a journalist, I wish to extend a special thanks to all of those men and women who have spoken to me over the years. Thank you for sharing your most intimate stories and experiences with me. A final thanks for the remarkable journalists, diplomatic staff, politicians and spies that I have met over the last decade. The spies know who they are.

Foreword

This book is a memoir. To paraphrase another soldier, Erich Maria Remarque, this book is 'neither an accusation nor a confession, and least of all an adventure'. For this is a book about conflict. It deals with the intensely personal conflict of a grieving parent. It describes the conflict between the individual citizen and those who wield power. It is an exploration of global conflict. It is a retelling of my experiences as an army officer, whistleblower, journalist and father. The book spans the period from 1996 to 2009. For the author, these dates bracket a sequence of formative, traumatic, life-changing events.

The chronology commences as the Balkan Wars of the 1990s draw to a close. The book opens with my experiences as an international election monitor for the Organisation for Security Co-Operation in Europe, (OSCE) in Bosnia Herzegovina during the crucial autumn elections of 1996. These elections were a critical provision of the Dayton Accords, and for many signaled the end of open hostilities in Bosnia. The narrative continues with my doctoral research – as a serving army officer – into women soldiers in the Irish armed forces. This research revealed unacceptable levels of bullying, sexual harassment and sexual assault of female personnel within the Irish military. The memoir also deals with my transition from soldier to whistleblower and journalist. The book charts some of my experiences as a journalist from the beginning of the US Global War on Terror (GWOT) – in the immediate aftermath of 9/11 – to the official ending of the GWOT in 2009. In parallel with these events, the book also details my experience as a parent coming to terms with the diagnosis of a serious illness in a beloved child.

The account given here of my experiences as army officer, whistleblower, journalist and father are based on actual events. Due to the lengthy time period involved and the complexity of events covered, this book is not an exhaustive account; it is based on my own personal experiences, diaries and letters.

Consistent with this account however, I have changed the names of individuals from time to time throughout the book in order to protect identities. In the opening phase of the book, which deals with my time in Bosnia, I have deliberately changed the names of those people that I worked with and lived with during my brief time there. The events themselves are true. However, I have changed some small details here and there to mask the identities of certain individuals in order to protect them from hostile scrutiny.

In order to protect the sensitivities of those with whom I served in the Irish armed forces, I have changed the names of many of the personnel with whom I served in various operational units and at Defence Forces Headquarters. In addition, I have created a small number of fictionalised characters in order to obscure the identities of a number of key players in my research process and its aftermath. These composite characters do not represent any real person with whom I served in the armed forces. The events that occurred, however, are factual and are true as described here.

In order to protect the anonymity and confidentiality of my research participants – the women who took part in my doctoral research – I have created a fictional cast of female soldiers. In the phase of the book that deals with the research and its consequences, I have also altered the interview responses of the research participants. The quotations I use in this book, whilst similar in tone and language to those elicited at research interviews, differ from the original responses obtained during the PhD process. It is the story of my own personal journey through the research process and my subsequent experiences as a whistleblower. To this end, most of the army personnel that appear in this phase of the book, male and female, are composite, amalgamated characters and do not represent any real persons.

A full and frank account of my academic research into women in the Irish armed forces is contained within my doctoral thesis, 'Sisters in Arms, The Status and Roles Assigned Female Personnel in the Irish Defence Forces'. This PhD thesis is held in the library of Dublin City University. A further account of the conditions of service, discrimination and bullying experienced by female and male soldiers in the Irish armed forces is contained within the report of the Study Review Group – an independent enquiry into the findings of my doctoral research initiated, at my request, by Michael Smith TD, Irish Minister for Defence in 2001. A full list of all of my academic articles and publications is available through the electronic academic archive at the Dublin Institute of Technology.

Whilst the majority of the army personnel who feature here are composite characters, a very small number of key players in these events have been identified by name. I am very proud to have served with these individuals and am very grateful to them for the positive role they played in my professional and personal development.

I have used a similar approach in writing about my experiences at Camps Delta and Echo, Guantanamo Bay, Cuba, the US military's Landstuhl Regional Medical Centre, Germany and the British army's former base at Bessbrook Mill, Northern Ireland. I employed the same narrative method in describing my interactions with US military personnel in Shannon Airport and US Missile Defence Agency staff at NATO Headquarters in Brussels, Belgium. Most of the key players are identified by name. However, I have sought to protect those who spoke to me off the record by going to significant lengths to mask their true identities.

I have named all of those with whom I interacted in Lebanon, Syria and Iraq where possible and where memory allows. The experiences described in these pages are based on actual events and real people. At the time of writing, many of my Syrian contacts have become central players in Syria's civil war. Some stand accused of war crimes and crimes against humanity.

The *Irish Times'* electronic archive contains all of the articles and features I have written over the years on the US Global War on Terror and on other security-, defence- and terror-related issues. My TV and radio interviews during this period are archived and cached in digital repositories and can be accessed through various online search engines.

In attempting to contextualise these professional experiences, I have made extensive reference to my own personal and family circumstances. I have done so in order to try and communicate a wider truth about conflict – personal and global – fatherhood and loss. I have tried to communicate the experience of becoming a parent to five children. I have tried to honestly communicate the experience of loss of parents, siblings and a precious daughter. I have tried to openly and frankly communicate the experience of having a child with special needs. I have also tried to communicate the perplexing and disturbing experience of being a whistleblower in contemporary Ireland – and my experience of whistleblower 'reprisal'. I make no apologies for including this account here. It is neither a confession nor an accusation. It is an experience that speaks for itself.

Prologue

South Lebanon, UN Position 6-40 Al Yatun, Operation Grapes of Wrath
April 1996

The Israeli artillery position known as 'Gate 12' has been firing at us for days now. Thousands of artillery shells pounding our positions. Israeli air force jets and helicopter gunships saturate the area with fire. I pinch myself. I have to keep reminding myself, amid the smoke and the havoc, I am in Lebanon. I am an officer in the Irish army. A UN peacekeeper. Here to keep the peace. But by now, the country is on fire. Peace, man.

I'm sick of it. Sick of being in uniform. I resolve to burn the filthy combats I've been wearing for over a week now. Two litres of diesel. That's all it takes. Little Mac, the tech sergeant who tends the diesel generators on Post 6-40 in Al Yatun, fills up my plastic container from the fuel tank. A scratched and scuffed plastic carton that once held orange squash. It reminds me for a split second of picnics with my mum and dad as a kid in Ireland. But that was a long time ago.

Today, the sun-bleached UN position at Al Yatun is the setting for my epiphany. I take the sloshing carton of diesel down to my billet, kicking up dust in the blinding midday sunshine and heat. Diesel evaporating on the back of my hand, the familiar kerosene smell drowning out the stench of human shit that permeates Al Yatun.

Earlier that day I had walked out of our neighbouring UN position in Qana. It was there, in the village of Qana, that I saw the remains of over one hundred Lebanese men, women and children laid out in the shade of a porta-cabin. Laid out on sheets and mats and plastic. Bits and pieces of bodies blown apart by Israeli artillery shells.

Children's clothes on ragdoll bodies. T-shirts with salutations in English and French. One little girl, eyes open, staring sightlessly past me. Her pink vest says 'Une Belle Histoire'. A small boy, the lower part of his face missing, wears a green T-shirt. It sings out, 'I Love My Baby Brother'. Flies are buzzing constantly in the heat. I feel sick.

I count my patrol members back into the armoured personnel carriers. Pat each one on the back as they hop up and mount the high-axled Sisu armoured vehicles. The radios are alive with traffic. The whirr and whistle and hiss of the radio sets play out over the vibration of the massive diesel engines.

I'm last in. I grip the metal handrail and swing up into the gloomy interior. Flak jacket and helmet soaked in sweat. Perspiration runs down the plastic pistol grip of the rifle. I instinctively rub my thumb over the safety catch release. Catch my forefinger over the automatic lock-out. Weapon safe. Sergeant Bracken grips my hand in his and with the other arranges the radio headset around the rim of my helmet. My crown of thorns.

The earplugs of the headset deaden the scene around me and Irish accents – clear of static, emotionless, calm – call out instructions over the net. I report my position to Operations and signal my intention to return to Al Yatun. The Ops officer breaks into the conversation and tells me I'm going home. 'Great news, Thomas – you're on the first flight out.'

Back in Al Yatun, I throw my rifle on the bed. I undo the chinstrap on the blue helmet and pull it off. My hair runs with sweat. I massage my scalp. I'm exhausted; I haven't slept for days. Night blurring into day through hundreds of hours of shelling and shooting. I resist the temptation to lie on the bed. I peel off my combats. They are filthy, stinking and caked in dust and God knows what.

I take my last bottle of water and carefully unscrew the cap. Naked, I pour the warm water over my head. Like John the Baptist in that dark filthy billet, I anoint myself. Hands shaking, I pour the hotel room miniature shampoo bottle into the palm of my right hand. I wash. And then, I pour the remainder of the water over myself. I climb into my last set of combats. Clean for the trip home to Ireland.

I go outside and bundle my dirty combats into the scorched and heat-blasted rain barrel. I take all the letters from home and dump them in on top – for good measure. Then the prayer to St Anthony, the St Christopher Medal and the relic of St Therese. I shove them in too. I think of my mum briefly and feel a short, sharp stab of guilt. She'd sent them to me. 'To watch over you my love.' But she's thousands of miles away. I get my second wind then and pour in the diesel. I light some rags. The barrel is ablaze. My opposite number comes crunching across the gravel. 'You alright?' He grins at me. He too is covered in dust and dirt. His eyes are red-rimmed from constant wiping and no sleep. 'The smoke is making my eyes water,' is my reply. We both laugh.

I drink whiskey in the Ops room until the convoy comes to take me to Beirut. I see Al Yatun in the rear-view mirror and I vow to myself never again. Never again will I get mixed up in something like this.

Dublin

April 1996

Twenty-four hours later, I'm walking up Grafton Street with my girlfriend.

Vienna

April 1996

The Dayton Peace Agreement, or the General Framework Agreement for Peace in Bosnia and Herzegovina, is implemented in the former Yugoslavia. Signed by the Republic of Bosnia and Herzegovina, the Republic of Croatia and the Federal Republic of Yugoslavia (FRY), a ceasefire of sorts is holding in Bosnia. In Vienna, the Organisation for Security Cooperation in Europe (OSCE) prepares the necessary plans for elections throughout Bosnia Herzegovina.

I read about the Dayton Peace Agreement in the *Irish Times*. It signals the end of the Balkan War in Europe. I'm still feeling restless, unsettled, after the Lebanon experience. Can't sleep. After three months at home, I decide it might be a good idea to go to Bosnia Herzegovina as an OSCE election monitor. International election monitors are required to physically oversee the election process – making sure that the ballot is properly organised and run – free from intimidation and interference. How interesting, to bear witness to the end of a war in Europe. As opposed to being in the midst of one in the Middle East. I'm thinking the experience might be 'therapeutic'.

I am deployed to Prijedor in the Republika Srpska (Serb) area, an autonomous region of the Bosnian Krajina. I discover later that, per head of population, Prijedor is reputed to have the highest concentration of war criminals of any municipality in the world.

Therapeutic indeed. My mum has a canary when I tell her. My dad throws his eyes up to heaven. My girlfriend buys me a drink.

Chapter 1

Welcome to Bosnia

'You are a very peculiar man.'

Vienna, Austria
September 1996

Just two hours by air from Dublin, Austria is strangely autumnal. In Dublin, the horse chestnuts are still green. In Vienna's Innere Stadt, the trees are already flaming yellow, red and golden as the leaves turn. I have no troops with me on this trip. Just me, myself, alone. I check in to the hotel that OSCE have block-booked for election monitors. My room overlooks the Danube. It is brown and fast-flowing. Not blue at all.

After a briefing on the next day's short flight to Sarajevo, I go into town. Into the central square, Stephansplatz. I gaze up at the serrated roof tiles and gargoyles that adorn Vienna's cathedral, the Stephansdom. At the corner of the square, at Graben and Kärntner Strasse, I come across the Stock im Eisen. An historic curiosity. A gnarled, medieval spruce tree that has been preserved and placed on public display.

Bound in metal hoops, the fossilised spruce is known in folklore as a 'nail tree' or Nagelbaum. Thousands of iron nails have been hammered into the ancient tree over the centuries. The martyred spruce is reputed to stand at the mythic heart of the old city. It is also reputed to attract Satan to its vicinity.

Pondering that, I decide to celebrate my birthday by going for a few drinks. Drinking is what soldiers do, after all. A little habit I've picked up in Lebanon. A foolproof way to avoid Satan and all his works.

I go to the Loos Bar, also known as 'the American Bar'. Frau Kohn, the owner, has restored the Loos to its original glory. Green and white chessboard marble floor. Gleaming mahogany bar counter. Onyx tiles and mirrors. I lose myself in this interior world. I order Wiener Schnitzel – of course – and potato salad. The waitress, high-browed and haughty with plaited platinum-blonde hair, brings me a half litre of Innstadt Weissbier.

She stares at me when I thank her in German. I eat in silence as the bar slowly fills. Three young Viennese women join me at the bar. They ask me about Ireland. I tell them it is my birthday. They ask me if I am a 'virgin'. All three staring at me intently. I find this an unexpected and unsettling turn of events. I explain to them, slowly and carefully, that this would not be considered a polite question in Dublin. Lotte, the group leader, exhales loudly and remarks that this is 'foolishness'. She presses home her enquiry. 'But you must be a virgin.'

I later realise that they are asking me if I am a Virgo. Because it is my birthday. I am unable to explain this misunderstanding. Konstanze tells me that I am 'a very peculiar man'. Ute insists we go dancing for my birthday. We find a bar with traditional Austrian folk music. It is the only dancing to be had in the city centre. They tease me at my inability to dance a polka – a dance they perform with alarming ease. They ask me if I even know any German. Feeling belligerent, I tell them I know one German word – *Anschluss*. Thankfully, they laugh. They then take me to see Hitler's old house, a kind of workman's shelter on Meldemannstraße in the Brigittenau district. We then get a taxi back into the centre of the old town. I watch as Ute vomits into the Donnerbrunnen Fountain in the Neuer Markt. Lotte is holding her blonde ponytails back as she retches. I call out, '*Auf wiedersehen*!' and take my leave of my newfound Austrian friends.

In the wee small hours I return to the hotel, which is locked. After much hammering and banging the concierge opens the door and peers out at me quizzically. I see a brass plaque over his chair which reads, '*Der Pförtner*'. He reluctantly allows me in and follows me to my room. He checks my name off a list on a clipboard in the crook of his arm. 'Aha. *Der ire Ire*.' I gather this is a less than complimentary term for 'Irishman'. He puts his finger to his lips and hisses at me, 'Singing now is *verboten*.' I get the message.

I awake the following morning with a pounding headache. I say a prayer for Lotte, Ute and Konstanze. Head thumping, I count out hundreds of deutsche marks and US dollar bills on the bed. I separate the notes and distribute them about my person in different pockets and bags as best I can. Time to go to Bosnia Herzegovina. Weighed down by various currencies in small denominations I take a taxi to the airport. *'Flughafen Wien,'* I tell the driver. He snorts and tells me he doesn't speak English. Another morning, another journey begins.

I check in with dozens of election monitors from all over Europe. I tag along with the Greeks. I meet two lawyers from Athens, Athena and Athena. One Athena is tall, the other shorter. So I call them Little Athena and Big Athena. We board a Swissair jet and I get the window.

The flight from Vienna to Sarajevo is short. Initially, I gaze down at the ordered patchwork quilt of Austrian countryside. Ponds, lakes and the odd metal roof wink and flash up at us as the European Union gives way to *Mitteleuropa*, which rolls out beneath us. We fly south and east through Hungarian airspace, the countryside below changing. Less patchwork. Less order. More forest. Now overhead Pecs, passing briefly through Croatian airspace and suddenly skirting Tuzla, Zenica and on toward Sarajevo.

The aircraft banks gently as we descend through Bosnian airpace. The terrain below suddenly changes from the brown and beige autumnal field pattern of Austria to jet-black Karst mountains and dark green forest. Like an illustration out of the Grimm's fairytales I read as a small boy in Dublin. I imagine trolls, witches and wolves in the valleys below. I know, in fact, that there is worse down there. I have a sudden recollection of an Irish army officer who was held hostage by the Serbs at the height of the conflict. I recall images of dozens of soldiers tied to trees and pylons during the NATO air campaign the previous winter. For some reason, the mental images remind me of the Stock im Eisen in Vienna.

The Swissair pilot announces our final approach to Sarajevo. Ears popping, I look through the window. Soviet-era apartment blocks brood grey in the distance. They shimmer a little through the late afternoon heat haze. Closer in to the city, I see terraces and rows of beautiful white-walled,

red-tiled villas. Not what I'd expected.

The roar of the engines now as we thump-clunk down on the runway. I see the Sarajevo skyline as we fast taxi to the terminal. It is like a set from *Star Trek*. Futuristic buildings, onion domes. On closer inspection, bullet holes, flak and blast damage. Missing windows everywhere. The familiar sight of wires and high-tension cables coiled and burned, looped around the bases of poles and pylons. This is reminding me of Beirut. Welcome to Bosnia.

When we disembark the aircraft, the Swissair jet taxis away immediately and is already airborne as a tractor approaches pulling a wooden cart containing our bags. We manhandle the bags down ourselves. I retrieve mine. My mum has tied a shiny red love heart around the handle so that it is easily identifiable on an airport carousel.

A French officer serving with NATO helps me to heft the bag down. 'Which one of the girls does this bag belong to?' he asks me. 'Err, it's mine,' I reply. He frowns at me and in a moment of presumably avuncular pity, he whispers to me, 'Avoid the Serb-held areas if you can. Don't get deployed to a Serb area. They are not happy.'

I'm digesting this new piece of information when we are called into a large tent. There is a Canadian major calling out names in a sing-song French accent, separating election monitors into groups. He calls out my name. He tells me that I am bound for the town of Prijedor. 'Where's that?' I enquire. Annoyed at the interruption, he glowers at me. 'It is in the Republika Srpska Region, 50km north-west of Banja Luka. Serb country.' His staff of NCOs are eyeing me curiously and grin broadly in unison at my obvious discomfort. 'Don't worry,' calls out the sergeant major, 'they'll really like you up there. They have not had many English-speaking visitors since the US and British bombing campaign. They'll be very keen, no doubt, to share with you their views.' I decide now to stop asking questions.

After a briefing and some bottles of lukewarm water, my group is marshalled out to the edge of the runway. A taciturn Norwegian air force corporal pulls our bags behind us on a hand trolley. We will fly to Banja Luka in a Royal Norwegian Air Force Hercules C-130 cargo aircraft. The Norwegians load pallets into the rear of the aircraft. They then signal for us to file up into the aircraft through the tailgate. They motion for us to sit in small canvas bucket seats which fold down along the sides of the aircraft. We sink into the canvas seats and buckle up, legs dangling over the spars below. I scan my fellow passengers and spot Big Athena and Little Athena on the other side, just opposite me. Big Athena gives me a big thumbs up. Little Athena is applying make-up with a tiny mirror.

And then, the roar of the four propeller engines as we start to taxi. Everything is vibrating and rattling as we sway and bump and whallop down the runway. Eventually, after what seems like a very long drive in the country, we creak up skyward and head north for Banja Luka. The pilots are visible to us in the cockpit. One has his feet crossed and resting along the side of the instrument panel. They are engaged in some hilarious discussion and laugh all the way to Banja Luka. They only pause from their discussion as we make our final approach. They spring into action then, twisting dials, pulling on levers and suddenly we are down. Almost imperceptibly gliding onto the runway as the sun sets in the west.

I think of Vienna and the American Bar now, many hundreds of miles away over the Dinaric and Julian Alps to the north. I have a brief vision of Lotte and Ute and Konstanze nursing their hangovers. I think of my girl-friend in Dublin.

We are met in Banja Luka by a detachment of British soldiers. The Brits belong to a battalion of the Royal Green Jackets. In contrast to our French and Canadian friends in Sarajevo, the Brits are positively cheery and ask us if we have tea bags and powdered milk. They ply us with British army standard-issue chocolate, biscuits, tea bags, powdered milk and marmalade of all things.

They drive us in convoy to Prijedor. I am dropped off at the house of a Serb family. I am billeted with them – their 'houseguest' – for the duration of the elections. I am met at the door of the house by Zoran and his son, Bojan.

Chapter 2

Breakfast in Bosnia

'No one will hurt you in the daytime. No one is permitted to
hurt you especially in the night-time.'

Prijedor, Bosnia

September 1996

Zoran and Bojan welcome me to their home. It is a large detached house surrounded by trees. A modern two-storey building – all white plasterwork and
an ornate red-tiled roof. A rambling climbing plant with variegated leaves
covers the walls on the ground floor. The climber graces the first-floor bal-
conies in a profusion of pink and white flowers. There are painted wooden
shutters on the upper windows and a large covered terrace adorns the first
floor. There are hanging baskets with multicoloured blossoms suspended
from the timber beams of the overhanging roof. I think briefly of Hansel and
Gretel.

Zoran resembles Zorba the Greek. He is a very large man with huge
hands. His face is burned brown by the sun. A white and grey beard gives him
a regal quality. Zoran's green eyes remind me of my father. Those green eyes
bore into mine. A full appraisal. He mutters something under his breath and
offers his hand. A firm handshake. Meanwhile, Bojan – pronounced 'Boyan'
– a seemingly shy twenty-year-old, hangs back, watching me nervously. Zoran
nods at Bojan and he too grips my hand, pumping it furiously in a more
enthusiastic greeting.

They lead me through the front door into a large hallway. The hallway is
painted white with a large central staircase with metal banisters. The floor is

shining marble. Family portraits and paintings decorate the walls. A large triptych hangs on the return of the stairwell. Jesus stares down at me forlornly from the upper landing. His hands outward and upward in supplication. The wounds of the crucifixion oozing blood. Mary's eyes meet mine, imploring. The Orthodox Christian images remind me of the Sacred Heart of Jesus statues at home in Ireland. This Serbian Jesus has a narrower face though. The blood flowing from his wounds is a vivid crimson. Fresh.

Zoran takes me by the elbow and motions me into the family room where I meet his wife and other children. Two girls, Milinka and Dragana, ten and eleven years old. They smile shyly at me. Zoran's wife Irena looks tired and drawn. She smiles faintly at me and I notice that she is pale, as though she has been indoors for a long time.

I am invited to sit at the family table – a huge timber affair covered with a starched cloth. We eat pickled vegetables, or *tursija*, followed by *cevapcici*, a kind of grilled minced meat. There is bread, salad and feta cheese. Zoran offers me *slivovitz* – home-brewed brandy. It is not unlike poitín and it burns its way down my throat. Everyone, including Bojan, who has been staring at me, smiles as I swallow it. The room comes to life and I feel grateful to this family who have taken me – a complete stranger – into their home. I am gradually made to feel at home, despite being a thousand miles from Dublin and a million light years from all that is familiar, constant and certain to me.

I look around the room and notice the wire trailing through the window into the garden. A diesel generator is humming outside. Zoran follows my gaze and explains in German that the electricity supply is sporadic. They get a few hours of electricity a day. The diesel generator has been turned on in my honour.

Irena explains to me that there is very little in the shops. She speaks in faltering German and Bojan helps with the odd English word. Everyone on the street grows something in their garden; fruit, vegetables. Everyone keeps a pig or some hens to provide the family with eggs and fresh meat during the winter.

Bojan takes me out into a scullery to the rear of the house. It is full of jars and large aluminium pots and pans. They are filled with fruit and vegetables. August and September is a time for pickling fruit and vegetables for the winter. I am beginning to understand that Zoran and Irena are almost self-sufficient when it comes to food. I ask Bojan where his father's farm is. Bojan laughs. 'Daddy is not a farmer. He worked in the concrete factory until the war is starting. We learn to do all of this together with our neighbours.'

I glance back into the family room. Zoran and Irena are talking gently to Milinka and Dragana – which translated, mean 'graceful one' and 'beloved one'. I get the briefest flash of insight into what they have been through in the war. Just four years ago, Zoran and Irena had lived normal suburban lives in Prijedor. Commuting to work. Shopping in the supermarket. Doing all of the things that any family in Dublin would be familiar with. The sacred daily rituals of family life. Those weekly routines intimately familiar to households all over Europe.

And then, in 1992, the war began. And in the four years that follow, this family has gone from normality to war. From cosmos to chaos. From serenity to anarchy. With all of the emotions associated with that roller coaster journey. When I look at Irena, I am reminded of the women I saw in Lebanon. When I look at her face, look into her eyes, I see fear.

I wonder how they feel just now, in the autumn of 1996, with a total stranger – from Ireland – under their roof. I think of the Volkswagen I saw in the front garden, covered in a tarpaulin. 'Daddy has not driven his car for four years,' Bojan tells me. 'He is waiting until everything is normal again. Waiting for when he can buy petrol.'

Irena brings the girls to bed. But not before they each solemnly shake hands with me. '*Dobra vecher*,' ('Goodnight') they solemnly intone.

Zoran sits at the table. I have given him the bottle of Jameson whiskey I brought from Dublin. He is examining the label with his glasses on. He engages in some hurried conversation with Bojan. He looks at me and grins again. '*Irska*. Not English. *Republika Irska, Republika Srpska*. Aye Orrr Ey.' I realise he is saying 'IRA'. I get a bear hug for my troubles. I have passed another test it seems.

After a glass of Jameson, Bojan is instructed to carry my suitcase up to my room. I am given the master bedroom. I look at the double bed and realise that I am to sleep in Zoran and Irena's bed. Zoran and Irena are sleeping in

Bojan's room. I object and am pushed gently into the room by Zoran. His finger to his lips, hushing a long, low 'sshhhh'. Silenced, the door closes gently behind me with the faintest murmur of timber on doorjamb.

The diesel generator's hum grows faint, splutters and coughs below. The lights flicker and the room falls into darkness. I unpack my bag in the moonlight and gather up my deutsche marks and dollars. I look guiltily at the crumpled notes. I had hidden them in the belief that they might be stolen from me. I think of Zoran and Irena sleeping on a fold-out bed in Bojan's room. I place the money in the drawer of the bedside locker.

The next morning I wake as Zoran knocks gently on the door. He says something in Serbian. '*Dobro utro*,' ('Good morning'). He opens the door a little and places a black coffee on the nightstand in the doorway. I drink the bitter coffee and go downstairs to wash myself in the scullery. There is no hot water. I wash and shave in cold water.

At eight o'clock Milomir arrives at the house. Milomir, or 'Milo', will be my driver for the next few weeks. He is about twenty-two years old. He wears faded Levis and a starched white shirt under a black sport jacket. I note his cufflinks and one earring. He is darker than Zoran and Bojan. Handsome. Tall. Confident. He is greeted at the door by Zoran, who kisses him and embraces him briefly. Bojan stands back and smiles shyly at Milomir. Milomir advances on him and playfully thumps his shoulder. He embraces Bojan then. Kissing him on both cheeks. He turns and looks at me. He pauses momentarily as he stares at me. He holds his hand out stiffly and utters a formal, '*Guten morgen*.'

Zoran speaks to him rapidly in Serb. Milomir looks at me anew. His eyes widen in surprise. '*Irska*? Irish?'

Bojan interjects, 'Not English. Not American!' I get another bear hug. Milomir's acrid aftershave makes my eyes water.

Then I meet Dragana. Another Dragana. Another 'beloved one'. Dragana is our interpreter. She is older than Milomir, in her late twenties. She has a long, livid scar on her face. It runs from her temple, down her cheek to her upper lip. When she smiles, only one side of her mouth responds. She eyes me coldly and speaks in perfect, slightly accented English. 'Welcome to Serbia.'

Milomir and Dragana will accompany me for the next few weeks as I visit around a dozen or so polling stations for the upcoming 'free and democratic elections' in Bosnia Herzegovina. The polling stations I am responsible for are dotted in and around Prijedor. Ljubija and Bosanski Novi to the west of the town. Dubica to the north. Bos Gradiska, Mrakovica, Kozarac and Omarska to the east.

Dragana is very different to Milomir. She is quiet. Speaks only when spoken to. She avoids eye contact. Milomir sweeps us out to his car – a silver Volkswagen Golf GTI, 1988 model. Alloy wheels. Spoilers and darkened windows. Milomir opens the passenger door for me and with a fluid, expansive gesture, invites me to sit on the velour seat. I climb in and notice the silver skull on top of the gear stick. Milomir, it would appear, is a boy racer. Dragana sits in the back. Sighs heavily, histrionically, and lights a cigarette. Milomir lights up as well and offers me one. I decline politely. Milomir looks puzzled. He opens the glove compartment and takes out a bottle of *slivovitz*. He takes a long pull on the bottle and offers it to me. I think, if I'm going to die in this car today, I might as well have a drink first. In for a penny, in for a pound. I take a deep swig on the *slivovitz* and feel it warm my belly. Breakfast in Bosnia.

Milomir takes us on a tour of Prijedor. He drives like a maniac. Smoking. Shouting in Serb. Even though there is very little traffic. Again, I am reminded of my father. A younger version perhaps.

Prijedor is a town of around 14,000 people. Milomir drives us through the old town, Stari Grad, at breakneck speed. Dragana rattles off a description of each street. 'Main street.' 'Side street.' 'Police building.' As we weave through the streets, Dragana makes languid observations, 'Notice the Ottoman and Austro-Hungarian architecture.'

We screech to a halt at a large modernist building. It is a cubist monstrosity – like one of the Ballymun towers perched precariously atop a massive concrete bunker. Apparently it was once a hotel. Now it functions as a kind of town hall. Municipal offices have been set up inside. It is where the OSCE election monitors are received by the mayor of Prijedor.

Dragana speaks. 'Milomir would like to introduce you to the mayor.' We enter the concrete and steel building with its small windows. The interior is gloomy with large, heavy wooden doors. The doors are painted dark brown. The walls are green. It reminds me of the public health clinic in Finglas village back in the 1970s. The air is thick with cigarette smoke. There are dour older men everywhere. Smoking. Sitting at desks. Glowering at us from office doorways. Eventually we are ushered to an office at the end of a long corridor. Our elderly escort knocks gingerly on the door. No reply. Milomir takes a drag on his cigarette and impatiently opens the door. He pushes me inside.

There are two men in the room. The mayor and another man. Dragana follows me in and announces in monotone. 'That is the mayor. That is a policeman.' The policeman is introduced to me as 'Simo'. Or Simo Drljaca – the 'Sheriff of Prijedor' – as I later discover. To me, he looks like any middle-aged man. Slightly overweight. Slightly disheveled. He looks me over without comment. He is expressionless. The mayor snaps something at Milomir. We have interrupted an important conversation.

The mayor then composes himself and smiles. Comes around his desk and embraces me. Kisses me on each cheek. He is speaking softly. Dragana announces from somewhere behind me, 'You are very welcome to Prijedor. I am at your disposal. No one will harm you here on my say so. No one will hurt you in the daytime. No one is permitted to hurt you especially in the night-time.'

Milomir says something in Serbian. The mayor looks at me. His eyes widen in surprise. I'm getting used to this now. He utters the words, '*Republika Irska*.' With his hands still on my shoulders, he continues speaking. Dragana translates for him and in her own mechanical way rhymes off the phrases, 'Not American, not English. You are Irish. You are welcome.' Even Simo walks toward me. Shakes hands with me and embraces me. He smells faintly of sweat and tobacco. He starts speaking in Serb. Dragana translates. 'Simo says, you are Irish. And the Irish have blood on their hands. The Irish understand. And you will understand that we, the Serbs, are not the new Germans.'

I'm absorbing this interesting observation and trying to compose a suitably pithy reply when the door opens behind us. Little Athena and Big Athena enter the room accompanied by their interpreter and driver. The mayor advances upon them, arms outstretched. He greets the Greek delegation effusively. Dragana translates, 'You are welcome, my Greek sisters. My daughters. Our true friends.'

The two Athenas accept his offer of cigarettes and puff merrily away as he informs them that they too will not be harmed 'in the daytime or even in the night-time'. The elderly concierge returns with a tray of glasses containing *slivovitz*. The mayor passes out the drinks and leads us in a Greek toast 'Eviva'. My second glass of brandy in less than two hours.

As we finish our drinks, Milomir is chatting enthusiastically with the other interpreter, Sofija. Sofija is tall and blonde. Over six feet tall. She dwarfs the two Athenas – even Big Athena. She stands with her hands on her hips and regards Milomir, eye to eye. Milomir repeatedly turns to me, winking conspiratorially.

The mayor's phone is ringing. We are ushered out to the corridor once more. Dragana and Sofija are conversing rapidly. Dragana announces, 'We are going to motel for coffee.' Milomir breaks into a run and shouts something. Dragana sighs. 'We are racing to the motel. Let's see who gets there first.'

It is a white-knuckle ride through the centre of Prijedor. We careen through the narrow streets. Cross over a bridge. Dragana observing, 'This is River Gomjenica. Now this is River Sana. Most famous river in *Republika Srpska*.' We eventually arrive at a riverside hotel. The Motel du Pont. The Athenas and Sofija arrive about five minutes later. Milomir is ecstatic. Sofija ignores him pointedly. The girls' driver is an older man. He remains in his car, preferring to smoke and read.

Milomir sits at the bar and orders a beer. Sofija and Dragana sit at a table in the dining room and carefully examine our lists of polling stations. The two Athenas speak fluent English. They are both lawyers in Athens. They quiz me about Ireland. They ask me what I do for a living in Ireland. When I tell them that I am a soldier, Dragana raises her head and stares at me. It is a hostile gaze. I look away and return to the conversation with the Greeks.

There is no menu in the motel. The proprietress brings us thick soup and bread. She also produces a tray with glasses of *slivovitz*. She thrusts the glasses into our hands and calls out the Serbian toast, '*Zivili*.' The Serbs and Greeks knock it back. I hesitate for a moment. Milomir clucks his disapproval as the maître d' asks something in Serbian – her eyebrows raised. 'Is this little one sick?' Dragana pokes me in the back as she translates. I take the hint and throw back my third glass of brandy of the morning.

We spend the day in convoy. Touring the polling booths. Meeting elderly mayors, presiding officers and polling clerks. Everyone is proud of their polling stations. In Bos Gradiska, the presiding officer is also the postman. He wears his postman's uniform proudly.

At the edge of each of the towns there are empty, gutted houses. Strange abstract symbols are painted on the entrances and gateposts. Some have been burned. I notice the tell-tale blast patterns of machine gun fire and mortar rounds on the plasterwork on many of the houses. The first-floor terraces destroyed, sagging and hanging down in twisted cords of reinforced steel rods and scorched concrete. Red-tiled rooftops burned and blackened. The roof timbers exposed like the ribs on rotting carcasses. Milomir whistles tunelessly and looks the other way. I ask Dragana about the houses and the painted symbols on the walls and doorways. 'These are the homes of some Muslims.' I ask her what has become of them. Dragana answers me in her flat monotone. 'They have gone to Belgrade to find work. The paint marks show them that their homes have been vandalised by NATO.' She does not bat an eyelid and stares at me, unblinking when I turn back to look at her.

Milomir points at the register of voters which has been supplied to me by OSCE. He says something while overtaking a truck on a blind bend. Dragana obliges me with a translation. 'Milo is asking you if you think the Muslims will come back to Prijedor for the elections. This is their right under Dayton. When they come, you can ask them what happened to their homes. You can ask them what they think of NATO.' Milomir nods his head enthusiastically and laughs. 'Fucking NATO.'

We get back to Prijedor late in the evening. Milomir and Dragana drop me at Zoran's door. They shake hands with me solemnly and bid me a formal 'Goodnight.' Little Athena and Big Athena are staying with another family across the road. They insist we go into town for dinner. According to Big Athena, 'The Irish and the Greeks – birds of a feather, stick together.'

Chapter 3

After Dark

'When one has been bitten by the snake, one fears the lizard.
One learns to fear all scaled creatures.'

Sofija's Restaurant, Prijedor, Bosnia
September 1996

Big Athena and Little Athena ask me to wait in the garden of their host family while they 'refresh their make-up'. The evening is warm and I sit at a carved wooden table in the shade of an elaborate pergola covered in blossoms and twisting entwined vines. The garden is full of fruit bushes. There is a row of beehives at the boundary wall. The air is heavy with the scent of flowers and the buzzing of insects. It reminds me of something. I cannot quite put my finger on it. But despite the idyllic scene, it makes me a little uncomfortable. The woman of the house, Radmila, approaches with more *slivovitz*. '*Zivili*.' We drink to each other's health. I'm becoming immune to the *slivovitz* or '*rakija*' as Radmila calls it. The *rakija* dampens down the discomfiting, unsettled feeling that has come over me.

I then notice an old lady sitting on a rocking chair in the shade of the front porch. I hadn't noticed her because she is dressed completely in black from head to toe. She wears a black headscarf. Her gnarled old hands clutch a walking stick. Her knuckles are swollen with rheumatoid arthritis. I call out to her and bid her good evening. '*Dobra vecher*.' She turns to look at me and stares blankly in my general direction. I see that she is blind. In fact, she has no eyes at all. Just sunken eyelids and scar tissue where once she had eyes. Her face is deeply lined. She slowly rises off her chair and calls me to her.

There's no one else around and I'm afraid that Granny will fall off the porch, so I approach her. I take her elbow as she struggles to her feet. She is mumbling away in Serbian as she gets her balance. She shuffles around to face me. She leans on me for stability and all the while mumbling and muttering, she places her hands on my face. She feels my face and becomes agitated. She sniffs at me and grabs my lapels. Now she is shrieking at me. She has stopped mumbling and is repeating the same word over and over. 'Darko. Darko. Darko.' I can't extricate myself for fear that she'll fall over.

Radmila comes running. Radmila is calling out *Majka* or 'Mother'. She gently takes the old lady's hands and dismisses me with a curt nod of her head. Radmila is crying. Tears rolling freely down her face. The old lady sinks into her chair and sobs inconsolably. She holds her head in her hands.

The Athenas arrive and rescue me. They kiss Granny's hands and embrace Radmila. The Greeks soothe them both with hugs and more kisses. Water is poured from a pitcher on the porch and Granny drinks up. Radmila will not look at me. I wonder what I've done wrong as the Greeks shove and push me down the garden path.

On the walk into town, as the sun sets, they tell me that Darko was Radmila's son. He is 'missing, believed dead' in the war. 'Senka', they tell me, is Radmila's mother. Darko's grandmother. Apparently Darko was a favourite. She waits in the garden for him sometimes. Expecting him to return from school and climb onto her lap. Any day now.

I remember now. The hum of insects in the garden. The buzz of flies in Lebanon as they rose up, fat and lazy from the bodies of the dead. Children lost in the ebb and flow of war. Big Athena interrupts my reverie with a poke in the back. 'Hello Ireland? Hello? Anyone at home? C'mon, it's dinner time.'

We take a shortcut into town. We walk along a track through a heavily wooded area. In the dying light, the track is like a tunnel. The heavy boughs meet overhead, enveloping us in a long, leafy archway. The leaves have turned. Red and yellow above, orange and brown underfoot.

We emerge into a large open area. In front of us, across the clearing, is Prijedor's train station. We pick our way across broken railway tracks. As we climb up on the platform of the train station, Big Athena explains to me about

Senka: 'Do you know what Senka means?' she asks me. 'It means shadow.' Little Athena observes that I am 'Darko's shadow.' They both laugh.

We walk though the train station and out onto the street. It is fully dark now. And, as in Lebanon, there are no streetlights. It is a profound, inky black. The streets are empty. Windows shuttered. I think of the mayor's reassurance that no one has permission to harm us. 'Especially in the night-time.'

By the time we have reached the old town, the Athenas have linked arms with me. A Greek on either side. We cross a pedestrian bridge over the river. The old town, or historic centre of Prijedor, is on a small island in the middle of the Sana River. The moon shines down on the cobbles as the Greeks direct me into the courtyard of a small restaurant. The lights are on inside. We open the creaking wooden door and enter. The old stone building is built in the Ottoman style; a low-ceilinged roof with heavy wooden beams visible. The room is half empty. The other patrons stare at us and the room falls silent. It is like the scene is straight out of a Hammer horror movie. I imagine Christopher Lee making a dramatic entrance. Instead, another heavy, ancient door creaks open. Vladimir, the owner, approaches us with open arms. He is accompanied by Sofija, the Greek girls' interpreter. She, it seems, is his daughter.

Vladimir grabs each of the Greek lawyers in turn, kissing them repeatedly. Sofija and the Greeks then embrace. They greet each other as though reunited after years of separation despite the fact that Sofija dropped them off at Radmila's house just over an hour ago. I'm mulling this over when the room falls silent again. Vladimir turns towards me. He is taller than Sofija and under the low ceiling he looks even bigger. In fact, he is built like the proverbial brick shithouse. He tut-tuts and speaks out loud in Serbian. His eyes are blank, devoid of expression as he stares at me. His hostility is evident.

Thankfully, Sofija intervenes and speaks Serbian to him. Rapid, staccato sentences. Vladimir's demeanour changes in an instant. His body relaxes visibly. He places one large paw on my shoulder and with the other he tousles my hair. *'Irska.' 'Republika Srpska. Republika Irska.'* I will encounter this reaction countless times. I will never tire of it. Thank God for Ireland. Saved by the shamrock once again. Mentally, I thank St Patrick and leprechauns and De

Valera and all things Irish for my repeated deliverance from hostile scrutiny.

Sofija guides us to a table. The Greeks tell me that I'm going to love the food. I realise now that they have adopted me. We drink to the Greek toast, '*Eviva*.' We drink to the Irish toast, '*Sláinte*.' Little Athena writes it down carefully in her little black notebook. Vladimir brings us a variety of Serbian dishes. Stuffed red peppers, '*punjene paprike*', stuffed cabbage or '*sarma*' and Serbian moussaka. There is plenty of red wine. The other guests have forgotten about us now and ignore us for the most part. As I look around the restaurant I notice that some of the younger diners have prosthethic limbs. And I notice one young man, laughing and drinking, red-faced with a livid scar similar to Dragana's.

The large wooden door creaks open again and a tall man enters. The hum of conversation in the restaurant dips a little as our fellow diners glance up at him. They quickly look away. No one engages him with eye contact. No friendly salutations. He scans the restaurant and spots our table. He fixes upon me and saunters towards our table. His hands are in his pockets.

Vladimir approaches and tries to divert the stranger with a menu. The man waves him aside and pulls a chair up to our table. The Greeks perk up at the new arrival and eye him curiously. He is tall and thin, with high cheekbones and a high forehead. Small eyes. Sofija falls silent. He introduces himself as Toma. He shakes hands with the Greeks. No kissing. He ignores Sofija and she ignores him. Her cheeks have reddened and there is the look of thunder on her face. Toma turns to me. 'Ah, the soldier,' he remarks as he offers me his hand. Evidently, he speaks a little English.

It seems he has also been talking to Dragana, my interpreter. He takes out a slim silver cigarette case and proffers it to me. I decline. He lights a cigarette and contemplates me once more. 'I am a policeman during the day,' he informs me. 'At night, I like to relax though. Now I am off duty, if that is the correct expression.'

I tell him that I am also 'off duty' and that I am in Bosnia as a civilian election monitor. Toma laughs and tells me that people are always curious about soldiers – 'Especially after NATO bombed us in our homes.' I explain to him that the Irish, '*Republika Irska*,' are not members of the NATO alliance. He raises his eyebrows a little. 'Is that so?' he remarks. 'Still though,' he continues, 'you look like them. When one has been bitten by the snake, one fears the lizard. One learns to fear all scaled creatures.' He laughs again. Sofija excuses herself and leaves the table. The Greeks are watching this exchange with interest.

Big Athena interrupts. 'So, what do you want with Little Tom?' she asks. Initially, I am surprised – and amazed at the coincidence – to hear that I have been designated 'Little Tom'. I have clearly met my match with the Greeks. And then I think, 'Of course – Big Toma, Little Tom.'

Toma exhales loudly and raises his eyes to heaven. 'And you, I presume, are now his lawyer?' Big Athena nods in the affirmative. 'Yes, and so is (Little) Athena.' She nods at Little Athena. Little Athena gives me a reassuring look. Toma sits forward and explains to me in broken English that he has been asked by Simo Drljaca to watch out for me. He elaborates: 'I am here to make sure that nothing happens to you after dark.' He opens his jacket and shows me a small semiautomatic pistol holstered at his waistband. Somehow, I am not reassured.

He orders *rakija* for everyone at the table. Vladimir complies but does not engage with Toma at all. Instead, he apologises to Big and Little Athena for Sofija's early departure. 'Sofija has a toothache.' Vladimir refuses to take any money for the meal. We excuse ourselves and thank Toma for the glass of *rakija*.

Toma expresses surprise at our hasty leave-taking. 'Let me give you a lift home. I insist.' We protest. Toma insists. He takes Little Athena by the arm and tells us to follow him. We go out to the cobbled square. There is a small police car parked there. Toma opens the front door to Little Athena. Bowing theatrically, he invites her to sit. The other Athena and I squeeze into the back seat. Toma starts the engine and grinning at me in the rear-view mirror he turns on the blue flashing lights. No siren though. In silence, he drives – in a manner not unlike Milomir – like a maniac to the street where we are billeted. The blue strobe light flashes and washes off the houses as he drops us off. I see curtains twitch in the darkness. Unseen eyes peering out in the darkness. Toma waves at the houses.

I say goodnight to the Greeks and silently, carefully enter through the front door of my own house. I slide the key into the lock, listening as the teeth glide over the sears. I twist the lock open and slip inside. As I close the door, I feel the eyes of Jesus staring down at me from the upper landing. I look up – expecting to see Mary there. Instead I see Zoran standing in the gloom. In his vest and underpants. He looks concerned. He nods at me in the darkness. He makes a circular motion in the air with his index finger – signifying the flashing lights of the police car. He looks at me quizzically. I whisper quietly that all is 'OK, OK.' He nods and disappears off to Bojan's room.

Chapter 4

Schweinfest

'They think you might be a spy.'

Banja Luka, Bosnia
September 1996

Each morning Milomir and Dragana collect me from Zoran's front porch. Each morning, Zoran and I sit on the front step and drink coffee. It fortifies me for the daily round of drinking and driving as we visit the various polling stations around Prijedor.

Our role as international monitors is to physically check that the voting infrastructure is in place for the election. Our physical presence is required for the duration of the poll. We are the eyes and ears of the international community. We are witnesses to the fledgling democratic process hammered out in the Dayton Accords. We are also here to observe the free and uninterrupted return of Bosniak Muslims and ethnic Croats to the region to cast their votes. We watch and listen. During our night-time encounters Toma tells me we are 'guests of greater Serbia'. He tells me repeatedly, as he inhales deeply on a cigarette, that we are 'guests of the nation'.

The polling stations themselves are coming along nicely. Polling booths are being installed in the school halls, municipal buildings and community centres from Prijedor central right out to the surrounding areas of Dubica, Bos Gradiska, Mrakovica and Kosarac. Election day, 14 September, is approaching fast.

The polling booths are remarkably similar to those I am familiar with at home. Crude timber constructions with black pencils suspended on bits of string. The layout of the polling stations is also strangely familiar. Tables laid out for polling clerks to mark voters off the register of electors. A top table for the presiding officer and other officials in the event of disputes. We are expected to attend as many of the polling stations as possible on election day – to ensure, as impartial international observers, that the vote is free and fair. The entire process reminds me of how much for granted this basic right is taken at home. In Ireland, voter turnout often hovers around 30 percent. In Bosnia, in 1996, after four years of war, voter turnout is expected to be high. We hope.

Each evening, myself and the Greek contingent – consisting of the two Athenian lawyers, Big Athena and Little Athena – cross the railway tracks and eat in Sofija's restaurant. And on most evenings Toma makes his appearance. He doesn't always sit with us. Very often he perches himself atop a barstool and watches us from a distance. When he does engage in conversation with us he always slips something into the conversation to indicate that he is aware of our daytime travels. 'The postmaster of Bos Gradiska tells me you visited today. He tells me you asked about the *Mudzahedini* who used to live there.' Toma tells me that the *Mudzahedini*, or mujahideen – as he refers to the ethnically Muslim Bosniaks who have fled the area – have 'probably gone to Mecca'.

One evening Toma follows me into the toilets. As I wash my hands he urinates against the ancient latrine with its high stench of piss and ammonia. He calls over his shoulder as I leave, 'You and your friends in NATO say that the Serbs are responsible for ethnic cleansing. Pity we are not so good at the toilet cleansing, hmm?' I close the door on his laughter.

On Friday, 6 September, all of the election monitors are summoned to an OSCE briefing in Banja Luka. Milomir relishes the drive. En route we overtake lines of ancient, rumbling articulated trucks along with tractors, horses and carts and all manner of improvised vehicles. Including a contraption that consists of an ancient motorcycle engine mounted on a three-wheeled timber frame. This rickety construction in turn pulls a large trailer behind it. An ancient man with a huge moustache and pipe is perched behind the engine and is steering the entire thing with a short metal stick. Like a rudder of sorts.

When we pass, Milomir blows his horn and shakes his fist at the old man. I close my eyes and mutter the rosary as we head towards blind bends and oncoming trucks on the wrong side of the road.

When we get to Banja Luka, my hands are slippery with sweat. But at least in the narrow city streets Milomir is forced to slow down somewhat. Banja Luka is in a state of reconstruction after the war. Situated on the River Vrbas, the city is recovering itself. Licking its wounds. As we drive into the town centre I note the bomb damage. The larger modernist buildings have been raked with shrapnel and damage from direct-fire weapons. The facades on some hotels and municipal buildings hang crazily from their fixings. In many cases they have subsided to one side and resemble the faces of stroke victims. Shutters and other fixings drooping and sliding street-ward. Missing windows like missing teeth, blown out by high explosives and small arms fire.

We eventually arrive at the municipal centre where the OSCE and NATO's IFOR, or Interim Force, Bosnia Herzegovina, are to give us a final briefing prior to election day. We come to a halt and Milomir pulls up the handbrake with a loud crunch. He kills the engine and lights a cigarette. I reach for the glove compartment and take a swig of the *slivovitz* there. Milomir smiles approvingly. Dragana lights up also and intones from the back seat, 'Milomir says you are becoming good Serb.' They both laugh. I head into the building for the OSCE briefing.

Row upon row of Humvee jeeps, British army Land Rovers and an assortment of other military vehicles are parked around the entrance to the building. American, British, Canadian and Czech troops stand around in groups watching the arrival of the international election monitors. I am asked for ID. I produce my passport and OSCE ID card to the US soldier at the entrance. He scrutinises it closely and then scrutinises me. He tells me that he is from Boston. The Murphy on his name tag tells me all I need to know about his ancestry. He tells me that he intends to go to Dublin on leave. I give him the names of pubs off Grafton Street. He scribbles them down and slaps me on the back as I enter the foyer.

There is a large table with glasses of *rakija* in the foyer. I have another brandy to fortify myself for the briefings. The hall resembles a large gym filled with old school tables and chairs. I sit next to some English election monitors as the briefing begins. The OSCE representative from Germany tells us that there is an expectation that Muslims and Croats may choose to return to their villages and towns within the Serb Krajina in order to vote. He introduces us to colleagues from the International Red Cross and the War Crimes Tribunal for the former Yugoslavia. They are hoping to cross-reference the electoral register – and those who might turn up to vote – with lists of those declared missing, presumed dead, during the war. There is a hope that if Muslims and others return to vote in the Republika Srpska area – and if they register to vote – that it might clear up some of the mystery surrounding their current whereabouts. We are asked to keep a close eye out for returnees.

According to the International Red Cross, approximately 5,200 Bosnian Muslims and Croats have disappeared from the area around Prijedor. I think of Dragana's matter-of-fact remark that these people had 'gone to Belgrade to find work'. I think of Toma's remark that they have 'gone to Mecca'.

In my mind's eye, I see the ruined houses outside Prijedor. I recall the porches overgrown with weeds. The red-tiled roofs scorched black. I am reminded of the strange symbols painted on the entrances and gateposts by Serb forces. I wonder if the former occupants of these now-empty homes will ever return. Somehow, I doubt it.

After the OSCE and Red Cross briefings we get a further update on the security situation from some Canadian officers deployed as part of NATO's IFOR. A Canadian major warns us that tensions within the Republika Srpska area are 'heightened' in advance of the elections. He also tells us that it is expected that irregular Serb forces – which have gone to ground since the ceasefire – are expected to re-emerge in the coming days and to put on some sort of display of strength or defiance. We are warned to 'avoid such situations if at all possible.'

In light of this escalation in the threat level, the Canadians also provide us with a somewhat belated briefing on mine awareness. A group of Canadian corporals and sergeants carry a large table into the room. They then carry in box after box of various types of unexploded ordnance, munitions and mines. I recognise most of the stuff straightaway and make a mental note of the exits.

My civilian counterparts move forward and, driven by curiosity, start to crowd around the table, 'ooh-ing' and 'ahh-ing' at the various explosive items on display. I nip back to the foyer and grab another *rakija*.

A Canadian regimental sergeant major then enters and in a booming voice orders everyone back. Silence descends on the room as the RSM starts his brief. I'm intrigued. I'm wondering if his contribution on mines and improvised explosive devices will teach me anything new. It does, as it happens.

The RSM clears his throat and takes an extendable silver pointer out of his combat jacket. He spends a great deal of time extending it to its full length. I'm pondering on the phallic imagery that this display – perhaps unwittingly – imparts, when he starts his presentation.

He points at each mine, improvised explosive device, unexploded bomb and booby trap in turn. With a loud tap of his pointer, he solemnly announces each item: 'Bomb.' 'Big bomb.' 'Small bomb.' 'Very dangerous here.' He repeats this mantra in accented English. He sounds like Inspector Clouseau. The election monitors are transfixed. A few hands go up. The RSM hesitates. 'Questions at the end, *s'il vous plaît*.' The crowd wait with baited breath.

The RSM concludes with what I think is good advice. He announces, 'Look, all this stuff will kill you. And we don't know where any of it is. Except that there is a lot of it. Every male of military service age was given an anti-personnel mine and an anti-tank mine. When the war started, everyone tried to hide them. So, some put them in the attic. Maybe in an old car. Maybe in the hedge. Who knows? So, in the absence of marked minefields, we don't know where any of this stuff is. It could be anywhere. So, don't get killed please.'

There is a stunned silence. An English monitor – an older man – stands up and demands, somewhat indignantly, to know if the RSM can offer any more specific advice in light of this threat. He does so in a clipped upper-class accent. This is pure theatre and I am enjoying myself immensely. The RSM stares at him and says, 'Well, maybe if you have false teeth. Wrap them in a – how you say, hanky – and put them in your pocket. There is not much else I can advise.' This earns the RSM an enthusiastic round of applause. I learn something new after all.

After the briefings we spill outside into the autumn sunshine. I bump into the two Athenas. Both are in very good humour. To break the monotony, the Athenas have agreed to take a lift back to Prijedor with Milomir and Dragana. Milomir looks like the cat who has swallowed the canary. He winks at me and gives me the three-fingered Serbian salute.

I am travelling with Sofija. She introduces me to the driver, Branislav or 'Branka' as he is affectionately known. Branka is driving an ancient Volkswagen Passat. The seats are covered in old blankets and Branka looks reassuringly elderly and grandfather-like. I am hoping that the drive home to Prijedor will not be a white-knuckle ride. Branka lights up his pipe and away we go. I leave the front seat to Sofija and they chat away in Serbian. Around halfway to Prijedor, I ask Branka about Dragana's scar.

Sofija looks at me in the rear-view mirror, then twists around in the front seat to speak to me directly. 'OK, I'll tell you. But, you cannot tell her that you know this. Dragana's boyfriend, Dragan, was killed in this war. He was a conscript when the war broke out and the Croats killed him and some other boys shortly after the war started.' I nod my head and mumble my regrets. Sofija continues. 'Dragana was heartbroken. And then, last October, Bosnian government forces shelled Prijedor with heavy artillery. Dragana was caught in the open with her father. They were hit with the same shell fragment. He was killed outright. Dragana's face is now what you see.'

Sofija explains to me that Dragana was treated by a local doctor and that because of the shortage of medical supplies and restrictions on movement, the wound could not be treated by a plastic surgeon. 'So, the war leaves the mark of Cain on her face. Then the British come to Prijedor and they take Dragana as an interpreter. Nobody speaks to Dragana about this because of how much she has suffered.'

By the time we get to Prijedor, I've a lot to think about. We pull up outside Zoran's house. Sofija opens the door for me. I'm child-locked into the back of the Passat. 'That's why Dragana doesn't like soldiers,' she whispers to me.

Milomir and Dragana are standing outside Radmila's house opposite us. Little Athena is puking into the road. Big Athena is holding her long black curly hair back as she vomits. The scene reminds me of the Austrian trio in Vienna. Radmila is giving out to Milomir about his driving.

That night we are joined in Sofija's restaurant by Dragana and Milomir. They are reluctant to accompany us. But, as we have only ten days to go in-country, they eventually agree to come along as our guests. Big Athena and Little Athena chat away to Dragana. Dragana ignores me completely. Milomir catches my eye repeatedly and makes cutting gestures at his face whilst nodding at Dragana. 'She is *baba korizma* – a witch. No one will fuck her now. Not with that face.' Milomir is quite drunk at this stage and delighted with his English. Dragana stares coldly at us. I pray that she has not overheard Milomir's words.

I tell Milomir to go fuck himself and get up to leave. Sofija intervenes and tells Milomir in no uncertain terms to go home. Milomir gives me the three fingered Serbian salute again – thumb, forefinger and middle finger. He waves his hand in my face and lurches off.

Toma enters as he leaves. He invites us all to a Schweinfest, 'in our honour'. Apparently, the mayor and Simo are anxious to throw us a party before the election. To acknowledge all that we have 'done for democracy in the *Republika Srpska*'. We are to meet him the following evening in the Old Town.

The next day, Saturday, 7 September 1996, is a day to remember. Election posters go up all over the town. They appear overnight. In the country lanes around Prijedor, posters proliferate as if by magic on telegraph poles and on trees along the forested roadways. It is very like Ireland.

On the Saturday afternoon, there is an open-air market in Prijedor's town centre. Myself and the Greeks decide to browse and see if we can buy some souvenir trinkets from our time in the Republika Srpska. As I move through the stalls, there is a loud commotion at the edge of the market. A small convoy of cars, covered in posters, loudspeakers on the roof, arrives with a revving of engines, horns blowing, brakes squealing. A man jumps out and the crowd surges forward. I try to catch a glimpse of him. He looks for all the world like an Irish showband star. Slightly overweight. Stuffed into a shiny mohair suit. And, incongruously, he is wearing make-up. Even I can see this from the rear of the crowd. He is hoisted shoulder-high onto the back of a flat-bed truck. He grabs a megaphone and he makes a brief, impassioned speech. Spontaneous cheers drown out his words.

Then, as quickly as he arrived, this mysterious Daniel O'Donnell looka-like is bundled away by his bodyguards and the convoy speeds out of the town centre.

Big Athena pushes her way through the crowd and hands me a poster. On it is a photograph of the man who has just been speaking. The man on the poster is wearing make-up too. Big Athena is out of breath with excitement. 'That was Arkan,' she tells me breathlessly.

Arkan, or Zeljko Raznatovic, is a notorious war criminal. Leader of a Serbian paramilitary unit known as Arkan's Tigers, Raznatovic is responsible for the murders of hundreds of innocent Bosnian Muslim and Croat civilians. For his ethnic cleansing in Vukovar and elsewhere, Arkan is indicted by the International Criminal Tribunal for the former Yugoslavia for crimes against humanity and breaches of the Geneva Convention. Arkan achieved interna-tional notoriety in 1992 when he was pictured by American photojournalist Ron Haviv holding up a tiger cub whilst posing in front of his paramilitary unit in Erdut, Croatia. Active in Prijedor until just nine months ago, Arkan has resurfaced just days before the elections. It is a sobering experience.

I scan the crowd. Not everyone is impressed with his appearance. One stall-holder stands grim-faced, his fists clenched, staring at the disappearing motorcade. He turns and notices me looking at him. His eyes are filled with rage. He shouts at myself and Athena. Athena translates for me. 'He is saying the war is over.' He looks away and, turning his back on us, begins noisily rear-ranging his jars of pickles and cured ham.

That evening myself, Milomir, Dragana, the two Athenas and Sofija meet Toma in the central square. He has invited some other election monitors – all Greeks – to the Schweinfest. The Greeks all greet one another like long-lost friends. There is the usual embracing and kissing. The arrival of the other Greeks dilutes the oppressive atmosphere. Toma has organised a minibus to take us to a roadside motel just outside Prijedor. He drives ahead, blue lights flashing in his tiny police car.

The proprietor of the motel meets us in the lobby with the obligatory tray of *slivovitz* and *rakija*. We carry on through to an open-air courtyard with trestle tables and long wooden benches. At the centre of the courtyard, over an open fire, a whole pig is roasting on a spit. The smell of roast pork mixes with the smell of the blossoms on the plants that clamber over the stone walls around the courtyard. It is an idyllic scene. A group of men come forward to greet us. They are all policemen apparently. And some mayoral officials from Prijedor. There are no women. Just us and this strange reception committee.

The policemen are mostly middle-aged. Squat, powerfully built, slightly overweight. They remind me of Arkan. Without the make-up. They are ruddy-faced after what looks like a long afternoon's drinking. They pass around large glasses of foaming *pivo* or Serbian beer. They encourage us loudly to drink. The beer is ice cold and tastes like a German pilsener. It breaks the tension.

The cops are good hosts and insist we sit as they pass around baskets of bread and plates of pickled vegetables and cured meats. The proprietor of the motel then reappears dressed in chef's whites. To roars of approval and a loud round of applause and whistles, he starts carving the roast pig. The chef shouts, '*Nema tice do prasice*' – a traditional Serb salutation. It is the signal to eat. The cops queue up like schoolboys with their plates. We join in.

The pork is delicious and we wash it down with more beer. The cops and mayoral officials are acquainting themselves with the Greeks. Occasionally, some of them look my way and give me quizzical glances. Eventually, one of them asks me a question. Dragana translates. 'He wants to know if you are English.' Dragana rattles off a few quick sentences in Serbian. I hear the words '*Republika Srpska, Rebulika Irska.*' On this occasion, however, there is no break in tension. No bear hugs. Just sullen looks from our hosts.

Toma sidles up to me and informs me in a whisper that his colleagues are 'curious about the soldier. They think you might be a spy.' Toma finds this highly amusing and is grinning at me from the keg of beer as he fills another jug of *pivo*.

The cops drink at a frenetic pace and begin an arm wrestling competition. The Greeks join in. Even Little Athena. She challenges one of the largest of the Serbs to a match. 'Miki' sits opposite her and takes her tiny hand in his huge paw. The Greeks take photographs as he pretends to struggle with her.

He groans loudly and eventually feigns defeat – the back of his hand slapping against the table.

As the evening wears on our hosts clear back the tables and Miki produces an accordion. He runs his hands up and down the buttons and keys and launches into a Serbian folk song. He plays song after song as his comrades join in, singing and hammering the tables in appreciation. They then stumble into the centre of the courtyard and begin a traditional Serbian dance or *kolo*. The Greeks join in as they grip each other around the waist with one hand, swinging wildly, clapping and stamping. I'm mesmerised and glad that I have not been asked to dance. Yet.

The cops then begin a Cossack dance of sorts. Miki leaps up onto one of the tables. Others join him and a struggle ensues. The music stops as Miki and another cop maul each other. Other fights break out spontaneously. I see Big Athena slap a policeman full in the face. Meanwhile, two other cops are rolling around on the cobbles. One is biting the other's ear and has drawn blood.

As the fight spreads, the Greeks make a bee-line towards the foyer of the motel. As they do so they fight a rearguard action with some of the police-men. Big Athena shouts over the melee to me, 'Come on Little Tom. Time to go.' I'm blocked, however, by one of Miki's colleagues. The one who'd been staring sullenly at me earlier. He is bearing down on me and mumbling in a sinister way. His eyes are unfocused. Milomir appears out of nowhere and punches him on the side of the head. He staggers and goes down like a ton of bricks. I make a break for it. As I do, I hear the splintering and cracking of wood as one of the tables collapses under the weight of the fighting.

As we exit the front of the motel, Toma shepherds us onto the minibus. As the engine starts up, the Serbs burst through the front entrance. Toma pulls out his automatic pistol and fires three rounds in the air in quick succession. The sudden loud cracks are accompanied by the revving of engines as the minibus screeches out of the driveway. I watch through the rear window as Toma runs across the car park to the tiny police car.

The following morning, I wake up with a phenomenal hangover.

Chapter 5

Omarska

'You in Ireland are killers also. Is that not true? Who are you to judge us?
Who are you to judge anyone?'

Omarska, Bosnia
September 1996

The final week in Prijedor goes by in a blur of last-minute checks on polling stations and poll registers. There are no signs of Muslim 'returnees'. The abandoned homes remain empty.

Milomir has not modified his driving style. We rally from village to village, station to station. I try to thank Milomir for rescuing me at the motel. He looks surprised. Dragana translates for me. 'It was a normal party. No problems.'

Toma disappears for several days. He finally reappears on the night before the elections. He sidles up to our table in Sofija's restaurant. He has a faded black eye, but otherwise appears none the worse for our nocturnal adventure the previous week. 'What a wonderful Schweinfest. Hmm?' It is more of a declaration than a question.

On election day, I go to Dubica and Bos Gradiska. The polling stations in both locations are reassuringly busy. Like election days in Ireland, convoys of cars ferry the elderly from the surrounding countryside to cast their votes. The atmosphere is very positive. There is a palpable feeling of excitement. A new beginning perhaps. There is hope that the election will draw a line under the violence of recent years. The missing Muslims do not show up to vote. There are no busloads of returnees from either Croatia or Belgrade for that matter. There is still a large gap in the electoral register. There are still many thousands of missing persons.

In Mrakovica, Milomir parks the car next to an old church. A tiny old woman dressed from head to toe in black – like Senka – approaches us with a small bunch of flowers. She is calling out to us in a beseeching manner. Almost wailing. Holding out the flowers. Her cries and lamentations are heartbreaking and I am stopped in my tracks. I fumble in my pockets and take out a handful of deutsche marks. Milomir gasps and cries out, 'No, no!' But it is too late and the old lady – surprisingly nimbly – snaps the money out of my hand with a deft pincer movement of forefinger and thumb. Dragana is shaking her head and looks around the village anxiously.

We enter the polling station and talk to the presiding officer. He is pleased with the turnout. We check the seals on the polling boxes and I make idle conversation with the IFOR troops providing security.

When we re-emerge onto the street, the car has been surrounded by a crowd of elderly ladies dressed from head to toe in black. There must be about thirty of them at least. They are all holding bunches of flowers in their claws. They spot me from a distance and charge in our direction. Milomir curses loudly. 'I fucking told you so.' His English seems to be improving dramatically.

We negotiate our way through the crowd of old ladies. Milomir puts the car in gear and we edge our way past them and, accelerating, he gives them the three-fingered Serb salute out the window. They wave the bunches of flowers angrily at us as we disappear out of the village. I ask Dragana if Milomir will take us to Omarska.

Omarska is the location of one of three concentration camps in the vicinity of Prijedor that operated during the war. The other death camps were located in Trnopolje and Kereterm. TV news images from the Omarska camp – featuring skeletal inmates – shocked the world in August 1992. The images, obtained by Channel 4 and ITN, were reminiscent of those taken at Nazi death camps during World War II. The international community expressed shock and horror that such atrocities could have taken place in central Europe. Especially after all that we had supposedly learned from the Holocaust. UN prosecutors specifically compare the death camps around

Prijedor as identical in almost every aspect to those run by the Nazis during the Third Reich. In the case of Bosnia, however – in this part of Bosnia – Muslims in the main replaced Jews as those destined by virtue of religion and ethnicity for torture and death.

I am particularly interested in Omarska because of the TV images I had seen in Dublin just four years earlier. Dragana translates my request for Milomir. But he had already begun to look at me when he heard the word Omarska. He speaks rapidly to Dragana. She in turn obliges with a translation. 'Milomir would prefer to take you to the World War II Memorial at Mrakovica. It speaks of all of the victims of war, Serbs and Partisans. Not just Croats or Muslims.' It is my second-last day in Bosnia and I feel I have little to lose. I insist. Milomir takes us to Omarska.

He drives us to the abandoned mine in Omarska. Outside the gates to the complex, Milomir slams on the brakes. The mine – where thousands of Muslims were detained during the war – is run down and overgrown. The outhouses and other buildings are in disrepair and there are signs warning of unexploded ordnance and antipersonnel mines. I think of the Canadian sergeant major's advice in Banja Luka.

Milomir is agitated and walks up and down by the car, smoking furiously. Dragana asks me if I've seen enough. In a rare moment of connection, Dragana looks me straight in the eye and asks me – implores me – to allow herself and Milomir to take me to the war memorial at Mrakovica. 'Everybody lost loved ones in this war,' she tells me. 'Not just Muslims and Croats. Serbs too.' Dragana's eyes have welled up with tears. It is the first time I have seen her express an emotion other than hostility. I agree to go to Mrakovica.

On the way to the memorial, Milomir conducts an angry tirade in Serbian. He uses the word *mudzahedini* (mujahideen) repeatedly. Dragana asks me if I have read about the mass murder and summary execution of Serb prisoners of war during the conflict. She asks me if I have heard about the beheadings by foreign 'Jihadis' of innocent Serb civilians. She asks me if I have heard about the ethnic cleansing of Serb families – whole family groups – by Croat 'special commando units' during the war. Dragana is at pains to point out to me that 'nobody has a monopoly on murder. Nobody is exclusively evil. Not Germans, not Russians even. Neither Serb nor Croat for that matter. Or Muslim. We are all killers.' She concludes her monologue on an uncomfortable note. 'You in Ireland are killers also. Is that not true? Who are you to judge us? Who are you to judge anyone?'

The Mrakovica Memorial is located in the Kozara National Park, which is located between the Sava, Sana, Una and Vrbas rivers. It is an area possessed of outstanding natural beauty. We fall silent as Milomir drives us there. Eventually we reach the deserted public car park at the site. It is an unusual monument to the dead. The memorial is designed by the artist Dusan Dzamonja. At its centre is a large angular tower – an enormous metal and concrete structure. What strikes me most, however, are a series of large concrete barriers that fan out in a sunray pattern from the centre of the memorial. The enormous concrete structures form open passages or corridors through which you must pass in order to reach the bronze centerpiece at the base of the tower. The names of thousands of Serb partisans who died fighting the Nazis, fighting fascism, are engraved there.

Consistent with the sunray pattern in the design of the memorial, the openings at the concrete entrances are wide. As you approach the centre, however, the passages grow narrower and more claustrophobic. In the final few metres, one has to squeeze through an increasingly narrow concrete gap. It is an uncomfortable and unnerving experience.

Even more so as Dragana leads me by the hand. As we squeeze through the final gap in the wall, Dragana turns to look at me. Her scar is still vivid in the shade of the concrete. Her face is flushed from the effort at forcing her way through the narrow aperture. She explains to me, 'This is the transition from life into death. It is supposed to be painful. But, you come from the darkness into light. Death is not the end.'

We emerge into the centre of the memorial. Dragana and I slap the dust of each other's clothing. The names of the dead are innumerable. Lots of Dragans, Draganas, Milomirs, Mikis and Zorans. Many of whom were butchered in Auschwitz or in the concentration camp at Jasenovac. Jasenovac was operated by Croats with the approval of the Nazis. Serbs who fought with the Allies as partisans along with Jews and Roma were murdered at Jasenovac in the most barbaric and sadistic manner. Dragana interrupts the stillness with another of her atonal announcements. 'The Serbs have now inherited the reputation of the Germans and Croats.'

When we return to the car, Milomir has calmed down somewhat. He drives us to an ice cream parlour on the outskirts of Prijedor. We eat our ice cream in silence.

In the following days, OSCE election monitors from all over Bosnia Herzegovina confirm a free and fair election at municipal and regional count centres throughout the country.

I spend the last night in Zoran's house helping him to dry walnuts on the first-floor veranda. He and Bojan have harvested thousands of walnuts and are drying them out on sheets suspended like hammocks from the roof beams and the timber frame of the covered terrace. Irena sits on a chair and watches us. She smiles as Milinka and Dragana run around and play on the terrace. The girls are very excited. Bojan explains to me that the walnuts are eaten during the Serb Orthodox Christmas celebrations. Zoran hands me a box of walnuts from the garden. He also gives me a bottle of *rakija*.

Bojan gives me a black beret as a souvenir. He tells me he was drafted to fight two years previously. I am very surprised. Bojan explains in German that he is now completing his high school education. 'Better late than never.'

Toma calls to the house in the police car and announces that he, and not Milomir, will give me a lift the following morning to the IFOR office in Prijedor where all of the OSCE monitors are to be transported back to Sarajevo. He tells me to be ready to go at 'eight o'clock sharp'.

The following morning, I leave at seven o'clock sharp with the two Athenas. I hope Toma doesn't mind being stood up. But I don't fancy that last drive with him.

We assemble at the IFOR office. It turns out that due to 'logistical problems' I am part of a group that will be taken out of Bosnia by road. Big Athena and Little Athena are flying to Sarajevo and we say our goodbyes at the side of the road. In turn, they give me a final embrace and a kiss on each cheek. Big Athena ruffles my hair and tells me, 'Take care yourself Little Tom.'

Milomir appears then and shakes my hand. I ask him about Dragana. He shakes his head and says, 'She is typical woman.' Milomir gives me a bottle of *rakija*. 'Because you like so much.' He then gives me the three-fingered salute and disappears into the crowd.

We board the bus. The route will take us through the Krajina, onward into Croatia, skirting west of Zagreb, through Slovenia and on to Vienna. I look out the rear-view window and see Toma pull up in his police car. He stands by the driver's door and I see him scan the groups of election monitors. He looks agitated. I catch his eye as we pull away with our IFOR escort. He stares at me and spits into the dust.

It is a long drive to Vienna from Prijedor. We pass through the border into Croatia and our IFOR escort waves us goodbye. The border crossing is a stark reminder of the war. The forest and ground around the crossing has been cleared for several hundred metres to create a no man's land. The Croatian troops at the border man reinforced steel and concrete positions and emerge only to pull away a tank stop and some barbed wire to allow us entry. Croatian police board the bus and examine our passports. As we leave the checkpoint, I see many more heavily camouflaged positions to the rear. Defence in depth.

Croatia in late '96 is similar to Bosnia Herzegovina. White painted villas with red-tiled roofs. Signs of reconstruction everywhere. And signs of the war. We ask the driver if we can stop for food. 'Wait until Slovenia,' is his reply. We pass through Croatian towns that are barely lit as night falls.

When we reach the border with Slovenia, the transformation is remarkable. We pass through what looks like a large motorway tollbooth. No concrete and steel gun positions here. Once through the border crossing we are on motorway. Indistinguishable from any autobahn in Austria or Germany. Slovenia has had a little longer to recover from its very brief involvement in the Balkan War.

About 2km from the border crossing the bus pulls into a motorway service station. The twenty-four-hour supermarket and restaurants gleam with brand-new fittings. The fridges are filled with Coke and 7Up. What strikes me most after seven weeks in Bosnia is how illuminated it is here. Lights everywhere. Strip lighting in the windows and out on the forecourts. Neon signage winking overhead. Lines of orange streetlights along the motorway stretching into the distance towards Austria.

We arrive in Vienna in the early hours of the morning. As it happens, I am able to fly to Zurich and then direct to Dublin with Aer Lingus. I'm home within a matter of hours. I ring my girlfriend from a callbox in Dublin airport. She asks me not to go away again for a while. She tells me she missed me.

On the way into the city centre the taxi driver asks me if I've been anywhere nice. I wouldn't know where to start so I tell him I've been to Majorca. He whistles 'Viva España' all the way to town. I think about where I have been. Home and dry, I realise I was not afraid. I have not experienced fear in Bosnia. In time and on reflection, I will conclude this absence of fear – my bravado – was a function of my innocence. Experiences at home will rob me of that innocence. It is in Ireland, in the bosom of family and in the peacetime routine of the Irish army, that I will fully experience doubt and fear. It is at home that I will fully come to know the hidden and destructive forces that often lie just beneath the surface.

The following Monday I report back to duty. The executive officer compliments me on my suntan and asks me if I've enjoyed my package holiday. There is no debriefing about Bosnia. There have been other developments in my absence. A new chapter in my life is opening up. The adjutant of the unit tells me that the commanding officer, 'after careful consideration', has given me permission to apply to do a doctorate in Dublin City University. He tells me that I'll need to apply through the chain of command to the Director of Training at Defence Forces Headquarters for formal, written approval from the general staff to conduct any doctoral research within the Defence Forces. With this information duly imparted to me, I am dismissed and ordered to report to the school commandant.

Chapter 6

Feminist Theory

'Girls can get any amount of information from most men. Get them going. Don't think there is anything ignoble about Army intelligence work. There is decidedly not. No army can move an inch or win the slightest victory without it. Help us move miles. Help us win victories. The work is as necessary – and as noble – as the regular scrapping. But – be careful! MOUTHS SHUT – EARS OPEN.' – Divisional Intelligence Officer, 1st Northern Division IRA, 25 July 1922

The Artillery School, Magee Barracks, Kildare Town

October 1996

So, seventy-two hours after Prijedor, I'm back in my home unit, at the School of Artillery in Magee Barracks, Kildare Town. Just the weekend to recover and then straight back to 'reality'. Although, it is the barrack routine that now feels increasingly unreal. I have no time to reflect on my experiences in Bosnia. Such as they are. The School Commandant gleefully informs me that after my continental holiday he has plans for me. I'm immediately detailed to supervise the unending cycle of annual tactical exercises and regimental shoots on the army's firing ranges in the Glen of Imaal in County Wicklow. As an instructor of gunnery, I'm responsible for teaching the language and skills of 'fire control' to the gunners, NCOs and officers that are detailed to attend the various courses in the school. The objective is to achieve 'the maximum exploitation of firepower' in all phases of offensive and defensive operations. In the late nineties, the Irish army is slowly but surely integrating into a range of European and international military and security agencies.

Ireland's military are already committed to the United Nations under the

UN's SAS or 'Standby Arrangement System'. The state has had decades of experience of peacekeeping and peace enforcement operations in blue-helmet missions. In the 1990s, however, the Irish military undergo a silent revolution. The army mantra in the nineties is 'integration and interoperability'. We integrate into the fledgling European Union Rapid Reaction Force. We eventually become members of the EU Nordic Battle Group. The appellation 'Nordic' makes me think of Vikings, swinging battle axes as they go berserk.

In addition, Prime Minister Bertie Ahern signs Ireland up to NATO's PfP or 'Partnership for Peace' program. This is a stepping stone to full NATO membership. Our pattern of integration is both local and global. Incremental, inexorable integration into EU battlegroups regionally, and NATO internationally. As a consequence, a strategic transformation takes place within Óglaigh na hÉireann's command, control and manoeuvre doctrine that copperfastens the Irish military's status and role within the EU's emerging military structures and within NATO. This process of integration and conventional militarisation takes place despite Ireland's explicit commitment to her stated policy of neutrality.

For military integration and interoperability to proceed smoothly, the Irish army must radically review and reconfigure its entire tactical and strategic posture. As an officer and lecturer in the School of Artillery, I find myself, by coincidence, at the heart of this profound change-management process. As a consequence, I learn a lot more about strategic doctrine, conventional combined arms tactics, ballistics and explosive natures than would normally have been expected. I also learn a great deal about CBRN or 'Chemical, Biological, Radiological and Nuclear' warfare. Weapons of mass destruction. Whilst all of this is very worthy, I'm slowly beginning to realise that the bulk of my new-found knowledge and skills have little application in the civilian world outside. Unless, of course, I'm considering a career as the human cannonball with a travelling circus.

Older, more experienced officers advise me to begin 'digging an escape tunnel'. As the Irish economy picks up, more and more officers of my rank are resigning their commissions and pursuing careers in the private sector. My plan is to complete a doctorate over the next four years or so in order to move on. After my experiences in Lebanon and Bosnia – despite the transformation that is taking place within the Irish army – I'm finding the barrack routine of the peace-time army to be limited and limiting.

My reasons for pursuing a doctorate are reasonably straightforward. In 1993, having spent two years as a probationary second lieutenant, I completed a Master's Degree in Communications in Dublin City University. The MA in Communications was a two-year course. I graduated just before I deployed to Lebanon in 1995. One of the semesters for the MA included a module in Feminist Theory. The module proved quite an eye-opener for me as a male army officer. It was an unexpected learning experience which would have profound implications for me, both personally and professionally. It would also have profound and unforeseen implications for the Irish armed forces. Feminism indeed.

The lectures in feminist theory gave me a thorough grounding in traditional, liberal and radical feminist perspectives. The module was perplexing and provocative. I found myself engaged in increasingly heated exchanges with the lecturer, Dr Maggie Gibbon. For her part, Maggie was a patient but persistent debater and teacher. Having exhausted all of my arguments to the effect that equality for women had 'surely been achieved' by 1994, Maggie made me slowly and painfully aware of the stark and persistent barriers to women's fullest participation in society. Obstacles for women which were still very much in place in Ireland in the 1990s. Maggie made me aware, as a young Irish man, and as a male officer in a male-dominated organisation, that structural inequality for Irish women was an everyday fact of life in our so-called Irish Republic. This was a troubling newsflash for me. After one particularly adversarial argument, Maggie invited me for a cup of coffee after class.

On that dark November night in 1994 – in the crowded canteen in DCU – Maggie asked me three simple questions. Three questions that would – unbeknownst to me – lead me directly into *terra incognita*. It was one of those moments where one can say, in hindsight, one's life changed. At the time however – like most people on the brink of an epiphany – I never saw it coming. Maggie put the questions to me in her soft, lilting Welsh accent. 'OK Tom, we may have to agree to disagree on some points, but I want you to complete a short exercise for me. Go to your workplace tomorrow and ask three questions. How many women are working in your organisation? How much are they being paid relative to their male peers? And finally, what are their promotion prospects compared to men in the organisation?'

Reflecting on what Maggie had asked me, I made initial enquiries. There were in fact approximately 100 women in the Irish army in 1994. Out of a total of almost 11,000 personnel. In relation to pay, these women were routinely barred from a host of military duties, such as border duties for example, that attracted extra pay and allowances. Army policies for female soldiers ensured that they were, de facto, paid less than their male colleagues. In addition, official army promotion criteria – including military service overseas and service in operational units at home – were aspects of army life from which women were formally excluded. Hence, dramatically fewer women than men were promoted. These initial, preliminary findings were troubling to say the least. They seemed to prove Maggie right. The findings challenged my perception of the army as a kind of brutal but fair meritocracy. This 'tough but fair' concept was one that I had firmly believed in throughout my military service to date.

I completed the MA in the summer of 1995 and deployed to Lebanon. By the autumn of 1996, having returned from Bosnia, here I am, ready to revisit the questions that Maggie had put to me in the canteen in DCU two years previously. I decide to pursue a doctorate investigating the status and roles assigned to female personnel in the Irish Defence Forces.

I apply in writing to the Director of Training to get permission to conduct research into the experiences of women in the Irish armed forces. By the autumn of 1996 there are still relatively few female soldiers in the army. The number has risen to around 130 or so, or approximately 1 percent of the overall strength of the army. The letter of application that I have written follows a tortuous course through the chain of command. First of all, it has to be signed-off by my commanding officer in the School of Artillery. Then it must go through the headquarters of the Curragh Command for referral on to the Director of Training at Defence Forces Headquarters.

Eventually, after a long wait, I get a written reply from the general staff. It is good news. According to the letter with an impressive file notation 'CC/A/CS3/8 – DA/CS3/L', I am told that, 'I am directed to inform you that D Trg [Director of Training] approves Lt Clonan's request to produce a Doctoral Thesis.' Great news indeed. But there are some conditions attached. According to paragraph two, the letter continues, 'Provided that (a) The work is not published (b) The exercise is funded by himself and (c) Any time off necessary is sanctioned.'

Despite the conditions imposed, I am delighted. I'm looking forward to the challenge and begin consultations with Maggie, who has agreed to be my research supervisor at Dublin City University. We negotiate a research design that comprises a thorough and comprehensive audit of the experiences of women in the Irish Defence Forces. This audit will – initially – consist of an in-depth examination of all of the written and documentary sources within the army as they apply to the service of female soldiers. These written or documentary sources include legislation such as the Defence Acts, Defence Forces regulations, standard operating procedures, orders, memoranda, boards of enquiry and all internal and external reviews of the organisation. The audit will be retrospective. Its starting point will begin shortly before the intake of the first female soldiers into the Irish Defence Forces in 1980.

The audit will also consist of a comparative analysis with the experiences of female soldiers in the US and British military during the same timeframe. I am accepted on to the postgraduate research register in DCU. I hope in time – if the office for postgraduate studies is satisfied with my work – to progress to the PhD register.

Thus, in addition to my duties in the School of Artillery, I commence my PhD research in earnest. I assiduously identify, retrieve and collate every single document within the army, air corps and naval service as they apply to women soldiers. Like a magpie, I build up a diverse but comprehensive collection of papers, reports and policies pertaining to women in the Irish armed forces. A distinct pattern is beginning to emerge.

In military archives, I gain access to the initial internal army reports that pre-empted the recruitment of the first women soldiers to the forces in 1980. In January 1978, a memo from the Secretary of the Department of Defence to the Chief of Staff of the Defence Forces outlines the concept for a 'Women's Service Corps'. According to the memo, women are to be strictly limited to non-combat duties to include, 'a. Clerical duties, b. Driving of light vehicles, c. Observer Corps duties, d. Welfare duties, e. Miscellaneous.' In paragraph three of the memo, the Department of Defence advises the chief of staff that the Women's Service Corps is intended to 'release male soldiers from certain duties in order to fill more active military functions'.

The general staff, duly informed, form a 'Committee on the Establishment of a Women's Service Corps WSC.' This committee submits its confidential report on 10 February 1978. The report's conclusions are ominous. On page eleven, paragraph four, entitled 'Pay', the report states, 'After full consideration of the matter, the majority of our members recommend that the basic rates of pay of members of the WSC should be less than those payable to men.'

The report also reaches some interesting conclusions on pregnancy and issues of maternity among Irish women soldiers. On page nine of the report, at paragraph three, entitled 'Pregnancy', it states, 'We are aware that pregnancy is not a ground for termination of service in the . . . Ban Garda and the Public Service generally. Nevertheless, in view of . . . the fact all military employment is of its nature physically demanding and requires a minimum standard of fitness at all times . . . we recommend that pregnancy should be included in Defence Forces Regulations as a reason for automatic termination of the service of members . . . for both officers and other ranks.'

Fortunately for those women soldiers who were eventually recruited to the army in 1980, these conditions of service proved impossible to impose – overtly. As such provisions were contrary to equality legislation enacted in the 1970s and 1980s – including the Anti-Discrimination (Pay) Act of 1975, the Employment Equality Act of 1977 and the Maternity Protection of Employees Act 1981 – the army's concept for a 'Women's Service Corps' was rejected by the government of the time in favour of 'general enlistment' for women to the Irish armed forces.

Despite this general enlistment and the appearance of an integrated approach for women within the Irish armed forces, the general staff still prescribed ways in which to – intentionally or otherwise – curtail women's participation in the army and to severely limit their career prospects.

In the first two years of my research I access many other disturbing and often contradictory documents within the Defence Forces. To me, they reveal a mindset on the part of a small, but powerful, cohort of senior officers in the Irish army that is hostile to women's service in our armed forces. One document in particular, the 1990 Defence Forces Headquarters 'Policy on the Deployment of Females in the Defence Forces', makes for sobering reading.

In the preamble and opening statement of the document, the authors state, at paragraph B, 'The General Staff acknowledge . . . and fully supports the concept of equality of opportunity in the areas where women are to be employed. Where possible, female personnel are encouraged to participate on an equal footing with their male colleagues in areas where they serve together.' So far, so good.

However, the policy statement continues to include a litany of exclusions and barriers to women's fullest participation in the core activities of the Irish armed forces. Under the heading 'Areas of Participation' at paragraph B, the document states, 'Specifically, women will not be posted to units in the Infantry, Artillery, Air Corps, nor to the Army Ranger Wing, Brigade Operations or Intelligence Staffs, nor in the case of (female) officers to the Operations Sections at Command HQs or Defence Forces HQ.'

No reason is given in the document as to why women soldiers and officers should be excluded from such service. I think of Maggie's lectures in which she describes received beliefs about women in some primitive societies – where females are believed to be inherently 'untrustworthy' or 'intellectually inferior' to males. I remember one lecture in which Maggie explained the origin of the Greek word *hyster* for womb. In the lecture, Maggie spoke of the belief in ancient Greek society that women – possessed of wombs – were therefore considered innately 'hysterical' and by implication 'naturally inferior' to their male counterparts.

I do not know why the Irish general staff feel that women are unsuited to such roles as intelligence gathering. I can only speculate. I do know, however, from other documents in military archives, that during the Irish War of

Independence, Irish women were considered especially suited to intelligence work and intelligence gathering. In a letter from the Intelligence Department of the 1st Northern Division of the IRA, on 25 July 1922, the Divisional Intelligence Officer writes to 'No. 23,' Miss Coyle, 'Girls can get any amount of information from most men. Get them going. Don't think there is anything ignoble about Army Intelligence Work. There is decidedly not. No army can move an inch or win the slightest victory without it. Help us move miles. Help us win victories. The work is as necessary – and as noble – as the regular scrapping. But – be careful! MOUTHS SHUT – EARS OPEN.'

I am particularly intrigued as to why the army feels that Irish women in the 1990s are unsuited to intelligence work. Especially given the hyperactive role that contemporary Irish women play in intelligence gathering among terrorist organisations within the state, such as the Provisional IRA. It is as though the general staff are suffering from a form of cognitive dissonance. On the one hand, they recognise the threat posed by women in terrorist organisations in Ireland – and by extension their skills and potential as combatants and intelligence operatives – and yet on the other hand, at the stroke of a pen, they see fit to disbar women from service in such roles within the army itself.

The 1990 Policy on the Deployment of Females in the Defence Forces contains a long list of very explicit and detailed prohibitions on female military service. Under the heading, 'Service Corps and Special Establishments, Paragraph (c) iii MP Corps', the document states, 'Women MPs will not serve in the No 1 Garrison MP Company at Government Buildings. They will not carry out gate security duties, nor pay escort duties, both of which essentially require the carrying of arms.' It is not clear from the document why 'women MPs' are unsuited to such duties. Nor is it clear why 'women MPs' ought to be excluded from the environs of Leinster House and Ireland's national parliament. Perhaps they might run amok with guns? Or, heaven forbid, provide a positive role model for women in a national parliament which is depressingly and overwhelmingly male dominated?

In relation to the Air Corps, the 1990 Policy Document contains fascinating stipulations and implied assumptions about female pilots. At 'Paragraph

C, iv Air Corps,' it states, 'Women will not be eligible to serve as pilots in the armed support role, nor take part in flying operations in Aid to the Civil Power Operations (Anti-Terror Operations).'

This exclusion was authored at a time when female pilots were routinely flying multiple fixed-wing and helicopter aircraft in the US Air Force and in the air forces of several other European Union member states. In 1990, women were well established as professional pilots in the commercial air industry, flying millions of passengers worldwide. And in 1990, female pilots in the US 101st Airborne Division's 'Screaming Eagles' – flying Blackhawk and Chinook helicopters – would participate in the largest helicopter air assaults since World War II on Iraqi troops in Kuwait and Basra. The Irish general staff's views on the capabilities of Irish female pilots seem to me to be grossly out of step with international best practice and experience. The Irish military authorities appear to be of the view that a pilot must be in possession of a penis to fly aircraft equipped with weapons.

The 1990 policy document also deals with the question of Irish female soldiers serving overseas. In paragraph (b) 'Areas of Participation', it states, 'Women will not serve with UN Forces abroad except at a designated Forces HQ, i.e. UNIFIL HQ (United Nations Interim Force in Lebanon Headquarters) Naquora, (Lebanon) . . . excluding service in IRISHBATT (Irish Battalion in Lebanon).' Reading this document, it appears Irish women are to be disbarred from peacekeeping operations in Irish uniform, with no prospect of interacting with civilian populations overseas.

This provision is breathtakingly short-sighted given the numbers of women and children with whom Irish soldiers directly interact. Many of those civilians who come into contact with Irish troops overseas are refugees, internally displaced persons or the innocent victims of military attacks. Many of these women and children are victims of sexual assault and rape. To suggest that Irish women ought have no role in dealing with these populations as peacekeepers – in a 1990 document – suggests a mindset at Defence Forces Headquarters that is gravely at variance with established best practice in international peacekeeping and peace-enforcement missions. To me, as an officer charged with seeking out best practice as it applies to tactical and strategic doctrine, this aspect of Defence Forces culture seems anachronistic and ill informed.

I also reflect on my experiences in Lebanon in 1996. I think of the female medics and drivers who went to the aid of the dead and dying. The army documents that I am accessing at home in Ireland speak of a profoundly patriarchal, paternalistic and misogynistic attitude towards female soldiers. The army documents filed in Dublin seem to ignore the reality of women's service overseas. My research supervisor in DCU urges caution and exhorts me to examine other documents, where possible, in order to achieve a balanced view. Maggie urges me to consult with the Defence Forces Equality Mission Statement. 'They must surely have one,' she tells me. The literature on equality of opportunity contains the uniform assumption that all modern organisations – particularly state-funded bodies – will have such documents. I enquire at work about our 'Equality Mission Statement.' I draw a blank. I get quizzical looks from HR officers at DFHQ.

The Defence Forces has no equality mission statement in 1996. The only policies it has in relation to female personnel, it appears, are explicitly discriminatory.

Chapter 7

Sisters in Arms

'There is a tendency to compensate for physical weakness in females by not detailing them for the most strenuous tasks. Added to this in the tactical training situation is an overly protective attitude from male colleagues . . . There is no doubt that some male officers and male soldiers are also physically weak. This may be due to their small stature . . .' – Staff Officer, Personnel Resources Section, Irish Defence Forces, Dublin, 4 February 1993

The School of Artillery, Magee Barracks, Kildare Town / Dublin City University, Glasnevin, Dublin

1997

At this point, the first year and a half of my research has consisted of an extraordinary paper trail. My investigation thus far has involved an in-depth examination of the history of women in combat both in Ireland and internationally along with a forensic examination of the conditions of service for female soldiers serving in the contemporary Irish armed forces. I spend a lot of time in Military Archives in the Cathal Brugha Barracks in Rathmines. I also spend a lot of time accessing documents at Defence Forces Headquarters – in Enlisted Personnel Section and at Officer's Records in Parkgate Street.

In my trawl of documents as they apply to women in the Defence Forces, I come across several written appeals, or attempts at redress, by female soldiers from within the organisation seeking to overturn the discriminatory policies that confront them within the Irish army. In response to specific queries raised by female soldiers, about the validity, legitimacy and *raison d'être* of exclusions to overseas service, the Adjutant General's Branch responds in a memo of May 1994. In this revealing memorandum, the Adjutant General's

Branch states at paragraph two, 'United Nations New York (UNNY) has stated in writing that no distinction is made with regard to the deployment of males and females in Peace-Keeping or Observer Missions. The decision on whether to assign females to duty with UN Missions is one for the Government of the troop contributing countries concerned.' At paragraph three, the Adjutant General's Branch memo states, 'The Defence Forces Policy on the deployment of females is based on the principle of Equality of Opportunity, therefore no individual is precluded from selection for overseas service on the basis of gender.'

This paragraph must surely have reassured Irish female soldiers who had the legitimate expectation and ambition of serving the Irish Republic over-seas. But, unfortunately, as in so many other Irish army documents of the time, there are conditions attaching to the notion of 'Equality of Opportunity'. At the end of paragraph three, the Adjutant General's Branch elaborates, 'However, Defence Forces Policy must not conflict with host nation policy.' At paragraph four, the memo continues, 'The following points will be addressed when considering the assignment of females, (a) Location and Host National Policy, (b) United Nations Policy (If Any), (c) Policy and Practice of other troop contributing nations, (d) National and local culture and religious norms, (e) The Role of Women in the particular society.'

I'm disturbed at the reasoning contained within the memo. If the interna-tional military were to take the 'national and local culture and religious norms' or 'role of women in the particular society' as prescriptions for the deployment of female troops – then no women soldiers would serve in Kuwait, Iraq, Saudi Arabia, Afghanistan, Lebanon, Western Sahara and so on. The list would be endless. While the Irish military authorities recognise the wide cultural differ-ences between Ireland and those often Islamic societies where we deploy our troops – they see eye-to-eye with Islamist cultural norms exclusively as they apply to women. Maggie is unsurprised.

According to my document search – and my own experience as an officer at the time – the contents of the the Irish Army's '1990 Policy on the Deployment of Females in the Defence Forces' are widely disseminated throughout the organisation. It causes a furore among female soldiers and officers. Many of these women write lengthy submissions and redress applications to have the policy amended or withdrawn. The general staff relents and in October 1991 – under the chief of staff's Convening Order of 30 September 1991 – it convenes an internal board to examine and report upon the 'Employment of Females in the Defence Forces'. The board assembles on 7 October 1991 at Defence Forces Headquarters. It consists of eight members. All of them are male. The board becomes known throughout the Irish army as the 'Beauty Board' because of its focus on female personnel. Thankfully, the board recommends the withdrawal of the 1990 Policy Statement. However, it does not replace it with an equality mission statement or a formal set of equality of opportunity guidelines similar to those in common usage by the international military.

Instead, the board reaches some interesting findings about women soldiers in general and small male soldiers in particular. One of the members of the board, a senior officer from 'Personnel Resources', pens the following in his submission, 'Physical Capacity, Personnel of the Defence Forces,' (PDF, PHY, PRS, 4 February 1993): 'There is a tendency to compensate for physical weakness in females by not detailing them for the most strenuous tasks. Added to this in the tactical training situation is an overly protective attitude from male colleagues . . . There is no doubt that some male officers and male soldiers are also physically weak. This may be due to their small stature . . . One only needs to contemplate a 4'10" female driving an armoured personnel carrier or a Man Diesel Truck, or the credibility of a 4'10" Platoon Sergeant to realise that some females will NOT be suited to a variety of appointments because of their physical stature.'

These observations are not borne out by the facts. The latest research in the US military – conducted by the US Army Research Institute of Environmental Medicine along with other military academic research institutions – shows that women have a uniformly positive impact on unit performance in both the training environment and the live operational environment at war.

The reality of women's actual experience of combat is at variance with the assumptions and conclusions reached by the Irish army's 'Beauty Board'. As part of the research process, I have accessed US military archives that state that over 40 percent of military commanders in the North Vietnamese Army and Viet Cong were women. The US military also records the activities of one particular Vietnamese woman, Din Le Tunn, who ran a 'sniper school for girls' at Min Top in Vietnam. These women, in the interests of concealment and economy, specialised in a technique of killing US troops with one shot, often beating survivors to death with their own weapons. Notions of 'girlishness' or assumptions of 'passivity' about women – or the mistaken association of strength and combat effectiveness with physical stature – are quickly dispelled by such accounts. Indeed, for US troops in Vietnam, the initial surprise, or 'culture shock' of encountering female enemy troops, or indeed enemy troops of small stature, was soon tempered by the knowledge that, man, woman or child, the enemy of either sex was equally deadly. This view however, learned at great cost on the contemporary battlefield, does not seem to be shared by my Irish army colleagues at Defence Forces Headquarters.

As my research into the status and roles assigned female personnel in the Irish Defence Forces continues, the findings are increasingly stark. The research process gathers momentum. The investigation, however, is making me feel increasingly uncomfortable. In terms of numbers alone, Irish women represent less than 1 percent of the army's strength in 1997. Meanwhile, women consist of around 11 percent of US and British army strengths. Fifteen percent of all NATO active military forces are female. The low numbers of women in the Irish army are all the more surprising given that, now, for the first time in the history of the state, we have a female commander-in-chief – President Mary Robinson. The army, rather than struggling to keep pace with change, seems determined, in its official reports and memoranda, to remain static with regard to the status of women within the ranks.

The research generates an enormous amount of written data. To date, my 'database management' has consisted of a primitive filing system in my old bedroom at home in Finglas. There simply isn't room anywhere else to accommodate the growing piles of documents, journal articles and photocopies of archival material. I take all of my notes the old-fashioned way, by hand. Pen and paper. I start to write up initial reports and the beginnings of chapters in my awkward, left-handed script.

One day, in June of 1997, I'm carrying a box of papers up to my old bedroom when I find my sister Pauline standing in the doorway. Pauline is just two years older than me. Taller than me, blonde and nonchalantly smoking a sneaky cigarette in my room. She is looking quizzically over my 'Alladin's cave of stuff'. Pauline looks at me with her pale blue eyes – one eyebrow raised. 'What's all this, little brother?' she asks me. I explain to her about the work in progress.

Pauline was a major role model for me when we were growing up in Finglas during the 1970s and early '80s. As my big sister with her exotic friends, Pauline was unassailably, impossibly cool in my eyes. Pauline introduced me to my first cigarette. She introduced me to my first drink. Giggling as we sneaked vodka from our dad's austere drinks cabinet – which consisted only of hard liquor. We sampled copious amounts of whiskey, vodka and gin. We didn't start out on beer or wine. Straight on to the hard stuff. She also introduced me to the music of Bob Dylan, Neil Young, The Doors. Pauline kept an eye on me as a teenager. She introduced me to her wide circle of friends – which was unusual, given that I was her annoying little brother. Pauline was, in short, a sort of guardian angel. When our parents were out, Pauline and I would sit next to the open window, smoking cigarettes, listening to Blue Oyster Cult on the record player. 'Don't Fear the Reaper' was one of Pauline's favourites. She liked the lyrics. And, she'd done *Romeo and Juliet* in the Leaving Cert. Despite her tough, cool, blonde exterior, Pauline was an old romantic at heart. I remember vividly the two of us, forever young, singing the lyrics as teenagers in our house in Finglas:

All our times have come
Here, but now they're gone
Seasons don't fear the reaper
Nor do the wind, the sun or the rain

Valentine is done
Here but now they're gone

Romeo and Juliet
Are together in eternity

For all my faults and irritating habits as a teenage boy, Pauline loved me. And I loved her. My cool big sister.

Pauline exhales now. A thin plume of blue smoke. She looks at me directly. 'You'll need to start typing this stuff up. You've got two left hands.' She looks around the room, stuffed with papers and notes. 'It'll take you forever. I'll type it up for you.' And so, Pauline becomes a collaborator and critic. As she types up the material, she grows more and more astonished by what she is reading and transcribing. 'Nana would go nuts if she read this,' she tells me. Our grandmother – Mairéad Begley, from Killorglin in Kerry, was in Cumann na mBan. She fought with the IRA in Dublin in the War of Independence. She taught in Scoil Bhríde – the all-Irish school founded by Louise Gavan Duffy. Nana taught every junior infant in Scoil Bhríde from 1917 to 1968. She was a republican down to her fingernails. She passed that republicanism and pride in Ireland on to us. She was also – I now realise after my module on feminist theory – a feminist. Pauline looks at me as she hands me the typewritten notes. 'I presume you know what you are doing, Thomas.'

In July of 1997, I am watching Sky News when I see a report from Prijedor. Simo Drljaca – the 'Sheriff of Prijedor' – has been shot dead by British troops during his arrest at Omarska on charges of war crimes. I remember his words to me from the previous year, in the mayor's office in Prijedor. When he spoke to me about the Irish 'having blood on their hands', I had not realised how much blood were on his. The hand that had gripped mine in the mayor's office.

At the end of my first academic year, I submit my research report to the office for postgraduate studies in Dublin City University. I also record my progress on my army annual confidential report or Army Form AF667. Each officer in the army is the subject of an annual 'confidential report' which charts his or her progress to date. This involves a formal interview with one's commanding officer in which the reporting officer gets the opportunity to comment on achievements during the reporting period. I proudly note to each and every one of my commanding officers during my PhD research the progress that I am making.

In December of 1997, I receive a letter from Bojan. It is the first contact I have had from the Krajina since I left Bosnia the previous year. He tells me that his mother, Irena, has died of cancer. In his letter he writes that she 'could not get treatment because of the war'. He also writes of Zoran's heartbreak. He tells me that Milinka and Dragana miss their mother. It is just another post script to the war in Bosnia. To war in general. It occurs to me how many such stories go unreported, remain untold. I think of the excitement of Milinka and Dragana as we dried the walnuts for Christmas. It will be a sad Christmas in Prijedor for Zoran and his family.

Chapter 8

DFHQ

'Don't fuck up. That's the brief.'

Defence Forces Headquarters, Parkgate Street, Dublin /
Dublin City University, Glasnevin, Dublin
1998

By 1998, after almost two years of research, I have amassed overwhelming and incontrovertible evidence that the Irish army is not a woman-friendly work environment. I am disappointed with the research outcomes. I'm also deeply worried about the findings. My beloved and eternally patient girlfriend, Aideen, is unsurprised when I tell her my big news. She smiles at me indulgently and tells me that she is glad that 'the penny has dropped'. I mull over the direction that the research is taking. I am proud of the Irish army. It is an extension of my family. And yet, my research to date tells me that there are deeply discriminatory systemic and systematic policies and practices within the organisation that function to restrict women's progress within the Irish military. The numbers of female soldiers recruited to the organisation are kept artificially low. Female soldiers are denied the requisite workplace experiences necessary for promotion and women leave the organisation at a disproportionately high rate by comparison with their male counterparts. The army, like many families it seems, is dysfunctional.

My supervisor Maggie is not surprised at the findings either. 'I hate to say I told you so,' she remarks at one point. But she is surprised at the level of discrimination – and its overt and explicit nature – at official levels within the army. The impact of this discrimination gives effect to a division of labour within the army on the basis of sex or gender. Having undertaken an exhaustive unit-by-unit audit of the army, air corps and naval service, I establish that only 17.1 percent of women soldiers are employed in front-line or operational roles attracting extra pay and allowances – such as border allowances or security duties. A whopping 82.9 percent are employed in lower-paid, menial roles such as waitresses in officer's messes, or as kitchen porters in cookhouses in army barracks across the country.

The summer of 1998 brings a number of significant developments for me. I get promoted to the rank of captain. And, in Dublin City University – between live-firing exercises, security duties and the odd stint guarding political prisoners as commander of the Portlaoise Prison Hospital Guard – I present my research progress to the office for postgraduate studies. I have now completed two full years of documentary and archival research. The findings are bleak. DCU are happy with my progress but are becoming increasingly concerned about the conditions imposed upon me by the military authorities in my original letter of application to the Director of Training at Defence Forces Headquarters. In particular, DCU are concerned about the condition at paragraph two: 'Provided the work is not published.'

I'm informed by the university that, in their opinion, to circulate my research findings for the purposes of examination – or to lodge the completed doctoral thesis to the library in DCU – would constitute a form of publication. I am advised that in order to proceed to the next stage of the research – and in order to progress to the PhD register – I must obtain written clarification and confirmation from the military authorities with regard to permission for the examination and publication of my research. In other words, I need to get permission from the chief of staff to have my work examined by the university. I also need to get written permission from the army to have the work lodged to DCU's library – as is the norm with doctoral theses.

In June of 1998, I look for an interview with the chief of staff. As an officer, I'm entitled to seek such an interview in exceptional circumstances. However, officers in the Irish armed forces rarely avail of this 'entitlement'. It is a bit like pulling the emergency cord on the train. If you are going to do it, you'd better have a pretty compelling reason for doing so. I am surprised at the speed of the chief of staff's response. I'm invited to meet him in his office.

The chief's suite of offices is in Parkgate Street at the very heart of Defence Forces Headquarters. The building is the former 'Headquarters, Ireland Command' of the British army. It is an imposing stone building. I'm met by a staff officer who ushers me into a waiting room. The door opens and the chief himself invites me in. He offers me a coffee, which he pours for me, and invites me to sit.

As lieutenant generals go, the chief is informal and approachable. He stirs his coffee and asks me slowly, carefully, measuring his words, in what way he can be of assistance to me. I'm extremely nervous about this meeting. I swallow hard and explain to him about my research and about the progress I have been making. I also explain to him the manner in which the prohibition on publication is blocking that progress and preventing me from completing the doctoral research. I have no idea how the general will react.

The chief probes me about the findings thus far. 'Well, young Clonan, I think it is of the utmost importance that you complete this research. Thoroughly. Leave no stone unturned. When you are finished, you'll need to give the general staff a full and final report.' I'm pinching myself. The chief is brief and to-the-point. 'I'll give you that written clarification today. You wait outside and my staff officer will give it to you. If you need anything else – just ask.' He smiles at me. 'There now. That wasn't so bad, was it?' He gives me a firm handshake. I salute and take my leave.

The staff officer directs me back into the waiting room. True to his word, the chief provides me with a letter of clarification within minutes. Addressed to the Registrar, Dublin City University, the letter is written in a clipped military style. At paragraph one the chief observes, 'In June of 1996, Captain Clonan sought and received permission to produce a PhD thesis on female personnel within the PDF . . . The letter states at paragraph two that permission was granted, 'provided the work is not published'. This is to confirm that the Defence Forces have no objections to the publication of the thesis for academic purposes. The thesis may be circulated to officers of the University and any internal and external examiners for the purposes of evaluation and examination. The thesis may also be held in the library of the University for reference purposes.'

As I read the letter, I feel relief flood through me. I get pins and needles. In providing this letter, the chief has ensured that I can complete the study and finalise the investigation. I am profoundly grateful to him. I feel in my heart and soul that the chief of staff's commitment will ultimately transform the workplace environment for female soldiers. I make copies of the letter for my own records and send the original by registered post to the registrar of DCU.

Maggie contacts me in due course and advises me that I have progressed to the PhD register. The next phase of the research can now begin. This phase will involve interviewing female soldiers – of all ranks – about their experiences of service within the Irish armed forces. These in-depth interviews take time to prepare. I expect to commence them in earnest over the coming winter of 1998 and into the spring of 1999.

Meanwhile, my time in the School of Artillery is drawing to a close. After almost ten years in the Curragh command, I am finally transferred to my native Dublin and the 2nd Field Artillery Regiment in McKee Barracks near the city centre. On my last night exercise with the school, I find myself sitting in a Land Rover with Sergeant Bracken – my friend and mentor with whom I'd served in Lebanon. Out on the Curragh plains under a full moon, I am unable to locate a battery of 105mm field guns that are training for night deployments.

'They must be here somewhere,' I remark. I'm staring at the map and the six-figure grid reference which indicates their current position. All I can see in front of me are ghostly gorse bushes, illuminated by moonlight. I decide to blow the horn on the Land Rover a couple of times to see if I can attract their attention. As soon as I do so, Sergeant Bracken sighs loudly, 'I wouldn't do that if I was you, sir.' And out of nowhere, hundreds of sheep emerge. Out of the darkness they come in single file, in groups and by the dozen. All headed for the Land Rover. I'm puzzled. Sergeant Bracken explains, 'They get fed with salt licks and water by farmers now and again. They blow the horn and the sheep come for the food. They think you have something for them.' Sure enough, I feel the Land Rover moving gently as it is nudged by sheep. There are now about two hundred or so pressing up against the vehicle. We are stranded in the middle.

That's when the gun battery finally appears. The school commandant and his staff officer also arrive. They are amused, to say the least, at my predicament. Sergeant Bracken looks wearily at me in the darkness. 'You can take the jackeen out of the city, but you can't knock any sense into him . . . sir.'

Two months later, I am appointed as a battery commander to the 2nd Field Artillery Regiment in McKee Barracks. My new CO is an exotic lieutenant colonel. Lt Col O'Brien has one all-consuming passion in life. That one passion being Lt Col O'Brien and his next promotion. As a result he micromanages the unit mercilessly, mithering his officers with a zeal bordering on obsessive. As he marches me in to meet him, the executive officer warns me that 'the CO could bore rats out of a barrel'.

Lt Col O'Brien appears disinterested in me and launches into a lengthy lecture on the requirement to remain 'vigilant' for 'negligence' and 'disloyalty to the CO' at all times. He pronounces each word carefully in his distinctive Belfast accent. Thankfully, as a respite from the CO's attentions, the unit is busy. One of my first duties is to act as a witness for the state in a criminal case involving one of the gunners. Apparently, on a Saturday night binge, the gunner in question has attacked a group of men outside a pub in Temple Bar. He's up for assault.

My job is to read out his army record as part of his defence. The gunner in question has had 'exemplary' service in the unit. I meet the gunner at the charge courts, near the Bridewell Garda Station. I ask him if he is OK. He looks OK. In fact he looks all too familiar with his surroundings and is on first-name terms with most of the felons and other offenders that throng the courtroom.

The arresting garda approaches me with a brown file. One of the gunner's victims has suffered a fractured skull. The charges against the soldier are now more serious. The garda is explaining to me that the case will probably be referred to a higher court. The gunner – having overheard this exchange – calls the garda a 'sneaky fucker' over my shoulder. The garda looks him in the eye and remarks, 'Yes, I suppose I am a sneaky fucker. And it's probably best you don't forget it.' Both smile beatifically at one another after this exchange.

I then spend a month in the High Court – again as a witness for the state

– in army deafness cases. My job is to clarify, if required, under cross-examination, whether or not claimants have suffered discrimination or loss of earnings arising from deafness. The deafness claims are a legacy issue within the Irish army backdating to a period when soldiers had insufficient hearing protection whilst firing weapons on the range. In other words, they had no hearing protection. Some of the old soldiers recall stuffing cigarette butts into their ears to protect them from the sound of rifle fire.

Years later, hundreds of soldiers suffer from tinnitus and hearing loss. The claims are working their way through the court system. Day after day I sit in on cases involving various older soldiers – heads cocked to one side as they try to follow court proceedings – and their claims against the state. One judge, clearly frustrated at the technical nature of the evidence before him, interrupts an expert witness who is describing hearing loss in terms of high-frequency sounds and decibels. He asks the claimant to explain 'in layman's terms' how the hearing loss affects him.

The old soldier looks him in the eye and tells him straight. 'Well, if I'm in the sitting room and the missus is in the kitchen, I can't hear what she's sayin' to me.' The judge ponders this and responds, 'If I might submit to you, Private Murphy, when my wife is in the kitchen, I sometimes cannot hear what she is saying to me.' Private Murphy considers this for a moment. The courtroom is hushed. Then he answers, 'Yeah, well with respect yer honour, I'd say your house is a lot bigger than my gaff.' He gets around 30,000 punts in compensation for his troubles.

Each day I report to the High Court in full No. 1 uniform. Sam Browne belt, medals and peaked cap. Each day I pass by two gardaí at the entrance who hold the door open for me. Presumably in honour of Michael Collins – 'The Big Fella' – they remark each time as I enter, 'Here comes the Little Fella.' They never tire of their joke. I'm highly amused, needless to say.

Apart from day trips to Dublin's courts, I'm also detailed on a regular basis for security duties in the capital. As part of the Brigade 'Stand-To,' I command a detachment of troops every ten days or so for a twenty-four-hour security duty. Based in Cathal Brugha Barracks in Rathmines, over a twenty-four-hour period, we patrol many of the city's vital installations, such as Dublin Airport, the cash distribution centre at the Central Bank in Sandyford and – from time to time – the transmitter in RTÉ along with other 'sensitive' locations.

On one such duty, I get a call from a classmate of mine who is a naval officer. He has just returned from an isolated farmhouse in the Wicklow Mountains. Answering an ad in the newspaper for thoroughbred Labrador pups, he had gone to this old lady's farm to buy a dog as a surprise for his wife and kids. But, as he tells me over the phone, when he gets there, the old lady invites him in for a cup of tea. There is a roaring fire in the fireplace – and the fire-surround is made up of antique US Navy sixteen-inch heavy shells. As my classmate drinks his tea, he notices that the shells are live. And, not only that, but they are 'sweating' next to the roaring fire. That's when he starts sweating. He tells me that if they had detonated – and they were highly unstable – the farmhouse and all of the barns and outhouses would have disappeared in the detonation. He and the old lady would have been the first Irish citizens in outer space. So, he manages to persuade the old lady to abandon her cosy seat by the fire and calls the Gardaí.

I'm still laughing at this when the radio comes to life. We are tasked with escorting the Explosive Ordnance Disposal team from Clancy Barracks to a County Wicklow farmhouse to 'make safe' a series of World War II naval shells 'discovered' in an old lady's sitting room. We're up there half the night. The last laugh is on me, it seems.

I'm also on duty on the day that the Omagh bombing takes place. I'm in the Stand-To room in the operations centre in Cathal Brugha Barracks, watching the images on Sky News. Twenty-nine dead. Two hundred and twenty-two injured. I'm watching images of people, with blood streaming down their faces, walking towards the TV cameras. Some are covered in masonry and dust from the explosions. It pulls me back to Lebanon two years previously. To the small towns and villages devastated by artillery and air strikes. I cannot believe that this scene is unfolding before my eyes in Ireland. I cannot believe that it is happening just weeks after Irish people on both parts of the island of Ireland had voted to ratify the Good Friday Agreement. I thought that we had achieved a peaceful end to the Troubles. I think of the words of Simo Drljaca – the 'Sheriff of Prijedor' – who had told me that the

Irish 'had blood on their hands'. I'm thinking that he may well be right.

In the meantime, my girlfriend and I decide to get married. Aideen also tells me that we'll need to buy a bigger house if we are going to have children. We have a lot to think about that summer.

Shortly after that, in August of 1998 – just a few months after my deployment to the 2nd Regiment – I'm summoned by my CO to his office. Lt Col O'Brien is an excitable man at the best of times. He doesn't like surprises. On this warm summer's evening, he is apoplectic. He is waving a piece of paper around as he speaks. I catch bits and pieces. 'Your career as an artillery officer is now over . . . mark my words . . . press office indeed.' Eventually, my commanding officer manages to inform me that I am to be transferred into the chief of staff's branch at Defence Forces Headquarters.

He informs me of this as though I am the next of kin being informed of a death in the family. He does not congratulate me. Rather, I am Stan Laurel to his Oliver Hardy as he drones on in his nasal northern accent about 'another fine mess' I've gotten him into. It seems – inconveniently for Lt Col O'Brien – that I am to be appointed as a staff officer to the chief of staff. Specifically, I am to be appointed to the Defence Forces Press Office as an accredited spokesperson for the army, naval service and air corps. Lt Col O'Brien appears bitterly disappointed at this apparent dereliction of duty on my part. I, however, am gobsmacked to say the least. Within months of being promoted to captain, I've been given my dream job at Defence Forces HQ. I try to contain my delight and try valiantly to express my regret at leaving Lt Col O'Brien's overbearing command. I consciously suppress a desire to skip out of his office like a giddy schoolboy.

Three years after completing my MA in Communications, the army has decided I might be useful in dealing with journalists. My appointment comes at a time of growing hostile public scrutiny of the organisation as the army struggles to deal with the increasingly expensive and increasingly controversial army deafness claims. In the autumn of 1998, on Ireland's national broadcaster, RTÉ Radio 1 – on the Gay Byrne show to be exact – the show's producers host a debate on 'Why do we need an army at all?' The general staff are rattled. It seems my MA in Communications – recorded on my AF667

'Annual Confidential Reports' – has brought me to the attention of the Director of Public Relations at this sensitive time for the Defence Forces. I'm posted into the appointment with clear instructions to assist in rehabilitating the image of the Irish army in the eyes of the general public.

The closing months of 1998 go by in a flash. I say goodbye to the Artillery Corps. I take up my new appointment and begin a very steep learning curve. I am introduced to the Director of Public Relations in my new office on the fourth floor of DFHQ in Dublin's Parkgate Street. I march in to the director's office and salute. Lieutenant Colonel Fitzgerald is famous throughout the army for his extensive overseas service. Lt Col Fitzgerald is a highly experienced senior officer and is highly regarded by every junior officer in the army. I am in awe of him. He invites me to sit and briefs me at length about the role of a Defence Forces press officer. 'You are the official voice of the army now. You must be conscious at all times that you represent the entirety of the Defence Forces. You must ensure that you are fully informed about all aspects of the mission and that you communicate clearly and accurately at all times. You are personally responsible for the public reputation of the Defence Forces.' No pressure. He advises me that I will be dealing with the local, national and international media on a daily basis. With Irish troops serving in seventeen countries worldwide, he tells me that I will be busy. 'Never a dull moment. Stay switched on and remember to think on your feet.' He dismisses me and tells me to report to Captain Reilly – the Defence Forces information officer.

I go into Captain Reilly's office. The office has the appearance of chaos. Files spilling out of filing cabinets. A massive desk covered in phones, a fax machine and a printer. Paper everywhere. Rolled-up socks next to one of the phones. A pair of shoes on top of the fax. An apple core on the floor. The captain looks up at me. He is a tall, gangling officer from the Midlands. His nickname is 'the Bodach', or 'the Giant', from the Irish myth, *Bodach an Cota Lachtna* (The Giant in the Grey Coat). 'Well, what did Fitz say to you?' he asks me. I tell him that 'Fitz' had told me to report to him for a more detailed brief. He looks at me again, and as all four phones in the office start ringing, he tells me, 'Don't fuck up. That's the brief.'

Chapter 9

Didn't I tell you not to fuck up?

'I left you on yourown for an hour.'

Defence Forces Press Office, DFHQ, Parkgate Street, Dublin
1998–1999

So I embark on that steep learning curve in the press office. I get my first mobile phone. A stubby Nokia that rings incessantly. The Bodach tells me to be careful what I say. Apart from that, it is pretty much up to me to learn the brief and figure out what to say to the eclectic mix of Irish and international journalists who constantly call my mobile number. My new 'friends'.

In December of 1998, after only a week or so in the press office, Fitz tells me that we are meeting some journalists in Lebanon. The journalists are going to do some colour pieces about the troops over the Christmas holiday. I hadn't expected to return to Lebanon this soon. It is two and a half years since I was last there. Two and a half years since the violence and the mayhem that convulsed the entire country. Two and a half years since I had spent so much time patrolling the shattered villages. Day and night, constantly under fire. My memory of that time is an unending loop of dead and dying Lebanese men, women and children. Innocent civilians pulled from the rubble of their homes by Irish troops. The Irish covered in dust. Walking like automatons through the heat and the bloodshed. 'Great!' I express delight at the prospect of the trip.

As myself and Fitz prepare to depart for Lebanon, President Bill Clinton authorises air strikes on Iraq. In Operation Desert Fox, the US and Britain pound targets in Iraq for seventy-two hours between 16 and 19 December.

The Middle East erupts in protest. There are ugly demonstrations in Beirut. Myself and Aideen are due to get married the following week. Despite the news reports and deteriorating situation in the Middle East, Aideen bids me a breezy *adieu* as I head to the airport and Beirut. It is just six days to our wedding. 'See you next week. Don't be late.'

My mum sneaks another set of rosary beads into my bag. I find it in my hand luggage and stuff it down the back of the taxi driver's seat on the way to the airport. I've mixed feelings about rosary beads and Lebanon. After check-in, I have a brief mad moment where I fleetingly consider walking out of the airport. I could give Lt Col Fitzgerald some sort of excuse. Feign food poisoning. The Fitz is busy smoking cigars in the last-chance smoking area. He shows me a report in the *Financial Times* about civil unrest and protests in downtown Beirut. He slaps me on the back. 'Beirut might be on fire when we get there young Thomas,' he tells me. He looks delighted. He rubs his hands and heads off to buy another paper. I feel reassured, sort of. Fitz returns with the *Irish Times* and tosses a bag of dry-roast peanuts at me. 'Get them into you,' he says. 'Breakfast is served.'

We fly to Heathrow and connect to Beirut with Middle East Airlines. The flight to Beirut lands at around seven in the evening local time. As the plane descends into Beirut, I catch sight of Lebanon once more. Lt Col Fitzgerald grins at me as we return our seats to the upright position and fasten our seat belts. I see the tracery of lights – Beirut appearing out of the darkness as we glide over the Mediterranean coastline on our final approach. The cabin crew buckle in and the lights go dim. The plane floats down smoothly and with a slight bump we arrive in Beirut.

As soon as we clear the aircraft, Fitz lights up another cigar. He inhales deeply. 'The smell of the Leb,' he says. 'You never forget it.' It's true. The warm, scented air brings me back. We eventually clear passport control and get a taxi to the Mayflower Hotel in the downtown Hamra District. The taxi driver takes a circuitous route. 'To avoid demonstration,' as he puts it. We see protestors throng the side streets a few blocks away. They are burning American flags. Fitz is completely unconcerned. Instead, he urges me to check in as quickly as possible in order to get to Beirut's Phoenicians Rugby Club for their annual Christmas dinner. We get there just in time.

This Christmas dinner in Beirut is slightly surreal. The dinner guests are mostly Irish and British expats. There are French and Lebanese guests also. The atmosphere is lively. The French delegation announce their intention to go to a nightclub. Fitz has no intention, however, of relinquishing his seat at the top table in the club. I tell him that I'm tired and slip away with the French. He calls after me, 'Young Thomas, you get to bed early – you need your beauty sleep.' I leave to a chorus of cheers and guffaws. Fitz is delighted.

Myself and the French – mostly Air France employees – travel across the city in a convoy of ancient, battered Mercedes taxis. I'm sitting in the front with the driver. We get to an abandoned car park. Everyone gets out. I'm looking around for the nightclub. The driver demands fifty dollars. I offer him ten. He leans over and opens the glove box. There is an ancient revolver inside. He points at it and then makes a mock pistol gesture at my head with his finger. I give him twenty dollars. He slams the glove box closed.

The French steer me across the car park to what looks like an extra-large manhole in the ground. In fact, it looks for all the world like those cellar openings through which beer companies deliver kegs of beer to pubs in Dublin. Only, there are two bouncers standing at this cellar entrance. The nightclub is a former underground air-raid shelter and missile silo. We descend the steps into the club. The music is deafening. The French introduce me to some friends. I resurrect my pidgin Arabic. The manager, Mahmoud, is impressed. I get free drink.

At one point, they open the roof of the nightclub. I have a hazy recollection of getting back to the Mayflower at around 7.30 AM. I've to meet the Fitz in reception at 8 AM. I manage to shave and change my clothes. I arrive into reception at 8.03 AM. Fitz points at his watch and tells me I'm late. He also tells me that I should be ashamed of myself. 'You had a full night's sleep,' he tells me. He adds, 'I didn't get in until midnight and I'm up and about before you.' I decide it is best not to speak too much.

We meet our journalists that morning in the airport and bring them south along the Coastal Highway to the Irish Battalion area. Tibnine is as I remembered it. Al Yatun remains unchanged. Just some new shell damage to some of the houses. There are little plaques here and there with wildflowers in water. Memorials to some of the families killed in Operation Grapes of Wrath. I say a Hail Mary for them.

We escort the journalists around the area of operations. They record interviews from the troops to be broadcast over the Christmas period at home. Their families will hear their voices over the radio as they eat their Christmas dinner.

After just forty-eight hours, it is time to leave once more. The artillery officers in Al Yatun invite me up for dinner. I eat in the villa once more. Khalid has long since gone. Another Lebanese youth announces the menu. 'Chicken in a flak jacket. White ting and green stuffs.' No major changes in the menu then.

That night, I go up on the roof and watch the sporadic rifle fire across the villages. It is generally very quiet. In the darkness, I see the menacing outline of the Israeli firebases on the ridgeline opposite. There is a small Christmas tree on the roof. The lights click as they wink on and off. I say a quick prayer for Sergeant Fuckin-Fuck. He shot himself in the armoury next to the villa during the last week of Operation Grapes of Wrath.

The next morning, we head north. Hours later we board MEA and are London bound. The following morning I am home. The day before Christmas Eve. I get married a few days later. My girlfriend says, 'I do.' I am the luckiest man on earth.

In January, I return to the routine of the press office. My learning curve is still steep. But I feel I'm getting there. The Bodach himself is gregarious enough when it suits him. When he is in good form, he is witty and can be charming. When he is in bad form, he is a hulking, sullen presence. Above all though, the Bodach is a schemer. Pacing up and down the office he is constantly plotting and strategising. Planning responses for the myriad crises that confront the organisation on a day-to-day basis at home and abroad.

Soldiers arrested for possession of drugs. Soldiers arrested for possession of firearms and membership of illegal or terrorist organisations. Soldiers arrested, charged and convicted for murder, rape, you name it. Soldiers involved in accidents, theft, misadventure. Soldiers killed or injured in the line of fire. The Bodach deals with each incident as it arises. He looks at me from time to time to make sure I'm listening and learning. On those rare moments when the phones stop ringing, he slumps into his chair and sighs loudly. 'It'd be a great fucking army if there were no soldiers in it.' That's his favourite refrain.

The journalists that call range from earnest foreign correspondents to local tabloid crime and security correspondents. I prefer the crime and security correspondents. They have a sense of humour. Some of the foreign correspondents are strangely devoid of humour. Almost like religious zealots. Some of them talk about themselves in the third person. One even describes herself as a member of a 'tribe'. She refers to herself and her colleagues as an exclusive collective: 'We tribe of war correspondents.' I'm tempted to say I belong to a 'Band of Brothers'.

We have troops in over a dozen countries internationally – from Afghanistan to Honduras, Kosovo to Lebanon. They are often caught up in fast-moving international events. As a consequence we get a lot of calls from all over the world. Robert Fisk makes contact from Lebanon or Syria from time to time. The majority of our international contacts are English speaking. We get a lot of queries from the BBC, Sky News, Fox, CNN. As situations vary, we help them to get correspondents across borders, into safe havens or simply to get interviews with high-value local contacts. Where we can, we organise interviews and pieces to camera with our own troops.

We feel a special duty of care towards Irish journalists. The Bodach has invented an ingenious system whereby we provide some training and support to Irish journalists deploying to hostile environments. We take them onto the rifle ranges in the Curragh and show them the effects of small arms fire on car doors, concrete blocks and so on. We show them mines, antipersonnel devices and improvised explosive devices. It is a sobering experience for most of them. We urge them all to get first aid training. The infantry officer involved in the firepower demonstration remarks to me that the first aid training is probably the most useful thing any of them will ever learn.

At the end of May, the reality of our service in Lebanon revisits us forcefully with the death of Private Billy Kedian in a mortar attack on his position in Brashit. He was unlucky. It is my first introduction to the bleak round of media interest in deaths overseas. We obtain his details from Enlisted Personnel Section. We release his photograph to the media. The news cycle grinds on as his body is repatriated and finally buried by his grieving family in his native County Mayo. As soldiers, we reflect on our own service in Lebanon with the news of Billy's death. We each silently recall the countless near misses and chance escapes we have had. It is a miracle that we have not lost more soldiers overseas.

Private Kedian's funeral is eventually overtaken by the ongoing business of the organisation; 1999 is filled with the usual incidents on land, sea and in the air for our personnel. The air corps rescue the crews of stricken trawlers – tossed in stormy seas off the south and west coasts in Atlantic gales. Classmates of mine, air corps pilots, in tiny Dauphin helicopters, struggle week after week in gale-force winds and heavy swells, hundreds of miles from safety, to pluck crew members off heaving vessels.

In one incident, a woman out walking falls to the base of a cliff. The air corps crew come to her rescue. As they are winching her aboard, a thermal blanket – a flimsy silver foil affair – is sucked up into the rotor wash and wraps around the blades. The chopper shudders and flails around the clifftop. The pilot tells me of the manic struggle to regain control of the aircraft. Eventually, they manage to airlift the woman to hospital. She survives. The chopper crew are traumatised. But they get back into the chopper and do the same thing, day after day, night after night. To my mind, the air corps pilots are unsung heroes. Beyond a shadow of a doubt.

In July of 1999, four of my colleagues in the air corps are killed whilst returning from one of these search and rescue missions. Their Dauphin helicopter clips a sand dune at Tramore beach near Waterford Airport. In the subsequent crash, all four crew are killed. We name the crew members, who are in their late twenties or early thirties, as Captain Dave O'Flaherty from Lucan in Dublin, Captain Michael Baker from Wexford, Sergeant Paddy Mooney from Meath and Corporal Niall Byrne from Dublin. Mick Baker was in my senior class in the Cadet School. Dave O'Flaherty leaves a wife and unborn daughter behind. Paddy Mooney and Niall Byrne also leave grieving families and loved ones behind.

On the day after the crash, I fly down to the site of the accident on the air corps Kingair Beechcraft. One of the pilots is a former classmate of mine, John Flanagan. He chats to me from the cockpit as we fly to Waterford. When we get there, we circle the crash site overhead. John and his air corps crewmates fall silent as we circle. The impact site and scorch marks are clearly visible from above. I say a silent prayer for our comrades and their families.

Throughout this tragic episode, myself and the Bodach attend the funerals and try to manage the media and photographers who cover them. For us and the media, it is business as usual. It is a sobering experience.

When it is all over, the Bodach makes me a cup of coffee. This is an unusual gesture from such a normally taciturn officer. 'There. You did all right,' is all he says. He also tells me that he hopes these will be our last funerals during our time in the press office. Sadly, that proves not to be the case.

Life goes on for the Defence Forces. The navy boards vessels all year round. One sailor loses a finger to a gutting knife in a heavy January swell. One unfortunate naval officer is attacked by an angry Spanish skipper in the hold of his vessel. The naval officer is inspecting the Spaniard's catch when he hears the skipper approach from behind. He is wielding a frozen eel. Like a baseball bat. Except with fishy eyes on it. At first the navy guy thinks this is a joke. But then the Spaniard smashes the eel into the bulkhead – missing his temple by milimetres. A frantic life or death struggle ensues. The naval officer narrowly avoids a fractured skull when the frozen eel snaps in two on a fish crate.

The Spaniard picks up the two shattered eel ends and advances again. Luckily, the remainder of the boarding party comes to his rescue. No shots are fired. Another day at sea for the Irish navy. Meanwhile, inland, navy divers recover a body from the water near Russborough House. The navy recovers bodies – usually young men who have died by suicide – on an almost weekly basis.

After a month or so, the Bodach decides it is safe to let me man the phones unsupervised. On a quiet Friday afternoon, I'm left alone with the four phones and the fax. I get a note from Operations to say that parts of the Coastal Highway in Lebanon have been closed due to heavy snowfall. The resupply convoy from Beirut to the Irish Battalion is stuck north of Sidon. Trucks filled with rations and supplies imported from Cyprus unable to move in the snow and ice. The battalion has run out of tea bags. That makes me laugh. I think of the tea drinkers in Camp Shamrock going cold turkey.

Then the phone rings. It is a journalist from one of Ireland's tabloid newspapers. 'Hiya Tom. Is the big lad there?' I reply in the negative and inform him proudly that I'm 'minding the shop'. He asks me if there is anything going on. He wants to know if I can give him something, 'anything' for the weekend. I'm feeling a bit giddy and remark – somewhat unwisely – that the battalion in Lebanon has run short of tea bags. My friend is suddenly interested. 'Say what now?' he asks.

I explain about the snow and so on. I hear him tapping away frantically on his keyboard at the other end of the phone. 'Leave this with me,' he says and slams down the phone. About fifteen minutes later I get a call from one of Ireland's two leading tea manufacturers. It is their chief executive, no less. He introduces himself and enquires with some concern about the welfare of our troops whom he's been told are 'cut off by the Israeli army and have no supplies'. Furthermore, he tells me that an Irish newspaper is organising an emergency airlift to Beirut International Airport with essential supplies for the beleaguered Irish soldiers there. After all, it is 'the least he can do' as an Irish citizen. His company are prepared to donate a dozen boxes of tea bags for the airlift – immediately.

I swallow hard and explain that there is no such emergency. That there must be some misunderstanding. He sounds relieved – if a bit puzzled. 'But the journalist who rang me was emphatic.' I assure him that all is OK. I thank him profusely for his concern.

Then the phones start ringing. Queries from all sorts of manufacturers of dried and canned goods. They all want to know when the 'emergency airlift' will take place. They all want to help the army. 'Our lads stuck out in the Leb.

Surrounded.' I am now panicking a bit. I assure them that all is well and that there is no such airlift.

After an hour or so, the journalist rings me again. 'You'll never guess what's happened,' he says. Before I can interrupt, he continues, 'One of the tea companies just pulled out of the airlift – but don't worry, the other tea company is only too delighted to come on board.' I eventually talk the journalist out of his version of events and all talk of airlifts – emergency or otherwise. I look at the clock. I've been on my own in the office for less than two hours. The journalist sounds very disappointed. He tells me not to worry though, that he'll give us a 'good run out on the front page on Saturday morning'.

The next morning, the headline appears. 'Storm in a Tea Cup – Irish troops run low on tea bags.' The Bodach rings me at home. 'I left you on your own for an hour. That's all. Just one hour. Didn't I tell you not to fuck up?'

On the Monday morning, the staff sergeant and the corporal clerk in the press office keep asking me if I would like any tea. At least someone is enjoying themselves. 'Ah go on, go on,' they chorus. 'You'll have some tea.' They laugh themselves sick at my expense. The Bodach shakes his head. Fitzy decides I need a break. I'm sent on a touch typing course in the School of Administration in the Curragh Camp. It is an intensive two-week course. A sergeant major patrols the room ensuring we complete our typing practices. Miraculously, at the end of the two weeks, I can touch type. Nearly forty words per minute. When I get back to the office the Bodach looks at me. 'Type something.' I type, 'The quick brown fox jumps over the lazy dog' with my eyes closed. 'Fucking hell,' the Bodach remarks. 'You're good for something at least.' After that, I get to type up all of our press releases. In truth, it is one of the best courses I've ever done in the army.

As the months go by, under the Bodach's watchful eye, I learn more and more about the tactics and strategy of crisis communication. It's an excellent learning environment as we're always in some sort of crisis or another. The Bodach never loses his head and is endlessly inventive in thinking of ways to get the army onto the news agenda in ways that highlight our missions overseas. He, like me, feels very strongly that Irish journalists do not really 'get it' or 'get the story' about the reality of Irish military involvement overseas. He is passionate about this lack of understanding, on the part of the Irish public, of the role of Ireland's armed forces abroad.

On the 24 March, NATO commences the Serb Air Campaign. Operation 'Allied Force' lasts for seventy-eight days with NATO air strikes all over Serbia. I think of Milomir and Dragana. I think of Bojan, Zoran, Dragana and Milinka. Hundreds of Serb civilians are killed in the air strikes. For our part, we have military observers in Kosovo and Belgrade. They give eyewitness accounts to the international media. In doing so, the world also learns of Ireland's role in the conflict. The Bodach is a genius. He forms a vast network of contacts in the international media. I'm learning fast.

Later that summer, the Irish Army deploys to Kosovo as part of KFOR or Kosovo Force. Even though it is a NATO-led operation, Irish troops participate as a result of our membership of Partnership for Peace – a NATO structure that allows us to engage in missions with a UN Security Council mandate.

The Bodach takes Irish journalists from RTÉ and TV3 to Kosovo with the troops. The Irish contingent rendezvous in Thessalonika in Greece. In convoy, the Irish then travel north, overland, to Kosovo. The Irish public gets previously unseen footage of the Irish army at work under NATO command in Europe. He also brings Irish journalists to Albania. They tour the refugee camps that have been set up for ethnic Albanian Kosovars fleeing the violence in Kosovo. Irish army officers are running the camps.

Meanwhile, I continue to escort journalists to Lebanon. I fly in and out of Beirut on Middle East Airlines from Heathrow. The MEA flights are almost always half empty. I wander around the huge airbus as we cross Europe towards the Middle East. Each trip back to the Lebanon is a pilgrimage of sorts. Each night-time landing reacquaints me with the heat of Beirut. The late evening air heavily scented with lilies and hyacinths as we emerge from the terminal buildings. The scent of the flowers mingling with exhaust fumes as we queue to get taxis to Place de la Martyr in downtown Beirut. I know that in Greek mythology, hyacinths are associated with death and the loss of innocence. How appropriate that they greet me on each arrival in Lebanon.

The long flights and the trips to the Middle East give me a chance to reflect on my research progress. During long stays in hotels in Lebanon and Syria, I get a chance to write up some of the findings from my interviews. I put my newfound typing skills to use. There are no phones to disturb me here. The findings themselves are disturbing enough.

Chapter 10

Girl Talk

'I don't think he was mentally fit for the task of training recruits. Do you?'

Despite the steep learning curve involved in my appointment to the Defence Forces Press Office, I continue my research investigation into women in the armed forces with a renewed sense of confidence and urgency. In 1999, the next phase of the research will involve in-depth interviews with female soldiers in order to fully explore the day-to-day experiences of women working in the Irish armed forces. As a researcher – particularly a male researcher – I need to find out from the women themselves, in their own words, precisely what it is like to serve as a female soldier in the Irish military.

This is going to be a difficult process. The academic literature on research methodology hypothesises that a male researcher – particularly a male officer associated with authority, in a hierarchical and male dominated organisation such as the military – will find it difficult, if not impossible to elicit frank or meaningful responses from female research participants. In particular, the academic literature assumes that women will not be inclined to discuss sensitive issues with a male researcher.

The academic literature is also limited as it applies to my own study in that it is laden with assumptions about researchers themselves. The dominant paradigm for research as presented in the academic literature describes researchers as academics or investigators who are normally resident in the academic setting. The literature describes researchers almost exclusively as academics of one form or another who leave the safety of the university in order to enter research settings – anthropologists visiting primitive societies or sociologists visiting factories, for example – and ultimately returning to the safety and sanctuary of the university to write up their findings and conclusions.

The literature does not deal with a researcher such as myself, who lives, works and soldiers with those whom he has chosen to study. As such, I am a member of the organisation that is being studied. And unlike Indiana Jones – or the anthropologists, sociologists, academic researchers or ethnographers I read about in academic literature – when I'm finished the research, I will not be able to return to the safety and serenity of some university campus. I'm going to have to live with the outcome of the study. I'm going to have to live with the implications of my research for the military authorities, for my female colleagues, and for myself. I have yet to meet an Irish academic who is subject to military law.

For their part, the military authorities give me every assistance possible. Every document I request, every report I seek out is given to me willingly and without question. My commanding officers throughout the four years of the research process afford me whatever flexibility they can so that I can keep working on the project. I receive constant encouragement from both male and female colleagues. I'm teased by my fellow officers from time to time about the work. Each officer is entitled to an annual uniform allowance in order to replace items of dress uniform such as the Sam Browne belt and other ceremonial items. Some of my peers in the 2nd Regiment ask me if I am going to order a skirt from the military tailor – such is my interest in matters relating to female personnel. This is a recurring joke among my peers, for it has become common knowledge that I am researching the work experiences of women in the Irish military.

By the summer of 1998, the numbers of women in the Defence Forces has increased. There are now approximately three hundred women in the army, navy and air corps. This is due to the fact that the government has lifted a recruitment embargo which has been in place since the early nineties. It is also evidence of a greater level of commitment towards equality on the part of individual unit commanders in terms of a larger number of women being recruited by regional command manpower officers. It is a positive development. However, by international standards, the level of female recruitment is still low.

This increase in numbers gives me a wider sample of women with which to commence interviews. I try to get a maximum variation sample. In other words, I try to interview as many women as I can with as wide a variety of military experience as is possible. I interview female officers who are senior to me in rank. In military parlance, they are my superiors. I also interview female officers from all three services of my own rank. I interview as many female soldiers as I can within the non-commissioned ranks; sergeants and corporals for the most part. I also interview female privates from every command area in the country. I interview women from every corps within the Irish military. From army corps such as infantry, cavalry, artillery, signals, engineering and medical corps through to naval units and units from the air corps. I interview women of varying ages and levels of education. I interview single women, married women, women with children and soldiers without children. I interview women who have served overseas and women who have served exclusively at home in Ireland. In total, I interview sixty women. This sample is approximately one-fifth of all women serving in the army at the time of the study.

The business of interviewing women for the research is a complicated one. First of all, I've got to identify female personnel who fit the profile of my maximum variation sample. Then, I've got to contact their commanding officers in order to obtain permission to conduct the research interview. In the army, you can't just turn up in a unit and start asking questions. You have to get permission to visit the unit in the first place and then provide an explanation as to why an interview is taking place. In addition to this process, there is the ethical dimension of consent. As an officer, a verbal request to a subordinate may constitute a lawful order. I'm conscious that I'm conducting these interviews as a researcher and not in my role as an army officer. I explain this to each interviewee. They are also interviewed on the basis of strict anonymity.

Between trips overseas with journalists and between the rough and tumble of the press office, I manage to interview a steady stream of research participants throughout the spring and summer of 1999. The women are for the most part eager to do the interviews. The majority of them in fact – some of them with almost twenty years' service – have never been interviewed before, either formally or informally, about their experiences in the Irish armed forces. They are extraordinarily frank and honest in airing their views. Collectively, they provide me with a shocking and brutal account of their experiences within the Irish military.

The process starts off predictably enough. There is a thematic approach to the interviews. We start off with a discussion of the manner in which women were recruited to the organisation, followed by a discussion of their military training and concluding with an exploration of the ways in which they are deployed in the army and their rate of progression and prospects for promotion.

As I interview each woman, they express negative views about the recruitment process. A total of forty-eight of them feel that the selection process is unfair towards women. Thirty of the women feel that there was a 'quota' system in place to keep the numbers of women recruited to the army low. I am not entirely surprised at these findings given that the numbers of women serving in the Irish armed forces are so low by international standards.

The discussion on military training is where the interviews take an entirely unexpected turn. It starts out on a slightly farcical note. One of the officers I interview tells me that during her cadet training in the early 1980s, she and the other women were withdrawn from heavy weapons training. Instead, they were given dress and deportment classes in the drill shed in the military college. In her office, she leans forward and tells me more. She is laughing so much, she wipes a tear from her eye.

'They wanted to see if we'd die if we fired a rifle. We didn't of course. But still they wouldn't let us do the 84 [anti-tank weapon] the 60 [mortar] or the GPMG SF [general-purpose machine gun, sustained fire role]. Instead we did a grooming course. They got an air hostess to come to the drill shed. She got us to march up and down balancing books on our heads. For posture. We enjoyed it. It was very beneficial in fact.' Sitting back behind her desk, she adds, 'The lads would have benefited from it.'

Another female officer tells me in a separate interview about the 'personal grooming' component of her military training. 'We did dress and deportment instead of heavy weapons training. We did everything, right down to putting on make-up. They gave us Lancôme samples. It did wonders for them. I've stayed with them ever since.'

For the other ranks, however – sergeants, corporals and privates – the training atmosphere they describe is more charged. They have a sharper, profoundly uncomfortable experience. One female soldier tells me of her recruit training in which one of her colleagues was referred to at all times as 'fat arse' by the training sergeant. 'He'd say, "C'mon, fat arse. Get up on the truck, get off the truck. Hey, fat arse, get your fat arse over here," and so on. She cried herself to sleep every night. We stuck together. We were having none of it. And we got her through it.'

Another woman tells me of her experience of training. 'At the start of the training the corporal and sergeant thought they were on to a good thing, with the three of us (females) in the platoon. When that didn't happen, when we didn't respond, it was abuse, abuse and more abuse.'

The interviews continue in this vein. They are a series of intense and blunt discussions with female soldiers in offices, orderly rooms, section rooms, training rooms and cafeterias all over the army. One woman looks me in the eye as she coldly recounts her training experience. 'The training was just a screw session. One sergeant was an out and out evil bastard. He hated women. He used to call us fat cunts, fat cows, useless pieces of shit. Some of the guys in the platoon would see this and start abusing us too. Having power over us was his happy hour. I don't think he was mentally fit for the task of training recruits. Do you?'

As I interview more women in the maximum variation sample, all of them report accounts of their military training that contain disturbing elements. There are reports of psychological and physical abuse of women right across the spectrum of rank and seniority. From female officers educated in the cadet school to the most junior private soldiers trained in barracks countrywide.

Even more worrying is the fact that these women also detail negative experiences of an explicitly sexual nature. They recount the use of inappropriate and sexually explicit language by their immediate superiors and include accounts and allegations of sexual harassment and sexual assault. Some of the women tell me things that they have not shared with family members or even their partners or husbands. I am stunned by the revelations. As a male officer, I've never experienced bullying or sexual assault myself. I've never considered it as a workplace phenomenon because I've never been targeted in this way. I'm also struck by the passion and the conviction of these women. They are outraged. For the majority of them, I am the first person with whom they have had the opportunity to discuss their experiences in detail.

Chapter 11

Sexual Harassment

'I would state, categorically, emphatically, to any woman in the army who is harassed, assaulted or raped, to inform the Garda Síochána. Forget about the military police. Otherwise, you will not be heard and you will not get justice.'

Defence Forces Headquarters, Dublin
1999

I talk to Maggie about the disturbing developments in the research. We discuss, in detail, the nature of the emerging themes around bullying and sexual harassment and assault. She is as shocked and concerned as I am. She refers me to the literature on research methodology that deals with 'unanticipated' or 'antithetical' outcomes within investigations and studies. The appropriate and ethical course of action, as outlined in the literature, is to include this emergent set of findings into the scope of the study and to fully investigate it. This is what I do.

And so, what begins as a general discussion on the training environment for women in the Irish armed forces turns into an audit of the bullying and sexual harassment of women as experienced by them during their day-to-day military life. As I progress with this line of inquiry, the women detail a litany of experiences that encompasses every level of such abuse. From verbal sexual harassment to sexual assault and allegations of rape. At the end of the research process, fifty-nine out of the sixty women I interview report some form of bullying, sexual harassment or sexual assault by male colleagues.

A sergeant with eighteen years of service in the army agrees to meet me for interview. She answers my questions mechanically at first. She becomes more animated when we discuss the training environment. Having invested almost two decades of her life in the Irish army, her understatement in relation to sexual harassment is poignant. 'Under military law we are all equal. In theory. But, I don't like the way the girls are treated, not as soldiers, but as women. What I mean here is sexual harassment. There is a huge amount of sexual harassment, especially amongst the younger women. But there is a terrible fear of complaining. Do you understand? Those that complain don't get a fair hearing. You get this attitude, if you can't take the heat, get out of the kitchen. You're in the army now.'

Out of the sixty women I interview, forty-eight express no confidence in the reporting procedures for sexual harassment and sexual assault within the army. One female officer with almost twenty years' experience tells me, 'If something happens, call the Gardaí. Don't bother with the military police. It is a waste of time.' Another female officer, who has just recently been commissioned, is thoroughly disillusioned. She gives me her view of officer training for women in no uncertain terms. 'There is a massive problem in the cadet school in relation to sexual harassment, intimidation and bullying. It is a huge problem. When females come out of the cadet school, their confidence, their self-esteem, their perceptions of themselves as women and their intelligence, worth – you name it – it is gone. Women are devalued and made to feel completely worthless. I couldn't recommend the army as a career to any woman. No fucking way.'

At the lower end of the scale – in terms of sexual harassment – the women are subjected to inappropriate comments about dress and clothing. One officer shrugs her shoulders, 'You get such an amount of comment on the way you dress – sexually explicit comment – that you just ignore it. Eventually, it goes in one ear and out the other. They say things to me like, "Look at the arse on her in those combats." You get conditioned to it though.' One young private tells me in barely a whisper, 'On a training session one time, I was around eleven stone then. The physical training instructor singled me out in front of everyone. He said I was an example of a big girl.' Her voice drops again. She is barely audible. 'Or words like that. I wouldn't like to say exactly what he said.'

After a long silence, she composes herself. 'They were the most offensive remarks I've ever heard. I grew up in a family of boys. I never heard anyone speak about a woman like that. And he did it to my face in front of the whole platoon.'

Sexually explicit language is sometimes aggravated by disinhibition. One soldier with seventeen years of service tells me that on one occasion, whilst serving in an overseas headquarters unit, she walked in on a male colleague who was reading a pornographic magazine in an office. 'He didn't miss a beat. In fact, he held it up and showed it to me. He said, "I know you'd be good at this."' She adds, 'This stuff is downright nasty. It is completely in-your-face overseas. Some of the girls I know would be suicide risks. Especially the vulnerable ones.'

Another young woman tells me about the day her recruit platoon were issued with their combat uniforms for the first time. She tells me how excited they were for that transformative moment when they put on a uniform for the first time. Change from civilians to soldiers. 'But, when the QM [quartermaster] handed me my combats, he tipped them off the hatch so that they fell on the floor. I had to lean down to pick them up. And as I did so, he said, for everyone's benefit, "If I was thirty years younger, you wouldn't bend down like that in front of me. I wouldn't be long giving you one up the arse."'

Other women, forced to live in barracks as recruits, were exposed to other, equally cruel forms of abuse. One woman tells me of her experiences in the training depot in the Curragh. 'I was on a work detail in the ammunition depot. The corporal came looking for me and called us all to attention. He then pointed some graffiti out to us. "Read this," he said. It was about me. Like "X" did the entire battalion. If you want a ride, call "X". He was laughing so hard he nearly split himself. I didn't think there was much point complaining to him. I complained to the CS (company sergeant). He said he had more important things to be dealing with.'

Another woman's experiences underpin the seeming desire on the part of some male soldiers to humiliate female colleagues. Her story also highlights the futility most female soldiers feel in relation to official complaints. 'When we were doing our recruit training, there were five females in the platoon. The sergeant put a poster up on the unit notice board. It was a cartoon of us, with our names written in underneath. We were naked from the waist up. And it showed the sergeant shouting at us. He's saying, "In the army, we get to do the nagging." It was left up there for ages. We eventually tore it down one night when we were doing details. The sergeant was really pissed off. He warned us that it was an offence under military law to deface or otherwise interfere with a unit notice board.'

A commissioned officer gives a similar account about her treatment at the hands of fellow officers in the University Service Army Complement, Renmore Barracks in Galway. Whilst a student in NUI Galway and living in USAC, Renmore, she was the subject of a series of obscene messages placed in her post box. When she complained about it, the situation deteriorated, with obscene messages scrawled on the door to her room. 'I complained again and again. But obscene drawings appeared on my door. I repainted the door myself. Several times. But then there was an atmosphere. I got a name for rocking the boat. Some of my classmates are still very touchy about it.'

For many women, the abuse does not stop when the training phase has completed. On passing out, or having been commissioned, many women report further provocations and challenges in their new units. One female soldier describes her first night on a twenty-four-hour security duty as a fully trained soldier. 'The BOS [barrack orderly sergeant] told me on my first guard duty, "I hope you don't fucking well think that just because you're a female that I won't be watching a blue movie tonight. Because that's what I do on twenty-four-hour duty. And I won't be stopping for you."'

Another female soldier is spared the prospect of having to be in the same room as men watching a porno movie while she is on duty when she is told by her NCO to go outside on patrol. 'I was on duty. The corporal told me to go outside, that the lads wanted to watch a certain film. So I went outside. But I was very uncomfortable, do you know? You know, on duty overnight with twelve guys watching a porno. But you learn to say nothing. It is hard enough to be one of the lads. To fit in. If you cause ripples you'll get a bad reputation for being a troublemaker. So you just grin and bear it. You mightn't get much of a hearing anyway. Officers come and go. They rely on the NCOs.'

The notion of not rocking the boat is something I'm familiar with as an army officer. But not in the context of sexual harassment. I recall vividly our lectures on leadership in the cadet school. One lecture in particular was given to us by our school commandant – a senior officer who later went on to become a member of the general staff. After lectures on leading by example and physical courage, he told us as young officer cadets that the most important characteristic in any leader, military or civilian, is moral courage. When confronted with a choice, always do the right thing. According to him, moral courage was more important and a greater challenge than physical courage.

Two female officers tell me of unfortunate experiences in the cadet school, however which reflect poorly on the army's institutional notions of 'moral courage'. For some officers, it seems, loyalty to the group far outweighs the imperative to tell the truth and to do the right thing. Both of the female officers' accounts corroborate one another. They both tell me of an incident where pornographic movies were being viewed in the cadet's mess on a particular channel on cable TV. One of the female officers, who was a cadet at the time, tells me that the female cadets approached one of the training officers to complain about the issue, 'after a showdown with the guys. Because it wasn't fair on the junior cadets. And it wasn't a good example either. We went to a senior officer to get it sorted out. The outcome was that all of the female cadets were paraded and given a dressing-down. We were told that we needed to sort it out ourselves. Then the guys in the class found out about it and the atmosphere got worse.'

The second female officer involved in this incident gives a similar account. 'We were paraded by the senior officer. We were all disciplined for "not handling it right". In other words, we got into the shit for complaining. The senior officer said that he wasn't going to intervene, that we had to manage these situations ourselves. And when the guys in the class got wind of it, they were obnoxious. One of them said to a junior cadet, "You'll learn to hate the females in your class too."'

Not all of the experiences recounted to me are entirely negative, however. Some of the women tell me of the sometimes unexpected support that they get from male colleagues. One officer tells me, 'When I was in Naqoura in

Lebanon, I logged on to the office computer. There was a screensaver of a naked woman. The IT guys replaced them all immediately. They were mortified. I was nearly going to insist they put Brad Pitt or George Clooney up as replacements. In the end, I think we scanned in something boring, like an Israeli tank or something.'

A sergeant tells a similar tale. 'I used to go play cards with the lads in the transport yard. They had cards with topless women on them. I told them to get another set, which they did. And that was that. They also took down all the dodgy posters.'

Overall, the women interviewed indicate that the practice of publicly displaying pornographic images in work spaces is declining. There are, however, still some die-hards. One woman summarises it eloquently. 'You don't see the page three stuff so much now. The majority of the guys would be scarlet if you caught them with that kind of thing on the walls. But you still get the odd exception. Usually way down in a back office in stores or something. One sleazy old bastard in our unit even asks you, "What do you think of the tits on her?"'

One officer indicates her zero tolerance approach. 'Just after I was commissioned, there'd be a scattering of posters of naked women about the place. I used to ignore them. Pretend they weren't there. Like, when you're the new officer, you don't want to make waves. But now I've completely clamped down. No way will I tolerate that now.'

Many of the women endure unwelcome advances, some of an explicitly sexual nature, when they are deployed to their units. One officer with around ten years' experience explains her situation to me. 'I've had poetry written and sent to me. I've had persistent invitations to lunch from a particular senior officer with whom I had a direct working relationship. He pestered me. I mean pestered me – for months. I couldn't believe it was happening to me. I got no support from my CO. He actually paraded me when I complained to him about it. He actually cautioned me that it was an offence under military law to make a false allegation against a superior. He told me to think about that. And don't get me wrong. Let there be no confusion here. That wasn't friendly advice. That was a threat. The army doesn't like to deal with these things head-on. They prefer to cover them up.'

Another female officer did, however, get what she felt was a satisfactory response from her CO. 'I received a lot of unwelcome attention from one senior officer. I got long letters. I even got photos of me that he'd taken when I was a cadet. Pictures from the cadet school Christmas dinner when he was a guest. It was weird. Creepy. I went in and told my CO. He was angry for me. He told me to keep the letters and keep a note in my diary of any further contact or incidents. He told me he'd put a stop to it immediately. He told me also that I could launch an official complaint and that he'd back me all the way. I just wanted it to stop. Thankfully it did. He just looks straight through me now. Ignores me, thank God.'

For others, however, there were less satisfactory results arising from their complaints about unwelcome and inappropriate sexual attention. As one soldier put it to me, 'I kept getting these obscene phone calls when I'd be on duty. Now, it had to be someone who knew when I was rostered. In other words, someone in the unit. I started to leave the phone off the hook. But that meant that I was non-contactable. And this was going on for weeks. I complained to the company sergeant. I suggested that we could monitor the calls and trace them. He told me that signals would say that was impossible. Now, even with my minimum of knowledge of these things, I knew this to be a barefaced lie. They just didn't want trouble in the unit. I caused one hell of a rumpus then. I gave my CS and the CO an ultimatum. They said that they would put in an LED phone with a caller-display. But they never did. And guess what. The calls stopped. But I had no way of finding out who was responsible in the first place.'

At the most serious end of the spectrum, twelve of the sixty women I interview make allegations of sexual assault. These disclosures include allegations of rape. It is a humbling moment to sit and listen to the women as they share these appalling experiences with me. They do so with great dignity. I can only imagine how difficult it is to discuss these matters. They are upset. They are angry. Angry at the perpetrators and angry at the dysfunctional reporting system within the army. I tell Aideen about these developments. She tells me I've got to finish the investigation and take it to the highest authorities. I tell my dad about the allegations of sexual harassment and sexual assault. I'm interested in his view as a retired policeman. He pulls long and hard on his cigarette and looks at me. 'If you make allegations like that, you'd better have your facts right. Belt and braces stuff. Make sure your back is covered.'

I don't tell my mum. She is too ill. She's just worried about my next trip to Lebanon or Syria or anywhere foreign. She keeps sprinkling holy water on me whenever I visit.

The women who are targets for sexual assault and rape tell me some of the saddest stories I have ever heard. They follow a pattern. The target is usually the victim of someone immediately senior to them. Very often, they are assaulted by the person to whom such assaults must be reported under Irish military law. It puts most of the women into an impossible catch-22 situation.

It is summed up by one rape victim. She describes in a simple but devastating way how many of the women feel.

'I was assaulted. I complained. I did not get equitable treatment. Women in the Irish army are not encouraged to report these issues. The Irish army is more concerned with its reputation than it is about whether or not a woman is raped. And if you do report an assault, the court sits in hell. Satan is the judge. I would state, categorically, emphatically, to any woman in the army who is harassed, assaulted or raped, to inform the Garda Síochana. Forget about the military police. Otherwise, you will not be heard and you will not get justice.'

Chapter 12

Farewell to Lebanon

'That'll put a stop to your gallop.'

Defence Forces Headquarters, Dublin / Irish Battalion, UNIFIL, Lebanon 1999–2000

While the research process steadily progresses, work continues at a frenetic pace within the press office. The Bodach decides to target local or regional Irish media in order to improve the army's public profile from the 'bottom up' or at 'grassroots level'. According to the Bodach, 'We need to get as many of 'em out to the Leb as we can.' He pitches this idea to the chief of staff and we get the green light to aggressively pursue a policy of escorting an increasing number of local and national journalists out to Lebanon. We target opinion leaders in as many regional newspapers and regional radio stations as we can. The general staff – normally shy of journalists – give us their full support. Anything to draw media attention away from the ongoing army deafness scandal at home. This means a dramatic increase in the number of visits to the Middle East undertaken by myself and the Bodach.

For their part, the journalists seem to enjoy the trips. Luckily, the trips are uneventful from an operational point of view. No one gets shot at or shelled. More importantly, the journalists get a chance to move around the area of operations and to actually see the exposed positions where Irish troops serve. They also get to see the Israeli hilltop firebases and to monitor some Hizbullah activity. The Irish journalists experience a kind of culture shock when they patrol with the troops and experience life in south Lebanon. They witness at first hand the chemistry that exists between the Irish and the

Lebanese – particularly the children. They file copy and broadcast from Camp Shamrock. The result is a shift in the type of coverage the Irish army gets at home. For the first time, in a long time, the media focus on the actual mission and role played by the Irish overseas. Court cases and other scandals melt into the background.

Shortly after my trip to Lebanon with Fitz, the Bodach comes up with another major master stroke. More evidence of his ingenuity. As we begin to accrue more and more positive press coverage in the Irish media, he decides it is timely to target the taoiseach, Bertie Ahern. And, for the first time in the history of the state, an Irish taoiseach is persuaded to visit Irish troops serving abroad in Lebanon.

In January of 1999, Ahern, accompanied by Celia Larkin, visits the battalion in south Lebanon. We get saturation coverage in all of the newspapers. Bertie and Celia appear on the front pages of all the national broadsheets and tabloids wearing Irish army flak jackets and helmets. The Bodach texts me from Camp Shamrock. 'We've got them wearing the green jersey now.' The positive coverage is picked up on radio and TV. Myself and Fitz man the phones back in DFHQ. They never stop ringing.

The only controversy about Bertie's visit to the Lebanon is raised on RTE's *Liveline*. Some old soldiers ring in complaining about the taoiseach and Celia Larkin wearing 'Irish army uniforms'. Joe Duffy, responding on air, asks if the Defence Forces Press Office might call the program and explain why the duo are wearing uniforms. Fitz looks at me and lights up a cigar. 'You ring them, young Clonan,' he advises. So, with Fitz listening to the radio in his office, I call *Liveline*. The researcher tells me I'll be up after the ad break and then I'll be live on air. Joe Duffy introduces me. 'We're joined now, live on air, by Captain Tom Clonan of the Defence Forces Press Office to exlain why Taoiseach Bertie Ahern and Celia Larkin are wearing uniforms in Lebanon.' I plough straight ahead. 'How'ya Joe,' I begin. I'm a bit nervous. Fitz raises his eyes to heaven and signals at me to keep talking. He's furiously puffing on his cigar now. I continue. 'The taoiseach is actually wearing a flak jacket and helmet for health and safety reasons.' I explain that in the live operational environment of south Lebanon, where the Irish are subject to attack without warning at any given moment, all personnel are issued with flak jackets and helmets for their personal protection. I go on to say that the Irish army has a duty of care to all visitors and that we provide flak jackets and helmets to all visitors including journalists and VIPs such as the taoiseach and Celia.

Fitz gives me the thumbs up through a haze of blue smoke. Then, a caller asks Joe if Bertie and Celia are sleeping in the same bed. Fitz goes white and gently closes the door of his office. I'm left alone with my thoughts on the taoiseach's sleeping arrangements. I have a brief, mad urge to tell the nation that they could be sleeping in 'bunk beds' for all I know. But then I think, I'll surely be asked who's sleeping on top. I abandon these thoughts to hear, with great relief, Joe Duffy thank me for our call. It seems we are not required to comment after all on the taoiseach's sleeping arrangements. They are 'private'.

The taoiseach is delighted with the images that come back from Lebanon. Like Tony Blair or Bill Clinton, Bertie Ahern realises the benefits of being photographed and filmed 'visiting the troops' overseas. For the first time probably since the Congo, we manage to put the Irish army centre-stage in the minds of the Irish public. For all the right reasons. The army's image as peace-keepers in hostile environments is reinforced in a powerful way. For the journalists, the photo opportunities afforded by the taoiseach's visits are media gold. For us, the taoiseach's presence guarantees media coverage of our troops' operational activities. Not an overweight soldier or a deafness claim to be seen. From a PR point of view, the visits are a win-win for us.

The taoiseach repeats the exercise by visiting our troops in Kosovo later in the year. He also travels to East Timor to visit Irish troops in our first peace-enforcement mission overseas in many years. He witnesses at first hand Irish Special Forces (the Army Ranger Wing) operating alongside Australian troops along the border with West Timor. The Irish troops are particularly successful at preventing the infiltration of pro-Jakarta militia into the villages and towns in their sector area.

During one of these trips, an operations officer calls into the press office. He is a senior officer – a nervous type – with big sticky-out ears. His nickname is 'Sam Maguire' due to the size of his ears. He is waving a piece of paper about. Apparently the pro-Jakarta militia captured and executed a UN soldier in Timor. And, as he breathlessly exclaims to us, 'They cut off his ears as trophies.' When he leaves the office, 'Pigeye', one of our clerks, looks over at me and remarks, dead-pan, 'If I was him, I'd stay well out of East Timor. He'd be a marked man with them ears on him.'

The taoiseach's visits to the troops represent highlights for us in the press office. The relationship with journalists is positive.

However, tragedy strikes too. On St Valentine's Day in 2000, I am in the office when the phones start hopping. Fitz comes into the office ashen-faced. We've lost four young men in Lebanon. Four young soldiers travelling to Beirut International Airport have been killed in a road traffic accident on the coastal highway, just south of Beirut. The soldiers are all aged between nineteen and twenty-three, and are all single.

We hold back details of the dead until the next of kin can be notified of their loss. Fitz sends me across the road to the Enlisted Personnel Section to collect their Single Administrative Documents, or SAD documents. These are forms filled in on personnel deploying overseas which contain all of their personal details, next of kin and so on. They are accessed in the event of death or injury.

I collect the files from the personnel officer. When I open them, I see the faces of the dead soldiers. Tragically killed on their way to the airport to go home on leave to visit their loved ones. I imagine their excitement as they got closer to Beirut. My heart goes out to the families. The black and white photographs of the young men are heartbreaking. They are so young; they look more like schoolboys than soldiers. Three of them, Privates Declan Deere, John Murphy and Matthew Lawlor, come from County Kildare. The fourth, Private Brendan Fitzpatrick, is from Portlaoise.

I'm at the air corps airfield, Casement Aerodrome in Baldonnel when the bodies are repatriated by the air corps Maritime Patrol Casa aircraft. The air corps have flown the bodies from London where they had arrived from Beirut earlier in the day. I am standing behind the bereaved families as the tailgate of the aircraft is lowered. There is an audible sigh of grief as the families get their first glimpse of the coffins inside the aircraft. They are inconsolable.

I think of my own service in Lebanon. I think of the fact that I got to come home. To see my family. The thoughts of dying so far from home fills me with an almost unbearable sadness. Again, myself and the Bodach attend the funerals and manage the media presence as best we can.

In April, I am again Lebanon-bound. This time with a team from RTÉ's *Prime Time*. The *Prime Time* crew are making a documentary on the 1980 Battle of At Tiri, which took place in the Irish Battalion area. The battle, which involved Irish troops and fighters from the Israeli-backed South Lebanese Army (SLA), lasted over a week and the Irish inflicted heavy casualties on the SLA.

After the incident, two Irish soldiers, Derek Smallhorn and Thomas Barrett, were abducted at gunpoint and executed by an SLA gunman, Mohammed Bazi. Their murders were committed as revenge killings in Lebanon's ongoing cycle of violence and mayhem.

I fly to Heathrow to meet the RTÉ crew. We meet up and fly British Airways to Beirut. As I'm boarding, Aideen texts me. 'We're pregnant.' When the cabin crew close the aircraft door and I fasten my seatbelt, I am still staring at the text. The air hostess asks me to turn off the phone as we taxi for take-off. As we cruise at 39,000 feet, I think of the new life – thousands of feet below, thousands of miles away – growing in Aideen's tummy. I have a few gin and tonics to steady my nerves. As the sun sets behind us and specks of high-altitude frost appear on the aircraft's windows, I think of the new speck of life I have left behind in Ireland. A tiny being, cells reproducing faster than the speed of this aircraft. My life has changed faster than the speed of thought. I have a few more gin and tonics.

When we land in Beirut, the cabin crew open the aircraft door. I feel the rush of heavily scented night air. I am dimly aware of the rush and hustle of Beirut rush-hour traffic on the Assad Highway into the centre of town. I'm aware of the staccato ring of Arabic about me. But none of it impacts on me in the same way. Something has shifted within me. A homing instinct has been switched on. I need to get home to this new life that we have created.

The next week or so in Lebanon is extremely hot. RTÉ film their reconstructions in the village of At Tiri. The producer, Janet Traynor, has managed to persuade John O'Mahony to travel out to Lebanon for the documentary.

John, a former soldier, was abducted by Bazi along with Smallhorn and Barrett. He was shot at point blank range in the same incident but somehow managed to survive. He was flown out of Lebanon in 1980 with serious injuries. This is his first time back to the country in almost twenty years. It is an emotional journey for him.

We visit the spot where he was abducted and shot. John is visibly upset. Again, I am reminded of those Irish who came to Lebanon, never to return home. John's emotional response to Lebanon, his grieving and loss, underscore the increasing unease I feel about being here. I am distracted. The RTÉ crew film reconstructions of the abduction using members of the Irish battalion on loan from Camp Shamrock. Janet Traynor has also persuaded some locals to act as members of the SLA. Both sets of actors play their parts with enthusiasm. The effect is unsettling. At the abduction scene, both Irish and Lebanese are fully in character. It is emotionally charged for all concerned. Both sides become heated in the final reconstruction. We have to step in and separate them. It is an eerie experience.

Throughout the filming, the area of operations is quiet. The villages baking in the strong summer sunshine. I sit in the shade of the armoured personnel carriers as the filming takes place. Occasionally, Israeli fighter jets pass high overhead. I squint into the sunshine to observe their flight pattern. To check for flares, sudden changes in direction, or the sonic boom I associate with bombing. After my experience of Operation Grapes of Wrath, I constantly expect to come under fire. I constantly expect the tranquility and shimmering heat to be ripped apart by gunfire and shelling. I feel myself instinctively fumbling about for the Motorola to report the position of aircraft or movement I observe in the Israeli firebases that are a constant, brooding presence above us. I notice that the young soldiers on this trip are oblivious to the aircraft. They are also oblivious to the Israeli compounds. They don't look up when there is movement on the ramparts. They ignore the telltale flashes of reflected sunlight as aiming devices rotate in our direction. They have not been under fire. Their ignorance is bliss. I wince each time I hear a new noise or detect an unfamiliar movement. I like to stand behind the armoured personnel carrier. I'm uncomfortable when RTÉ point their cameras towards Israel.

The final two days of filming are of cutaway shots of the Irish battalion's area of operations. These wide panoramic shots will give viewers at home an idea of the terrain in which Irish soldiers serve. The sun-bleached villages, the bleak scorched wadis. The cameraman, Nick Dolan, is especially talented. He has an eye for detail. He invites me to look at the footage he has taken through the viewfinder of the camera. I'm amazed at how small everything looks. It is almost impossible to communicate Lebanon. It is virtually impossible to understand it. It requires physical presence.

When we get back to Dublin, Aideen is waiting for me at the airport. On the drive into the city centre, I place my hand on her tummy. Like Doubting Thomas placing his fingers into the wounds of Christ. I tell my mother and father. My dad remarks, 'That'll put a stop to your gallop.'

A few weeks later, on 24 May 2000, the Israeli military announces it is withdrawing its forces from south Lebanon after two decades of occupation. By the end of the following day, the Israelis have abandoned their positions. All of the Israeli compounds and firebases that I had patrolled for months on end are gone in less than twenty-four hours. The Cuckoo's Nest, Haddathah Compound, Brashit Compound. All gone. Deserted. The Israelis withdraw south to the border with Israel. The Lebanese are ecstatic. Hizbollah are in the ascendant. They grow bolder and more confident. They are in full control of south Lebanon. Their power and influence supersedes that of the Lebanese government in Beirut.

Fitz laughs when he hears that the Israelis have withdrawn. He was one of the first Irish peacekeepers to serve in Lebanon in the mid-1970s. He stretches out in his office and lights a cigar. 'My work in Lebanon is complete.' A week or so later he is transferred to UN Headquarters in New York. He is replaced by Lieutenant Colonel Dermot Earley. I am lucky with my commanding officers in the press office. Dermot Earley is an informal, approachable and highly competent senior officer. He gives me every encouragement and allows me to continue to proactively network with journalists. He encourages me to use my initiative. 'Just keep me in the loop,' he says.

At around the same time, the Bodach announces his retirement from the army. '*Slán tamaill*' or 'goodbye for now' are his final words to me. I'm actively thinking about retirement myself. With our first baby due in December, I realise that I need a more family-friendly occupation. In army terms, after two years in the chief of staff's branch, I'm now staring down the barrel of a lengthy overseas mission. As a captain, I haven't been deployed with troops for almost four years. There are a number of overseas appointments that I'm now liable for. A year in Kosovo or further afield will not be consistent with new fatherhood. With the PhD in its final phase, I start applying for academic jobs.

Lieutenant Colonel Earley is helpful in this regard. He is the father of six children himself. He has a photograph of himself and his wife and children on his desk at all times. His son, Dermot Junior, is also an army officer. He gives me paternal advice on my army career path and its impact on family life. He agrees to act as a referee on my applications for academic jobs. He also gives me continued support for my ongoing research into female personnel. Reacting to my accounts of the interviews with women soldiers, he is highly supportive. He offers sound, compelling, advice. He cautions me to dot my 'i's and cross my 't's with regard to the investigation. 'You've got to make sure that your report is bulletproof. Make the strongest possible case. The army will do the rest.'

I scan the papers every week for academic posts. Meanwhile, Aideen's tummy is swelling. I can feel the ripples of movement in there at night. Things are changing rapidly.

My last trip to Lebanon takes place in August 2000. I'm escorting a party of journalists who are touring the recently 'liberated' area of south Lebanon along the border with Israel. The Irish have moved forward to newly constructed UN positions along the border with Israel. The firbases are empty. They are being slowly but surely dismantled by the UN. Locals have ransacked some of them. With their perimeter defences sagging and eroded, the compounds have deteriorated astonishingly rapidly. The radio masts, antennae and weapon ports have all been gutted. There is Arabic graffiti everywhere. There is the stench of stale urine in what remains of the burned-out concrete bunkers.

There is also unexploded ordnance. In addition, some of the compounds have been booby trapped. We escort the journalists into the abandoned Israeli positions only after they have been swept by the battalion's ordnance officer. While the journalists pore over the charred remains, I stand up on what is left of the ramparts and look back at the Irish positions. I see Al Yatun in the distance. UN flags hanging limp in the midday heat. The massive white gabions with 'UN' in black lettering are clearly visible. Below the rampart I see steel rods – red and white-striped gun-aiming posts – driven into the rock. A permanent reminder of the fields of fire the Israelis had marked when firing on our positions and on the homes and villages around us.

On our last day in the battalion area, I'm invited – for the last time – up to Al Yatun. I travel up from battalion headquarters in the water truck. Bouncing and clattering over the cattlegrid into Al Yatun, the radios come to life. As we swing into the vehicle park, the Irish Battalion Mobile Reserve are running to their vehicles. A loud series of detonations have broken the relatively peaceful silence of recent months. The SISUs move out towards Brashit.

The operations officer at battalion headquarters gets me on the radio. I'm recalled to bring the journalists out to Brashit. A company of troops give me a lift back to Shamrock. From there, we're taken by armoured vehicle to Brashit. We dismount at a track below the abandoned compound. Three small children have been killed by an abandoned Israeli device. They must have picked it up.

The children are torn apart by the blast. Bloodstained clothing and rubble are scattered all over the track. Another child, wounded in the blast, screams shrilly. Like a rabbit or a small animal caught in a trap. The cries are impossibly high-pitched. The medics are working furiously on this little girl. Strewn around her on the ground is her shredded clothing. A dainty little shoe. And the torn-open packaging of bandages. She is surrounded by Red Crescent medics. They are squatting around her. One of the medics taps a syringe with his finger and gently rubs her arm. They close in around her as the medic pushes the plunger on the syringe. The cries increase in pitch briefly and subside.

The journalists are struck dumb for once. The dead children are only recognisable as human remains because of what is left of their clothing.

We eventually get back to battalion headquarters. I pack my bags in Lebanon for the last time. The next morning we drive up the Coastal Highway. A sergeant from Headquarters Company is driving the minibus. He plays Johnny Cash all the way to Beirut. 'I fell in to a burning ring of fire.'

A few days later, the Irish battalion creates a mine awareness program for Lebanese children. The ordnance personnel travel to all of the schools and the orphanage at Tibnine. They hand out leaflets in Arabic that contain photographs of the dozens of different types of explosive device that litter the area of operations.

The fax machine in the office in Parkgate Street buzzes to life as one of the leaflets hums and zips through the printer. I look at the black and white images of white phosphorous shells, grenades, mines and mortar rounds. In black and white, their ugliness in relief.

Aideen calls me. There is a letter for me at home. I'm invited to interview for a lecturing post at the Institute of Technology, Tallaght. I leave the leaflet on the table. I change into civvies and cycle through Dublin 8 to our little house off Meath Street.

Chapter 13

Farewell to Arms

'Not that bullshit about the women again. Are you still going on
about the fucking women?'

Institute of Technology, Tallaght, Dublin / Defence Forces Headquarters, Dublin
Spring 2001

During my appointment to the press office throughout 1999 and 2000, I
complete the final phase of my doctoral research. The interviews with my
female colleagues haunt me. They also fill me with a deep sense of respect for
them. Despite the many obstacles placed before them in the workplace – discriminatory policies and practices that impact on every aspect of their service
– the women are determined to stay in the Defence Forces and strive for promotion. Against all the odds. That they do this, in the context of unaccept-
ably high levels of bullying, sexual harassment and sexual assault, marks them
as the most remarkable of soldiers.

   In the spring of 2000, whilst shuttling back and forth from Syria and
Lebanon, I manage to write up my doctoral thesis and present for examination. The Viva examination takes place in a room in DCU's Business School.
After an exhaustive cross-examination, I am told that I have passed, subject to
a series of revisions and re-editing. Over the summer, I complete the revisions
and resubmit the work. The university have been very careful to ensure that I
satisfy the most exacting, ethical, methodological and theoretical tests of the
thesis. Such are the work's findings and conclusions, it is essential that it withstand the most rigorous scrutiny. So stark are its results, there is a requirement
that the work be robust and have sufficient academic, intellectual and factual

integrity to withstand any subsequent challenge or interrogation.

Finally, after a four-year journey, the doctoral thesis is lodged to the library in DCU as per the parameters for publication as laid down in the chief of staff's letter of clarification of June 1998. In November, myself and Aideen – who is heavily pregnant – attend the graduation in DCU. Later that month, I interview for the position of lecturer in communication theory in the Institute of Technology, Tallaght. I am successful and am informed by the human resources manager that I will commence employment in December of 2000. HR also inform me, as is standard with all academics, I must undergo a period of one year's probation. During this probationary year, my ongoing employment is subject to my satisfactory performance and overall suitability for retention as a lecturer in a third-level institution.

As soon as I receive the confirmation letter from IT Tallaght, I apply for permission to retire from the army. My awfully big adventure with the army, which began in the cadet school at the Curragh in 1989 and which has brought me to Lebanon, Bosnia and Syria, is drawing to a close. The army has encouraged me, mentored me, educated me. It has been my family for over a decade. I will miss my comrades in arms. Those that I trained with, soldiered with, laughed and cried with.

Officers Records reply that permission is granted by the chief of staff to retire. I undergo an exit medical in St Bricin's Military Hospital. I am given a retired officer's identity card and am offered associate membership of the officer's mess in McKee Barracks. I hand in all of my webbing and kit to the quartermaster in the 2nd Field Regiment in McKee. He takes my helmet and what remains of my combat uniforms into the stores. He ticks off each item. The list includes the binoculars that I used in Lebanon to scan the opposing ridgelines and Israeli firebases. He asks me if I still have the combats I had been issued for service overseas. I think of them burning in a barrel of diesel in Al Yatun as Israeli drones flew overhead. 'I lost them.' He grunts. 'You'll be deducted for those.'

Whilst I shuffle off the trappings of military service, I make strenuous efforts to bring the contents of my PhD to the attention of the military authorities. Once the revised doctoral thesis has been signed off by the external examiners and has been lodged to the library in DCU, I am now in a position to present the final version to the general staff. Over the entire four years of the research project, I have appraised my immediate superiors of my progress, both formally and informally. I have been told throughout by successive commanding officers to ensure that the report is fully executed, fully completed and containing a comprehensive account of the issues confronting female personnel in order that the military authorities be fully informed and appraised of the problems within the organisation.

Once the thesis is complete, I make an application through my colleagues in the chief of staff's branch to have a personal interview with the chief of staff in order to present my findings, conclusions and recommendations to him. The chief of staff who wrote my letter of clarification in 1998 subsequently retired. Indeed, his successor has just retired and in November of 2000 there is a newly appointed chief of staff in army headquarters. Like the Pope in Rome, the new chief of staff brings with him a new set of staff officers and there is a period of transition and change in DFHQ.

As a result of this change at the top of the organisation, DFHQ is in flux when I make my request to see the chief of staff. My colleagues and other staff officers at DFHQ ask me for some time to make the necessary arrangements. One senior officer informs me that 'the chief is on a steep learning curve. He needs to read himself into the brief. Just give him a couple of weeks to settle in and find his feet, and then you can appraise him fully of your report.' There are a lot of competing demands on the incoming chief of staff's time.

I use the delay to summarise the doctoral thesis and configure it as a Power Point presentation. The doctoral thesis is over three hundred pages long as it stands. I summarise the main points and condense its main findings into a punchy, twenty-page document. I edit one version as a stand-alone discursive document. I edit another version as a slide presentation. I wait anxiously for my opportunity to expose the appalling conditions of service, bullying and sexual harassment and assault endured by female soldiers to the chief of s taff.

The weeks slip by. Despite repeated attempts on my part, I am not given access to the chief to discuss the research. I impress upon my superiors in

DFHQ the serious and pressing nature of my concerns. They again reassure me that all will be well and that the chief will give the matter his full attention 'in due course'.

Days later, I am lecturing in IT Tallaght. I keep in touch with my colleagues, however. I tell them that when the chief of staff is available, I will come into DFHQ on my own time to make the presentation.

My probationary year in Tallaght starts abruptly. The head of school who was part of the interview panel greets me in his office. 'Are you ready to go?' he asks. I'm lecturing on business communications to a large group of first-year students. He walks me down the corridor and ushers me into a large lecture hall. And there they are. Around two hundred young men and women eyeing me skeptically – the new guy. The school head introduces me and mischievously tells them that 'Dr Clonan has come straight from the army, so pay attention.' This draws a mock intake of breath from the group and some laughter. The school head takes his leave and I'm on my own. My mind goes temporarily blank, so I slip into a routine I've used for years when addressing military groups. I clear my throat and ask if everyone can hear me. No answer, just some nervous giggles and a lot of texting going on. I seize the moment and ask everyone to turn off their mobile phones. This gets their attention.

Amid much muttering and rustling, dozens of mobiles are shoved into pockets, bags and under seats. They look at me with renewed interest. This army guy is obviously a ball-breaker. I launch into a description of some of the classic models of communication favoured by business studies theorists when a mobile phone rings loudly.

I stop mid-sentence and scan the room. The phone continues to ring loudly; the cheeky ringtone accompanied by the loud buzzing courtesy of the vibration mode. As if it wasn't loud enough to begin with. The students look down at me – halfway between curious and entertained. How will the military hard-ass deal with this provocation? The phone continues to ring defiantly. There is total silence. All eyes are on me. They know, and I know, that the manner in which I deal with this issue will set the tone for the remainder of the academic year. Probably even for the rest of my academic career in Tallaght. I ask in a quiet, but I think authoritative voice, 'Would the person who owns that phone, please have the courtesy to switch it off. I'm trying to give a lecture here.'

That's when I realise that the offending phone is in fact my own phone. Ringing loudly from inside the leather suitcase that my mum bought me as a graduation gift. Realisation that it's my phone sweeps through the room like an electric current. They spontaneously burst into laughter and I get a round of applause, as, red-faced, I reach into the bag to switch it off. I think of the first lesson in communications I am delivering – 'first impressions last'.

The school head meets me later. 'How did it go this morning? I'm sure you made your mark on them. Great to have a bit of military efficiency around here.'

Making sure each day to set my phone to silent, I get into the rhythm of lecturing and research. I begin to submit papers for research journals and journals in communication. The school head encourages me to submit chapters of my PhD for academic publication. It is 'publish or perish' it seems.

For my part, I'm particularly interested in the dilemma of researching from within an organisation. The academic literature does not deal with this phenomenon in sufficient detail. I read up about other researchers who have conducted research from the inside of organisations and other institutional settings. Most, however, are academics who briefly gain access to the 'inside' but are destined to return to the sanctuary of the university or academic setting. Erving Goffman, for example, the eminent American sociologist who was briefly committed to a psychiatric institution, writes about the experience and describes the 'total institution,' where behaviour is prescribed, uniform and carefully regulated. Reflecting on my military service, his 1961 work, *Asylums: Essays on the Social Situation of Mental Patients and Other Inmates*, has echoes of the army for me. This seminal work is considered an 'ethnography of the concept of the total institution'. I see parallels in the sociological examination of the social circumstances of mental patients in a 'total institution' such as a psychiatric hospital and the plight of women in a male-dominated, patriarchal military organisation such as the Irish Defence Forces.

I'm also interested in the work of John Van Maanen, a sociologist who joined the NYPD to investigate its internal culture during the 1970s. He enriched his research into the experiences of police recruits and rookie cops with his own experiences and participant observation as a cop. His works, which include the memorably titled essay 'The Asshole: A View of Policing From the Street', gives the reader a rich and deeply insightful view of the workplace culture of New York cops in the 1970s. Van Maanen's work strikes a chord with me as it seems to reflect the processes in which I was engaged as a soldier and researcher – without the protection and immunity from prosecution under military law enjoyed by most academics.

There are advantages and disadvantages to this type of research. As an insider, I had full access to the reality of military life for both men and women alike. I had unfettered access to the unvarnished truth. I have reached a number of conclusions based on this research. I now consider archival material to be almost completely unreliable as truthful representations of the reality of the 'contested' experiences of women. Whether they be in the army, the Gardaí or in Magdalene laundries for that matter. Equally unreliable and misleading are official documents and records which purport to demonstrate realities on the ground. I know from my own research – involving exhaustive interviews and human audit – that the real experiences of workers are often far removed from those descriptions contained in official reports. I believe, based on my own experiences, that many such documents are a carefully constructed whitewash.

I think especially of the women I interviewed in Lebanon. One woman in particular, a private soldier, was working as a waitress in the officer's mess at battalion headquarters in Camp Shamrock – a job she despised. 'I'm a fully trained soldier,' she told me. 'Yet here I am, checking the freezer every day to make sure there's enough fucking ice cream in it for the officers.' She also told me how she wrote letters home to her family in Ireland, almost every day, where she fabricated stories about patrols and sentry duty. 'I wrote home telling them about the villages and the people I was meeting. I hadn't the heart to tell them that I was working as a fucking skivvy in the officer's mess. I was so ashamed. So I made all that stuff up to keep them happy and keep myself sane.' Responding to official army policy at that time, which proscribed the work of Irish women outside the camp as a result of 'local cultural conditions', she had this to say. 'The Arabs don't have a fucking problem with us. They take our money and our blood in transfusions – no problem. It's the fuckers who are running this camp who have a problem with women. They're the real fucking Arabs if you ask me.'

Part of my learning curve as an academic is in seeking out ways to communicate the wider findings of my doctoral research to an academic audience. I decide to write a paper for the *Irish Journal of Sociology* on my research methodology. To try and describe the experience of being an insider researcher in a highly regulated 'total institution' such as the military. The experience of being a military researcher subject to military law and the Official Secrets Act. I make contact with Professor Tom Inglis in the Department of Sociology in University College, Dublin. He welcomes my submission of a paper, which I have titled 'The Inside View of the Irish Defence Forces: Implications for Methodology'. Like all academic papers, it is subject to review. I continue all the while to lecture in Tallaght. I enjoy the interactions with the students. They are irreverent. They call me 'Tom' without blinking. Nobody calls me 'Dr Clonan'. It is different to my own college experience. These students are buoyant, confident, assertive. They are noisy. They are full of energy and optimism. Full of humour. Full of life. It is life-affirming to witness it at first hand.

Despite this, I'm still fretting and worrying about the conditions being endured in the army by female soldiers. I lie awake in the early hours agonising over the correct course of action. Each time, I recall the assurances of my former colleagues at DFHQ. 'Leave it with us. We'll arrange for you to talk to the chief of staff when he has settled in.' I resolve to call them regularly to remind them of their promise.

Meanwhile, Aideen has reached her due date. Our little baby, it seems, has no intention of joining us just yet. Life changes suddenly for us about a week later. I wake up in the bed at around 1 AM. Aideen is walking up and down in the darkness, packing a bag. 'What's wrong with you?' I ask her. 'My water's just broke. Get dressed.' I ask her 'Are you sure?' She laughs at me and minutes later we are driving – as calmly as I can – to the Coombe.

After a twelve-hour labour, our baby arrives. Our first baby. Born just two weeks before Christmas. We call him Darach. Or 'Oak Tree'. A mighty oak someday. But, for now, our little acorn.

Two days later, we drive from the Coombe Maternity Hospital back to our house. Nothing will ever be the same again. I continue to lecture in Tallaght. My learning curve there has now been augmented by new skills at home including swift nappy changes and identifying the meanings of different cries and yelps. I'm also punch drunk from sleep deprivation, all day, every day, from the endless round of night feeds and interrupted sleep. My father looks at me and laughs. 'Welcome to the real world.'

Christmas comes and goes. During night feeds, standing at the microwave under a full moon, I comfort myself with the thought that approximately 120,000 Irish people become parents each year. So, somewhere in Ireland, there is someone else standing in front of a microwave at three in the morning – watching a bottle of milk go round and round. Waiting for it to 'ping' so that they can go back to bed. Even if there's little or no sleep.

One February morning, I'm sitting in my office feeling a bit groggy from lack of sleep when my phone rings. I recognise the number as Defence Forces Headquarters. Curious, I answer the call. A staff officer from DFHQ is on the line. He greets me breezily and asks me if I have a moment. I close over the door of the office and tell him I can speak. He tells me that, 'The chief would like to see you. He'd like you to come in to DFHQ to talk about something that has cropped up. Something of a sensitive nature shall we say. It's right up your street.' At last, I'm thinking, they want to talk about the research. Act on its findings. Sort the whole sorry, sordid mess out. For good. For everyone's benefit. I confirm that I can come in immediately. The staff officer tells me that the chief will be available the following morning.

I tell Aideen about the meeting. She is happy for me. 'Good to have some sort of resolution. Some sort of closure,' she calls out to me from the tiny kitchen of our house. I'm holding Darach as she says it. He's asleep – for once. It is the calm before the storm. In more ways than one. After a very short maternity leave, Aideen – a busy hospital doctor – is due to return to full-time work. The brief spell of tranquillity and domestic bliss which we have enjoyed following Darach's birth is coming to a close. Aideen will return to the manic work routine of Irish hospital medicine. And, unbeknownst to me, I'm about to enter the twilight zone. I'm about to go on a surreal safari with a general staff who develop an acute phobic reaction to my research findings.

And so, the following day, at the appointed hour, I drive in to DFHQ. The soldiers on the front gate recognise me immediately and wave me in. After all, it has only been a month or so since I retired. I decide to be cheeky and park right at the front door of DFHQ – where the minister for defence and chief of staff park their staff cars. I walk through the granite entrance. Carved into the stone arch overhead are the familiar words, 'Headquarters, Ireland Command'. I've never walked under this arch as a civilian before. I have a spring in my step. The guys on the reception desk smile up at me and wave me towards the lift. I know where I'm going anyhow.

The lift reaches the third floor and the doors open. The staff officer, a senior officer I know well, is waiting for me. He laughs and tells me to 'Get a haircut – civvie.' We go to his office and I start to open my briefcase. I'm taking out my laptop and I mention that I've got all of the relevant information on Power Point. The staff officer cocks his head to one side. A cloud passes briefly over his eyes. 'What's that now, Tom?' he asks me.

I reply, 'I've done up a Power Point presentation on the doctoral research for the chief. I've got it all here. I'm ready to go.' I'm about to ask if there is a projector and screen in the chief's office when the senior officer cuts me short. 'Oh, no Thomas. There's been a misunderstanding. You're not here to talk about that stuff about the women. No. Not at all. Forget about that stuff. You're here to give the chief your views on whether or not we should outsource our crisis management function to a PR consultant.'

I'm a bit confused. I'm also feeling a bit frustrated. 'Well, you'll need the services of a crisis communication consultant if you don't deal with the situation involving the women and the bullying and sexual harassment.' Things are going wrong now. The temperature in the room drops to freezing point. The senior officer looks at me and sighs. 'Not that bullshit about the women again. Are you still going on about the fucking women?'

I'm temporarily stunned by the sudden switch to expletives. It knocks me off balance. It is as though this is happening in slow motion. I feel a little disassociated. There is no way I'm going to talk to the chief of staff about PR consultants and crisis communication. I try again. I try to be as reasonable as I can. 'Look, I was told I'd be briefing the chief on my research into the women. There are serious problems to be addressed. Allegations of discrimination, bullying, sexual harassment, sexual assault. Allegations of rape.'

The senior officer points his finger at me. 'I'm telling you now to forget about it Tom. Fucking drop it. You are an academic now. Living in an ivory tower. Unlike you, we have to live in the real world. Have you forgotten what the women are like? We'll deal with the fucking women. And we'll deal with it our own way.' I try to protest once more, but I am now being ushered towards the door, I'm literally being shown the door. As we walk back to the lift, the senior officer states in no uncertain manner his 'disappointment' in me. 'I didn't think you'd turn into a civilian that fucking quickly.'

I try one last time. 'Please. Listen to me. Just deal with the issues raised in my research. The chief has the perfect opportunity. He is new to the job. He has no historical responsibility for what has gone before. He can be the first chief of staff to sort these issues out for once and for all. It is the army's own study for Christ's sake.' The lift arrives. The senior officer leans towards me and says very forcefully. 'Forget about it. This conversation is over. Now fuck off, Tom.'

I'm numb. I cannot believe this is happening. I cannot believe the forceful manner in which I have been rebutted. I walk past the guys on the reception desk and drive out the gate. The sentry on the gate salutes me. It will be almost a decade before I enter a military barracks again.

On the quays, stuck in traffic, Aideen calls me. 'How did the meeting go?' she asks. 'Not very well,' is all I can manage. I think of all of the women that I interviewed. I think of the confidence they placed in me. I cannot accept that the discrimination and ongoing bullying and harassment will continue unchecked. I feel sick to the pit of my stomach.

Chapter 14

Ivory Tower

'No one of any real importance reads the *Sunday World*.'

Summer 2001

After the disastrous meeting at DFHQ, I explore every avenue of approach open to me in order to secure a meeting with the chief of staff. I call his personal staff officer several times to make an appointment to see the chief. The staff officer is apologetic and tells me that the chief has a very hectic schedule. He promises to see what he can do.

My main contacts are gone. Fitz is in UN Headquarters in New York. Dermot Earley is in London at the Royal College of Defence Studies. I have no senior officer – with sufficient clout – through whom I can seek access to the chief of staff. I am extremely frustrated.

In addition to adjusting to life with Darach, I continue to throw myself into my work as an academic in Tallaght. I'm conscious that I am on probation. The advice 'publish or perish' rings in my ears. I submit conference papers. I have a paper accepted at Kiel University in Germany. My paper, 'Women, Combat and the Use of Force', is well received. I submit another paper to the University of Aarhus in Denmark. They accept my paper 'Irish Women's Participation in the Liberation of the Irish State'. It is also well received and at the conference I meet many academic peers who have conducted research into the status and role of women in other European armies. They express the view that such research in Europe is routine and highly regarded. None of them, it seems, have been told to 'fuck off' in quite the same way that I have. Mind you, none of them were serving soldiers either when they conducted the research. They express puzzlement and some sympathy when I explain to them the outcome of my research. A German colleague observes – somewhat presciently – 'Don't worry about your findings. The truth will always out.'

Flying back from Aarhus, I connect to Stansted. Aideen texts me as I board the Dublin-bound flight. We are pregnant again. I am now getting used to receiving life-altering newsflashes in dreary airport departure lounges.

When I get home there is more news. My mum's cancer has returned and she is no longer in remission. She is suffering from Multiple Myeloma. From what I can gather, her condition will be 'managed', but that there will be no 'heroic measures'. She is only sixty-five. My mum tells me that she has refused the option of a bone marrow transplant as she is too tired. 'I couldn't face it, my love.'

My father tells me not to worry. 'You are always worrying. Worrying about nothing. Forget about it.' I do of course worry about it. I fret. I make dozens of phone calls. I practically stalk my mum's GP with enquiries and suggestions about oncologists and geriatricians who might proactively manage her condition. They each tell me, patiently but firmly, that they are doing all they can.

My dad gets wind of some of these phone calls. He warns me off. He tells me to mind my own business. 'Leave your mother alone,' he tells me. 'She has enough on her plate without your interference. You think you know it all. You know nothing.' I suspect he is as upset as I am.

I complete my first six months of probation in the Institute of Technology, Tallaght. Darach is a bonny baby. All is well. For now.

In the early summer I get an unexpected call from an ex-army colleague. We served together in the artillery corps and were good friends. He is also that rare thing in the officer corps of the Irish army – a fellow Dubliner and Northsider to boot. The adjutant of our unit used to joke that not only were my friend and I from 'north of the Liffey', we were also both from 'north of the Tolka'. By coincidence, my friend's mother had known my father when they were younger, growing up not far from each other in Drumcondra. I'm delighted to hear from him. It turns out that he has decided to pursue an MA in Communications in DCU. The same postgraduate degree that propelled me into the Defence Forces Press Office. My friend calls me on the phone and asks if he can interview me in relation to his dissertation. His research is focused on the workings of the Defence Forces Press Office.

I'm delighted to help him in any way I can and to catch up on any army gossip. I've been out of the loop, as it were, for a few months now. He calls to my house. He greets Aideen warmly and smiles at baby Darach. He brings a bottle of red wine – châteauneuf-du-Pape. As I play with Darach on my lap, he interviews me for his dissertation. He asks me about the working routine in the press office. Afterwards, he asks me how my own research, my doctoral research, has progressed. I tell him that I am concerned about it. I tell him that the general staff have serious questions to answer in relation to my research into female soldiers.

After a while, my friend excuses himself and leaves. He has a long drive home as he now lives near the Curragh Camp. I wave goodbye to him from the front door of the house. Darach is asleep in my arms now. Probably bored to sleep with talk of research and dissertations.

In August, I receive a phone call from another ex-army colleague, Declan Power. Declan is a freelance journalist and is working with the *Sunday World*. We make some small talk over the phone about the good old days. After some polite chat, Declan gets to the point. He's been working on a story about allegations of rape at an Army Reserve training camp in the Glen of Imaal, County Wicklow. In working through the story and interviewing soldiers about the allegations, he tells me that more than one female soldier has mentioned my research to him. Whilst Declan would have known that I had undertaken research into women in the army, he would not have been aware of the stark findings in relation to bullying, harassment and allegations of sexual assault and rape. Declan asks me a straight question. 'Tom, does your research deal with sexual assault and rape?' I confirm that it does.

At the time of this phone call, Declan is working as a part-time lecturer in Dublin City University and is completing an MPhil there. He has full access to the library in DCU and full access to my doctoral thesis, which is lodged there as per the agreement reached with the chief of staff. Declan tells me he will go and have a look at it. I think of the German academic's prediction that the findings of my research would inevitably find their way into the wider public domain. I recall specifically his words on academic theses. 'Academic research is a matter of public record. Once lodged to the library, it is an accessible, searchable database. Even though it is in an academic repository, it is irrevocably placed within the public domain. It is like giving birth to a child. Once you put your work on the record, it takes on a life of its own. You know longer control it.'

Declan calls me the following day on Friday, 3 August. He tells me that he's had a look at the findings on bullying, harassment and sexual assault. He tells me that the *Sunday World* newspaper is keen to run with the story. Declan, like myself when I conducted the research, is shocked and disgusted with the results. He thinks it is a big story. An important story. I thank Declan for paying me the courtesy of letting me know that the story will be published that Sunday.

I agonise once more over the issue. On the one hand, I feel a sense of relief that the findings of the research will make their way into the public domain. On the other hand, I feel a sense of loyalty to my colleagues at DFHQ despite the harsh treatment I had received earlier in the year.

Having mulled the issue over for an hour or two, I call my father and ask his advice. He listens to my dilemma. My dad doesn't beat about the bush. 'You did the doctorate. It's your call. I presume you know what you are doing. I suppose you know what you have got yourself into. Do what you think is the right thing to do. And leave your mother out of it. Don't be worrying her. She's sick.'

Based on this advice, I resolve to contact the military authorities once more. To see if I can appeal to reason. I speak to a staff officer at DFHQ that Friday afternoon. The staff officer in question is familiar with my research. 'The woman study,' he calls it. I tell him that the thesis and its findings in relation to bullying, harassment and sexual assault has been seen by the *Sunday World*. 'So what?' is his reply.

I tell him that the *Sunday World* are going to run with the story that week. That it will be a huge, breaking news story. I tell him that the army needs to prepare itself for the inevitable negative public reaction. I remind him that the research was facilitated by the army itself and that the very existence of the thesis reflects a desire on the part of the military authorities to end the mistreatment of female personnel.

In fact, I point out to him, that by taking 'ownership' of the doctoral thesis, the general staff would legitimately hold the high moral ground in relation to this difficult story. I try every ounce of my powers of persuasion to sell the idea to the staff officer that it is in the general staff's interest to embrace the thesis and its findings. After all, none of the research could have taken place without their permission and support throughout the research process. The staff officer pauses on the other end of the line. He tells me that he will have to wait and see what the *Sunday World* publishes on Sunday. He also makes two other remarks that give me pause for thought.

'If this is about women, there'll be no public interest in it. So calm down Thomas. You don't really think that *Sunday World* readers will be interested in an academic thesis, do you? And anyway, no one of any real importance reads the *Sunday World*.' I can still hear his laughter long after he hangs up the phone. Well, at least I tried.

Chapter 15

Breaking News

'We've dealt with you politely up to now and you have not learned your lesson. Now you are going to face the fucking consequences. You declared war with your ambush today. Now it is guerilla warfare. Make no mistake about it Clonan, this is war and we are going to use every dirty trick in the book against you.'

Dublin

August 2001

Two days later, the *Sunday World* boasts a headline in huge white capitals set against a black background: 'Army Rocked With New "Orgies" Shocker'. Running across the headline is a strapline, 'Female Recruits have FCA Summer Camps – Something like Ibiza uncovered.' In the story, the *Sunday World* deals with an investigation by Gardaí into an alleged assault on a female soldier at an Army Reserve training camp in Ballymullen Barracks in Tralee. Under a second headline, 'Top brass is already reeling from a string of sex scandals', the article then lists some of the main findings of my doctoral research. In black and white, my research is now out in the wider public domain.

The following day, I make contact with Defence Forces Headquarters yet again. I imagine they will be angry. They are very angry indeed. But, they are not angry with the *Sunday World*. They are angry with me. I suppose that it is easier for them to be angry with me. I'm told that they have nothing to say to me. I advise them as best I can that the story will likely be picked up and seized upon by other media in the aftermath of the *Sunday World's* revelations. Given the tone of the exchange, I get the impression that I am irrevocably considered persona non grata. In spite of this, I send an email to the staff officer with the summarised version of the main findings of the doctoral research. This executive summary also contains all of the positive findings about the army that are contained within the doctoral research. Whilst I keep a copy of the email sent, and I receive no reply from DFHQ.

In the following days the remainder of the print media pick up on the story. I get a call from Jim Cusack, the security editor of the *Irish Times*. He tells me that he considers the story to be not just of national importance, but of international significance. The *Irish Times* covers the story over a full page under the headline, 'Former captain finds an Army where aggrieved women soldiers appear to be seen but not heard'.

The *Irish Independent* also follows up on the story. Samantha McCaughren writes about the findings of the doctoral thesis under the headline, 'Woman branded a trouble maker for speaking out on common problem'. In a story labeled 'exclusive' in the *Sunday Independent*, Declan Power follows up yet again with a major analysis piece under the headline, 'Army a sexual "minefield" for women. says survey'. Eventually the story gets saturation coverage in the print media – among broadsheets and tabloids alike. Conor Kavanagh, writing in the *Irish Daily Star*, deals with the doctoral thesis under the heading, 'Sex Ordeal for Women in the Army'.

In responding to the coverage in the press, the army's spokesperson is quoted in the *Irish Times* as follows: 'Replying to some of the points raised in the thesis, a spokesman for the Defence Forces said . . . the thesis was an "academic work" and that the research had "not been made available to the Defence Forces"'. This is, of course, untrue. It is a lie.

In addition, Jim Cusack is told by the military authorities that the thesis is 'bullshit'. He is told this by a senior officer at Defence Forces Headquarters. After the *Irish Times* publish the report, Jim Cusack – whom I know well through my duties as Defence Forces Press Officer for the previous two years – contacts me at home to say that the army are very hostile about the story. He tells me that one senior officer in particular kept repeating the word 'bullshit' to describe the research. Jim tells me that he only stopped using the word 'bullshit' when asked if this was his 'on the record' response to the research.

When I read the army's statement in the *Irish Times* to the effect that the work had 'not been made available to the Defence Forces', I ring them again. The response I get is frosty to say the least. I ask the staff officer on the line if they have received the executive summary that I have sent them by email. He replies that they have indeed received it and that it is 'bullshit'. In the meantime, the army sends a senior legal officer to DCU. The legal officer in question gains admission to the library and signs out the thesis.

Arising from the coverage of the doctoral thesis in the print media, the following days are a blur of radio and TV interviews. Given the army's cold and negative response to the research and their claim that I have not made the research 'available' to them, I spend a lot of time on air trying to defend my reputation as a retired army officer and as an academic and researcher. I am especially conscious, given that I am on probation in the Institute of Technology, Tallaght, that my reputation as an ethical researcher and the integrity of my academic qualifications are now subject to hostile scrutiny in the full glare of media publicity. I find the process intimidating and deeply disturbing.

In the middle of all of this I get a phone call out of the blue from a former colleague and staff officer at Defence Forces Headquarters. He tells me that the army think that I'm a 'wanker'. He also tells me that the army feels that its back is up against the wall. He goes on to say that, 'When your back is up against the wall, character assassination is a legitimate tactic. When you can't go for the ball, you go for the man.' I feel sick. I feel out of my depth. I don't know who to turn to for advice. Everything is happening so quickly and so publicly, I do not feel in control. It is as stressful as coming under fire in Lebanon. Every time the phone rings, I am invited to participate in yet another media interview. I'm interviewed on RTÉ radio and television. I'm interviewed on TV3. The army refuse to appear in studio with me. Their spokespersons continuously repeat the assertion that I have in some way 'concealed' the research and its findings from them. The opposite, in fact, is the case.

The implication over repeated interviews is that I have in some way fabricated the research and falsified its findings. The advocacy groups and equality agencies that purport to advocate for women and who campaign against gender-based violence are completely silent throughout this public interrogation of my PhD. I receive no public support whatsoever. None of my army friends call to ask me if I am OK. In fact, I find myself utterly isolated.

At this point, another, more sinister development takes place. I receive silent phone calls. When I answer the phone, the caller hangs up. I also receive obscene phone calls and threatening and abusive calls from withheld numbers. 'You're fucked, Clonan,' is a phrase that is repeated very often. As is the phrase, 'Who the fuck do you think you are?' About a week into the media frenzy, one of my sisters calls me. She too has received obscene phone messages. One caller leaves a voicemail on her phone which repeats the message I have become so familiar with, 'Clonan, you're fucked.' All of these events are happening as the media spotlight focuses on me with ever-greater intensity.

Things come to a head on Friday, 17 August in two separate but parallel developments. I am at home when I receive a call on my mobile phone from Michael Smith, the Fianna Fáil Minister for Defence. He asks me if I am free to talk. He expresses bewilderment and surprise at the media furore over the research and its findings. He also expresses disbelief at the insistence by the military authorities that the PhD was somehow concealed from them. I inform him as to the exact mechanism by which I sought and received written permission from the director of training to conduct the research. I also inform him of the manner in which I received written clarification from the chief of staff as to the manner in which it could be examined and the manner in which he directed I lodge it to the library in DCU – consistent with all other PhDs.

The minister sounds sympathetic. Unlike the military authorities, he is neither hostile nor rude. He tells me that he has 'no control' over the conditions imposed upon me by the military authorities. I tell him how stressful the whole situation is, for both me and my family. He asks me a direct question. 'What do you want me to do about it as minister?' I ask him to make sure that any inquiry into my research and its findings be independent – and carried out by people who are qualified to investigate such issues. The minister gives me his word. And, true to his word, he announces shortly thereafter that he will launch an official, independent inquiry into my research – the Study Review Group.

Later that morning, I am once more interviewed by Bryan Dobson on RTÉ Radio 1 and quizzed about renewed army claims that I have concealed the research from the military authorities. An army spokesman on the program repeats the assertion that I am 'refusing' to disclose its contents to the general staff and that I had in some way conducted my activities in secret and without authorisation. This is the last straw for me. I state, live on air, that I am in possession of two letters – one from the director of training, and one from the chief of staff himself – giving me explicit written permission to conduct the research and directing me to lodge the thesis to the library in DCU. The existence of the letters contradict the army's position that they knew nothing about the research – an adversarial and confrontational position that they have adopted since the story first broke. For the first time since the military authorities sought to muddy the waters, I feel somewhat vindicated.

After the radio program, I switch on my mobile. After a minute or two it buzzes out a few message notifications. I look at the screen. A couple of missed calls and some texts. A text from Aideen, telling me that her scan is normal. The obstetrician has taken a screen grab of our little one and printed it off for me so that I can look at it later.

The other texts are a mix of things. One from my sister Pauline saying 'Well done' and saying that she heard me on the radio. A voicemail from IT Tallaght about a staff meeting for the coming academic year. The phone buzzes again. Another voicemail. I dial into it as I unlock the car. The voicemail is broken up a little. But I can make out the anger in the voice. I get a garbled, 'Who the fuck do you think you are?' I immediately hang up.

I head for home. When I get there, Aideen is waiting for me with the grainy black and grey printout of our tiny baby. It is little more than a bean at this stage. That's what it looks like to me. I don't mention the voicemail. We have decided to take a few days' holiday. To get away from it all, so to speak. I don't want to ruin the moment. I also feel that the minister's promise of an independent inquiry, along with the radio interview, which seemed to clarify matters somewhat, means that I can draw a line under the situation for a few days. I'm hoping the 'war' is over.

We are going to France for a short break. Away from Ireland. No radio or newspapers for a week or two. A chance to pause for reflection. To try and make sense of everything that has happened in the last week.

We have already packed the car. We strap Darach into his baby seat in the back. Aideen squeezes in beside him. She is breastfeeding at the moment. If he wakes, she'll be next to him. We're driving to Cork. We'll overnight there and in the morning take the ferry to Roscoff in France.

I call my Dad as we head out onto the N7. He tells me that my mum is in bed. Resting. He tells me not to worry about the problems with the army. He's heard an announcement on the radio that the minister for defence is to set up an independent review of the research. 'Everything will be all right,' he tells me. 'Enjoy your holiday.'

We are only out of the city when Darach wakes up. Crying for a feed. I look in the rearview mirror as Aideen holds him to her and feeds him. I hear the snuffling noises as he tries to latch on. Eventually his cries subside and his eyes glaze over, closing gently. I catch Aideen's eye in the rearview mirror. She smiles at me.

My phone rings once more. As I'm driving, I tap the answer key on the car kit with my index finger. I notice as I do so that the number displayed is from Defence Forces Headquarters. The caller is one of the staff officers that I have dealt with in recent weeks. Up until now he has maintained an air of indifference to my offers of help.

This afternoon, however, his voice is thick with anger. His voice comes over the speakerphone. He does not mince his words. 'I suppose you think you are so fucking clever with your interview on the radio today. You are a fucking amateur, Clonan.' I cannot believe my ears. The minister's promise of an independent inquiry into the research does not seem to have dampened down the anger towards me. If anything, it seems to have enraged the army even further. I interrupt the caller and tell him to calm down and to stop using bad language. I should have hung up. But I have this forlorn hope that I can reason with him. He ignores my plea and continues in the same vein. 'We've dealt with you politely up to now and you have not learned your lesson. Now you are going to face the fucking consequences. Now it is guerilla warfare. Make no mistake about it Clonan, this is war and we are going to use every dirty trick in the book against you.' I feel Aideen's hand on my shoulder. She has leaned forward and tells me to hang up. I hang up.

We continue our journey in silence. Aideen eventually speaks up. 'This is not over. Those guys are not going to go away. You'll need to be very careful, Thomas.' That night in Cork, I call my brother in Dublin and ask him to keep an eye on the newspapers for me. The story shows no sign of abating.

The following morning as we head for the ferry, we pull into a petrol station in Ringaskiddy. I scan the papers on the newsstand. The *Irish Daily Star* has a picture of me at my graduation. In my uniform. Smiling at the camera. The headline above it reads, 'Inquiry Sought Over Army Sex Report'. The *Irish Examiner* also contains a report on the ongoing situation. The newspaper coverage also notes the fact that I had demonstrated clearly that I had received explicit and written permission from the military authorities to carry out the research.

As the ferry sails out of Cork harbor, I breathe a sigh of relief. As Ireland slips out of view I feel a mix of conflicting emotions. I realise I am at the centre of a national controversy. While I am confident that an independent inquiry will vindicate my findings – and vindicate my reputation – I am at a loss to understand the vitriolic and malicious response I have experienced from my former comrades. I feel that I have gone from the heart of the organisation which I feel to be an extension of my family, to the status of pariah. For what? For doing the right thing. For uncovering the systematic abuse of female soldiers. As we edge out further into the Atlantic and the coastline recedes, I think Ireland to be a strange country. No country for those who speak truth to power.

After the overnight voyage, we reach France. Another republic. Another planet. I get a call from my brother as we drive south towards Bordeaux. The story is still being covered in the Sunday papers. *Ireland on Sunday* runs a cartoon by 'Del on Sunday' which features a row of glum-faced female soldiers standing to attention before a sergeant major who is presiding over a 'Sexual

Assault Course'. The *Sunday Independent* also carries a follow-up piece of analysis by Declan Power. This is the third Sunday in a row that Declan has dealt with the story.

Finally, during the following week, the story eventually starts to recede from the national press. In the *Irish Times*, Patsy McGarry reports that the army finally agrees that there is a problem within its ranks. Under the headline 'Army Chief Promises to Uncover Harassment', the chief of staff states, 'My aim is to uncover the nature and extent of the problem and then to identify intervention measures to deal with it.' He also states, 'Harassment or bullying of any kind within the Defence Forces is entirely unacceptable and will not be tolerated.' I only wish someone would communicate that to certain staff officers in DFHQ in their dealings with me and my family.

Finally, by the end of August, as we return from France, the minister for defence keeps his word and the *Irish Independent* confirms that an 'outside agency' will lead the investigation into my research and its findings. This Study Review Group will independently explore the questions prompted by my research. On 30 August, the security editor of the *Irish Independent* reports that the group will be headed up by Dr Eileen Doyle. Under the heading, 'Consultant to Assist Inquiry on Bullying', Brady writes, 'She will assist . . . the study of claims which were made by a former army captain . . . Dr Tom Clonan, in his doctoral thesis in communications for Dublin City University.' I am over the moon to see that there will be a competent and independent oversight of the investigation.

I notice something else when I return home. Now, when I call any of my friends in the army, the phone usually rings out. Or else they simply hang up when they hear my voice. No one returns calls when I leave messages. Army friends that I trained with. Army friends that I had served overseas with. Once again, I'm puzzled at this new and unforeseen development. Even those friends that came to our wedding. Friends who were on my guard of honour the day I married Aideen. Some of my closest friends in the army – even they have gone to ground.

There are a few notable exceptions. But, for now, for the most part, I am incommunicado. In fact, as I will discover over time, I've been sent to Coventry. I am bitterly disappointed with this development. Disappointed in those of my so-called friends who have frozen me out. One of them – a childhood friend, a school friend and army colleague – tells my sister that he will not invite me to his wedding as I'd be 'an embarrassment'. When she tells me this, I wonder what sort of 'embarrassment' is caused by someone who highlights the sexual abuse of women. Maybe I'm better off to be excluded from the company of such individuals. It is nevertheless deeply hurtful. But it is also a revelation. It makes me reassess my understanding of friendship. It is a harsh lesson, but a lesson nonetheless.

In early September, I am walking on Grafton Street with Darach in his buggy. He is nervous of the street performers and squirms in his straps as we pass clowns and other street acts. Aideen is walking alongside me. Her bump is showing now. I bend down to reassure Darach. I snuggle him and rearrange his blankets. As I stand up, I am confronted by a man standing very close to me. He has interposed himself between myself and Aideen and is now poking me in the chest with his index finger. It is happening so quickly, I have no time to react. As I steady myself and try to make sense of what he is saying, I recognise him. He is a senior officer that I served with at one point in the Artillery Corps. His face is a mask of anger and as he stabs my chest with his finger, he repeats, again and again, 'You are a fucking disgrace. You are a fucking disgrace to the corps.' In an instant he is gone. Aideen and I are in shock. My hands are shaking.

I scan the crowded street, but he has disappeared as quickly as he appeared. It is the stuff of nightmares. Aideen is shaken also. I cannot believe that this has happened in broad daylight, on Grafton Street. In my hometown, out walking with my family. It compounds the sense of dread that I have felt since I received the phone call promising me 'guerilla warfare' and 'every dirty trick in the book'.

I'm at a loss as to what to do over the Grafton Street incident. I call yet another senior officer at DFHQ and explain what has happened. I ask him to please talk to the powers that be and to communicate to them the invidious position in which I find myself. The senior officer interrupts me and tells me that the officer in question 'obviously didn't get an 'A' in his courtesy and etiquette exams'. He also seems to find my account of what has happened inordinately funny. He tells me to lighten up. I am speechless.

Chapter 16

Iodine Tablets

'It's bad enough having to listen to your bullshit without having to read it as well.'

The 9/11 Attacks
September 2001

A week or so after the Grafton Street incident, I am working on a research project when a colleague in IT Tallaght approaches me in my cubicle. It is a shared working area. Hana, an economist from Egypt, is distraught. 'Come quickly. Something is happening in New York.'

We go to the canteen area and watch images of a passenger jet striking the Twin Towers in New York. The images are played and replayed over and over again. Like everyone else, I'm thinking that this is some sort of a tragic civil aviation accident. When images of the second passenger jet strike are played, the room falls silent. There is an audible gasp as the aircraft hits the building – the blossom of flames and plume of smoke. The images are replayed over and over as the text straplines on Sky News struggle to keep pace with events.

Over the following twenty-four hours, the US goes into lockdown. It is several hours before news of President Bush's whereabouts become clear. US airspace is temporarily closed. Aer Lingus flights to the US are cancelled or diverted.

Over the next seventy-two hours, talk of Islamist extremists begins to emerge. The words Al Qaeda and the name Osama Bin Laden are associated with the attack. Five years after the massacre at Qana, Bin Laden's subsequent Fatwa, or declaration of war, on the US has led to these suicide attacks. Little did we know in April of 1996 as we struggled to come to terms with the slaughter of the men, women and children in South Lebanon that the Qana massacre and Bin Laden's subsequent promise of revenge would spawn the mass murder of thousands of innocents in New York. Within a week, President Bush coins the term 'Global War on Terror'.

Over the coming days, 'Al Qaeda', 'Global War on Terror' and 'Weapons of Mass Destruction' become household terms. On the national day of mourning for the Twin Tower attacks, Aideen and I walk from our home to the US Embassy in Ballsbridge. We sign the book of condolences as Darach sleeps in his buggy. He is oblivious to the changing world around him.

Then a peculiar thing happens. Something completely unexpected. On 27 September, Minister for State at the Department of Public Enterprise, Joe Jacobs, with responsibility for Ireland's emergency response in the event of a terrorist attack similar to those in New York, gives an interview on the *Marian Finucane Show* on RTÉ radio. Minister Jacobs is quizzed about Ireland's emergency preparedness and he states live on air that Irish people ought to take iodine tablets in the event of a nuclear attack. His performance on air, where he appeared unsure and unclear about procedures in the event of a terrorist attack, set against the atmosphere of paranoia following the 9/11 attacks, sparks a major national debate on terrorism and nuclear, chemical and biological weapons of mass destruction. Minister Jacobs adds to the fear, panic and hysteria surrounding the issue by giving a poor interview. At one point, he mistakenly calls Ireland a 'small nuclear country' instead of a 'small neutral country'. The interview does not inspire confidence.

The interview also comes at a time when there are a spate of anthrax attacks across the eastern seaboard of the United States. 'WMDs' are the topic of the day. Whilst this mini-drama unfolds, I'm at home changing nappies when the phone rings. The call is from RTÉ radio. The *Today with Pat Kenny* show wants to know if I can talk about weapons of mass destruction in the wake of Minister Jacob's interview. I think about it for a split second. As an army officer, I'm a qualified CBRN (Chemical, Biological, Radiological and Nuclear) warfare specialist. So I know all about WMDs as it happens. In fact, as far back as 1990, during Operations Desert Shield and Desert Storm, the

Irish Defence Forces re-emphasised their training in chemical and biological warfare. At the time, Irish troops in Lebanon were within range of Scud missile attacks from Iraq, where Saddam Hussein was believed to be poised to fire chemical warheads.

Having discussed the issues raised by Minister Jacobs on Marian Finucane's show with the researcher, I am invited into RTÉ to do an interview on WMDs with Pat Kenny. The interview goes well. Pat Kenny whom I have never met before, immediately puts me at my ease. He welcomes me into the studio with a warm handshake and tells me to relax. I'm nervously awaiting the red light for our live exchange. Pat engages me in conversation during the ad break, asking me about various chemical weapons. When the interview begins, I've relaxed. He gives me the space to answer questions and take unexpected or novel directions. The result is a lively radio exchange that illuminates the precise differences between nuclear, chemical and biological attacks. A number of listeners text in to ask questions. One such query is from an elderly lady who wants to know if she can get a nuclear, biological and chemical protection suit for her poodle. It is a funny question. But such is her sincerity and her concern for her only companion, her query strikes a poignant note. It also underscores the Irish government's inability to communicate clearly in a time of crisis.

Time and time again, I note how the Irish government's reaction in a crisis is to increase fear in the population, to increase uncertainty and stress and to communicate in a patronising and arrogant fashion. The Jacobs radio performance is emblematic of that tendency. It will be echoed years later by Taoiseach Brian Cowen's appalling crisis communications and media relations at the height of the banking collapse.

After the interview, I am contacted by Cliff Taylor at the *Irish Times* foreign desk. He asks me if I can type. Thanks to that stern sergeant major in the School of Administration, I can still touch type to a speed of about forty words per minute. Cliff asks me if I can write eight hundred words on what I've been talking about on radio. In that moment, my career as a journalist begins.

The following day my analysis piece on nuclear, biological and chemical weapons appears in the *Irish Times*. I have to pinch myself. My mum calls me and tells me she is proud of me. She cuts out the article and keeps it in her bedside locker. She spends more and more time in bed now as her condition deteriorates.

I ask my dad if he has read the piece. He tells me, 'It's bad enough having to listen to your bullshit without having to read it as well.' I take that as a weird sort of compliment as he implies he has actually read it.

A couple of days later, towards the end of September, I'm at home with Aideen and baby Darach when I get a call from Jim Cusack, security editor of the *Irish Times*. He tells me that he has something that I really need to see. He gives me directions to his house and I drive over to meet him. He opens a garage door at the rear of his house and invites me in. He makes me coffee and hands me a document. He asks me what I think of it. I recognise it straightaway as a military briefing document from DFHQ.

My heart sinks as I read a series of false allegations about me. The document, which has been leaked by persons unknown to Jim Cusack and a number of other Irish journalists, alleges that I have been involved in a 'planned and assisted' attack on the army's reputation. It comes hard on the heels of allegations that I had somehow falsified my research into women in the army and fabricated the findings of my investigation. A wave of nausea rises within me. If this material is published in the national press at a time when I am still on probation as an academic, I fear I will finally and irrevocably lose my reputation and ultimately my job. With my character assassinated in this manner, my career would be destroyed. It seems to me that the 'guerilla war' is not over. It is clear to me that I am still the subject of a very vigorous campaign of dirty tricks. I feel very tired.

Jim Cusack has given me the opportunity to respond to the allegations. I am able to refute them all.

Nevertheless, I go home to Aideen feeling completely deflated. I am worried sick. Months after I thought the issue had been resolved, months after the minister had announced an independent inquiry into my research, I had thought that the confrontation with the military authorities had ended. Yet, here I am, once again, having to refute claims that my research and qualifications are somehow suspect. Despite the fact that I have done nothing wrong. All that I have done is to highlight wrongdoing. The situation is Kafkaesque. A recurring nightmare.

When I tell Aideen about the latest development, she is emphatic. 'We've got to get help, Thomas.' She is holding Darach in her arms. 'If we don't put a stop to this, who knows what they'll do next.' Following this discussion, I contact a solicitor in the city centre. He agrees to meet me the following Monday.

I had never contemplated availing of the services of a solicitor before. Never in my wildest dreams did I imagine that I would find myself in a solicitor's office, outlining the events that have led to me taking this most reluctant of steps.

The solicitor takes a comprehensive history of the events of the last four and a half years. To be honest, it is the first time since this whole sad, sorry episode began that I finally get a full hearing. It is therapeutic to tell the story out loud to a third party. The solicitor gets it straightaway. I tell the story in chronological order, addressing the facts along with the peer-review processes involved in a PhD. I address the complex conditions around publication imposed upon me by the general staff. The manner in which the solicitor takes the history is a revelation to me; he is a skilled listener. He questions me forensically about each stage of the experience. Crosschecks dates with me. Crosschecks who said what to whom and when. He skillfully elicits the chronology of events from me with all of its nuances and the stark set of outcomes that now confront me and my family.

The solicitor thinks that we have a very strong case for libel and defamation. We embark on a course of action that brings me into legal conflict with my former employers. It is not a decision I take lightly. However, as a family, Aideen and I feel we have no choice.

The solicitor warns me that libel and defamation is a difficult case to take to court. The burden of proof resides entirely with myself. I must demonstrate to the court that publication of libellous or defamatory material has taken place. I must also be able to show who the authors of such publication are. And finally, I must show how it has damaged me. The solicitor warns me that if I lose the case, I will be liable not only for my own costs, but also the costs of the state, whom I am suing. It is a big risk to take.

Aideen and I discuss the high stakes that have been outlined to us. She is breastfeeding our little boy in the waiting room of the solicitor's office on the quays. The traffic passes slowly outside. An occasional truck rumbles by on its way to the docks. There is just me and Aideen and the baby. We know that this is a huge step to take. Again, we reach the conclusion that we have no choice. The dye has been cast. A doubt has been created about my integrity. My livelihood, along with our security and stability, is at risk. There appears to us to be no other remedy. We instruct our solicitor to take a case against the state.

We decide to take the case to the circuit court. We are not interested in money or compensation, only in the vindication of my good name and reputation. We are interested only in asserting my right to pursue my career as an academic – or journalist for that matter – without further interference or harassment.

Seán, our solicitor, shakes hands with us when we tell him of our decision. He is confident. We are terrified. On balance, though, I find the experience empowering. It puts a distance between ourselves and the military for the first time.

Seán also warns us that it may take some time for the case to be heard in court. The case of 'Tom Clonan (Plaintiff) against the Minister For Defence, Ireland and the Attorney General (Defendants)' will take four years to get to court.

One of the immediate effects of initiating court proceedings is that there is a temporary cessation in mischief or interference from any quarter regarding the research.

I tell my father about the decision to initiate court proceedings. He pulls a little harder on his cigarette and exhales loudly. 'I hope you have a good legal team. You'll need it.' My mum tells me that everything will be all right. She reassures me that I have done the right thing.

Meanwhile, the Study Review Group headed up by Dr Eileen Doyle begins its work. In the first week of October, just days after seeking legal advice, I get a call from the chief of staff's personal staff. 'Is that you, Clonan?' is the greeting. I reply in the affirmative. 'You are to be brought before the Doyle commission to answer for yourself,' is his next remark. I ask him if this an invitation to cooperate with the Study Review Group. He states, 'I think I've made myself perfectly clear.' He adds, 'Here is a date for your diary.' His voice is filled with barely concealed contempt. I am taken aback by his attitude. I ask him, as politely as I can, to contact me in writing if he has any requests for me. He hangs up. And that is the last I hear from the army for a very long time.

Later that week, I get a phone call from a senior counsel, Paulyn Marrinan Quinn. The former Insurance Ombudsman, Paulyn calls me out of the blue. She introduces herself over the phone with her distinctive voice and explains who she is. She also tells me that she has been watching my situation with interest. She invites me to deliver a lecture on a course she is delivering on conflict resolution with Trinity College at the Milltown Institute. It is the first contact of support I have received since the entire unfortunate saga began. Paulyn's confidence in me has a powerful impact on me. I feel at some level that there are others out there who understand precisely the nature of the situation that confronts me. It is good to know that there are others who know what happens when one challenges the powers that be in Ireland. I am grateful that she has reached out to me in this way.

That weekend, on 7 October, the United States, with support from British and Australian allies, invades Afghanistan. Operation Enduring Freedom begins in earnest on that Sunday with air and missile strikes on targets throughout Afghanistan. I'm at home with Aideen and Darach when news begins to filter through of the outbreak of war. My phone rings. RTÉ asks me to come into studio for the *Six One News* to 'explain to viewers what is happening in Afghanistan'. I try to sound as calm and nonchalant as possible and say, 'Yeah, sure. See you later.'

I've never been on TV before. I ring my dad and mum and tell them I'm going to be on the television. My dad says, 'Don't make a balls of it.' Mum says she'll say a decade of the Rosary. I iron a shirt and flick through the channels. I see the American aircraft carrier the USS *Enterprise* firing cruise missiles into Afghan airspace. The Sky News reporter is breathlessly announcing volley after volley of missile strikes 'deep into Afghan territory'.

The US are stripping out whatever air defence and command and control assets the Taliban possess. It is a clear precursor to a ground offensive. I'm confident I can give a context to the images being beamed into people's homes. As I race up to RTÉ's studios in Donnybrook, I recall briefly what it is like to come under air and rocket attack. I recall the vibration and noise. The intensity. The heat.

It is my first time in the RTÉ news studio. A broadcasting assistant splodges some foundation on my cheeks and licking her fingers tries to smooth down some of my hair. I'm reminded of my mother. 'Jesus Christ,' I think to myself. 'I'm going live on the telly.' I barely have time to take in the RTÉ News studio. I've seen it so many times on TV myself. I just have enough time to register the desk and the chair and how small it all is when a man puts a microphone on my lapel. Suddenly, someone is counting down – 'And five, and four and three and two and one.' The red light comes on in the studio and the signature tune starts up. The presenter pipes up. 'Tonight, the United States is at war. This afternoon, US forces have commenced attacks on targets throughout Afghanistan.' There are pictures of missile strikes and fighter jets taking off aircraft carriers. My heart is pounding. 'And joining us in studio to discuss all of this is security expert, Dr Tom Clonan.' Fuck me, I'm on, is all I have time to think. The presenter swivels his chair dramatically towards me and asks, 'Just what is going on this evening, Tom?' I clear my throat. My first words ever on live TV.

'Well, the US are using the Starship Enterprise to attack targets in Afghanistan.' The presenter's eyes widen for a split second. And then, I'm not sure if I've really said Starship Enterprise or USS *Enterprise*. But, there is a niggling doubt there. I see Spock's ears sprouting on the presenter's head in my imagination. I force myself to concentrate.

I continue talking about command and control, air defence assets and so on. The presenter relaxes and the interview continues like a game of table tennis. Questions served, answers fly back. TV is a lot faster than radio. I mean, it is extremely fast. I don't know if many people realise just how short that slot is. You've got to be really prepped. You've got to have a few key points that you are going to hit.

I do dozens more interviews throughout October, November and December. Cliff Taylor and Peter Murtagh in the *Irish Times* ask me to do more analysis. My features appear in the foreign pages and migrate from time to time into the opinion and editorial, or op-ed section of the paper. Eventually I'm styled 'The *Irish Times* Security Analyst'. Strangely, throughout this time, I never set foot inside the *Irish Times* building on D'Olier Street. I work remotely, from home.

Through this period, because I've been frozen out by the Irish army – I'm still in Coventry it seems – I start to network with the various military attachés in a number of key embassies in Dublin and London. I establish contact with the US, British, Israeli, Palestinian, French and Iranian embassies along with the embassies of Russia, Syria, India and Pakistan. My network of contacts within the embassies grows rapidly. My contacts vary from embassy to embassy. Sometimes the contact is with a military attaché. Sometimes with a 'counsellor for public diplomacy'. Sometimes it is with press officers. More often than not, it is with the ambassadors themselves.

They, in turn, connect me with dozens of invaluable contacts within organisations such as NATO, the UN and in particular within the US and UK foreign policy establishment. In this way, I evolve a rapidly growing network of information sources, often primary sources, against which I can cross-check, compare, verify information to either confirm or refute rapidly moving combat situations abroad. I also make invaluable contacts within Non-Governmental Organisations such as Amnesty International and Transparency International. The NGOs in turn refer me on to a host of non-state information sources.

This is very busy work. Intense, but highly rewarding. After a short time, some of my contacts begin to make discreet enquiries about other contacts, from other embassies, within my network.

December 2001 sees US invasion forces, reinforced by the Northern

Alliance, take Kabul. I continue to write analysis features for the *Irish Times*. December is also our second family Christmas. Baby Darach is one year old. Santa brings him his presents. That Christmas night is a magical time. It reminds me of so many happy childhood memories. It reminds me of my parents and all that they did for us. Those countless Christmas mornings with my brother and my sisters in Ballygall Avenue. Charging down the stairs at six in the morning. Seeing, but not quite believing, the presents under the tree.

Darach gets a little plastic walker. He hauls himself upright and does a comical wiggling walk across the wooden floor. As he leans into the walker, he loses his balance and accelerates. He comes to a crashing halt in the branches of the Christmas tree. He repeats the exercise over and over and creates an unbroken skidmark, toddler height, along the walls and hallway. His little fingerprints everywhere. His first steps. His journey beginning as he navigates the world beyond the rug in the sitting room of our family home.

Chapter 17

The Doyle Report

'You've been vindicated. That doesn't always happen with government reports.'

January 2002

The war in Afghanistan settles down. The US and its allies adopt an occupation routine which is similar in many respects to that of the Soviet occupation two decades earlier. Operation Enduring Freedom is conducted from heavily fortified bases throughout the country, such as Camp Bastion, or from the massive headquarters in Bagram. Not unlike the heavily fortified Russian 'Hedgehog' positions of the Soviet occupation. As the allies settle into their defensive routine, the Taliban – in much the same way as the mujahideen harassed the Soviets – mount roadside bomb and guerrilla attacks on US and British troops.

The first of over a million US troops begin to transit through Shannon Airport in Ireland on their way to the war in Afghanistan. At Shannon, the US troops are allowed to disembark and visit the bars in the duty-free area whilst their chartered aircraft are refuelled. A pint of Guinness in County Clare, which for many young US soldiers is their last safe moment before Afghanistan, becomes a rite of passage for a new generation of US troops going to war. Many of the young soldiers and marines in County Clare are too young to buy beer in the US. Many more of them will return home via Shannon in coffins. Unlike the highly visible human chain of US combat uniforms that flows and ebbs through Shannon, the coffins of those killed in action are unseen. They lie in the darkened holds of US aircraft. Out of sight.

As the Taliban ramp up their attacks on the US invasion forces, they rely more and more on roadside bombs and car bombs as a method of attack. Whilst the majority of US soldiers injured in Vietnam fell victim to gunshot wounds or shrapnel injuries in jungle firefights, the majority of US and British soldiers killed in Afghanistan fall victim to roadside bombs or improvised explosive devices (IEDs). This is a tactic that the Taliban have learned from the provisional IRA and their campaign of violence against the British army in Northern Ireland. As I immerse myself in writing opinion and analysis pieces on the nascent war on terror, I cannot help but observe the centrality of Ireland to the evolving global conflict.

It is clear to me that the template for the Global War on Terror was forged on Irish soil. Among the ditches and hedgerows of Fermanagh, Tyrone and South Armagh, the Provisional IRA perfected the type of asymmetrical warfare favoured by twenty-first-century jihadis. They also pioneered the use of car bombs and high explosives in attacks on city-centre targets and financial districts. Their 1996 Canary Wharf attack in London provides a precedent of sorts for Al Qaeda's 9/11 attacks against the New York World Trade Centre just four years later. In the 1970s, '80s and '90s, Ireland becomes a laboratory for counterterrorism operations and the emerging surveillance society. In the first decade of the new millennium, the principles of counterinsurgency, developed in Ireland, form the central tenets of the Global War on Terror.

In Northern Ireland however, British soldiers and RUC officers generally did not move by road in South Armagh. They travelled almost exclusively by helicopter within the so-called 'murder triangle' of South Armagh, Fermanagh and South Tyrone. Hundreds of British troops and RUC officers were killed in this area during the Troubles. Victims of sniper fire and booby-trap bombs or IEDs. North of this area, troops and police travelled in heavily armoured Land Rovers to counter the threat posed by the Provisional IRA.

In Afghanistan, however, in 2002, as Blair and Bush fight a 'cut-price' war known as 'invasion-lite', British troops routinely travel around Helmand Province and elsewhere in soft-skinned vehicles such as 'snatch' Land Rovers. As a consequence, due to a lack of sufficient armoured protection and insufficient helicopter support, hundreds of young soldiers are blown to pieces by

Taliban roadside bombs. Whenever VIP visitors from the US or UK visit the troops, they move exclusively in heavy 'up-armoured' vehicles and helicopters. The boys and girls from inner-city London, Birmingham, Sheffield and Glasgow, however, die in their scores due to a lack of appropriate equipment and vehicles.

Many tens of thousands more are injured in the roadside bomb attacks – a unique feature of the war in Afghanistan. The injuries they receive are horrific. Gross blunt trauma complicated by the force of high explosives. The signature characteristics of these attacks are severe head injuries often accompanied by limb separation and, in many cases, multiple amputations. Many of the injured are cognitively impaired after the attacks and will require decades of high support and intensive care at home in Britain and the US.

Over a third of all of the combatants will suffer from Combat Stress Reaction (CSR), formerly known as Post-Traumatic Stress Disorder. Thousands of Afghan civilians will also perish in the war. Most of them are killed by the Taliban and their supporters in bomb and gun attacks. But a growing number are killed in NATO airstrikes. This is NATO's first foreign war. Like wars fought by colonial powers in Asia and Afghanistan in previous centuries, NATO's war quickly settles into a grinding war of attrition.

In 2002, the Irish government, despite our stated neutrality, sends Irish soldiers to Afghanistan. The first wave of Irish troops are ordnance officers – bomb disposal experts with years of experience of dealing with IRA roadside bombs and IEDs along with those encountered by the Irish in Lebanon of Hizbullah or Israeli manufacture.

The Irish troops, members of the Irish Defence Forces, in Irish uniform with the Irish tricolour on their sleeves, form a part of the US-inspired 'Joint Improvised Explosive Device Defeat Organisation' or JIEDDO for short, at NATO Headquarters in Kabul. The Irish become a critical part of the US's war on the Taliban and their roadside bombs and IED attacks.

With thousands of US troops streaming through Shannon on a daily basis as they deploy for combat in Afghanistan and with hundreds of thousands of US military over-flights passing through Irish airspace on their way to the war, Ireland becomes an integral part of the US's Global War on Terror.

Seventy-five percent of transatlantic air traffic passes through Irish airspace. In a special deal worked out between the Irish government and the US administration, the Irish taxpayer pays the onward navigation costs and aviation authority fees for the transit of US military aircraft as they go to war. This agreement costs the Irish taxpayer thousands of Euro on a daily basis – a direct financial contribution to the Global War on Terror.

In 2002, 'neutral' Ireland is providing troops, vital logistics and air support and material support for the war in Afghanistan. We are, whether the general public realises it or not, at war. In an unprecedented move, the American military at US Europe Command Headquarters in Stuttgart assign a permanent staff officer to Shannon Airport. Shannon is officially a 'virtual' US airbase. In 2002, NATO designates its army in Afghanistan the 'International Security Assistance Force' or ISAF. On NATO's official ISAF website, Ireland and the Irish flag is listed as a member of the 'coalition of the willing' who are participating in the Global War on Terror in NATO's first war on the Asian continent.

In February, Aideen and I make another dash to the Coombe. After an alarmingly short labour, Eoghan is born. Outside the doors of the maternity hospital among all the anxious mums to be, pacing up and down in their pajamas and amid the throng of smokers, I call my parents. I tell them about Eoghan's arrival. My dad tells me that my mum is too weak to come to the phone, but that she is thrilled. Everything about Eoghan's labour and birth is normal. He is a perfectly healthy baby boy. Our little family is growing. Darach is toddling and stumbling around the house. The high-tide mark of dirty little fingerprints is now moving up the walls as he gets taller.

The months that follow are a blur of night feeds, nappy changing and general chaos. We have never before suffered as much from lack of sleep. We have never been happier.

A lecturer position in the School of Media, in the city-centre campus of the Dublin Institute of Technology (DIT), is advertised in February. I apply for the job and am invited for interview. I do the interview as though underwater due to chronic lack of sleep. Two small babies at home means that after the interview, I'm so exhausted that I feel an almost irresistible temptation to lie down on the floor of the waiting room to get some sleep. I sleep in my car in the car park instead.

Miraculously, I get the lecturing job in DIT. I say goodbye to my colleagues in IT Tallaght. Hana tells me it is 'the hand of Allah' that has moved me to the city centre. We have a good laugh at this. *Allah Akbar*.

There is also another very positive development at this point. The Study Review Group, chaired by Dr Eileen Doyle, which has been investigating my PhD research in the army, makes its first report. The independent inquiry fully vindicates my findings. The sense of relief is unbelievable. I am very grateful to Eileen Doyle. I am grateful to her for her thoroughness and for her integrity. And for her tenacity, because the army is not an easy environment to navigate. It is a difficult workplace to fully explore, especially as a civilian. Eileen Doyle and her team, however, not only vindicate my findings, but also record an unacceptable level of bullying among male soldiers.

The preliminary findings of the Study Review Group are reported widely in the Irish media. RTE Radio's *News at One* invite me into studio to give my reaction to the findings. During an ad break, I'm ushered into studio. Sean O'Rourke, the presenter, looks up from his notes and smiles at me. 'You must feel relieved,' he says. 'You've been vindicated. That doesn't always happen with government reports.' The red light comes on and Sean launches into his introduction. I welcome the report's findings. To tell the truth, I'm relieved. Something is going to be done about the bullying.

When I get out of studio, I turn on my mobile phone. I have some texts from my family. My sister Pauline teases me, 'Was that you on the radio? Sounding too grown up to be my little brother.' I have one voicemail. I dial into my mailbox. The voice on the other end is brief and to the point. 'You might think this is over. It's not fucking over. Make no mistake about it, Clonan. You haven't heard the last of this.' The line clicks and goes dead.

Summer arrives, and with it a renewed debate on Saddam Hussein's regime in Iraq. Claims and counter claims are made during the summer months about whether or not Saddam possesses weapons of mass destruction. UN inspection teams scour the country, searching for evidence of nuclear, biological or chemical weapons. There is a growing debate about a possible invasion of Iraq. There is a proliferation of articles in the international media pondering the question of whether or not George Bush will invade Iraq. 'Will he or won't he?' is the recurring question of the summer. There are countless debates in the United Nations and wrangling over resolutions and timelines.

In the meantime, in July 2002, the US Embassy in Dublin invites me to a NATO seminar in Brussels. This is an opportunity to expand my contact of networks within NATO, particularly as the US seems poised to invade another country. I'm on the early-morning flight from Dublin Airport to Brussels. I tiptoe out of the house as Aideen and the babies sleep. I kiss each one gently so as not to wake them. The taxi driver whistles and smokes all the way out to the airport. I check in and join the huge queue for the security check. Five in the morning is rush hour at Dublin Airport. I look around at my fellow travellers. Men and women in business suits. Looking as tired as I feel. As we shuffle towards the security scanners, word passes through the queue that we have to take our jackets and belts off. There is much sighing in the queue as weary travellers start peeling off jackets and folding them in the crooks of their arms, struggling with laptops and briefcases.

Then we hear that we have to take off our shoes. This provokes a susurration of indignant, urgent whispering. As we edge closer to the scanners, a guy in the crowd stares at me. He points his finger at me and declares for everyone's benefit, 'That's him. That's the fucker on the TV that keeps talkin' about bleedin' terrorists and fuckin' hijackers.' A mutinous muttering breaks out in the queue. They look at me accusingly. The heckler, emboldened by the reaction of the grumpy queue, continues, 'Yeah, this is your bleedin' fault. If it wasn't for the likes of you, we wouldn't have to strip off. Next thing we'll be going through in our jocks.' Pondering this unpleasant mental image, I wearily take off my own shoes. The security team on the scanner are grinning broadly as I go through the pat-down search on the air side of the scanner. The searcher bids me a 'top of the morning to you' as I go through. Meanwhile, 'angry man' is still staring accusingly at me as he heads off past the perfume shops and shoe-shine stands that line the route to the departure gates.

Chapter 18

We Break Things and Kill People

'That's our job.'

Brussels, Belgium

Spring 2002

After the short flight to Brussels, I make my way to the US Embassy on Boulevard du Régent in the downtown district. The street is lined with tank stops and there are a series of security measures in place around the building. I am directed through a security cordon manned by Belgian police. Having scrutinised my passport, they direct me to the embassy perimeter. I'm met inside the building by Morgan Kulla, who is the public diplomacy officer in the US Embassy in Dublin. I've met Morgan many times in Dublin and we've had lunch together several times in Ballsbridge. She introduces me to her colleagues in Brussels.

Over coffee, the Americans brief me on their various diplomatic roles in Brussels. In addition to their embassy to Belgium, they also have an ambassador at NATO and an ambassador to the European Union. We have an open and free-ranging discussion about their views on the EU and the various European players in Brussels and at the UN. The US are conscious of growing French criticism of their intentions to invade Iraq. Morgan and her colleagues discuss the issues with me in a lively, debating style. I'm impressed by their intimate knowledge of European affairs in general and the individual nuances of EU member state politics in particular. The embassy staff are mostly female and strike me as idealistic; passionate about the role of US foreign policy in the world. They argue with me about Saddam's regime. They argue with each other. It is a frank exchange of views.

Later, they take me to meet their embassy staff in NATO headquarters. They introduce me to Victoria Nuland, who is on the US Embassy staff at NATO. Victoria gets straight to the point about Afghanistan and Iraq. She tells me that the US are grateful for the assistance they are getting from Ireland in 'prosecuting the Global War on Terror'. She also tells me that she thinks we could, and should, be doing a lot more.

During the afternoon, I am briefed by a series of senior US military officers about the possible impending invasion of Iraq. Only they don't talk about it in terms of a 'possiblity'. They talk about the invasion of Iraq as a certainty. When I quiz one senior officer about the ongoing debate at the UN about weapons inspectors and UN Security Council resolutions, he waves his hand dismissively. 'Look, Tom. I'm a soldier. We break things and kill people. That's our job. Period. I don't really have a view on what's going down in New York just now. What's going on in the UN if you really ask me, is a circus.' He pauses, and looking me in the eye, he tells me the following: 'Look, Tom, you were in the military. You seem like a good guy. Let me lay it out straight for you. The United States of America is going to invade Iraq in 2003. And it is not gonna be just air strikes. Do you know what I mean? We are going to go in there in a big way. It is going to be an awesome thing to behold. On the ground. And it is gonna happen in March.' I'm scribbling notes furiously as he speaks. He reminds me that this is an off-the-record background briefing. He also throws me his card. He has written a telephone number on it in biro. 'That's my cell phone, Tom. When the shit hits the fan, I'm gonna be down range in Iraq. But you can get me on this number anytime if you have any more questions on our operations there.'

When I get home, I write a series of articles on the countdown to war in Iraq. My dad reckons the Americans would be mad to invade Iraq. I suspect he is right. I also suspect, however, that the invasion of Iraq is a done deal.

My mum is spending more and more time in bed. She is undergoing chemotherapy and has lost her beautiful hair. Mum went with my sister Pauline to have a wig fitted. Pauline tells me that the experience was positive. 'They were so nice to mammy.' Pauline's eyes well up as she tells me about the wig and about the other ladies that were there for similar fittings. I give Pauline a hug. I then put on the wig myself. It makes my mum laugh.

On 24 September, Tony Blair's government publishes the 'September Dossier'. Titled, 'Iraq's Weapons of Mass Destruction: The Assessment of the British Government', the document makes the case for an invasion of Iraq based on the premise that Saddam is concealing a formidable array of weapons of mass destruction for imminent use against the West. Blair recalls parliament to discuss the document.

Peter Murtagh contacts me and asks me to take a look at the dossier. He also asks me for eight hundred words of analysis of its contents and findings. Once more, I silently thank the sergeant major in the School of Administration for teaching me how to type. I download the document. While Darach plays at my feet and Eoghan sleeps in his cot, I read the dossier. The first thing that strikes me is that the document is not a military text. It does not conform to the conventions of military writing, an international style guide used by military, intelligence and security force agencies. The language used is also peculiarly non-military. It does not employ the terse, spare style that is drummed into military officers the world over. Instead, it mobilises emotive language to 'persuade' the reader that Saddam poses a clear and present danger to the US and its allies. The document even uses photographs of the 1988 Halabja massacre in Iraq, where Saddam used chemical weapons in a genocidal attack which killed thousands of Kurdish men, women and children, to illustrate what 'might' happen in the immediate future.

I write my analysis and the *Irish Times* publish my criticisms and observations about what would later be termed the 'Dodgy Dossier'. I point out in the piece that the document contains no new evidence or imperative for invasion. I comment on the timing of the release of the report and the emotive impact it will have on US and British calls for a pre-emptive invasion of Iraq.

My dad calls me and tells me that the US will never invade Iraq. He tells me 'they're not that fucking stupid'. I note from the call that he has read my piece in the *Irish Times*. His comments are as close as I'll get to praise from him. He doesn't agree with my assessment and belief that the US are hell-bent on invading Iraq irrespective of the causes or the consequences. Hana calls me and tells me that George Bush Junior wants to kill Saddam 'because Saddam try to kill George Bush Senior'. Hana tells me about a previous plot by Saddam to assassinate George Bush Senior during a visit to the Middle East. 'He try to kill the Daddy. Now he must die. It is the hand of Allah,' he adds. He also adds – for emphasis – 'The big fish always eat the little fish.'

On 23 October, a heavily armed group of some forty Chechen separatists storm the Dubrovka Theater in Moscow. The Chechens take over nine hundred Muscovites hostage. The musical *Nord Ost* is playing to a packed house when the Chechens enter the building and hold everyone at gunpoint. The hostage-takers are very heavily armed with over 100kg of high explosives, one hundred hand grenades, eighteen AK-47 Kalashnikov Assault Rifles and twenty automatic pistols. They seal off the building and threaten to kill hostages.

I'm at home when the incident unfolds. The *Irish Times* call me and ask me for a real-time analysis of the options open to the Russian security forces and the likely or possible consequences. My immediate, instinctive reaction is to think 'bloodbath'. Given the Russian's modus operandi when it comes to internal security matters – their heavy-handedness and apparent insensitivity to civilian casualties – I'm convinced that the siege will be ended by force and will be a mass-casualty incident. I suspect that neither side will be interested in negotiation or compromise. Neither side, I suspect, will give much thought to the civilians trapped inside. The problem with writing about such fast-moving incidents is precisely that – they are fast-moving. So, writing during the afternoon for a five o'clock deadline presents a number of challenges. Apart from the time pressure created by the deadline along with the practical challenges posed by frantic research, fact checking and making contact with sources, there is the issue of timing itself.

Having consulted all of my sources, both primary and secondary, the final version of what I write, in the short time-frame allowed, must make sense tomorrow afternoon when people have bought the paper. Irrespective of the actual outcomes and events in the coming twenty-four hours. This is the dilemma in providing such analysis. Whatever copy you submit, whether at five or six on any given day, will be minutely scrutinised twenty-four hours later when events will invariably have moved on quite considerably. Herein lies an intellectual challenge. The analysis that is submitted has got to be plausible regardless of what actually happens. This is a risky business and it is very difficult to write about fast-moving situations, especially where detail is often scant, without leaving hostages to fortune all over the copy. Luckily for me, my instincts are usually good and my predictions normally correct.

I contact the Russian Embassy in Dublin. They are reluctant to comment on the evolving situation in Moscow. They advise me to talk to their military attaché in London. The military attaché is polite but not particularly helpful. Like many military officers, he is reluctant to engage in the risky business of speculating outcomes. Nor is he happy to say what assets are at the disposal of the security forces in Moscow. I'm sure he knows precisely what those assets are – but he is no doubt concerned about communicating any of this to a journalist. This is all very understandable. But while he is very polite, he is as vague as hell. Next to useless to me.

I work away on other contacts and eventually get to speak to a retired Russian security forces officer who is now working as an academic. He and I discuss the evolving situation and reach the same bleak conclusions.

As I'm writing up my copy and going through the usual scenarios about outer and inner cordons and so on, the phone rings. The number is blocked. I take the call – always a gamble given my recent experiences with some of my former army colleagues – and a husky voice greets me at the other end. The line is crackly. It sounds long distance. The man on the other end, in a heavily accented voice, tells me, 'Sleeping gas.' Only it sounds more like, 'Sleeeping gaz.' 'If you want to know how we will stop the terrorists in the House of Culture – it will be swift. We will pump sleeping gas into the sewer and kill them like the rats in the sewer.'

I try to ask the caller some more questions but he tells me his English is not so good and keeps repeating the phrases 'sleeping gas' and 'sewer rats'.

I think it over in my mind. It sounds so bizarre and outlandish. Like a Batman movie or a Marvel Comic storyline. So I disregard it. Two days later, at around five in the morning, the Russians pump an aerosol anasthaetic, possibly fentanyl, into the theatre. At the same time, Spetsnaz Special Forces storm the building and start shooting the hostage-takers. The incident is over in a few chaotic hours. Over 170 people, including almost all the hostage-takers, are killed. Seven hundred are injured. It's a massacre all right. But not quite as I'd imagined. I've also missed an exclusive from a mysterious source.

In November, I fly back to Brussels for another, more in-depth briefing in NATO Headquarters. I'm introduced to a group of senior US and UK military officers who are part of a 'joint planning cell' for operations in Iraq. They talk about start lines and the logistical challenges of the coming war. They talk about when, and not if, the invasion will start. At the departure lounge in Charleroi Airport, I get a text from Aideen. We are pregnant. Again. I look around me at the styrofoam coffee cups on the tables and the lines of weary travellers queuing to board aircraft for destinations all over Europe. Who knows what personal drama is being played out in any of these journeys. I wonder if we will have a girl.

On Christmas Eve I call my mother and father repeatedly. There is no answer. I strap the babies into the car and we head over to Ballygall Avenue. It is around six in the evening. The house is in total darkness. I turn the key in the front door and call out for my parents. My dad answers from above, his voice wracked by coughing. He's in bed with the flu. On the flat of his back.

My mum is in bed in the other room. She is asleep. 'Don't disturb your mother,' my father rasps. She's very weak. I look at her in the gloom. Tiny in the bed. Bald from chemo. Like an infant. Regressing. She is pitifully thin. I make my dad a cup of tea. He lights up in the dark. His face lit up by the glow of his cigarette as he inhales, I notice how thin he has become.

I go back downstairs in the silent house and think of all of the Christmases I have spent here as a child. Dad asks me not to bring the kids into the house as they'll wake my mum. 'She needs to sleep.' Dad apologises. He is too sick to come downstairs to say hello, or goodbye. I wish him a Happy Christmas. I close the front door behind me.

Chapter 19

Grey Lady

'I mean, there's freakin' journalists all over the goddamn world writing about us now in their goddamn newspapers. Saying any and everything about what we're gonna do and not gonna do in Iraq. Course, none of 'em ever think to call up and ask us what we are actually gonna do.'

Dublin Institute of Technology, Aungier Street, Dublin
January 2003

In January of 2003, the Bodach contacts me unexpectedly to say that the army are going to have to go public and admit that they have a serious problem with bullying. There also seems to be evidence of serious problems with bullying among male soldiers. Garda investigations also reveal that there are instances of male rape within the army.

A couple of days later, on one of those really bright frosty days in January, I walk up Camden Street to get a coffee. The chill and the winter sunshine are invigorating. The strong sunlight plays over car windscreens in the traffic, reflecting off shop windows. It is a pet day. A Dublin bus honks its horn at me. I shield my eyes and through the glare see the driver beckon towards me.

The bus pulls awkwardly into the kerb, airbrakes hissing, its hazard lights winking. The driver's window is open. 'How'ya Tom,' the driver says. He knows me somehow. 'Can you come in to my office for a minute for a chat?' He is leaning out of the driver's window. He bangs the side panel with his open palm – indicating that the bus is his 'office'.

I think about all of the abusive calls and texts I've received from angry soldiers. I'm second-guessing the guy's motives. Trying to work out if he is hostile or friendly. In the end, I think of all of the things I've learned from acting on impulse. Instinct takes over and – rightly or wrongly – I walk around as the doors whoosh open. I hop up the steps into the single-decker bus. The driver opens his little hatch and directs me to a bench seat half-way down the bus. He sits opposite me. 'Thanks, Tom,' the driver says. He takes off his sunglasses and offers me his hand. It is a firm handshake.

'It's a delicate matter,' he says. 'It's about a family member.' He tells me that a member of the family, a young man, had shot himself in Lebanon a couple of years earlier. He takes a faded newspaper clipping out of his wallet and shows it to me. A newspaper article details the soldier's death. An army inquiry proving inconclusive. The young man's face looks out at me from his photograph. I recognise the standard shot taken for the Single Administrative Document.

'You see, Tom, we just can't get our heads around this at all. He was a really happy-go-lucky guy. Lots of girlfriends. Very popular. Everything to live for. So we could never figure out why he did this . . . thing.' I start to speak but the bus driver holds up his hand. He asks me to wait. He steadies himself. He looks me in the eye and with obvious great effort starts to speak again. His voice is almost inaudible this time. 'Tom. He was due home on leave. His mother was expecting him. And his girlfriend. He rang home just days before. Full of life. Full of the joys of coming home on leave. And, then, on the day he was supposed to come home, he shoots himself. Puts the barrel of a rifle into his mouth and shoots himself. Can you imagine that, Tom? Why would any-one do that?'

The bus driver's shoulders are stooped. He is shrinking into his seat as he talks to me. 'Of course, after the funeral. When the rest of the lads came home from the Leb, I started hearing things. In the pub. When the lads had a few pints on them. They said something had happened. I didn't take any notice of it. But I kept on hearing the same thing. That he'd been raped. How could that happen, Tom?'

I don't know what to say. The bus driver places his hands on the metal rail on the seatback in front of him. He knits his fingers together and lowers his forehead onto his hands. He is silent. 'Sorry about this, Tom. But I know your background. And I know you from the newspapers.' He looks at me. 'Could he have been raped?'

I think about the stories that the women have told me. I know that it could be true. I tell him as much. He falls silent once more. His eyes well up as he stares out of the window into the morning sunshine. We are bound together in this moment by an inexplicable death in Lebanon, so many thousands of miles away. 'Right,' he says. He wipes his eyes on the back of his hand. The radio in the driver's cab is squawking. He apologises to me. 'Gotta get going.' We exchange numbers. I tell him to call me any time. If there is anything I can do.

Meanwhile, Darach is now running around the house. Tearing around like a wild thing. Lots of bumps and bruises as he toddles and waddles. His first words tumbling out in a stream of questions. 'What's that? What's this?' His dirty finger marks are everywhere. Nothing is safe. The CD collection is scattered across the floor. *Bob Dylan's Greatest Hits* has been carefully posted through the cracks in the floorboards along with about a half dozen other CDs.

Eoghan is bum-shuffling along the wooden floors. Drooling with new teeth. Bright pink cheeks. Trying to keep up with his brother. He starts to pull himself up on the furniture. Occasionally burping milk onto the couches. Pushing mushed up food in between the cushions, like buried treasure. He bum-shuffles less when he gets a grip with his pink fists on the edges of chairs and sofas. Then he pulls himself up, preferring to hand-rail along the furniture. Following Darach's trail of destruction.

On 9 January we take Eoghan to his developmental check-up with the local public health nurse. This is a formality. She tells me, 'Just a quick check on his developmental milestones.' She smiles at me reassuringly and admires Eoghan in his dungarees. His little striped socks poking out. His feet wriggling and twisting with pleasure as I distract him with a toy mouse. The district nurse goes about her business. She repeats a couple of hearing and eyesight tests. 'He's easily distracted,' I tell her. 'He's excited.' She smiles at me. She asks me if it is OK to strip him down to his nappy.

I hold Eoghan in my arms as the nurse examines him. His delicate white skin is soft, smelling of baby powder. She gently massages his pudgy little arms and legs. She looks at me as the sunlight streams through the window. 'This is probably nothing. But I think we should make an appointment for Eoghan to see the paediatrician in the next week or so. Eoghan's muscle tone is just a little low. It's probably nothing. Nothing to be worried about.'

On 5 February, General Colin Powell, now US Secretary of State, addresses a plenary session of the UN Security Council, citing evidence of an acceleration in Saddam's WMD program as compelling evidence for the invasion of Iraq. Much of Powell's speech is based on information contained in the UK's 'Dodgy Dossier' – the 'intelligence file' which subsequently turns out to be nothing more than a plagiarised version of a research paper by an American graduate student, Ibrahim al-Marashi. Powell's speech is a pivotal moment and sharpens the international rhetoric and debate about the war in Iraq.

US Defence Secretary Donald Rumsfeld, a hawkish, right-wing neoconservative, ramps up his notion of 'invasion lite' – an 'on the cheap' invasion of Iraq – a stripped-down version of Desert Storm in 1991. According to Rumsfeld's plan, the US would invade Iraq with a tiny invasion force of about 130,000 troops backed up by a small number of British and other coalition troops. Nothing like the invasion force of over one million under Stormin' Norman Schwarzkopf a decade earlier.

In an unusual move, on 25 February the US Chief of Staff of the Armed Forces, General Erik Shinseki, tells an Armed Forces Committee hearing in Washington that a force of several hundred thousand troops would be required to keep the peace in Iraq. Both Shinseki and Marine General Anthony Zinni, former head of US Central Command, are unanimous in their view that there would be a requirement for a massive invasion and occupation force in Iraq. Both generals – two of the most senior commanders in the US military – also predict the apocalyptic violence that will break out in post-invasion Iraq. President Bush, Vice President Cheney and Donald Rumsfeld, however, overrule their opinions. In this case, the radical neocons knew better. After all, not only are they deregulating warfare and making it profitable – they are also deregulating the US financial system. To make them more 'fit for purpose'. Both endeavours will ultimately result in widespread suffering on an almost unprecedented level.

I'm busy doing the round of radio and TV interviews on RTÉ and the BBC, along with interviews on Today FM and Newstalk, as the countdown to war continues. I'm able to predict the certainty of war with some confidence based on ongoing conversations I am having with senior US military commanders and planners who are busy preparing for invasion.

At the end of February, my mum is admitted to hospital. Only days after she had been to our home on a rare visit. My dad managed to get her out of bed to come and see Eoghan on his first birthday. I have a photograph of my mum holding Eoghan. She is shockingly thin and gaunt. She is smiling faintly though. Even her wig seems oversized at this point. It is the last time I speak to her.

Mum is taken to the accident and emergency unit in the Mater Hospital. She is forced to sit there for almost twenty-four hours in a plastic bucket seat. My sisters Pauline and Marie give her whatever comfort they can as night turns to day and A&E fills with drunks and drug addicts. Amid the noise and confusion, my mum has a stroke. She never recovers. But she finally gets a bed.

After a few days in the Mater, they wheel my mum into a single room to allow her to die in some privacy. She is no longer conscious. I visit every day when I can. I hold her hand. The skin almost translucent. Her breathing laboured. Pauline is with her when she slips away on 13 March.

The funeral takes place on 18 March. I am numb. After the coffin is lowered into the ground and as we walk away from the freshly turned grave, I switch on my mobile phone. The phone buzzes and beeps as dozens of messages and voicemail notifications chirp out at me. It seems that the US invasion of Iraq is finally underway. The *Irish Times* ask me for a big analysis piece. Peter Murtagh asks me if I can get 1,400 words to him by six or so, outlining the likely invasion plans of the US. I don't tell him that my mum has just died. I'm too numb. I am grateful for the distraction.

I go straight from the graveyard to my office and start working. Due to the time delay, it is morning on the east coast of the US. I call some of my contact numbers. I get someone in Central Command (Centcom). 'Who is this, sir?' the operator asks me. 'Captain Tom Clonan, *Irish Times* security analyst,'

I reply. 'I want to ask some questions about the invasion plans.' The operator clears his throat and asks me to 'wait one'. I'm passed through a couple of switchboard operators and finally end up with a single, faint ring tone. The number rings for what seems an age over a faint, crackly line. 'Beeeeeep. Beeeep. Beeeep.' I'm about to hang up in frustration when suddenly, some-one picks up.

'Hello, Centcom here,' is the greeting. I hear a lot of background noise. Keyboards clicking, voices issuing what sound like warning orders. 'Er, Captain Tom Clonan here, *Irish Times*,' I repeat myself for what seems like the hundredth time. There is a pregnant pause at the other end of the line. 'Captain Clonan from the *Irish Times*? Not Captain Rowan from Intel?' I try again. 'Er, no. I'm Captain Tom Clonan. Eh, I'm a journalist in Dublin.' Something, somewhere along the line has got lost in translation. I've inadver-tently been transferred straight through to invasion headquarters. The voice at the other end is incredulous. 'You're a freakin' journalist? How'd you get on here?' I explain once more who I am and ask, somewhat tentatively, if Centcom might give me a few lines on their invasion plans.

The officer at the other end coughs out loud. 'You want me to tell you our invasion plans? Are you goddamn nuts?' I apologise and say that I know he must be busy. The senior officer at the other end of the line is laughing now. 'Busy? Are you freakin' serious? Man, let me break this down for you real sim-ple, OK? The United States is about to go to war. This is the eve of battle. And you drop a dime and expect me to reveal her war plans? Uh-huh, no sir. The United States of America is not in the habit of revealing her war plans on the eve of battle. Don't tell me you're surprised. I mean, hey, you are a military guy. What would you say?' I apologise again. The noise behind the colonel is increasing in pitch and fever. 'Sorry, Tom, we've got some missile strikes goin' off here.'

He sounds like he is about to hang up, so I make one last desperate plea. 'Look, one old soldier to another. I'm under pressure to get some copy into the *Irish Times* this afternoon, and well, even just for background, can I run my scenario past you?' The colonel laughs again. A good sign? 'OK man, you know what, you are a blast. I mean, there's freakin' journalists all over the goddamn world writing about us now in their goddamn newspapers. Saying any and everything about what we're gonna do and not gonna do in Iraq. Course, none of 'em ever think to call up and ask us what we are actually gonna do. So, I'm gonna cut you some slack here. You tell me what you think we're gonna do? I'm all ears. Shoot.' And so, over the crackly line, from my home office in the attic in Booterstown, I tell the colonel that I think the US 3rd Infantry Division are going to make a dash up Highway 1 towards Baghdad. I also tell him that the US 1st Armoured Division and the 1st (UK) Armoured Division will carry out concurrent and parallel armoured advances. The colonel lets out a whistle. 'Well, son,' he says, 'you're in the goddamn ball park. Now go write your newspaper. You're not wrong. What did you say your name was again?' We exchange numbers over a surreal conversation about Irish grandparents. Then the phone clicks dead.

I do my copy, confident in the knowledge that I'm 'in the ball park'. So to speak. And, I've made a new friend at US Central Command. That will prove useful in the coming weeks and months. And years, as it turns out.

The following day, Baghdad is hit by missile and rocket strikes. I'm feeding a bottle to Eoghan on my lap when I see the pictures of Baghdad promo'd for the *Six One News* on RTÉ. Darach wants to watch *Scooby Doo*. I think that the Iraq invasion is a bit scarier than Shaggy and Thelma all right, but I've got to see what's happening. The presenter's voice booms out, 'Tonight, the United States unleashes its war of shock and awe on Saddam Hussein's regime in Baghdad.'

The children fall silent as I turn up the volume. I see the familiar tracer fire rip through the night sky of Baghdad at unseen US aircraft high above the cloud base. The city rocks with deafening explosions. The palm tree fronds in the foreground of the panning camera shot blow in the blast and shock wave of a nearby explosion. Eoghan starts to cry.

The following weeks go by in a blur. I'm in Tesco doing the weekly shop and as I reach up for bread or tea or milk, I hear my mother's voice whispering in my ear. Softly. 'I love you, Thomas.' Or just a plaintive 'Thomas.' Like she used to whisper in my ear when I was a small boy. In the mornings, when it was time to go to school, she'd come silently into the bedroom and whisper our names into our ears to wake us. Gently. She was such a gentle lady. I think that now she is my guardian angel. I've had no time to process her passing. Within hours of her funeral I'm flat-out writing about the war in Iraq. No time to absorb. But I hear her voice from time to time.

I tell Aideen about my new 'angel'. Aideen looks at me and rummages about for her battered and much-thumbed copy of the *ICD-10 Classification of Mental and Behavioural Disorders*. 'Look at the page on 'Symptoms of Grieving,' she tells me. I flick through to the page. It says in black and white. 'During the grieving process, a close relative may experience brief auditory or visual hallucinations about the deceased loved one. This is normal. Some describe the auditory hallucination as a whispering in the ear. This is normal in the first few weeks after death.' 'Aha,' I think. Not a guardian angel. More 'an auditory hallucination'. Mum seems a little further away now. A little more dead than before. But I still see her in my mind's eye, calling out to me. Mouthing the words, 'I love you.' I miss her so much.

But dead or no, guardian angel or hallucination, I have no time to reflect. The weeks in March, April and May are a blur of writing for the *Irish Times* and an unending daily conveyor belt of TV and radio interviews on the rapid US advance on Baghdad. Each day is the same. I get up at 5.30 AM and monitor the news from the night before. Then I shower and go out to the TV3 studios in Ballymount. I do an almost daily slot on TV 3's *Ireland AM*, a morning current affairs show with Mark Cagney. I'm usually on at a few minutes past seven. Doing the first daily analysis package on the war. Then I run out to the car, taking the studio make-up off with Darach and Eoghan's baby wipes.

After that, I drive hell for leather through rush-hour traffic for RTÉ's studios and *Morning Ireland* on RTÉ radio 1. I do a quick slot there. Grab a coffee and catch up on latest developments before slotting into *Today with Pat Kenny* for 10 AM. I then do my lectures and student supervision at DIT. Dashing home from town, I then go to the crèche and collect Darach and Eoghan. Aideen is working late at the hospital on most evenings. I feed the boys, change them and do another eight hundred words for tomorrow's *Irish Times*. When that has gone in at around four in the afternoon, I make the dinner. Then it's back out to do *Prime Time* on RTÉ TV or *The Tonight Show with Vincent Browne* on RTÉ radio after ten at night. These are eighteen-hour days. I'm running on adrenaline. It is nuts and I shouldn't be doing it. Aideen tells me to stop and reflect on what I'm doing. She tells me, correctly, that it is not normal behaviour. I think I'm doing it to bury the grief over my mum's death. My behaviour and work rate are pathological

Aideen calls me during one of these frenetic days. I've to go to the Coombe immediately. There is something wrong. When I get there, Aideen is in tears. Our little girl has stopped moving. There is no heartbeat and Aideen is induced. Our little girl is stillborn at full term. 'Cord accident' is the term used to describe her death. She is tiny. And looks so much like the boys. We bury our little girl in the Angels plot in Glasnevin.

Pauline brings my dad to the funeral service. He is himself. He needs to get outside quickly to smoke. He tells me that in his day, there were no funerals for stillborn babies. He tells me about limbo. He tells me not to worry, that 'Your mother will look after Liadain.' He asks me what Liadain means. 'The Grey Lady' I tell him.

I have no auditory hallucinations about Liadain. I never heard her voice. I just held her tiny hand. However briefly.

Pauline brings my dad home. She winks at me as they leave. 'Don't mind him,' is all she says. As she leads him back to his car, the sun shines on her blonde hair. It gives a halo effect. She looks like a guardian angel. I still think of me and Pauline listening to her record collection all those years ago in Ballygall Avenue. We were so cool. Back when we were teenagers, we used to imagine what we'd do as adults – as grown-ups. We never imagined a day like today.

Aideen and I are distraught. I am haunted by Liadain. We are haunted together. We carry on.

Marian Richardson and Pat Kenny in RTÉ give me a little card the next time I'm in studio. Everyone shakes hands with me. Peter Murtagh sends me a card. He tells me to take it easy for a few days. The *Irish Times* send us a bouquet of flowers. A neighbour gives us a climbing rose. I plant it next to our gable wall. It thrives and produces beautiful red roses. My little darling will never see them. I will never see her lean gracefully in to inhale their scent. I think of Senka waiting for Darko under the scent of roses in her garden in Bosnia. He'll never come home from school. Neither will Liadain. I have to banish such thoughts. For they are unbearable. I entrust her to my mother's hands. I hope there is a heaven. Or even a limbo. I'd happily go to limbo to be with Liadain for all eternity.

Chapter 20

Mission Accomplished

'OK, asshole. I don't know what your major fuckin' malfunction is, OK?
But I'm not your mommy. This is 100 percent mace. Law enforcement
grade. Now fuck off before I call security.'

San Diego, California

May 2003

The daily grind of TV and radio and newspaper continues. I also deliver my
lecture load in DIT. Teaching journalism to journalism students. It helps if
you have industry experience. I'm getting that in spades.

A news editor in RTÉ tells me that there has been some negative feedback
about me from the Irish army. They've obviously spotted me on TV and
radio. A staff officer at DFHQ is briefing news editors and other journalists
– anyone who is prepared to listen – that I'm 'not qualified' to comment on
military matters. The Defence Forces have even taken the unusual step of
offering the services of serving army officers to act as 'military analysts' on television news bulletins. I bump into a few of them on the RTÉ campus. It cannot be easy for them, though. With Irish troops serving alongside US soldiers
in Afghanistan, it must be hard to offer a critique of the military tactics of an
ally in the field. A few journalists approach me and ask me what I ever did to
the army. 'They seem really pissed off at you.' I've enough on my plate to give
any thought to these comments. But, deep down, on a subconscious level,
they make me uneasy. Unseen hands working behind the scenes, anonymous
voices briefing negatively about me.

Things ease up in April after US forces seize Baghdad and consolidate their hold there. On 9 April, US forces topple the twelve-metre-high statue of Saddam in Firdos Square. US forces begin to establish forward operating bases throughout the city. General Jay Garner and his team arrive in Baghdad and begin plans for reconstruction. One senior officer who accompanies Garner tells me that Iraq is 'completely destroyed. Busted. We're in one of Saddam's palaces and there isn't even running water. Never mind an air conditioner. The air force and the army sure did a job on Iraq.'

I'm reminded of the US Marine officer in NATO headquarters the year before. 'We break things and kill people.' Mission accomplished.

I get a brief breather from the war and submit an academic paper for the International Communication Association in the US. They accept my paper and I travel to the US in May. The conference is held in San Diego. Before I travel, I have lunch with my contact in the US Embassy and we have a 'frank exchange of views' about the progress of the war in Iraq. In other words, we have a lively argument. My contact bids me farewell. As she does so, she turns around and calls out to me over the heavy traffic in Ballsbridge. 'Don't forget to try the salt water taffy in San Diego. It's a local delicacy.' She smiles and waves goodbye. I'm still smiling and waving when it dawns on me that I've never discussed my trip to San Diego with her. Since 9/11, it seems all travel to and from the US is routinely monitored. The world is changing in subtle but profound ways.

I fly direct to Los Angeles from Dublin with Aer Lingus. It is a twelve-hour flight. As we rumble down the runway and reach that point where we lose contact with the ground, I close my eyes and think of my baby Liadain. I hope she is with my mother. The plane actually passes over her burial place in Dardistown Cemetery next to the airport. I know she would be smiling as I depart the country over her own point of departure from this life. At 38,000 feet I walk around the plane. It is the first time in weeks that I've had the chance to think. I think about my mum. I think about Liadain. I think about Aideen and the boys. In that strange space between heaven and earth. Cruising high above all that is familiar and familial. I ask the air hostess for a gin and tonic. And another. And another. I think of the marathon drinking sessions I had as a young officer in Al Yatun. The gin gives me a pleasant numb buzz. I press the call button for another. The air hostess comes down to me and puts her fingers to her lips. Most of the passengers are sleeping now.

I follow her to the rear galley of the aircraft. She pulls back a curtain. Another air hostess sits behind it, reading a glossy magazine. She looks at me with a raised eyebrow. Hostess No. 1 opens up a steel door. 'That's where the gin is.' She opens another. 'That's where the tonic is.' And finally, she opens a catering bin. 'That's the ice.' She puts her hands on her hips and in a terrifying voice tells me, 'Now help yourself.' The other hostess smiles beatifically at me as Hostess No. 1 supervises my first attempt at 'self-service' at 38,000 feet. 'Now, stop pressing that button and don't be waking anyone up,' is her final comment.

When I get to Los Angeles, there is a short connecting flight to San Diego. The small commuter plane is piloted by two blonde women who laugh and gossip all the way down the Pacific coast. They effortlessy guide the plane through a long, graceful half circle. We come in to land, descending between two massive office blocks. The women at the controls never skip a beat. They chat and giggle all the way down. The air steward, who is very camp and very helpful, catches my eye. He raises his eyebrows theatrically and nods at the pilots. 'Girl talk,' he says to me as the wheels thump onto the tarmac.

The taxi driver who brings me to the hotel is from Afghanistan. He tells me that the war has 'fucked up Afghanistan'. He also tells me that Iraq is 'fucked'. 'Why you think I come to San Diego to drive this heap of shit?'

I deliver my paper titled 'Impact of Official Secrets Act on Academic Researchers'. There are a surprisingly large number of military researchers at the conference. We exchange cards. They are almost all pursuing PhD research within the US military establishment on a very wide spectrum of issues; from gay and lesbian military service to transgendered military experiences and the impact of foreign service on military families. They ask me about my own research. I tell them about the findings of the research and the subsequent reaction of the military authorities. They look puzzled. 'Don't you guys need to do research to get promoted?' None of them, it seems, has been verbally or physically abused for their academic inquiries. On the contrary, it would seem they have been encouraged. The most senior of their group, a US navy captain, is surprised at the reaction of the Irish military authorities to what the Americans consider 'routine' research. She raises her eyebrows. 'What a fucked up army.'

At the end of one of the conference sessions, the organisers announce a book sale in the basement of the hotel. I decide to go down and have a look. I keep getting static shocks as I move around the hotel from lift buttons and electric light switches. I wonder at the range of materials used in the construction of the hotel with its polypropylene carpets, plastic handrails and nylon wallpaper. My hair is literally standing on end as I summon a lift to the basement.

I get into the 'elevator' and 'ride' to the basement. The door pings open and I see a sight that roots me to the spot. There, among the bookstands and stationery counters, is my mother. Impossible. She's dead, I remind myself. I step out of the lift open-mouthed. Gawping at her. She moves along a bookshelf, stacking academic periodicals. I think of Aideen's warning about visual hallucinations. I pinch myself. This elegant older lady is the spitting image of my mum. She moves like her. Same hair even. I wander over to get a bit closer and pick up some journals whilst trying to look nonchalant. Her hands. Even her hands are like mum's. The same fine tracery of blue veins under the fine lined parchment of her skin. Freckles too.

The old lady turns to look at me. She fixes me with her pale blue eyes. I am speechless. It is as though mum has returned from beyond the grave. From beyond the great divide. Or maybe she faked her own death and ran off to join a travelling bookfair in California. I wouldn't blame her. The weather is so much better here. But that's impossible anyway. I saw how thin mum had become. Nevertheless, I'm transfixed by her.

Mum speaks to me. Or, rather, this random old lady speaks to me. 'Can I help you son?' It's definitely not mum. Because this lady has a voice gravelly with decades of heavy smoking. I'm not sure what to say. So I tell her straight out. 'If you don't mind me saying,' I begin. Her eyes narrow a little. The poor old dear. Probably a little hard of hearing I think. I raise my voice a little. 'You look very like someone I know. Someone dead.' I just manage to croak, 'My mother actually.' I'm croaking a bit because I feel so emotional. But the little

Getting paid to read the papers. Captain Tom Clonan, Defence Forces Press Officer, December 1998.

Lieutenant Tom Clonan's OSCE Election Supervisor Identity Card. Bosnia Herzegovina, September 1996.

Captain Tom Clonan, *Passeport de Service*, Official Passport, 1998–2001.

Slight misunderstanding. Tom Clonan and Syrian Arab Army (SAA) Guards, Syrian Foreign Ministry, Damascus, Syria, February 2009.

Landstuhl Regional Medical Centre, the US military's European ER and the first stop for thousands of US soldiers seriously wounded on the battlefields of Afghanistan and Iraq, March 2006.

British army Chinook helicopter dismantles the last British army observation post in south Armagh, June 2006.

Last of British army foot patrols (2nd Battalion, Princess of Wales's Royal Regiment) at end of Operation Banner (August 1969–July 2007), Bessbrook Mill, south Armagh, June 2006.

Above: British army briefing and threat assessment, Bessbrook Mill, south Armagh, June 2006. Subversive threat 'Low'. Media alert 'High'.

Right: British army engineers dismantle Observation Post 'Golf 40' in south Armagh, June 2006.

British army Lynx helicopter at Observation Post 'Golf 40', Croslieve Hill, south Armagh, June 2006.

In the hot seat. Cheeky pose in President Bashar al-Assad's seat in one of his ministries, Damascus, Syria, February 2009.

Is that a real gun, mister? Tom Clonan and short-range anti-armour weapon (SRAAW), south Armagh, June 2006.

Tom Clonan pictured at the entrance (or 'Sally Port') to Camp Delta, US Naval Station, Guantanamo Bay, Cuba, October 2005.

Main entrance (Sally Port) to Camp Delta, US Naval Station, Guantanamo Bay, Cuba, October 2005. Notice the sign on the right of the guard tower reads, 'No Photography'.

An arrow indicating the direction of Mecca (*Makkah*), imprinted on floor of a cell in Camp Delta, US Naval Station, Guantanamo Bay, Cuba, October 2005. Direction arrows such as these were supposed to 'aid prayer' for detainees.

Left: A rare view of cells inside Camp Delta, US Naval Station, Guantanamo Bay, Cuba, October 2005.
Right: 'The Golden Arches.' McDonald's Drive-Thru, US Naval Station, Guantanamo Bay, Cuba, October 2005.

Love at first sight.
Eoghan Clonan (aged 10) and
'Superdog' Duke, Irish Dogs for
the Disabled, Fiddler's Brook,
Blarney, County Cork,
June 2012.

Checking on the reindeer.
'Superdog' Duke, Eoghan,
Ailbhe, Darach and Rossa
Clonan, Phoenix Park, Dublin,
Christmas Eve 2012.

old lady is one step ahead of me. She steps back and takes a little key ring out of her bookstore bib. 'OK, asshole,' she says. 'I don't know what your major fuckin' malfunction is, OK? But I'm not your mommy.' She holds up the key fob. 'This is 100 percent mace. Law enforcement grade. Now fuck off before I call security.' I beat a hasty retreat, bumping into other academics as I do so. The evil old granny eyes me beadily as I hasten back to the elevator. I stab at the buttons repeatedly, heart hammering in my ribcage. The last thing I see is the granny talking to a burly security guard whilst she points at me. The doors close and I go immediately to the seventeenth floor and the safety of my room. I pour myself a stiff Jack Daniels. The phone rings. Aideen has called from Ireland. 'Having a nice time?'

The next day, I'm invited to lunch by some of the US navy grad students at the conference. They tell me that even though I'm a 'Bulletstop' (US navy slang for a soldier) they'll take me out to see some of the best US navy seafood bars in San Diego. 'Just don't touch anything and don't get sick.' We take a taxi to a bar and grill downtown. The dim-lit bar is tended by a foul mouthed ex-US navy coxswain who looks like Popeye – right down to the anchor tattoos on his arms. 'Whaddya want?' he asks me. He excuses his foul language to my friend, who is a lieutenant commander, and refers to her as 'ma'am.' This sounds strange next to 'motherfuckin' this and motherfuckin' that.' He ignores me for the rest of the afternoon – save occasionally to glare at me menacingly with his bloodshot eyes.

The lieutenant commander is inordinately proud of her own PhD research which is focused on patterns of sexual harassment among naval crews deployed at sea for prolonged periods of time. She tells me over a few drinks that the incidence of sexual harassment is relatively 'stable' irrespective of length of time spent at sea. She constantly refers to the ship as a 'weapon system'. The others giggle when I ask them why they call the ships 'weapon systems'. 'That's what they are dumbass!' They find my question hilarious. They don't refer to the ship as 'she'. They simply refer to it as a weapon. As one of them clarifies for me, 'It's a great big killing machine. What did you expect us to call it? Home sweet home?' Again, more laughter.

After an hour or two of eating and drinking and comparing research notes, the women decide it is a good time to show me some more Navy bars. The bars are 'interesting'. One is called the Hole. Another, the 'Star Bar.' In one particular bar there's a large gaggle of male naval officers there already – getting seriously drunk. 'We are in port,' they explain. They ask me what part of Britain I'm from. I explain I'm Irish. There is much backslapping. I have a flashback to the Serbs in Prijedor. Still, it's nice to be Irish.

After a few whiskeys they tell me they've got something to show me. They go to a side room and haul out what looks like a rolled-up carpet. They are all laughing uproariously as they stretch it out on the floor and unroll the top five or six feet of material. I see the tops of capital letters. I can make out an 'M' and an 'A'. 'Mission Accomplished,' it says. Of course. This is the banner that was hanging from the bridge of the aircraft carrier *Abraham Lincoln* when President Bush had landed on it a few weeks previously to announce the 'end' of the war in Iraq.

At the beginning of May, Bush, in a carefully choreographed television stunt, had landed on the carrier as a passenger in a Lockheed S-3 Viking jet. In front of the cameras, Bush hopped out of the aircraft and announced, in grave tones, 'Major combat operations in Iraq have ended.' He said this as the 'Mission Accomplished' banner hovered above him. In front of the world's media, he continued, 'In the battle of Iraq, the United States and our allies have prevailed.'

The guys and girls of the US Navy are laughing uncontrollably. 'Mission Accomplished. Fuckin' A.' One stands theatrically to attention and salutes the banner on the floor. They roll it up again and push it back into the side room next to the bar. In the few weeks since Bush has declared the war over, more than forty US soldiers and marines have been killed in action in Iraq – victims to an energetic Sunni uprising. Hundreds more have been wounded in the vicious insurgency predicted by the general staff only months earlier. The irony is not lost on the naval officers.

I fly back to Dublin.

Chapter 21

Neuromuscular Disorder

Temple Street Children's Hospital, Dublin

Summer 2003

A month later, Aideen and I are sitting in front of a pediatric neurologist who tells us that Eoghan has a 'neuromuscular disorder'. Eoghan is sitting on the floor of the neurologist's office chewing a building block. He is teething. The words 'neuromuscular' and 'disorder' hang in the air. I have no idea what they mean. The doctor continues talking. He is not unkind. He is delicate. Empathetic. I see his lips moving but, to be honest, I cannot really hear what he is saying. Aideen is asking him medical questions. Eoghan needs to have an MRI scan. I manage to hear that. The doctor is making appointments in Temple Street Children's Hospital. I've heard the name of the hospital so many times. I didn't realise the role it was going to play in our lives. We shake hands with the doctor and walk out to the car. When I say walk, I think we walked. We were on autopilot. In shock. Walking like robots. Putting one foot in front of the other, because our lives have just changed irrevocably.

We strap Eoghan into the car. Aideen looks frightened. 'He could have a brain tumour. Oh, Thomas. We could lose our baby.' We hold each other in the car. In the car park. Eoghan smiles at us and wiggles his toes when we turn to look at him.

We get an appointment for an MRI scan the following week. Eoghan is sedated and his tiny body is still. He lies there in his little cotton vest, wrapped in towels so that he fits onto the stretcher that will be rolled into the MRI scanner. He looks tiny as he goes into the bore of the massive magnetic device.

It is distressing. We are allowed to sit still in the MRI suite during the scan. It takes about forty minutes. There is a cacophony of loud bangs, ticks, clacks and buzzing as the scanner images our baby's brain and neuromuscular systems. His tiny brain and spine are being read, measured, assessed. I feel sick. I pray to Liadain to watch over him. I pray to my mum. I'd even pray to the granny who threatened me in San Diego.

When it is over, the technicians advise us that we will be given an appointment to discuss the results. They are kind. Sympathetic. We try to read their faces. They are inscrutable. We are sick with worry. We wait a few more hours in Temple Street as the chemical sedation wears off. Eoghan's blue eyes flutter open. We take turns to hold him.

The pediatrician meets us a few days later. Neurologists have a massive caseload in Ireland. There simply are not enough of them. He sits us down and opens Eoghan's chart. The waiting is agonising. 'Eoghan's scan shows evidence of demyelination of his nervous system.' The doctor explains what a myelin sheath is to me. It is an outer covering or layer which protects nerve cells and facilitates the transmission of signals from the cerebral cortex throughout the nervous system. Without the myelin sheath, which is similar in some ways to the outer insulation layer on electric cables, the system cannot function. Signals from the brain are degraded and are not transmitted to the relevant systems.

I understand this much. But what has happened to Eoghan? The doctor tells us that for some reason, Eoghan's system is demyelinating. The myelin sheath is compromised. The doctor is patient. He is kind. He takes time to answer my rapid-fire questions. I'm struggling to fully understand the implications of this. It doesn't sound good. Not good at all. Aideen is squeezing my hand very tightly. White-knuckled.

If Eoghan continues to lose myelin sheath for whatever reason, he could lose 'multiple functions'. Breathing could be compromised. We could lose our little boy.

The conversation continues. It is a bleak discussion. The doctor tells us as gently and as diplomatically as he can that Eoghan's quality of life will be affected by his neuromuscular condition. He emphasises over and over that there is no certainty in these matters. We have no idea as to the cause of the demyelination. Nor do we know if the process is just commenced or is ongoing. We have no timeline. Only the knowledge that there is something wrong. Something hidden. Something that has announced itself to us unbidden, without warning. Out of the blue. We agree to genetic testing of ourselves and Eoghan.

Eoghan will have more MRI scans to track and monitor his myelin sheath. In order to detect any changes. In order to measure the progress of his neuro-muscular disorder. In the meantime, the scan indicates that it is unlikely that Eoghan will walk. Unlikely that he will dress himself. Unlikely that he will be continent or able to control his bladder. He may or may not be able to eat independently. His future is up in the air. I'm holding him in my arms as we speak. His head on my shoulder as he sleeps. Wisps of blond hair over my shoulder. His breathing steady. I feel the heat of his body on mine.

Our heads are spinning. We list the appointments that need to be made. Muscle biopsy. Lumbar puncture. My fingers press against his tiny spine, I trace my index finger over the tiny ridges and bumps through his baby gro. Physiotherapy. Occupational therapy. Speech therapy. Surgical assessments. Eoghan faces a constellation of challenges. He sleeps away on my shoulder.

My head is still spinning as we walk to the car. All bets are off. All expectations on hold. There is a fundamental shift in our understanding of Eoghan's future. I am so afraid I feel physically sick. I feel helpless. I break out into a cold sweat. Aideen is silent. She looks at me in the car. She speaks slowly, deliberately. 'We are not going to just sit back and let this happen. We are not going to let this define Eoghan's future. We are going to do whatever it takes.' Aideen has commenced battle. Heaven help anyone who gets in her way. We are at war.

The other war escalates as the insurgency in Iraq gathers in momentum. Over two hundred US soldiers are killed in action over the summer months. Young men and women; sons and daughters of parents somewhere in what the US military refers to as 'CONUS' or the 'Continental United States.' Their bodies transit home through Irish airspace. Dead Americans, dead kids criss-crossing Irish skies while we go about our business below. Oblivious. Tens of thousands of Iraqi men, women and children are also slaughtered in the quagmire. I continue to write analysis for the *Irish Times*. 'Mission Accomplished' morphs into 'Mission Impossible'.

Towards the end of November I deliver an academic paper in the University of Sussex on the 'Political Economy of War Reporting'. It seems like a topical issue since Britain is at war. The audience of young students seem to have only a passing interest in the war. One asks me who Osama Bing Laden is.

On the way home, Aideen texts me. We are pregnant again. I immediately think of Liadain. At 38,000 feet on the short flight home to Dublin, I look out the window at the stars winking in the night sky. I think of her out there somewhere in the inky black. I pray that she watches over her new baby sibling. I pray that all will be well.

In December we get an invitation from the US Embassy to dine with the US Ambassador James Kenny and his special guests Newt Gingrich and his wife, Callista. A former speaker of the US House of Representatives and high-profile right-wing Republican politician, Gingrich has been tasked by President Bush to assess emerging threats to the United States 'out to 2020 and beyond'. President Bush has appointed him as a key member of the Hart-Rudman Commission. The Hart-Rudman Commission is officially known as the US Commission on National Security for the Twenty-first Century. Gingrich is interested in a 'frank exchange of views' with me in my capacity as a retired army officer and a 'key opinion leader' in Ireland with regard to defence and security. With our experience of terrorism in Ireland – our own, seminal version of 'asymmetrical warfare' – Gingrich is interested in the Irish perspective on terror threats to the US. My contact in the US Embassy tells me to 'read up a little' about Gingrich before we meet for dinner. He advises me to look up 'Newt.org'. I check out Newt's website.

Newt Gingrich's website is a breezy homage to the great man himself.

Penned, presumably, by himself or his staff. Nevertheless, it gives me a useful insight into the man, his background and his mission. Gingrich is an historian with an interest in military matters. He has never served in the military and was not drafted for Vietnam. Over the years, I've met many historians with a fascination for military matters. They are usually quite frightening. They tend to combine an almost perfect ignorance about soldiering with an absolutist certainty about military matters. They also tend to have an unshakeable belief in archive material and 'official' military records. Having served in the military and having compiled 'official military records', I do not share their belief in the sanctity of archive material. In fact, my own research shows conclusively that official military records bear only the flimsiest of relationships to the truth.

Aideen and I change the boys for bed. I've nailed a plank to the side of Eoghan's cot so that he doesn't roll out of bed. As he gets bigger, he has lost a little gross motor function and can easily fall out of bed. I think the nailed plank is a pragmatic solution. Aideen thinks it looks like something out of a Ceauşescu orphanage. Needs must.

The boys are prodigious pukers. So, before we head to the ambassador's residence in the Phoenix Park, I need to disinfect the car with Dettol as it smells like a dead cat. Aideen and I check each other out for milk stains. Remarkably, my one suit has no tell-tale milky stains on the shoulder or on my tie. We are suited, booted and ready to go.

When we get to the ambassador's residence, there is a security check at the gate. An extendable mirror is pushed under the car to check for explosives. I idly wonder if they'll find a dead cat stuck to the chassis somewhere. The security guy motions for me to roll down the window. He starts to speak and involuntarily inhales a good lung-full of stale baby vomit, which has been amplified by the car's heater. 'Excuse me sir but . . . Jesus . . . OK . . . *cough* . . . you guys are good to go.'

We park and are met by Ambassador Kenny and his wife at the front door of the residence. It is a beautiful period building dating from 1776. The ambassador explains to myself and Aideen that the house became a full US Embassy when Ireland became a republic in 1949. As we walk into the entrance hall, Ambassador Kenny remarks on the shared influences between the US and the Irish Republic from the French Republican ideal. '*Liberté, égalité* and *fraternité*.' The ambassador notices that Aideen is pregnant. 'Or in your case, *liberté, égalité* and *maternité*.' We are off to a good start.

Ambassador Kenny introduces us to his wife. We shake hands and exchange pleasantries. The Kennys extend to us a warm and sincere welcome into their home. Newt Gingrich and Callista enter the hall and we are introduced. Gingrich is a bear of a man and almost shakes my arm off. He's done his homework. He waves a huge paw around the room. 'Colonel John Blaquiere, Chief Secretary of the British government and Bailiff of the Phoenix Park designed this place. You can sense the history here.'

He shakes hands enthusiastically with Aideen and congratulates her on our fourth baby-to-be. I'm introduced to Callista. She is a tall blonde woman with striking looks. I have a fleeting flash memory of a picture of Newt on his website, playing with grandchildren on his knee. I am inspired. I say to Callista, 'Lovely to meet you. And may I say, you don't look a bit like a grandmother.' There is a frozen silence. Callista responds icily, 'That was Newt's first wife.' 'Ah, I see,' is all I can manage. Aideen pokes me in the back.

We have dinner. Ambassador Kenny is a great host. Gingrich is sitting next to me and when coffee is served, he announces loudly that it is time for 'a frank exchange of views'. Ambassador Kenny jumps straight in and challenges Gingrich to explain his 'neoconservative' views on third-level education. Gingrich seems to relish the provocative line of questioning and holds forth. He gives a no-holds-barred description of a twenty-first-century vision for university education. 'The world's top forty corporations will agree a hierarchy of essential learning outcomes, useful for the economy and so on. Then, guys and girls all over the world can just simply log on to our global corporate university and achieve these learning goals. No need for your fancy Ivy League universities. No need for big endowments or a rich daddy to get you into college. The world's corporations will democratise education and make it available to all the world's citizens.' I'm not sure if Newt is taking the mickey here, but he looks serious. He is also now staring at me intently. I realise, I am to respond.

'Well,' I croak. 'That's an interesting idea.' He slaps me on the back in something not far off a Heimlich maneuver. 'I like it. Interesting idea. C'mon Tom, get off the fence. Tell me what you really think.' The ambassador hops in and describes it as a 'nightmare' vision. Gingrich laughs this off. 'Nightmare. Really?' He looks at me again. 'Tom. True or false. Let me guess. Your own education institution, is, I betcha looking at ways to tailor courses towards economic outputs. In other words, seeking ways to commodify knowedge and transform the university into an engine for economic growth.' I think about it for a split second. He's right. He slaps me on the back again. 'Told ya.'

We retire to the sitting room. Newt and I share a couch. He looks at me again. 'I'm interested in what you have to say about our wars in Iraq and Afghanistan. And we don't have much time. So I want you to be frank. Tell me what you really think. Everything else is just horseshit.' Aideen is talking to Callista and Mrs Kenny over by the fireplace. Gingrich stirs his drink and addresses me once more. I'm interested in what you've got to say because I hear you're not a yes man. I've heard about your research in the military. Shook up the old ladies on the general staff I hear.' He's done his homework all right.

I tell him about my views on the invasion force in Iraq. I tell him I think it is too small at less than 100,000 ground troops. Iraq has a land area roughly the size of France and a population of twenty million; I tell him I believe that the territory is too big for such a small occupation force. I remind him of the numbers of armed British security forces in Northern Ireland during the Troubles. It was relatively ineffectual even in a tiny territory with a small population of less than one million. I remind him that at the height of the Troubles, between British Army, Ulster Defence Regiment and Royal Ulster Constabulary members, there were approximately 60,000 armed forces in the province. That number was unable to pacify the Provisional IRA, which had only a few hundred active service members at any one time. Gingrich continues to swirl his drink. 'And Afghanistan?' he asks.

I tell him that the US is going to have to talk to the Taliban. Sooner rather than later. I remind him that even Margaret Thatcher talked to the

Provisional IRA. I express the view that it is only through dialogue that a settlement can be reached. I also warn him about NATO forces in Afghanistan becoming part of the problem as opposed to part of the solution with regard to radical, fundamental Islamist rhetoric and ideology.

Gingrich thanks me for being 'up front'. He fixes me with his cold blue eyes once more and tells me emphatically, 'Yeah. We'll talk to the Taliban probably at some point. But not until after we've dealt with Al Qaeda. Make no mistake about it Tom, 9/11 was an attack on our people and our way of life. They made enemies of themselves. They put themselves in that frame. And we will deal with them without prejudice. This is gonna be the long war.'

We take our leave and drive home. The moon over the Phoenix Park illuminates a herd of fallow deer in the lee of some trees. Aideen tells me that our baby has just moved. The tiny bean is moving. Aideen's hand is on her tummy. Cradling the new life inside. I reflect on my conversation with Gingrich. His words 'the long war' stick in my mind. I wonder about the world that my children will inhabit.

I think of my mum on Christmas Eve. I light a candle for her. I light a candle for Liadain. I light a candle for our unborn baby. We hang stockings on the boy's beds. Eoghan's plank is handy for that.

Chapter 22

Investigations

'A romantic mid-week break?'

January 2004

In January, Eoghan gets an appointment for a second MRI in Temple Street. A 'reasonable' amount of time has elapsed since his first scan. A second MRI scan after this interval of time will determine whether or not the demyelination process has continued. It will tell us if Eoghan's condition is stable or progressive. To put it simply, brutally, the results of this test will tell us whether Eoghan is likely to survive or not. The test results may or may not tell us something about Eoghan's prognosis. What kind of life he might lead. Whether or not he will live. And for how long.

As we go about the daily routines of nappy changes, feeds, housework, grocery shopping and work, the dread knowledge is always there. Everpresent: Eoghan is in danger. The hardest part is not knowing what precisely the risk is. Not having a diagnosis. Everything is up in the air. The feeling of helplessness is almost impossible to cope with.

Eoghan is a beautiful boy. The chemistry between himself and Darach is beautiful also. They are inseparable. They eat together, sleep together, 'talk' to each other. The conversations consist of Darach's first words and Eoghan's squeals. They wrestle each other on the floor. They share bottles together on a beanbag in front of the fire.

In Temple Street, we go to the MRI suite. The massive General Electric MRI scanner is like a prop from a science fiction movie. It is a huge grey metal and plastic device. It takes up almost half of the suite with its sheer size. To all intents and purposes it resembles an ancient Irish passage tomb. There is a large squat circular dome containing a passage or 'bore' into which the patient is fed by way of a stretcher on runners. The dome contains arrays of radio frequency coils, powerful magnets and gradient coils. Adults often experience feelings of panic and claustrophobia when they are placed inside the machine. They are usually fed head first into the MRI, almost fully enclosed in the bore.

The confined space coupled with the loud noise of the machine combine to make the experience of scanning a frightening one for most patients. Many require chemical sedation in order to endure the experience.

Eoghan is sedated. We stroke his hair as he falls into a deep sleep. The technicians place him onto the adult-sized stretcher. A pair of red LED lights form a crosshair to help them position Eoghan's head and neck. He is swaddled in a cellular blanket. His little pink cheeks glow in the alien light just inside the scanning chamber. The technicians work quickly, efficiently and gently. They slide Eoghan into the aperture of the bore and his little body disappears inside. His tiny feet are visible just inside. Tigger chases a butterfly on his little yellow socks.

We hold hands as the machine clicks and burrs into life. The scanner bangs and hammers its way through its program. Time seems frozen. The technicians work away behind their glass screen. We watch them from time to time, trying to see any tell-tale signs on their faces. As usual, they are impassive.

Eventually the program reaches its conclusion. The technician comes in and tells us that the imaging has worked well and that Eoghan was perfectly still. We lift him up in his blanket and cradle him tightly.

We then take him upstairs for a lumbar puncture. While he is sedated, the team decide it is a good time to draw some cerebrospinal fluid for analysis. Eoghan is placed on a table for the procedure. The team busy themselves. They open the poppers on his little vest and raise it up over his nappy. The doctor runs his index finger over the ridges of Eoghan's tiny spine. I'm feeling sick. I'm feeling dizzy. Aideen watches intently.

The doctor settles on a site on Eoghan's back. An impossibly large needle is taken from its packaging. The doctor gently aligns the needlepoint along the spine and begins a slow push through soft tissue, deep into our baby's spinal cord. Eoghan does not move. The doctor is all concentration. The seconds tick by like hours. He sighs and flexes slightly, and slowly, slowly draws up the syringe. Eoghan cries out. I hold his head and kiss his hairline. I whisper to him that everything is all right.

The procedure is successful. A sample for analysis has been successfully harvested. We are limp with exhaustion. Eoghan cries out for us. We hold him in turns. Eventually he can take a bottle.

When the boys are in bed, we sit on the couch together and hold hands. Someone on RTÉ is talking about queues for Prada handbags in Brown Thomas.

The war in Iraq rages on. Over fifty coalition troops are killed in January alone. The US military innovates a new medical evacuation system to get their injured and dying off the battlefield as quickly as possible. When hit by sniper fire or injured in roadside bomb blasts, US soldiers are treated on the spot by forward surgical teams who deploy by helicopter to the scene of the attack. The injured are operated on in the field by senior trauma surgeons. The gross blunt trauma injuries inflicted by improvised explosive devices lead to innovations in the treatment of such wounds. Surgeons now routinely saw open the skulls and crania of victims to allow the brain to swell. They also cut the fascia on limb injuries to allow swelling to take place in the hope of avoiding amputation. The wounded are then stabilised and flown by chopper to Baghdad International Airport.

From Baghdad, the injured and dying are ferried by air to Ramstein Airbase in Germany in nightly shuttle flights. These nocturnal flights are essentially airborne intensive care units. The troops – young men and women – are sedated and ventilated for the relatively short flight to Germany. On arrival at Ramstein, the patients are transferred to the US Army's Regional Medical Hospital in Landstuhl, Germany. Many of the wounded are still wearing the tattered combat uniforms they had on when hit in Tikrit, Fallujah or downtown Baghdad. The medical evacuation pathway from battlefield to hospital is normally less than twenty-four hours. The survival rate for wounded is much higher than in previous wars because of the rapid transit time to a fully equipped hospital with intensive care facilities. A complicating factor of this, however, is that many, suffering from catastrophic brain injuries, survive to confront almost impossible challenges on their return to the United States.

A large cohort of the young soldiers – like Eoghan – find themselves in the bore of an MRI scanner within hours of being on foot patrol in Iraq. Of that cohort, a majority – like Eoghan – find their neuromuscular systems compromised and damaged. In a bizarre linkage to Eoghan's fate, many of the latest innovations in the treatment of neuromuscular injury are utilising the experience gained and the research data gathered at Landsthuhl. Eoghan may in time benefit directly from medical advances arising from the wars in Iraq and Afghanistan.

In February, we are called back to get the results of Eoghan's second MRI scan. The results show that the process of demyelination seems 'static' or 'stable'. There has been no change. This suggests that Eoghan's 'disease', whatever that might be, is not progressing. He may be in remission. His condition we are told, may have reached a plateau. There are no guarantees however. There is no certainty about the future. The disease may kick off again. It may yet progress. We try not to think about that prospect. We try to concentrate on the here and now. The lumbar puncture is also relatively inconclusive. The spinal fluid reveals little to indicate a precise diagnosis. The uncertainty, the doubt, is difficult to cope with. We tuck Eoghan up with his teddy bears.

Eoghan's cot with the improvised plank attached has now been replaced with a wooden bunkbed. Darach sleeps overhead. Often in the mornings we find Darach and Eoghan sleeping together, topsy-turvy in the lower bed. Darach will have climbed down during the night and snuggled in with his brother.

In March we make our way once more into Temple Street Children's Hospital. We follow the now familiar routine. The struggle to find a parking space. The rush and stress of having to feed the parking meter. The process of booking in at reception in the hospital. The queues of anxious mums and dads with their children. Some walking, some skipping, some running. Some pitifully quiet and held close by frantic parents.

Then the visit to the phlebotomy room to have blood samples taken. A lollipop after the needles. Eoghan is a little soldier. He smiles up at us throughout. He snuggles into us after each investigation.

On this day we are scheduled for a muscle biopsy. Yet again Eoghan is stripped down to his vest and nappy. The poppers on his little vest are opened. The registrar identifies a small spot on Eoghan's thigh. This will be the site where a needle biopsy will harvest a tiny piece of Eoghan's thigh muscle. We've been asked to make sure that it is at least four hours since Eoghan's last breastfeed. He is a little upset. Unsettled. The room is brightly lit. The heat amplifies the hospital smell of antiseptic fluid. The noise from the busy corridor outside is the backdrop as Eoghan is anaesthetised. Sedated. His breathing grows deeper as he goes limp in the crook of my arm.

The team move quickly, efficiently. They gently take Eoghan from me. They swab his inner thigh and mark the entry point. The needle biopsy is taken by means of a hollow metal device – not unlike a small apple corer. The registrar pushes the device into Eoghan's soft white skin. The pudgy little thigh gives way under the pressure. A small trickle of blood runs down his thigh. Scarlet against white. I find my fists are clenched. My teeth are clenched. I want to run screaming from the room. The registrar works the needle biopsy in a tight clockwise motion. She pushes further to ensure contact with the thigh muscle. Then, after what seems an age, she extracts the device.

The nurse applies pressure to the wound and dresses it. The needle biopsy is placed on a tray and taken for analysis. The biopsy will test for proteins present in the muscle which might give further clues as to Eoghan's diagnosis. It feels like another shot in the dark.

Meanwhile, my phone buzzes continuously in my pocket. When I go out into the blessed cool air outside the hospital I see that I have dozens of missed calls and text messages. Ten improvised explosive devices have been detonated on Spanish commuter trains in Madrid. I take notes on the train stations and timing of the blasts. They come just two and a half years after the 9/11 attacks. The timing and nature of IEDs, containing high explosives, detonators and timers, suggest a coordinated terror attack. The *Irish Times* ask me to provide an analysis piece on the effect of high explosives in a confined space. I write about limb separation, the pulping of internal organs, shattering of bones secondary to the blast effect. And the awful burn and blast injuries. Injuries I have seen myself – up close and personal. I predict a high death toll.

The following day it emerges that 191 commuters are dead. Almost two thousand injured. Innocent civilians from seventeen different countries.

Eoghan's thigh is sore for a while. He gives out a high shrill cry when I change his dressing. We get an appointment for another series of investigations. This time it is an electromyogram and a nerve conduction study.

We troop back into Temple Street Children's Hospital. Yet again, we go through the ritual search for a car parking space. Circling the block several times. Eventually getting a spot. Reversing in as stressed-out rush-hour drivers honk their horns and shake their fists. Check in at reception. Down to phlebotomy for more blood samples. Another lollipop after the needles.

Eoghan, with big heavy tears flowing down his baby pink cheeks. Electrodes attached to his skin as electrical current is passed in order to test conductivity levels in his peripheral nervous system.

The nerve conduction study is hell. Eoghan is held as two needles are inserted into the muscle of his arm. Sedation is not possible as it will compromise the test. Eoghan's tiny body wriggles and bucks as the needles go in. He starts to scream. A high-pitched, piercing scream. It does not sound human. He sounds like a tiny animal in distress. *In extremis.* I see his eyes screwed tightly shut with the pain. Then opening and rolling, his eyes trying to search out for Aideen and I. Searching for us. Wriggling and struggling against the grip and the pain. I feel the adrenaline course through me. The fight or flight impulse is almost unbearable. My stomach is a tight hard ball of pain.

Eventually it is over. Eoghan is drenched in sweat. We all are. We walk him up and down the corridor in our arms. His cries and sobs eventually subside.

The muscle biopsy, nerve conduction tests and electromyography are inconclusive. They confirm a neuromuscular abnormality. However, they do not provide us with a diagnosis.

Aideen and I hold each other in the dark at night. We wonder what will happen. Aideen's tummy is swollen as she reaches the final trimester of her pregnancy. We are exhausted from the investigations, the uncertainty, the interrupted sleep and the worry. We have countless sleepless nights.

On one of these sleepless nights we resolve to try and get a conclusive answer. We research muscle myopathy online. There is a muscle myopathy expert in Hammersmith Children's Hospital, London. At four in the morning we book flights to London. We contact the hospital and tell them that we are en route. Miraculously, we get an appointment with the professor.

We cradle Eoghan in our arms on the early-morning flight to London. The Aer Lingus hostess asks us if we are having a 'romantic mid-week break'. We take the Heathrow Express train-link into the city centre. We take the Tube to White City.

The professor greets us and reviews Eoghan's notes and charts. He holds Eoghan in his arms and plays with him for a while. Eventually he turns Eoghan upside down, flipping him gently over and over a few times. Eoghan's little body flexes a little each time. The Professor remarks to us that Eoghan is a 'little fighter'. You see he attempts to flex and coordinate.' He tells us that in his opinion, Eoghan's symptoms resemble those of Pelizaeus Merzbacher Disease or PMD. It is, he tells us, a rare disease of the central nervous system. Onset is usually during early infancy. 'Nystagmus' or rapid and rhythmic involuntary eye movements, are also associated with PMD. Eoghan matches many of the symptoms.

The professor tells us that many children with the disease survive into adulthood. Many have normal life expectancy. Some, however, die in early adolescence or as young adults. I only catch snatches of the prognosis. Aideen listens intently.

But at least we now have a diagnosis. We have three words to describe what has happened to our baby. Pelizaeus Merzbacher Disease or PMD.

The professor tells us that Eoghan will benefit a great deal from physiotherapy. He recommends the Peto Institute in Budapest, Hungary.

While in London, I contact the MOD to enquire about the medical treatment of British troops returning from the wars in Afghanistan and Iraq. They tell me that almost 65 percent of those wounded in action suffer traumatic brain injuries. They require MRI scanning to track and image the damage to their neuromuscular systems. Many require intensive physiotherapy to develop and maintain gross motor function. The MOD tell me in a cheery email that 'significant advances' are being made in the treatment of brain injury that will directly benefit those in the general population who are suffering from neuromuscular disorders. I have mixed emotions.

Chapter 23

White Lady

'Imagine, Dr Clonan – from that place which brings forth life,
they unleash the death.'

Dublin

2004

When we get back from London I do some online research about the Peto
Institute in Budapest. The institute was set up by András Pető as the National
Institute of Motor Therapy in the 1950s in communist-controlled Hungary.
Pető had a passion for physical rehabilitation and evolved an educational
model of intervention based on physiotherapy and learning for children with
disabilities and mobility issues. The pioneering centre combines a structured
regime of intensive physiotherapy alongside positively reinforced teaching
goals to enhance the physical mobility and function of children with neuromuscular disorders. This hybrid mix of teaching and physio is known as 'conducting' and its practitioners 'conductors'.

The Peto Institute has a website where conductors advertise for work. I
scan the list. Hungarian names. Surname first, Christian name second in the
Hungarian style. Lutaran, Zsuzsanna; Gyongosi, Dori; Weisz, Viktoria. I click
on Viktoria's profile. Reading through it I see she has worked with a family in
Ireland. I send her an email and describe Eoghan's symptoms and diagnosis.

Viktoria gets back to me in a few days. She addresses me as 'Clonan'. She
writes in a matter-of-fact manner. Blunt. I learn that this is the mode of
address used by Hungarians in general and conductors in particular. 'OK
Clonan, I will come to this Dublin and work with this boy, Eoghan.'

Viktoria will come and work with us for six weeks. She will do six to eight hours of physiotherapy and play with Eoghan each day. In return, we offer her a bed and all her meals. The conductors charge a fee of around €120 per day. We hope that in return we can sleep at night.

I am still busy with the war in Iraq. The insurgency there is claiming the lives of hundreds more US troops as the months roll by. In 2004 alone, the US and its allies will lose almost one thousand troops killed in action. Many tens of thousands more will be seriously injured. Thousands continue to suffer traumatic brain injuries and loss of limbs. All over the US and Britain, young men and women are learning how to walk and talk again. Infantilised by their injuries, they are rendered helpless and dependent. There is an enormous and growing demand for physiotherapy, occupational therapy and speech therapy for the wounded to live independently again.

The Sunni-led insurgency intensifies and the US fight urban operations in Fallujah and throughout the so-called 'Sunni Triangle' around Mosul and Tikrit. The Al Anbar province along the border with Syria becomes another flashpoint. Al Qaeda and other Sunni factions grow in strength and capability.

Meanwhile, in the central and southern districts of Iraq, Shia tensions rise. Moqtada al Sadr, described as a 'self-styled firebrand cleric' assumes a leadership role among the Shia population in parts of Baghdad and in Najaf and Kerbala. A second front seems to open up in the US occupation of Iraq. Battle lines are drawn across the country. An unanticipated outcome of the war there is the creation of a country divided – and armed by the US – along ethnic lines. The US military did a comprehensive job of destroying the Iraqi military, police and civil structures. In an attempt to rebuild Iraq on the cheap, the US arms the Kurds to the north in a de facto, semi-autonomous region.

They arm the Shia in the centre and south. The Shia, now armed for the first time since Saddam's ousting, and with assistance from Iran, begin to organise themselves and prepare for the eventual US withdrawal. The Shia are arming for the inevitable power struggle against the Sunni minority. The Sunni, for their part, are hyperactive in the insurgency. Al Qaeda is active in the country and 2004 sees the beginning of a spiral of violence which includes

Al Qaeda-inspired kidnappings and beheadings. American Nick Berg and Irish passport-holder Ken Bigley are abducted and decapitated on camera.

In a parallel development, the US military begins to arm more moderate Sunni groups along the border with Syria and Jordan in its 'Sons of Iraq' program. Iraq is wittingly or unwittingly being armed for civil war and a possible wider war in the Middle East between Iranian-backed Shia interests and Saudi and Gulf ('Gulfis') state-backed Sunni factions.

Aideen is tired. In May, I drive her to the Coombe as she holds her tummy in the car. She tells me to get moving. I drive in the bus lanes – hazards flashing. After a very short labour, Ailbhe arrives. A little girl. 'The White Lady.' A sister for Eoghan and Darach. A sister for Liadain, our little angel in heaven. Ailbhe has wisps of curly red hair on her head. They produce a hazy coreolis effect. She is the most beautiful girl in the world – my *cheri amour*.

It is a very busy household. We prepare a cot for Ailbhe in our bedroom. The spare room is set aside for Viktoria when she arrives.

Meanwhile, images of torture emerge from Abu Ghraib. Pictures of Private Lynndie England are flashed around the world. She and other reservists are photographed abusing Iraqi boys and men who are interned without charge or trial in US-run detention centres. The iconic image of the hooded prisoner goes global. It becomes a metaphor for the United States's abuse of Iraq.

I write in the *Irish Times* about allegations of the systematic abuse, including sexual abuse and rape of young Iraqi men and boys. The systematic and systemic abuse reminds me of the dysfunctional de facto system of abuse I uncovered in our own military. I know that the stories are plausible; I've seen it before.

I'm averaging about one feature per week in the *Irish Times* at this point as the Global War on Terror continues apace. It is a strange experience as a freelance contributor. I write from home mostly. In the attic, where I have improvised a little office. An old chest of drawers is my filing cabinet. It is stuffed full of reference sheets now. Items from *Jane's World Armies* or *Jane's World Aircraft* along with specification sheets for weapons systems from Boeing or Grumman. I've got an old portable TV on top of the chest of drawers so that I can monitor breaking news on Sky News and Al Jazeera. I listen to news and current affairs on the BBC and RTÉ on an old radio – a boom box I bought in the 1980s with my first paycheque as a teacher.

There are bits of paper all over the floor and on the spare bed. These are my notes. Hastily scribbled down whenever I hear something of interest. I get the *Telegraph* newspaper every day also. It is the only newspaper that faithfully lists the individual units of the British and US military involved in every engagement and operation in the ongoing war. I, in turn, make contact with the public affairs officers of each unit and quiz them about events. Often, because of the time difference, these conversations take place late at night or in the early hours of the morning while the babies sleep below. Between midnight bottle feeds and nocturnal conversations on war, I'm half dead during the daylight hours. I've barely set foot in the *Irish Times* itself. Only once, when my editor Peter Murtagh invited me into D'Olier Street to give me a tour of the newspaper offices and introduce me to the editor. Apart from that, my scribbling and writing takes place in isolation. I submit copy electronically. Miraculously, the articles appear in the *Irish Times*. I still have to pinch myself from time to time.

Ironically, simple as it may sound, I never see my TV appearances. I mostly appear live on *Ireland AM* on TV3 or on RTÉ news bulletins. I do some prerecorded pieces for *Prime Time* on RTÉ. It is odd talking straight into a camera lens and not interacting with a presenter. One night, after cycling home from DIT in the city centre, I manage to catch one of these prerecorded pieces on TV. Darach is still awake for some reason and he stares at me on the TV. 'There's daddy,' I tell him. He looks at me with his big green eyes and tells me, 'That's not you, daddy, that's a man.' I'm put firmly in my place.

In the middle of all this I get a call from Big Athena. She is now working as a general legal counsel for the War Crimes Tribunal for former Yugoslavia. She calls me on her cellphone from Prijedor. 'Hey Little Tom – guess where I am?' She is in Sofija's restaurant. Sofija's dad is still there. Sofija is in the US. 'Learning more English,' she laughs. She tells me that Toma – Big Tom – shot himself about a year ago. They found his body in the rear seat of his tiny police car. Apparently he'd stretched himself out so that his feet were between the front seats. 'One shot,' Athena tells me. 'He swallowed his own bullet.' She also tells me that a team of investigators have found a mass grave at Omarska. At more or less the same spot I visited on election day, just eight years previously. 'Imagine, Tom. They killed two thousand people in Prijedor. Men, women and children.' I think of Bojan. I cannot reconcile my memory of Bojan and Zoran – their gentle nature, their hospitality – with this knowledge.

Eoghan's nystagmus improves after a visit to an eye specialist in Temple Street. Eoghan is also acquiring language and some impressive singing skills. He loves to sing with Darach. The two of them strapped in the back of the car or rolling around on the floor together. Darach's play provides Eoghan with some natural physiotherapy until Viktoria arrives.

In August, my mysterious Russian contact calls me again. In heavily accented English he tells me to turn on Sky News. Two Russian passenger flights out of Moscow have disappeared off radar not long after take-off. Russian authorities have located the wreckage and are trying to establish the cause of two simultaneous crashes. That makes me suspicious. My caller tells me that the Russians have found traces of RDX in the wreckage. RDX (or Research Development Explosives) is a form of high explosive, a variant of Semtex or P4 – plastic explosives. 'Dimitri', as he calls himself, rings me from a withheld number and tells me that the Russians have identified a number of Chechen women on the flight lists. Two to be precise. One on each flight. They have made further enquiries.

Dimitri tells me that the women are believed to have concealed the RDX in a body cavity. He says 'vagina' to be precise. In order that there be no confusion. Apparently, the women, on their separate flights, each went into the toilet and removed the RDX from their vaginas. As soon as the seatbelt signs went off in fact. Dimitri waxes lyrical. 'Imagine, Dr Clonan – from that place which brings forth life, they unleash the death.' Indeed. The women then used the power source in their mobile phones to detonate the explosives. If detonated next to the hull of the aircraft, even a small amount of plastic explosives is enough to destroy a large aircraft in flight. Such a detonation would cause catastrophic failure of the aircraft structure.

I imagine the women queuing to board their flights. I imagine them, like the 9/11 bombers, looking around at their fellow passengers. Family groups. Business travellers. Students. People arriving. Departing. It is a depressing scenario. Dimitri tells me that the 'terrorists will pay'. I assume he means innocent Chechens. I put this to him. He grunts, 'Don't be so fucking naïve, doctor.' He relents then and tells me that we should meet up in London for a drink. 'I know some people that you should meet,' he tells me. 'You would be finding them very interesting.'

Ailbhe feeds well and unlike the boys sleeps most nights. I no longer feel dizzy all day, but nonetheless I do regularly fantasise about lying down on the floor and getting some sleep. Especially in DIT, where my office is carpeted. I reckon it would probably look bad though.

Pauline calls me in my office. 'Where are you now, Thomas?' she asks me. She sounds odd. I tell her I'm in DIT. Pauline tells me that she needs to speak to me and that it is urgent. I tell her I'll meet her in a coffee shop on Aungier Street. I make my way across the road to the coffee shop. 'Sugar and Spice.' It is run by some guys from North Africa. They greet me in Arabic. This is our routine. We have some banter. Then I see Pauline walking up the street. The sun reflected in her blonde hair. She comes into the coffee shop, hesitantly.

The proprietor, Ali, pulls out a chair for Pauline. She doesn't even see him. She has tears in her eyes. My beautiful older sister is crying. I'm wondering what has happened. She leans forward and takes my hands in hers. 'Thomas, I have cancer. Oh, Thomas, what am I going to do?' I'm trying to take in her words when she looks at me and tells me, 'Thomas, I found a lump on my breast. They biopsied it and it is cancer. Thomas. I think it could kill me.' She is distraught.

The chatter of the coffee shop continues uninterrupted. The heavens open up outside. The traffic hisses and splashes by through puddles. The coffee machine splutters and coughs hot milk into lattes and cappuccinos. What is there to say? 'You'll be OK, Pauline. You'll make it.' Pauline wipes her eyes. She takes a tissue from her handbag and dabs at the mascara that has run over her cheekbone. 'I'm sorry for crying, Thomas,' she tells me. I squeeze her hand. 'You'll be just fine,' I tell her. She looks at me with her clear blue eyes and, tears brimming once more, tells me, 'I'm not so sure.'

And so Pauline begins her journey of investigations and chemotherapy. Her husband and her two small boys are brought ever closer together in the centrifugal pull of her illness. In this maelstrom, they support and nurture each other through the pain, worry and fear. Pauline loses her hair and, like my mother, has a wig fitted. We text each other and joke about the wig. I tease her about my mum's wig which my dad has kept at home. The grandchildren delight in wearing my poor departed mother's wig around the house in macabre dress-up games. I tell Pauline that she can use mum's old wig. She texts me that she is going for 'blonde bombshell' as opposed to 'bouffant'. When we next meet, Pauline has a blonde bob. She looks great. She tells me over coffee, 'It gets very hot under here.' She tells me that her treatment is going well. We are all praying hard for her. It is difficult to imagine Pauline as 'ill'. The illness of a sibling is a very particular experience. It is different to the experience of my mum's cancer. My brain keeps telling me that it is simply impossible. Emotionally, the feeling of helplessness is sadly familiar.

Viktoria comes to Ireland to work with Eoghan. We've never met. I drive out to Dublin Airport and wait in arrivals with a cardboard sign on which I've printed 'VIKTORIA' in large block capitals. It is a nerve-wracking wait as passengers come out in single file and groups. Various nationalities. Anxious families are reunited in the arrivals hall. Grandparents hug grandchildren. The atmosphere is electric. I'm tense. I keep texting Aideen. Updating her on the arrival of someone – a complete stranger – who is going to spend so much time with little Eoghan. He's at home in his vest and nappy. Propped up behind a pillow on the couch watching videos of *Bear in the Big Blue House*. He's dribbling milk all over the couch. Oblivious to the impending arrival of Viktoria.

I'm texting away when all of a sudden someone tugs on my cardboard sign. It is Viktoria. Dressed entirely in black with the biggest suitcase I've ever seen. Even bigger than those massive suitcases I saw in the airport in Beirut, usually covered in plastic wrap, for entire families emigrating to the United States. It looks like a coffin on wheels. She sees my eyes wander over the suitcase. 'Tracksuits,' she informs me. She tells me in slightly accented but perfect

English that, 'We will be working hard, me and Eoghan.' She pronounces Eoghan as 'Oven'. She has her hands on her hips and her head is cocked sideways. I think the better of correcting her pronunciation.

I drive Viktoria through Drumcondra and across the city to Booterstown. She asks me, 'Where is the opera house?' I reply that there is, 'Ahem, err, none.' Viktoria looks at me shocked. 'No opera house?' She adds, as we cross the Liffey, 'Is this the river? A Hungarian could easily spit across this so-called river.' When we get home, Viktoria embraces Aideen as I manhandle the coffin up the stairs. It won't fit into the boxroom. I hear laughter downstairs and the clink of glasses. Viktoria begins her stay with us by producing a bottle of Unicum, a Hungarian spirit. It tastes like aftershave. Smells like disinfectant. Burns like hell as it goes down. She also produces several bottles of Hungarian red wine called 'Bull's Blood' and a shoebox containing several salted sausages. 'Clonans,' she announces in the Hungarian habit of addressing us by our surnames. 'Clonans, I hope you are not on some healthy diet nonsense, because every night for dinner we will have Unicum, wine and the sausage.'

Later that night, much later, Viktoria unpacks the behemoth and fills the boxroom with her tracksuits and dozens of books and papers. The house is now officially full to overflowing. Before she goes to sleep she knocks on the door of our room. She is theatrically winding an old-fashioned mechanical alarm clock. 'Goodnight, Clonans. Sleep well for we will have an early start for Oven.'

The next morning at around 6 AM, I hear loud clattering alarm bells from Viktoria's room. She emerges from the boxroom, muttering and cursing in Hungarian. After her shower, as we all weave around each other to take turns in the bathroom, Viktoria does some stretching on the landing. She has her foot wedged high on the banisters and is grunting and heaving as she cracks bones in her hips and her lower back. She is truly terrifying. 'Clonan,' she orders me, 'prepare Oven for the assessment.'

Viktoria and Eoghan hit it off immediately. She squats on the floor beside Eoghan, wearing a red tracksuit similar to the ones I used to see on Soviet Olympic athletes on our TV in Finglas during the 1970s – all that's missing is 'CCCP'. They eye each other up. Eoghan reaches out to touch her face, his fingers quivering with the intention tremor that is a consequence of his neuromuscular condition. His blue eyes dance with curiosity and the nystagmus which is also secondary to the disease. They hold each other in direct eye contact as Eoghan's fingers explore Viktoria's chin and lips. She pretends to bite his finger and he squeals with delight. Viktoria holds up Eoghan's favourite teddy bear and waves it over her head. He instinctively reaches for it and begins to fall over. Viktoria grips Eoghan's hips and steadies him. 'Feel it here, Oven,' she intones, and the assessment begins.

Watching Viktoria at work, I note that she is methodical and consistent in her approach. She identifies goals for Eoghan during her initial six-week stay. She will teach Eoghan to sit up and to dress and undress himself independently. The therapy is a mix of teaching and physiotherapy through play. Each set of movements required for Eoghan's physiotherapy goals are broken down into little steps. For each of these steps, Viktoria devises games that she plays with Eoghan, repeating the movements until he does them unconsciously himself. The process is carefully considered and plotted. Each step of the way is punctuated by little rewards and constant positive reinforcement. Eoghan flourishes. Viktoria and Eoghan form a very strong bond over the days and weeks. She no longer calls him 'Oven' but 'Pumpkin'. 'Come here my little pumpkin.' To the casual observer, they seem to be immersed in a world of imagination and play. Rolling around on the floor, crawling up and down the stairs or stretching out and reaching for bubbles that Viktoria blows across the grass in the back garden.

After two weeks, Viktoria meets me in the hallway as I'm coming in from work. 'OK, Clonan, watch this.' She claps her hands. 'Oven, get dressed.' Eoghan is sitting on the floor in the living room in his nappy. He looks up at me and as I watch, he pulls his white cotton vest over his head and wriggles into it. He pokes his fat little arms out through the sleeves. His curly golden hair pops out of the neck and he smiles up at me triumphantly. Viktoria claps her hands again and Eoghan rolls over sideways. As Viktoria encourages and cajoles him in a mixture of English and Hungarian, Eoghan manages to pull a little pair of shorts over his nappy. It is indescribable. Aideen comes up behind me and puts her hand on my shoulder. She has already witnessed the miracle.

For the first time in a long time, I no longer feel afraid. Fear is being replaced by hope. Viktoria looks up, her face flushed. 'Unicum, Clonans – let's have a drink, huh?'

Chapter 24

Beslan

'My name is Nick Berg. My father's name is Michael. My mother's name is Susan. I have a brother and sister, David and Sarah.'

Dublin

2004

As the weeks roll by, Viktoria and Eoghan continue to bond. Eoghan gains gross and fine motor function through hours of one-on-one play and physiotherapy. Viktoria becomes a part of the family and we learn how to curse and swear in Hungarian. Eoghan learns to be more and more independent. The conducting complements the physiotherapy and occupational therapy that Eoghan is receiving in the CRC. Eoghan gets the physical, psychological and emotional benefit of Viktoria's single-minded and complete love and attention. We sleep at night.

On 1 September 2004, we get confirmation from our local primary school, St Mary's, that they will guarantee Eoghan a place in September 2006. They also tell us that they are confident that they will be able to get a special needs assistant for Eoghan so that he can attend mainstream school. We are over the moon with the news. Eoghan will go to school with all of the other little boys in our community. We want him to be a fully participating citizen in this republic. We want him to realise his fullest potential and make his contribution to our society. We bring Eoghan to the school in his special buggy to show him the playground. Eoghan clenches his little fists in excitement.

Viktoria is a news junkie. Whenever she is not working with Eoghan, she is glued to Sky or Euro News. When we get back to the house after Eoghan's visit to St Mary's, Viktoria calls me to the sitting room. She is distraught. 'Clonan, look at this.' Sky is covering a breaking story about a school in a small town in North Ossetia, in Russia, just 30km from the regional capital Vladikavkaz. School Number One, Beslan. A large group of armed men and women – over thirty in all – have stormed Beslan's school on its celebratory opening day of term. The building is crammed with over a thousand proud parents and children celebrating the first day of the school year. Over eight hundred are taken hostage by the armed group.

Viktoria puts her hand over her mouth and rocks to and fro as footage of regional police and part-time soldiers is shown live from the scene. To me it looks like chaos. There is no cordon around the school. The camera crews are too close. All hell seems to have broken loose. There are armed civilians milling around in front of the school among groups of soldiers and police. Nobody seems to be in charge. I see a local paramilitary police unit standing around the periphery of the action. The letters OMON are clearly visible on their rag-tag uniforms. OMON or Otryad Militsii Osobogo Naznacheniya is an infamous regional police unit found throughout the former Soviet Union and its satellite states. They are notorious for their incompetence, brutality and indiscriminate use of force. I hear the television news presenter refer to them as 'Russian Special Forces sent to end the siege.' I cannot believe my ears. They confidently predict an end to the siege as soon as the 'special forces' are in position. I know instinctively that the situation will end badly and that, like the Moscow theatre siege, the casualty figures will be enormous.

OMON were previously involved in the tragic Budennovsk Hospital siege of June 1995. In that incident, Chechen separatists led by Shamil Basayev stormed the hospital in Budyonnovsk in much the same way that the Beslan school has been taken. In a shambolic response, a nadir for Russian security forces, Yeltsin ordered three separate assaults on the building. Hundreds of hostages were killed and the Chechens escaped. As I watch the chaos unfold on TV, I can see only one outcome to this disaster.

My phone starts ringing. The *Irish Times* ask me for analysis of the evolving situation. As I head up to my attic office to work up the feature, I know that my predictions will be dire. I cast aside happy thoughts of Eoghan's first day at school and focus on another school and other children thousands of miles away in Ossetia.

The siege ends just forty-eight hours later with over three hundred dead and almost eight hundred seriously injured. The Islamist hostage takers show no inhibitions in the taking of life. Most of the dead are innocent children. I'm in RTÉ doing live radio on *Today with Pat Kenny* when the siege comes to its bloody conclusion. We watch the distressing scenes on the TV monitor in studio as semi-naked and exhausted children, many covered in blood, run and stagger from the school. The footage is almost unbearable. I feel my stomach turn somersaults as I give a live estimate of the situation. I couch it in remote military language. I slip into the patois and vernacular of the army. I hear myself using terms such as 'maximum exploitation of firepower' as the militia try to 'exploit an entry point or foothold' within the school. I talk about the effects of high explosives on the children – many of whom were organised into sibling groups by the hijackers. Involuntarily, images of sibling groups I had seen slaughtered in Lebanon spring to mind. I feel a cold sweat. I feel nauseous. I keep going. And then it's over. The broadcasting assistant holds open the door and I tiptoe out of studio. The next item is a book review. The producer looks at me as I go past. She tells me to go upstairs and get a coffee. I appreciate the kindness.

Viktoria flies home a couple of weeks later. Before she goes, we plan another six-week block of therapy for Eoghan in September. She kisses baby Ailbhe, squeezes 'Oven' and shakes hands formally with Darach. The house returns to something approaching normality.

The wars in Iraq and Afghanistan grind on. Iraq shows no sign of stabilising and the insurgency gains momentum. I write several analysis pieces for the *Irish Times* that are increasingly pessimistic about the long-term prospects for success of the US military strategy there. In 2004, in Iraq alone, over nine hundred coalition troops are killed in action. Thousands more are seriously injured and require medical evacuation to the United States and Britain. All the while, hundreds of thousands more young men and women are funnelled through Shannon Airport on their way to the battlefield. As this huge army of invasion moves through Ireland on its way to the death, destruction and mayhem that is Iraq and Afghanistan, many Irish people seem oblivious. With the Celtic Tiger roaring, many journalists and commentators are fixated on rising property prices and our 'boom'.

The violence in Iraq takes a very disturbing turn in 2004. In May, Nick Berg, a US citizen working in Iraq, is abducted by a group with links to an Islamist extremist organisation called Muntada al Munsar. Berg, who is Jewish, is subsequently executed by the group. His execution is filmed. The digital recording is posted on the internet and delivered to a number of media outlets in Iraq and the Middle East. I am doing physiotherapy exercises and stretches with Eoghan when my mobile rings. A colleague and friend who is the security editor of a rival newspaper tells me that he has something I should take a look at. He tells me that he has a copy of the execution and decapitation video of Nick Berg and wonders if I would take a look at it to see what I think.

I go up to the attic and fire up the computer. I check through my inbox and open the email and attachment. I double click on the short video and there is Nick Berg. He is sitting on the floor of a room somewhere in Iraq, facing the camera. He is wearing an orange jumpsuit – similar to the ones worn by prisoners in the US detention facility at Guantanamo Bay. Berg appears to be sedated or drugged in some way. Behind him are five armed and masked men who read a statement condemning the US invasion of Iraq. Berg is permitted to speak. If the video is genuine, his final words are deeply upsetting. He confirms his identity. 'My name is Nick Berg. My father's name is Michael. My mother's name is Susan. I have a brother and sister, David and Sarah.' I think of Berg's family in the US. Their suffering is unimaginable.

The beheading itself is particularly gruesome. Most decapitations involve cutting the victim's throat from the front. Most ritual killings of this kind are similar to the manner in which cattle are slaughtered according to Halal rites. The carotid arteries are severed and the victim loses consciousness almost immediately. It is a relatively painless, though incredibly traumatic, way to die. In Berg's case, however, the masked men hold him roughly, pinning him to the floor face down. In a particularly cowardly and barbaric act, one of the men produces a knife and appears to assault Berg from behind. In the unfolding film, the perpetrator appears to saw at the base of Berg's neck. Berg's high-pitched screams become more and more frantic. The appalling images are the very distillation of evil and hatred.

I believe that the footage sends a message to Islamist audiences that might not be picked up by western viewers. The manner of his execution is deliberately inhumane. By hacking at his neck, the perpetrators must saw through the knuckle bone at its base, severing head from spine before severing the carotid arteries in the throat. This method of decapitation causes more pain and distress to the victim. It also sends a clear signal to an Islamist audience – familiar with Halal slaughter rituals – that the victim is considered subhuman. It is sub-bestial. Berg is given a death that you would not give to a dog.

There are aspects to the video that give me pause for thought with regard to its authenticity. Berg is remarkably still in the film. Moving only occasionally. But his voice is clear. I feel he may have been sedated by Muntada al Munsar in order to facilitate the filming of the murder. The sedation perhaps makes him more compliant with his kidnappers and he does not struggle or resist. In the most cynical and heartbreaking of interpretations, I conclude that he has been sedated to stay on camera throughout the entire appalling episode. The result is a powerful terror tool for Islamist resistance groups in Iraq. From a propaganda perspective, however, I feel it will ultimately backfire on Muntada al Munsar, as it shows all too clearly the reprehensible and unjustifiable actions of Islamist groups such as Al Qaeda. I am confident that it will inevitably undermine whatever peripheral support for such groups that exists among ordinary Muslims.

I write about the killing in the *Irish Times*. I am deeply shocked by the images and am haunted by them. I wish now that I hadn't viewed the video, as it has resurrected other memories. On my way to the crèche to collect Darach and Ailbhe, I feel sickened by what I have seen. I wonder at the world they are growing up in – where violence begets violence. I think that with Nick Berg's murder, the war in Iraq has reached a nadir. But things continue to deteriorate.

In June, a US helicopter engineer, Paul Marshall Johnson, is abducted and beheaded near Riyadh in Saudi Arabia. His grisly execution is filmed and posted on the internet. Just days later, on 22 June, a south Korean citizen, Kim

Sun-il, is also beheaded on camera. During Viktoria's visit in September, insurgents decapitate more US hostages. Eugene Armstrong is executed on 20 September. The following day, his fellow prisoner and hostage, Jack Hensley, is beheaded on film. Both clips are released to the international media for maximum terror effect. The killings are an obscenity. They take place in the context of growing savagery within Iraq – a descent into violence and abuse that is killing hundreds of thousands of innocent Iraqi men, women and children. The spiral of violence will eventually kill millions of innocent civilians – direct and indirect casualties of the Global War on Terror.

In October, insurgents murder Ken Bigley, an English citizen and civil engineer from Liverpool. His abduction and captivity have generated much media interest. For in addition to filming the execution of victims, Islamist groups – in this case the so-called Sunni Muslim Tawhid and Jihad in Iraq – are now releasing footage of their victims pleading for their lives. The images of Bigley begging for his life and pleading for UK Prime Minister, Tony Blair's direct intervention in his case are heartbreaking and carry with them a powerful terror effect. As propaganda tools, however, the films ultimately contain within them the seeds for the erosion of any support for such groups by right-minded people, irrespective of religious or political beliefs.

Bigley's family undertake herculean efforts to save his life. His brother secures condemnations of his abduction and demands for his release from the Palestinian leader Yasser Arafat and Libyan President Colonel Gadaffi, among others. As Bigley's elderly mother, Lil, is Dublin-born, it emerges that he is entitled to Irish citizenship. The Irish government move with alacrity and issue him with an Irish passport *in absentia*. The Irish government join the international chorus of appeals for his release on the basis of his Irish nationality – and Ireland's self-declared non-involvement in the Global War on Terror.

Ultimately, these pleas fall on deaf ears and Bigley is executed on 7 October. Like the other cases, I write about the execution in the *Irish Times* and provide comment and analysis on TV and radio. My distant analysis no doubt sounds remote, clinical, unfeeling. I find the whole exercise profoundly disturbing and dispiriting.

Within two weeks, another criminal group in Iraq abduct Irishwoman Margaret Hassan. Originally from Ireland, Margaret is a long-time resident of Iraq. She is abducted in broad daylight by an armed gang. They seem highly organised. I provide written analysis of the events for the *Irish Times*. Given that her abduction occurs hard on the heels of the other killings, I am pessimistic about Margaret's chances of survival.

A contact sends me the full-length version of a film of Margaret Hassan pleading for her life. In a now sickeningly familiar pattern, the footage has been released to media outlets internationally. I slip up to the attic and watch the images. The sound quality on the film is poor and I strain to hear the audio over the domestic sounds of my own family filtering up through the house below. What strikes me about Margaret is her soft voice. The kindness and intelligence in her beautiful face. The familiar Irish accent is shocking in the context of the film. The fear on her face is terrifying to behold. She had been abducted on her way to work in the CARE organisation – a non-governmental organisation that sought to assist ordinary Iraqi citizens by providing them with much-needed medical care and other services. Margaret's hair and make-up are still relatively unruffled in this first video. I think of Margaret getting ready for work that morning; doing her hair and putting on her face. The situation that her captors have placed her in is unthinkable. It is unwarranted and unjustifiable.

The Irish government make strenuous efforts to have Margaret released. The Department of Foreign Affairs leave no stone unturned in their efforts to rescue her. Senior gardaí and members of the Irish army's Ranger Wing become involved. To no avail. Margaret is eventually murdered on or around 2 November. She is not decapitated, however. Apparently she is executed with a pistol shot to the head. Her killing is another expression of evil in a country plunged into chaos by the allied invasion, and where human life has become cheap, if not worthless.

I meet Pauline in early December. She looks tired, pale, drawn. She tells me that she is responding well to her treatment. She is looking forward to Christmas.

There is great excitement in the house as Christmas approaches. In an act of defiance, I put up the decorations at the end of November. I put lights up on the big conifer in the front garden. I've always loved this time of the year. The darkest month, the shortest day – the end of winter relieved by bright lights and feasting. I trust in the wisdom of our celtic forebears who celebrated the winter solstice with abandon. The kids are very excited. They want Lego and train sets. It will be Ailbhe's first Christmas. After two boys, it is a curious novelty to walk through the pink aisles in the toy shops.

I visit my dad on Christmas Day. The kids run around the house. Wrecking the place. He is oblivious. His second Christmas without my mum. He is sitting on the couch, in his usual spot, smoking furiously, when I notice a copy of the *Irish Times* on the chair beside him. I have an article in the copy he has kept beside him. Some end of year round-up of the military situation in Iraq. I ask him if he has read it. He looks at the paper quizzically and then looks at me. He puts down his cigarette and narrows his eyes, focusing on me directly. I have his fullest attention it seems. 'Let me tell you something straight, Thomas, I don't buy that newspaper for any of the bullshit that you might write in it. The only reason I get the *Irish Times* is because of the television listings.' He picks up the paper and shakes it in my direction. A cloud of ash falls off it, adding to the haze of smoke around him. I think he is in bad form. 'Look, a whole week of television listings here. Never mind your stuff.' I look at him appraisingly. My dad. Sitting there on the couch, all skin and bone. He looks a bit like Steptoe, from the BBC series *Steptoe and Son*. He is as ornery for sure. More ornery than usual. Probably lonely.

When we get home, Aideen puts her hand on my shoulder once more. 'Don't mind him. He's just upset.' Later, when the kids are in bed, exhausted and sleeping, myself and Aideen open a bottle of wine and turn on the TV. And there it is. A *Steptoe and Son* Christmas special. It gives us both a laugh.

Chapter 25

Court Case

'I hope you've a good fucking solicitor.'

January 2005

After Christmas, the Asian tsunami hits the low-lying coastal regions of India, Indonesia, Malaysia, Thailand, Sri Lanka, Thailand and Myanmar. As we sleep on St Stephen's night, the Sumatra Andaman earthquake erupts in the Indian Ocean. The subsequent wave surges kill over a quarter of a million people. The apocalypse is given saturation coverage. There is demand for disaster response and emergency preparedness analysis. Many of the rapid responders are military. The US launches Operation Unified Assistance to help the victims.

US Aircraft Carrier Strike Group Nine is dispatched to the area to render assistance and relief. Led by the aircraft carrier *Abraham Lincoln*, the US presses forty-eight military helicopters into action to support the victims of the tsunami. Within ten days there are twenty-four US navy ships in the affected region. Each ship provides almost 100,000 gallons of fresh drinking water to the stricken population per day.

It is a welcome relief to write and comment on the resupply, evacuation and search and rescue capabilities of Sea Horse and Blackhawk helicopters as opposed to describing their offensive characteristics. I can skip over the weapon systems and concentrate on payload and precious human cargo. I find it therapeutic to comment in this way. I'm beginning to realise how toxic and corrosive the running commentary on global war has become. The international rescue effort restores some faith in humanity.

In February we hold graduation ceremonies in DIT. They are held in St Patrick's Cathedral in Christchurch, not far from our Aungier Street campus. The ancient limestone church, over eight hundred years old, is a perfect venue for graduations. It is both dignified and atmospheric. The gloomy gothic interior is illuminated by spectacular stained-glass windows. The atmosphere is heightened by flying buttresses overhead and soaring stone arches. The nave and transepts are filled with historical burial plates, brass plaques, military flags and inscriptions of all sorts. I'm wandering around, idly exploring the various nooks and crannies as the parents and extended families of the graduates slowly fill up the space. It is always a joyful and moving occasion for families and friends. A milestone of celebration, achievement and completion. There is an excited cacophony of laughter, chatter and conversation inside the church. The noise is amplified by the stone walls, echoing and reverberating, the volume rising and falling.

One of my DIT colleagues interrupts me from my reverie and nods her head towards the side entrance. The ceremony is about to begin. Time to join the academic procession. I'm wearing my academic gown from DCU. A red and yellow cape. All part of the spectacle. I join my similarly robed academic colleagues and we get in line for our march up the centre of the cathedral.

As we make our way up the aisle, the cathedral falls silent. A small chamber orchestra from DIT's Conservatory of Music performs a suite of classical music. The atmosphere intensifies. We take our seats at the head of the nave. The president of DIT takes to the pulpit, or rather a lectern, at the edge of the central altar. He welcomes the families into the cathedral and invites the students to stand and give their parents, families and significant others a round of applause for all of the support they have given them over the years. I look back at all of the happy faces. Filled with expectation, optimism, hope.

Silence descends again and the president calls the graduates forward. 'I now call upon the Bachelor of Arts in Journalism, class of 2004, to come forward and receive their degrees.' I hear a shuffling from the seats behind me as the stewards and ushers direct the graduating students towards the podium to receive their parchments. They proceed up the central aisle in single file. I turn to look at them. They are almost all young women. They are all dressed up for this special day. Full make-up. Hair done. I can smell a wave of perfume as they approach. Parents among the pews stand up and take flash photographs of their loved ones. That's when it hits me.

Out of left field, I think of little Liadain. My own little girl. My own precious one. The thought comes unbidden. Unexpectedly. I realise in that moment what Aideen and I have lost. Our little girl, who would be almost two years old now, had she survived, will never graduate. I will never get to see her walk, talk or achieve all of those sacred milestones that we as parents might have shared with her.

I look at the young women as they teeter up to the podium on their high heels. Turning around, smiling at family members. A deep grieving fills me. A terrible sadness. I want to get up and leave. It is all I can do not to stand up and make straight for the nearest exit. I am determined to retain control. I bite my lip. I try to suppress thoughts of Liadain.

In May, we celebrate Ailbhe's first birthday. She is a little bundle of energy with red curls. Despite her size, she rules the roost. She crawls, stands and walks before her first birthday. She is a fiery, determined little spirit. My solicitor calls me and tells me that we finally have a court date for my libel action against the Minister for Defence and the Attorney General. The case is scheduled for hearing in the circuit civil court at the end of the month. He tells me not to worry about it. All will be well.

I had almost forgotten about the court case. The wheels of justice grind slowly in Ireland and it has taken almost four years for the action to be heard. I tell my Dad about the upcoming case. He looks at me with his beady eyes. He's having another bad day. 'I hope you've a good fucking solicitor,' is his only comment.

In an incident reminiscent of the bad old days, I get a phone call from one of my former colleagues on the Friday before the court case. He calls me on my mobile. I get so many calls from journalists and contacts, I don't give it a second thought and answer the call. The voice on the other end is hostile. There are no pleasantries or greetings. There is no 'How are you?' or 'How is your family?' Instead, the voice on the other end – which I instantly recognise, and which makes my blood run cold – gets straight down to business.

'Are you still going to go through with this fucking court case?' I reply wearily that I have no choice. My caller interrupts me. 'Get a fucking hold of yourself, Clonan. You've subpoenaed soldiers for this case. Good men with families and careers and reputations. Are you really going to drag them through this fucking thing?'

I put it to my caller that I too have a family and a career and a reputation to protect. He snorts at the other end. 'Don't hide behind your family, Clonan. Don't hide behind your wife and kids and that fucking handicapped son of yours.' I cannot think straight now. My head begins to pound. Ridiculous as it might sound, all I can think of to say is, 'That is reprehensible.' He replies instantly. He is faster on his feet than I am. 'Never mind reprehensible, you'd better make sure your solicitor is on form next week. Because you are for the high jump, Clonan. You're fucked.' He terminates the call and I sit in the car perspiring. My heart is pounding. Fear. Rage. The anger rising within me makes me feel sick to the core. It takes a long time to fully recover and continue my journey home.

On the day of the court case, Aideen and I meet my solicitor in his offices on Arran Quay. We assemble for the hearing outside the designated courtroom. Solicitors, barristers and clients mill about. My senior counsel is waiting outside. He smiles when he sees me. He shakes my hand and reassures me that all will be well. He tells me not to be nervous and to tell the truth. That's all I have to do. Tell the truth.

I'm waiting with Aideen for proceedings to begin. We wait at the periphery of the proceedings as stenographers, clerks and legal people take their seats. Everyone seems to know exactly where to go except us. I feel a hand on my elbow. My older brother has arrived to give me moral support. It is good to see him there. He has brought my dad. He is outside having a last cigarette before proceedings begin. He shuffles in. My dad has come along to 'see what happens'. He is stick-thin. His movements are slow and unsure. Things start happening in the courtroom.

The state is corralling its witnesses on the other side of the room. I see about six or seven guys in uniform including my former friend and colleague – the one who had called to my house to interview me for his dissertation a few summers previously. My dad spies him and shuffles forward to shake hands with him. Like me, he mistakenly thinks that he is there to support me. My dad shakes hands with him. He knows him as my friend. He knows his mum. It is the most natural thing in the world for my father to greet him. My dad still hasn't grasped the fact that my former friend is not in court in a friendly capacity, and tries to make conversation with him. My brother sees the scenario unfold and moves discreetly towards my dad and diverts him away. For me it is a sad little vignette. My dad appears a little confused. I think he's going to shake hands with all of the army guys. Some of them look away, embarrassed. My brother gently ushers my dad away from them and leads him over to a seat in the courtroom.

The judge enters the court and the case is on. I'm cross-examined by my own senior counsel. Under questioning, I tell the story of my PhD. I tell the story of the manner in which I received written permission from the military authorities to pursue the doctoral research in the Defence Forces and the manner in which I conducted the investigation. I also outline the unexpected findings that I uncovered in relation to the bullying, harassment, sexual assault and alleged attempted rape of women in the Defence Forces. My senior counsel then leads me through questions about the aftermath of the research and the manner in which I was instructed by the chief of staff to lodge the doctoral thesis to the library in DCU.

I go through the entire sorry narrative. It feels good to tell the truth. To know that now, at last, the truth of what happened is out. It is an unnerving experience, but I feel that in some respects it is like an exorcism. I address the court about the manner in which the findings of my research were published in the national press by journalists and the manner in which the military authorities behaved towards me afterwards. I detail the abuse, the vitriol and the isolation I experienced. I also outline the threats I received. I recall the conversation in which I was told that 'every dirty trick in the book' would be used against me. I recall being told that I had started a 'war', a 'dirty war', and that 'guerrilla' tactics would follow.

My senior counsel then brings me to the matter of the briefing document, which was leaked to a number of journalists in October 2001. Under oath, I rebut all of the claims made within the document about me. Including those that suggested I had 'concealed' my research activities from the military authorities or that I had engaged in a 'planned and 'assisted' effort to embarrass the army. The judge makes no comment during the proceedings. She listens to me carefully throughout and fixes me with full eye contact at all times. I feel that I am being heard. I feel that I am being listened to.

The court adjourns for lunch and I go for a coffee with Aideen. We are silent. It has been very stressful and traumatic for us both to go back over the events in question. We feel emotionally drained. We are also worried about the costs involved. We are just a couple with a young family. Our resources are limited. We do not have the support of any organisation or advocacy group. We are on our own. The military authorities, on the other hand, have access to the full resources of the state. Financial costs are not a concern for them. As is usual with libel cases in Ireland, we are acutely aware that if we lose the action, we will be personally liable for all of our own costs and all of the costs incurred by the state. It is a David and Goliath situation. If we lose this case after three or four days in court, we could be looking at a debt of hundreds of thousands of euro. It is a sobering and terrifying prospect. Aideen smiles at me. 'We are doing the right thing.' We hold hands and walk across the cobbles of Smithfield and back into court.

We meet our solicitor on the way into the courtroom. He tells me that, despite my evidence that morning, the state is tight-lipped and do not appear interested in a settlement. We had hoped that the state might settle on the day of the court case and offer some sort of apology. But that does not seem to be in prospect. The army seem keen to fight me in court. This appears to be a fight to the bitter end. The consequences for myself and Aideen – if we lose – are potentially disastrous.

When the court reconvenes I am cross-examined by the state's senior counsel. It's extremely trying to go over the evidence that I have given that morning. I feel anxious during the cross-examination. It is hostile. It is repetitive. As the end of the day approaches, at around 3.30 in the afternoon, the state's senior counsel sighs and announces to the court that he wishes to introduce into evidence a tape recording that was made of myself. The recording was not included in discovery to us. The state, it seems, has pulled a rabbit out of a hat. My senior counsel objects and describes the tactic as 'underhand'. Dirty tricks indeed.

There are some exchanges between my legal team and the judge. We seek an adjournment so that we can listen to the audio tape. My mind is reeling as I consider what might be on this recording. We have had no prior knowledge or warning that something like this would be introduced into proceedings. The words from the threatening phone call I had received the previous Friday are ringing in my ears, 'You are for the high jump, Clonan. You're fucked.'

The judge grants us an adjournment to listen to the tape. It turns out that the tape in question is simply a recording of the research interview I had given my former friend on the day he called to my home.

My solicitor and senior counsel advise me that the state wish to rely on a paragraph in the recording in which I am heard to comment that the military authorities have 'serious questions' to answer in relation to the treatment of female personnel. The comment was made by me in answer to a conversational question put to me by my former friend in relation to the status of my own research.

In truth, I am relieved. There is nothing sinister on the recording. Just standard research questions and answers followed by some casual conversation. In fact, the introduction of the tape results in a positive outcome for us. My legal team inform me that the state has taken advantage of the adjournment to approach us with a view to a settlement. In the small briefing room where we had adjourned to listen to the tape, my legal team advise myself and Aideen that we've done our utmost to tell the truth. We have 'fought the good fight'. Our resources, however, are finite.

My solicitor advises me that if we continue the case for two or three more days, it could, potentially, be unsustainably costly for us in the event of losing. We think about it long and hard. We are contemplating the wager of tens, perhaps hundreds of thousands of euro on the outcome of the case. In the worst case scenario, we would have to sell our family home to meet the costs of losing. We agonise over the decision. During our deliberations, the state offers to make a contribution to our costs in taking the case. It is a modest amount of money. A four-figure sum. My solicitor reassures us that to settle the case is not to lose. 'It's a draw,' he tells us. We shake hands and agree to settle with the state. Having witnessed the state's 'underhand' tactics, myself and Aideen feel that settling the case is the right thing to do.

After the adjournment, the lawyers inform the judge that the matter has been settled. She expresses satisfaction that the matter has been settled amicably. She smiles at myself and Aideen as we leave the courtroom.

The following day there is some newspaper coverage of the case. One report states that the case was 'dropped'. We know, however, that the case was not dropped. It was settled.

We try as best we can to put the court case behind us. It has trawled up some of the deeply unpleasant experiences that we had been through around the time of the publication of the research. Experiences, it unfortunately transpires, that are common to most whistleblowers in Ireland. Experiences that are described in the growing international research on the phenomenon of whistleblowing as 'whistleblower reprisal'. In the days that follow the case, I have time to reflect on the behaviour of my former colleagues and 'friends' in and out of court. Their strategy was described by my senior counsel on the day as 'underhand'. Underhand seems apt.

Chapter 26

GTMO

'Because, I'm an asshole.'

Dublin

June 2005

I'm cycling into DIT when I meet a solicitor friend, a fellow cyclist, at the traffic lights on Baggot Street. He congratulates me on the court case. 'Libel cases can be difficult to settle,' he tells me as the lights go green. 'The state could have bogged you down for days and days. Expensive business.' I'm beginning to realise we had a very lucky escape. I draw a line under the experience. Any curiosity I have ever had about the inside of a courtroom has been more than satisfied.

I throw myself into work. As the war in Iraq continues with shocking loss of life on all sides, there is mounting concern in Ireland about the use of Shannon as a virtual air base and logistics stopover for the US military. By June 2005, just two years after the invasion of Iraq, almost half a million US troops have transited through Shannon on their way to Operation Iraqi Freedom and Operation Enduring Freedom in Afghanistan. There is a growing awareness on the part of the Irish public as to the significance of Shannon in the US war effort.

Groups such as CND and the Irish Peace and Neutrality Alliance (PANA) protest and write regularly in the national press about their concerns. These groups argue that the use of Shannon by such troops is a violation of our neutrality and neutral status. The government deny that the US troops are armed. On the contrary, Bertie Ahern's Fianna Fáil-led government argue that the troops are passing through Shannon in civilian charter aircraft and that the airlines in question are paying full landing fees and navigation costs to the Irish exchequer. One junior minister in Ahern's government describes the transit of US troops as 'good for business'.

The Irish anti-war movement focuses on US planes on the ground at Shannon. They methodically log aircraft landing and taking off from the regional airport. They diligently record the numbers of troops passing through Shannon and keep the issue high on the news agenda. Two years previously, in February 2003, a number of protestors managed to successfully get through the security fence at Shannon and damage a US Navy C-40A Clipper logistics plane. The protestors seriously damaged the militarised Boeing 737 with hammers and metal bolt cutters. They justified their actions on the basis of Section 6(2) of the 1991 Criminal Damage Act, and argued in court that they had a lawful excuse to 'damage . . . the property in question . . . in order to protect himself or another or property belonging to himself or another . . . and the act or acts alleged to constitute the offence were reasonable in the circumstances as he believed them to be.' In other words, the protestors argued that they damaged the aircraft in order to protect the lives of innocent Iraqi civilians. Their defence was accepted in court and they were unanimously acquitted of any offences by a Dublin jury.

The focus of the anti-war movement on aircraft, on the ground, at Shannon is heightened yet again in June of 2005 in the run-up to the Salthill Air Show. The organisers of the show are featuring a US UH 60 Blackhawk helicopter and an RAF Tornado fighter jet. These aircraft are in use in Afghanistan and Iraq and their inclusion in the air show causes a furore among protestors.

I do a little background research and discover that, in fact, there is another, possibly more serious issue at play with regard to US military aircraft in Irish airspace. On 25 June, I write an analysis piece in the *Irish Times* that shows that the Irish taxpayer is paying up to €10,000 per day for the en-route navigation costs and air traffic control management of thousands of US high-altitude bombers, refuelling aircraft and other airborne weapon systems travelling through Irish airspace. In other words, the Irish taxpayer is making a direct financial contribution to the wars in Iraq and Afghanistan. Under a European Union agreement, 'Eurocontrol,' to which Ireland is a signatory, the Irish government has agreed to pay the navigation fees and air traffic control levies for US military aircraft passing through our airspace. Since 75 percent of all European-US air traffic passes through Irish airspace, this presents the Irish taxpayer with a significant bill. Figures obtained from the Irish Aviation Authority reveal that in 2004 alone, €3.6 million in navigation fees for US military aircraft heading to or from the battle space in Iraq and Afghanistan had been charged to the Department of Finance.

I write in my article that protestors should not focus only on aircraft on the ground at Shannon, but that they should also look up towards the equally significant events occurring at higher altitudes.

When the article is published I get an immediate and strong response. The first is from elements in the anti-war movement who assume that because I was in the army and because I write about defence and security in the *Irish Times*, I condone the high-altitude flights. They do not seem to be able to distinguish between description and advocacy. They shoot the messenger. I get angry emails and texts from some high-profile individuals within the movement who accuse me of being a 'military moron' and a 'cheerleader' for the wars in Iraq and Afghanistan.

I also get an angry phone call from my current contact in the US Embassy. X calls me and tells me that my article is a 'disgrace' and that I have 'misled' the Irish public on the facts about the use of Irish airspace by US military aircraft. I tell X to point out precisely the inaccuracies in the piece and that I'll happily rectify them if required. I also encourage him to write to the *Irish Times* to outline his concerns. X laughs it off. 'We need to meet for an exchange of views.' I tell him I'm available straightaway and we meet in Roly's Bistro, directly opposite the US Embassy.

X arrives at Roly's. Whilst we've dealt with each other over the phone and by email, we've never met face to face before. X is well known by the waiters and we are shown to a discreet table in the corner on the ground floor. He sits opposite me and places his elbows on the starched white tablecloth. He clasps his fingers together and exhales. 'Tom. You are an asshole.' He looks at me directly then and we both laugh. We have what can only be described as a lively discussion which ranges over the rights and wrongs of the Global War on Terror, freedom of the press and Irish neutrality.

As has been the case with all of my previous interactions with the US Embassy, staff in Dublin and elsewhere, I am struck by their willingness to engage in candid discussion and lively argument. I am also struck by their ideological commitment to US foreign policy and their passionate defence of US initiatives; good, bad or indifferent. I also note the amount of disclosure that US officials are prepared to offer. Without exception, I find them at ease with off-the-record briefing and more than willing and confident to go on the record when requested. Crucially, they are all capable of agreeing to disagree and all, without exception, have a healthy sense of humour. They are intellectually curious about Ireland and very well briefed on Irish attitudes and cultural orientation. In fact, they are the very opposite of the stereotyped caricatures of US citizens that feature in most Irish media platforms, which typically characterise Americans as insular, dogmatic and almost completely ignorant of cultures outside of the continental United States. The US public servants that I have come in contact with are cosmopolitan, passionate about their work and very well briefed.

X and I continue our argument well into the late afternoon. X tells me that he still disagrees with what I might consider 'newsworthy' but that we all have to 'live and let live'. I'm assuming he still thinks I'm an asshole.

As we put on our coats and head back out into the bright June sunshine, X asks me if I'd be interested in learning more about the Global War on Terror. 'Do you wanna go down-range?' he asks me. This is US-speak for a trip to Iraq or Afghanistan. To be honest, I'm not interested in a dog and pony show in Iraq or Afghanistan as an embedded journalist. As a professional soldier and as a military press officer, I've seen that, done that and worn the T-shirt. I ask him if I could go to Guantanamo Bay. To see the prison. He looks at me and tells me to leave it with him. 'Why did you have to pick the most controversial goddamn thing?' he asks me. 'Because, I'm an asshole,' I reply.

The following day, I get a text from X. 'Pack your bags, Tom. You're going to GTMO.' GTMO is the US military abbreviation for Guantanamo Bay, Cuba.

The trip to GTMO will last approximately one week and I'm scheduled to travel in early October. I pitch the idea to Peter Murtagh in the *Irish Times*. He is enthusiastic. GTMO is a huge story, particularly after the highlighted abuses of Iraqi and Afghan prisoners in Abu Ghraib in Iraq and Bagram Airbase in Afghanistan. There is also growing controversy over news that prisoners in GTMO have gone on hunger strike. News of coordinated hunger strikes among the prisoners in GTMO is strongly denied by the US authorities. I note that the US authorities do not use the term 'prisoners' and elect to use the word 'detainees' for inmates at GTMO. Peter confirms to me that the *Irish Times* will pay for my flights to and from GTMO. The US authorities will provide my accommodation while I am staying at the US naval base at the southern tip of Cuba.

Getting to GTMO, however, is a complex process. Officially known as the US Naval Station, Guantanamo Bay, Cuba, GTMO is the oldest military base outside the continental United States. According to the US authorities, it is also the only US military base located within a communist country. The US originally leased Guantanamo bay from the Cubans in 1903 for use as a coal refuelling station for its fleet operating in the south Atlantic, Gulf of Mexico and the Caribbean Sea. A century later, the base is still of crucial strategic importance to the US.

When people, including myself, think of GTMO, they are informed by the now-infamous TV pictures of Camp X Ray, which feature blindfolded prisoners in orange jumpsuits held at gunpoint in wire cages in the open air. People, therefore, imagine Guantanamo as a confined space housed in some bleak and tiny backwater. In fact, GTMO is one of America's largest military bases and consists of forty-five square miles of land and water. In an ironic twist, given its dark purpose and even darker international reputation, Guantanamo is an area of exceptional natural beauty. Guantanamo Bay itself consists of a sheltered deep-sea port, a little over two square miles in area, that services the US Navy Atlantic Fleet and US Coastguard vessels operating on drug interdiction missions throughout the Bahamas, Antilles and the Caribbean.

The business of getting to GTMO requires me to jump through a number of hoops. When I confirm that I will travel to Cuba, X asks me to pop in to him in the embassy. He asks me to bring my passport and some other documentation with me. I duly oblige. I go through the usual security at the embassy's front entrance. X takes me down into the bowels of the embassy where I'm photographed and processed for an 'I' visa. This is a working visa which allows me to engage in journalism while in the United States. This process takes a long time and involves a lot of form filling.

There are some questions I recall as a student applying for a J1 working visa to the US in the 1980s. 'Have you ever been a member of the Nazi Party?' and so on. However, the forms have been updated since then. Presumably in the aftermath of 9/11. I'm asked if I've ever been a party to an armed conflict. 'Yes.' I'm asked if I've ever had firearms training or training with high explosives. 'Yes.' I'm asked if I've ever been a member of an armed organisation. 'Yes' again. All of this training and experience is courtesy of the Irish Defence Forces. However, there is no facility on the form to explain why one might answer 'Yes' to any of these leading questions. No 'Please explain' option. X reassures me on this point. 'Don't worry, Tom.' He tells me to always tell the 'truth and the whole truth' when filling out US Homeland Security or US Immigration forms. 'Those bureaucracy guys don't like it if you give an inconsistent answer between forms.'

As it turns out, no one seems to pay any attention to my declarations of proficiency in firearms and explosives or my participation in armed conflicts. I'm relieved.

I get my visa. Meanwhile, the Joint Task Force Guantanamo make contact with me from Cuba. They ask me to provide them with a scanned copy of my passport. They also ask me to confirm my gender and to provide supporting documentation if necessary. They also ask me for my PPS number and require me to sign a copy of the 'Ground Rules'. This is a lengthy document which they email to me. It contains a litany of dos and don'ts on GTMO. I am not allowed to approach, talk to or photograph any of the prisoners. I am also advised that if I reveal anything about the 'security measures' on Guantanamo Bay, or if I reveal the exact location of 'Camp Delta' or if I reveal anything of 'operational or intelligence significance' during or after my stay, I will be subject to criminal prosecution.

I ask X about this last provision. 'If I let something slip, you know, inadvertently in my articles, the US will hardly seek to extradite me to face charges?' X, who looks very like Ned Flanders from *The Simpsons*, considers this for a moment. He answers me cheerfully. 'Don't worry about extradition, Tom, they'll just pick you up when you come to Disneyland, Florida some time down the line.' I sign the document and fax it back to JTF GTMO. X is delighted with his joke – I presume it is a joke – and hums 'Zippy De Doo Dah, Zippy De Day', every time we meet subsequently.

I eventually get a letter from JTF GTMO which tells me that I have been accepted for travel and provides some tips for my impending stay in Guantanamo. On page one of the factsheet, I am told that I must not, under any circumstances, bring 'weapons of any type' with me, as this may lead to a 'serious misunderstanding'. I am also advised to get inoculated for 'immune serum globulin, tetanus-diphtheria, oral polio, typhoid, yellow fever and malaria'.

I am also required to submit a list of all electronic equipment I will be bringing to GTMO, including mobile phone, digital camera and laptop. In addition, I must submit myself to a Security Review Panel at the end of my stay. The Security Review Panel, I am informed, will consist of a 'J3 or Operations Officer', a 'J2 or Intelligence Officer' along with another 'agency official' as required. The Security Review Panel will ask me about my stay prior to departure. I am also required to hand over my laptop, phone and camera for the overnight period before departure in order that they can be inspected and scanned. I'm sure they'll find my DIT lecture notes on journalism theory of great interest.

The *Irish Times* book flights for me from Dublin to New York. I will connect at JFK and from there to Fort Lauderdale, Florida. The return flights are similar. Jet Blue, an American budget airline, and Aer Lingus. The flights from Florida, however, are a different matter. I am to fly from Fort Lauderdale to Guantanamo in a chartered aircraft. Namely, a small, twin-propeller aircraft, which will make the final four-hour flight from Florida to Guantanamo Bay.

It strikes me as a long way to fly in such a small aircraft. Guantanamo is situated at the south-western tip of Cuba, approximately five hundred miles south of Havana at the opposite end of the island. The closest 'friendly' airport to Guantanamo is approximately two hundred miles to the south-west at Kingstown, Jamaica, or hundred and fifty miles south-east at Port au Prince in Haiti. When I look at the route the flight will take, I notice it goes straight through the Bermuda Triangle. I'm beginning to develop a fear of flying at the thoughts of this final leg of the journey. X reassures me. 'Hey, Tom,' he says cheerily, 'why don't you look up the Bermuda Triangle on the US Department of Commerce, National Oceanic and Atmospheric Administration website? That'll tell you all you need to know.'

I duly look it up. The website doesn't reassure me. Nor does it banish my newfound fear of flying. Its opening line is enough: 'For decades, the Atlantic Ocean's fabled Bermuda Triangle has captured the human imagination with unexplained disappearances of ships, planes, and people. Some speculate that unknown and mysterious forces account for the unexplained disappearances, such as extraterrestrials capturing humans for study; the influence of the lost continent of Atlantis; vortices that suck objects into other dimensions. Some explanations are grounded in science. These include oceanic flatulence (methane gas erupting from ocean sediments) and disruptions in geomagnetic lines of flux.'

'Holy Shit,' I say to myself. Or, as my departed mother would have said, 'Jesus, Mary and Joseph.'

The weeks fly by. During the last week of August, Hurricane Katrina hits New Orleans and practically destroys the city. Over 1,800 people die in the disaster and Katrina inflicts over $81 billion worth of damage during the storm. I watch as US military units patrol the shattered city's streets. Helicopters hover along the skyline. It is hard to distinguish New Orleans from Baghdad or Fallujah.

The tropical storm season off the Florida coast continues to worry the US authorities with several near misses in the aftermath of Hurricane Katrina.

In the interim, Viktoria arrives back in Dublin to do another six-week block of physiotherapy with Eoghan. She works with him every day. The therapy has all sorts of direct and indirect benefits for Eoghan. As I work in the attic, writing to deadline, I hear them below laughing and giggling as they play. Every now and again I hear Viktoria call encouragement to Eoghan. 'Come Oven, do it yourself!' This becomes a catchphrase for Eoghan as we encourage him to become more independent, autonomous. His crawling improves. His muscle tone improves. He wrestles on the floor with Darach. They are very pleased with Eoghan's progress at the CRC. During hydrotherapy sessions in the pool there, Eoghan is able to flip himself over on to his tummy and over again on to his back. His gross motor function has progressed in leaps and bounds. During physiotherapy sessions in the gym in the CRC, I look up at the ceiling. There, along the top of the wall, in block capital letters, I see the words, 'DO IT YOURSELF'. Eoghan's gross motor and fine motor development will hopefully allow him to achieve this simple goal. He is a determined little man.

Darach starts school at the beginning of September. Another milestone. The school run is now incorporated into our hectic schedule. With Aideen's busy work routine, I do most of the cooking and most of the school pick-ups and drop-offs. I'm on the clock constantly. Cycling in and out to DIT, delivering lectures, attending meetings. I pop in and out of studios in Donnybrook and travel all over the city centre doing radio and TV interviews. Every other day I try to get up into the attic to write to another deadline. I manage also to keep my academic publication up to date. As a lecturer in journalism, I feel it is important, vital, to have one foot in the academic world and one foot firmly in the world of real-time journalism. It keeps me on my toes. The students benefit from my freelance experience. I'm immersed in a world of deadline-driven media and have to pitch and sell every word, every interview to disinterested, harassed and time-pressured editors. This is the media landscape that most of my graduates will have to navigate.

I collect Darach every day from school. His little hand in mine as we walk along the Rock Road. It occurs to me as we meet neighbours each day, neighbours who become friends, that one really starts to knit very closely into the neighbourhood when the kids start school. Booterstown is an especially inclusive, friendly and warm community.

The day before I fly to New York en route to GTMO, I spend most of the day cooking. I freeze several dinners and make sure there is enough milk, bread and vegetables on hand for the week. I pack my bag. I make sure I'm not carrying any weapons. I don't want a 'serious misunderstanding' when I arrive in GTMO.

At our last supper before I depart, I unwisely let slip to Aideen and Viktoria that I'm a bit nervous about the last leg of the flight. I tell them about the oceanic flatulence and the geomagnetic flux lines. I even mention the extraterrestrials. I express deep misgivings about flying for four hours through the Bermuda Triangle, during the tropical storm season, in a tiny plane. Aideen throws her eyes up to heaven. 'Do you want me to show you the relevant section in the *ICD-10 Classification of Mental and Behavioural Disorders*?' she asks me, eyebrows raised slightly. Meanwhile, Viktoria is staring at me intently. 'Clonan, you believe in goblins?' She bursts out laughing at me. When I protest, they both laugh. Cold comfort.

Chapter 27

Cuba

'I hope you're not some sort of fucking comedian, sir.
This isn't the laughter lounge, buddy.'

US Naval Station, Guantanamo Bay, Cuba
October 2005

I depart for Dublin Airport at some ungodly hour. The taxi driver asks me where I'm off to. 'Guantanamo Bay,' I reply. 'Ah,' he says. 'Goin' on a bit of a holiday are ye?' I'm not sure if he is taking the mickey or not, so I just nod.

I check in at the Aer Lingus desk and head through security. No one blames me for having to take their shoes off this morning, thankfully. US Immigration have a permanent facility in Dublin Airport by way of a special agreement with the Irish government. So it is possible to clear US immigration before you even board your flight to the US.

I take the escalator down to the US Immigration clearance area. There are a number of forms to be filled in, including one where you are asked to state at what address – including zip code no less – you will be resident during your stay in the US. I think of X's words in the US Embassy. 'Always tell the truth, the whole truth,' on US documents. So I write on the form, 'Address: Camp Delta, US Naval Station, Guantanamo Bay, Cuba'. I don't know what the zip code is. I get in the queue and am called to the immigration counter by a rather brusque immigration official. He flips open my passport and scans the details. He then looks at the form I have filled in. He pauses. He looks up and gazes at me in a neutral, bordering on bored manner. 'Why did you put that address on the form?' he asks me. 'Eh, because, that's where I'll be staying,' I

231

reply. He looks at me again. 'Holy shit,' he mutters and stamps my forms and passport. I'm on my way.

When we land in JFK, I walk briskly through the terminal heading for the connections area. When I get to the Jet Blue desk, the lady takes my passport and scans my travel details on screen. 'Oh, Mr Clonan,' she says, 'can you go over to the wall there and call Homeland Security?' I look around, and sure enough, there is a phone mounted on the wall, with a sign overhead, 'Homeland Security'. I wander over, a little self-consciously, and pick up the receiver. 'Is that you Mr Clonan?' a voice immediately speaks into my ear. I'm impressed.

'Eh, yes,' I reply. 'Could you please remain where you are sir,' the voice instructs me. I wait and sure enough a couple of guys in suits emerge from an alarmed door along the corridor and beckon me to follow them. I go through the door and into a parallel universe. This is the part of the airport that passengers don't normally get to see. I imagine this is where illegal immigrants, terror suspects and drugs traffickers are taken when they disembark from flights. I'm ushered into an interview room. Man No. 1 stands at the door. Just like in the movies. Man No. 2 sits down and opens a file. I wonder will he offer me a cigarette. Instead, he takes out a copy of the form I filled in at Dublin Airport. 'Did you fill this in, sir?' he asks. 'Yes,' I reply. 'And, sir, can you explain to me and my colleague here, why you put "Camp Delta, Guantanamo Bay" down as your, ah, place of residence?' His colleague interrupts. 'I hope you're not some sort of fucking comedian, sir. This isn't the laughter lounge, buddy.' I'm a bit taken aback by the last comment, but I plough on. 'Eh, I put it down, because that's where I'm going.' Man No. 2 is about to interrupt, but I continue nonetheless. 'I've been invited there by the US government.'

There is a long pause. 'No shit?' says Man No. 1 at the door. I get the feeling that he is the bad cop. His voice dripping with sarcasm, Man No. 1 continues, 'And, uh, is this invitation anything to do with your self-declared proficiency in firearms and high explosives?' I frown now as I recall ticking 'Yes' to all of those boxes on the visa form.

Good cop asks me gently, as though I might be a bit simple, if I have any evidence to support my 'ah, claim'. I reach for my briefcase and they both jump. I jump. 'I'm just getting my letter of invitation out here,' I reassure them. They watch me like a hawk as I slowly reach in and produce hard copies of my email correspondence with JTF GTMO and X at the US Embassy in Dublin. They both pore over them for a few minutes. I clear my throat. 'And, er, I was in the Irish Army. That's where I learned to shoot.' They look at me, eyebrows raised. 'Shoot, did you say?' 'Yes,' I reply and then, thinking I might as well be hung for a sheep as a lamb, I add for effect, 'And I learned all about explosive natures.' The guys look at each other meaningfully. 'Excuse us for a moment, sir.'

They go outside and eventually return after some heated whispering in the corridor. I hear doors slam and swing open again. Phone calls are being made. I think I hear the phrase 'nut job' being used at one point. Eventually they return and, smiling broadly, announce, 'Welcome to the United States, sir.' I'm relieved.

They race back to the Jet Blue desk with me and make sure I'm boarded on time. They tell me that when I get to Fort Lauderdale for my connecting flight, that I must pick up a phone and call Homeland Security once more. 'Our colleagues in Florida will look after you, sir.' We shake hands.

The flight to Fort Lauderdale is uneventful. After take-off, I look down as we ascend over New Jersey. I see the shoreline below where I worked as a busboy, waiter and gas station attendant as a student on a J1 visa during the 1980s. I think about how much the US has changed since then.

When we land in Florida, I do as instructed and head for the now familiar Homeland Security phone mounted on the wall. I pick up the receiver and press the call button. After a few rings, the phone answers. 'Homeland' is the off-hand greeting. 'Eh, my name is Tom Clonan – I was told to call you.' The Homeland Security guy responds immediately. 'Oh, yeah, we've been expecting you.' He tells me to wait, tells me he'll pick me up and bring me to the charter plane. Just like New York, he emerges through an alarmed door in the corridor. He holds it open and waves to me. He swipes me through the door with a guest tag and hands it to me to put around my neck. 'So,' he says, 'Guantanamo? What you doin' there?' I tell him I'm a journalist. He lets out a whistle. 'I don't like journalists much,' he tells me. 'But, I tell you what I don't like even more?' I nod encouragement at him. 'I don't like this fuckin' prison camp out in Guantanamo. No sir. I don't fuckin' like it. Not one little bit.' As we walk along, he tells me his name and shows me his badge. He gives me a card. 'You write in your paper in Ireland that we don't all approve of Guantanamo. Here, use my name if you like.' I am very surprised. I'm beginning to understand a little more about the US and the concept of freedom of speech. As we walk through the parallel universe towards the charter plane area, I reflect on whether or not an Irish public servant would speak as freely. I reflect on whether or not Ireland is a country where the frank expression of views is tolerated as readily. I ask him if he isn't nervous about criticising US policy as a member of Homeland Security. He looks at me in amazement. 'Are you serious? If George Bush walked in here right now, I'd tell him the exact same fuckin' thing, make no mistake.' His voice is now raised. I'm beginning to like this guy.

By the time we get to the check-in desk, or what could loosely be described as a check-in desk, my tour guide has moved on to other areas of US policy that he is unhappy about. He stops suddenly and shakes my hand. 'Great to have met you. Best of luck.' He disappears down the corridor and leaves me to my own devices. There is a huge weighing scales at the desk. A few minutes later a very large, very tall man approaches. I mean really, really, really tall. He is a giant. He is at least seven feet tall and is built like a weight lifter. He is wearing dark glasses, indoors, and is chewing gum. 'Uhhh,' he grunts at me. He motions to the weighing scales and breathes heavily. He's not much for conversation. I hop up on the scales. He writes down the result. 11kg. He weighs my bag.

Some more gum-chewing guys arrive. No one says a word. No one looks at me. There is no conversation as everyone gets weighed. I get the impression that my fellow passengers have been through this ritual before. As far as I can gather they are civilian 'contractors' working in Guantanamo Bay. I learn later that some of them are translators and professional interrogators. Some are members of 'unspecified agencies'.

The big pilot is joined by a small, dapper man. He announces himself as our captain. He is dressed with meticulous care in a pilot's uniform covered in braid and shiny buottons. He looks like a child in a kid's costume. The big guy is heaving and hauling our bags out to the plane. The plane is tiny. And I mean really tiny. The plane sinks down on the nose wheel at the front when the bags go in. I try to board as I just want to get this over with. But the captain holds me back. 'Wait now,' he says in a singsong voice. The big guy then manhandles and pushes himself through the door. He goes in backwards and then, crab-like, moves sideways into the cockpit. He strains and squeezes between the pilot's seats and collapses into one of them. The entire plane groans and squeaks on the wheels. The nose is noticeably pointing at the ground. I feel a growing sense of panic. I'm shoved in next and shown where to sit. The taciturn passengers all climb and clamber aboard and take their assigned seats. Some of the bags are shoved around to balance out the weight. The captain walks around, outside the plane, head cocked to one side, making sure the plane isn't too lopsided.

He then gets in, hauls up the steps and slips in beside his perspiring co-pilot. The big guy's shirt is now stuck to his back with sweat. The aircraft starts up and begins to vibrate alarmingly. First one propeller, then the second whirs into life. We lurch forward and head towards the runway. We join a queue of other light aircraft who in turn take off between larger jets queuing on another apron. The large jets tower over us. Our plane looks and sounds like a mosquito. Eventually it is our turn. The big guy becomes energised and I watch him stab at buttons in the cockpit and he is suddenly all movement. Graceful even.

We race down the runway and the take-off is more rapid than I expect. We're up in seconds. The plane is also ascending quite steeply. The engines seem to be straining. The wind catches us also and we begin weaving and bouncing around a bit. The runway flashes past and we are suddenly flying over the ocean. The big guy comes over the PA. He is shouting. 'It's gonna be rough, ladies. Enjoy it while you can.'

We are buffeted and bounced around the sky for the next four hours. The plane flies east out to sea and then south, skirting Cuban airspace. We fly through Bahamian airspace and finally descend to Guantanamo Bay through the 'Windward Passage' – a strait of water between Haiti and Cuba that connects the Caribbean Sea to the Atlantic Ocean. It's windy, all right. It feels like we are in a tumble dryer. I look up from time to time at the big guy and the captain. They seem unconcerned, talking and joking all the while. The captain occasionally slaps the big guy's meaty shoulder. Little and large.

We land with a bump and come to an abrupt halt. It is a rough concrete landing strip. The engines stop. The sudden silence feels strange. My ears are still popping and buzzing after the noise. My silent copassengers gather up their gear rapidly and exit the aircraft without a word or a backward glance. The big guy struggles and finally extricates himself from the cockpit. I watch him amble across the runway to a small, single-storey building. I think I see a Starbucks Coffee sign, but imagine it might be a mirage of some sort.

A female marine officer pokes her head in the door. 'You the Irish guy?' she asks. I nod and she asks me for my letter of invitation and ground clearance certificate. She asks for my passport. With the paperwork in order, she motions for me to follow her off the plane. 'Welcome to Cuba,' she smiles at me. I could kiss the ground. A strange impulse for Guantanamo.

She brings me over to a Humvee and drives me through a number of security measures to the edge of the airfield. There are huge crabs everywhere. Walking and running around on spindly legs. My host spots me looking at them. 'Don't pay those guys any heed. They're harmless. Land crabs is what they're called.' She weaves the Humvee in and around the crabs and informs me that we're heading for the 'Combined Bachelors Quarters' or the CBQ. This is going to be my home for the next week. 'The CBQ is where we house all the single or unaccompanied soldiers and officers during their tour of duty to GTMO.' She tells me that there is a lot of wildlife on the base. 'We've got land crabs, snakes, spiders, lizards, manatees. All sorts of critters.'

The CBQ is a large complex of apartments and courtyards. There are a number of dining halls and cafeterias dotted about. It is, for all the world, like the halls of residence on any university campus. Except, this is Guantanamo Bay. The lieutenant explains to me that the naval station is effectively split into two main areas divided by a deep channel or inlet which runs north-south right up to the border with Cuba. She points up to where the border

with Cuba lies, just north of the road we are travelling on. Guantanamo is sep-
arated from Cuba proper by a seventeen-and-a-half-mile fence which is
patrolled on one side by US marines and on the other by Cuba's 'Frontier
Brigade'. A series of fortified watchtowers with sensitive listening and surveillance equipment line both sides of the frontier. The so-called 'North Gate'
operates as a sort of 'Checkpoint Charlie' between Cuba and Guantanamo at
the northern tip of the base. The senior US commander on the base meets
regularly with his Cuban counterpart through the North Gate to discuss matters of mutual interest and to defuse local tensions.

The lieutenant drops me off at a single-storey block of offices. There to
meet me is a tall officer, a captain. He introduces himself and we shake hands.
'Call me Jim,' he tells me. Captain Jim in turn introduces me to another staff
officer. 'This is Sheila.' Sheila is tall and blonde and slightly older than Jim. I'd
put her in her late thirties or early forties. She informs me that she and Jim are
my 'J2' and 'J3' guides for the trip. In other words, Jim is the J3 or operations
officer and Sheila is the J2 intelligence officer. Sheila and Jim will form my
Security Review Panel at the end of the trip. They usher me into a large office
and give me a comprehensive briefing and overview of the base.

They go through the timeline of the camp. Established in 2002, as Camp
X Ray, Guantanamo Bay now consists of five Halliburton-constructed camps
known collectively as Camps Delta and Echo. I will be visiting each of them.
They tell me that there are currently 505 detainees in total on the naval station.

They also remind me of the ground rules and tell me that at first light, we
will be heading over to the other side of the naval station and Camp Delta
itself. We'll be taking a ferry over the river and inlet that bisect the base and
will spend the day visiting Camps Delta and Echo. The following day, I'll be
given an interview with the major general in command of Joint Task Force
Guantanamo. After that, I'll be given access to some of the investigative and
administrative reviews that are ongoing within the camp. I am reminded once
more that I must under no circumstances attempt to communicate with the
'detainees'. Jim and Sheila also inform me that we will be accompanied at all
times in Camp Delta by an 'individual from an agency' who I will only know

on a first-name basis. This is intriguing. I ask them which agency. They reply that they 'never discuss agencies'.

They also remind me of how 'dangerous' the detainees are. They give me a printout of death threats made to guards and their families by various detainees over the years. They inform me that of the 240 detainees so far repatriated to their home countries, many have 'returned to violence'. One former detainee has assassinated a judge in Afghanistan, for example, and others have been killed in action in operations involving US troops in Afghanistan and Iraq.

Jim chews on a toothpick as he speaks. Occasionally using it as a pointer to emphasise a particular detail. Sheila is much more reserved and watches me closely throughout the briefing. I ask a lot of questions about the security measures employed. I am interested to compare them with the security measures employed in Portlaoise Prison: Ireland's own maximum-security prison for political prisoners and terror suspects. They express some surprise at this. 'Ireland has a military prison?' they ask. They are incredulous when I tell them that Ireland is the only country in the European Union to operate a maximum-security prison manned by police, army and prison officers. Sheila looks at me with interest. 'That's far out, Tom. We wouldn't be able to sell that state-side.'

'Hell no,' Captain Jim agrees. 'Americans wouldn't tolerate the United States Army being used to lock up citizens. All hell would break loose.'

Before we finish, Captain Jim produces a small plastic implement and shows it to me. 'Do you know what this is, Tommy boy?' he asks me. It is a small plastic eating utensil. A fork at one end and a spoon at the other. The round edge of the spoon has been shaped into a crude point. 'That, my friend,' he explains, 'is a spork. United States standard-issue plastic eating utensil.' He goes on to explain, 'One of the detainees got his hands on this here spork, and as you can see, fashioned it into a deadly weapon. Now, weapons on Guantanamo, especially deadly weapons like this, can lead to . . .' He pauses for effect. 'Serious misunderstandings.' I could have finished the sentence myself, having heard the mantra several times now. Captain Jim continues, 'The detainee in question planned to kill his guards with this here spork, get through the fence and make his way once more to wage jihad against the United States of America.' I try to imagine the desperate scene of a detainee breaking out of Camp Delta with a spork. How would he get off the naval station? Swim? I imagine a detainee staring at the vast expanse of the Atlantic Ocean or the Caribbean. Armed only with an orange jumpsuit and a spork. It sounds like a forlorn exercise. It seems that US and Irish threat assessments differ somewhat. I keep my opinion to myself.

After our briefing, Sheila and Jim accompany me to the CBQ. Jim hefts my bag over his shoulder and helps me deposit it in my room. I've got a bed, en-suite bathroom and a TV with satellite and cable. There is also a fridge in the room and it is full of cans of draft Guinness. Jim smiles at me when I open the fridge. 'We figured you'd like Guinness, bein' Irish and all.'

After I settle in, Sheila and Jim tell me that there is a barbecue in the courtyard every night and that I'm invited along. 'Make yourself at home.'

Hundreds of personnel live in the CBQ. Mostly young soldiers and marines. When they are not on duty, pulling guard shifts in Camp Delta or on the perimeter fence, the troops like to let their hair down. I am introduced to a group of soldiers, young men and women, who are firing up the barbecue. I get a great welcome. 'Hey, you're the Irish guy. We've got Guinness here.'

The young soldiers are very hospitable and I am made to feel at home in their company. After a couple of burgers and a few beers, they all start to speak freely. The young soldiers are articulate and unafraid to voice their opinions – even in front of Captain Jim and Sheila. Some express the view that Guantanamo is a necessary evil. Others argue that it ought to be closed down immediately; that it is bringing the US into disrepute. Others joke that 'it sure beats the hell out of serving in Iraq.' Everyone laughs at that observation. Sheila and Jim argue the point with all and sundry. I am surprised at the ease with which all ranks mingle with each other. I am surprised also at the manner in which all shades of opinion are voiced and shared.

The barbecue is sputtering and smoking. It is not quite hot enough. The barbecue has been jerry-rigged out of a metal grate perched over some concrete cavity blocks. Some of the marines are tinkering about with it and one guy is trying to heat the coals by fanning them furiously with a piece of cardboard. I spot a bottle of barbecue lighting fluid on the ground. 'Here, let me have a go,' I say. Emboldened by Guinness and my having survived the flight through the Bermuda Triangle, I slosh the fluid liberally over the coals which hiss as the red glow is doused – temporarily. I continue to pour the whole bottle in. One of the marines takes exception. 'Aww, man, you've put it out.' I then borrow Sheila's lighter and ignite it over the coals. There is an enormous 'whoosh' and a tongue of flame shoots straight up. The heat is scorching. The guy with the cardboard beats a hasty retreat. The flame burns iridescent yellow and orange, flaring out our night vision. Eventually it settles and the coals glow a fierce red – like a workman's brazier. The marines look at me with a newfound respect. 'That was fuckin' awesome, little guy.' The others join in. 'Fuckin' A, man, fuckin' A.' Sheila throws her eyes up to heaven.

My first night on Guantanamo is surreal; drinking Guinness in the glow of a communal barbecue with young soldiers from all over the United States. I pick up a lot of information about the manner in which the prisoners are detained and guarded. I learn a lot about the relationships that form between the soldiers and their enemies. I'm surprised at how much the troops disclose to me. Later, much later, I make my way back to my apartment, tripping over spindly land crabs as I go.

Chapter 28

Camp Delta

'CAMP DELTA 1 MAXIMUM SECURITY
HONOUR BOUND TO DEFEND FREEDOM'

Camp Delta, Guantanamo Bay, Cuba

October 2005

I wake up the following morning with a severe headache. The first thing that hits me is the intense heat. Despite the fact that the sun is not yet over the horizon, the temperature is already in the low thirties. I have a cold shower and gather together my laptop, digital camera and a digital recorder and microphone. I wander outside and see the glowing tip of Sheila's first cigarette of the day. She looks unaffected by our late night. Not a hair out of place. Captain Jim is in the back of the Humvee. He's lying back with his beret pulled down over his eyes. The movement of the toothpick between his teeth is the only evidence of life. He doesn't greet me. Just lies there, sighing occasionally and working his jaw muscles.

Sheila winks at me and we head for the jetty and the inlet that divides the naval station. We join a queue of vehicles at the ferry crossing. Sheila tells me that there are thousands of US navy personnel and their families living on the other side of the base. As we board the ferry, she tells me to look out for manatees in the water. 'We get dolphins here also,' she tells me. Captain Jim leans over the rail, staring sullenly into the water. Apart from soldiers in uniform, there are around a dozen or so civilians on the ferry. They deliberately avoid eye contact with me and they stay well away from our little group. Sheila tells me that they are civilian contractors, 'mostly'.

We arrive on the other side of the inlet and disembark. The sight that greets me as we drive up from the harbour takes me by surprise. As we exit the dock area, the streetscape changes to that of suburban United States. The road markings, road signage, and street furniture are standard-issue Americana. Even the traffic lights suspended mid-street are classic American fixtures. I feel like pinching myself. This is not the Guantanamo Bay I had imagined. I had imagined some sort of barren penal colony.

We drive past a carefully tended golf course, and immaculate baseball and football fields, towards what can only be described as a regular American 'downtown' district. More traffic lights and stop signs, and a massive shopping mall appears. The traffic is heavier here. I spy a yellow school bus full of kids on their way to school. Opposite the shopping mall there are neat wooden street signs painted white with black lettering. They direct the eye to row upon row of neat, detached suburban houses with white wooden picket fences. It reminds me of *Desperate Housewives*'s Wisteria Lane.

I look back at the shopping mall. There is an illuminated McDonald's sign attached to the main entrance. A mix of civilians and soldiers throng the entrance to the mall. It is like anywhere, USA. Shoppers carrying bags of groceries and newspapers, mingle with US troops in the concourse and carpark.

Jim comes to life. 'Hey, Tom,' he addresses me for the first time today. 'We'll grab some McDonald's after Camp Delta.'

We pass through the downtown area of the naval station and move through a series of 'security measures' that I am not allowed to describe here. Nor am I permitted to describe the route we take, the distance involved or any other detail. Suffice to say, the Stepford quality of Guantanamo is reinforced when we crest a ridge and down below us lie Camp Delta and Camp Echo below.

Sheila pulls over to allow me take in the sight. This is it. This is Guantanamo Bay. I have a sudden vision of Sheila handing me an orange jumpsuit and announcing, 'Welcome to GTMO, asshole – now put this on.' X in the Dublin Embassy would have enjoyed that.

'Hey, Tom, wake up, you're daydreaming.' I'm interrupted in my reverie as Sheila elbows me in the ribs. We roar off down the hill to our reception committee. We dismount outside the perimeter of the camp. It reminds me of Coolmoney Camp in the Glen of Imaal, the Irish army's training camp in County Wicklow. Camp Delta consists of row upon row of squat buildings with flat roofs housing the prisoners, or 'detainees'. The perimeter fence consists of a double set of chain-link barriers topped with coils of razor wire. Portions of the inner chain-link fence are screened by what looks like heavy PVC or tarpaulin and camouflage netting. Every hundred metres or so there are guard towers dotted along the fence. I'm describing this as Sheila invites me to take photographs at this point. She seems unconcerned about images of the fence.

There is a sign which clearly states, 'No Photography'. A soldier up in the guard tower watches me taking pictures. He simply smiles at me. On each of the gates to the camp, there is a sign which states, 'CAMP DELTA 1 MAXIMUM SECURITY HONOUR BOUND TO DEFEND FREEDOM'. It seems like a contradiction in terms to see the word 'freedom' emblazoned on a sign fixed to a prison gate. The prison gates are called 'Sally Ports'. Marine Corps Sergeant Major Sanchez emerges from our Sally Port and introduces himself. He has an entourage of troops who act as a security party whilst escorting us through the camp. The troops have removed their nametags and have put black masking tape over their unit and rank insignia. Aha. This is something that the Irish Army do in Portlaoise Prison. The idea in Ireland is to anonymise the military guard and to prevent individual identification and reprisals against soldiers' families by dissident republicans or other criminal elements. It is also designed to minimise the risk of threats and intimidation among off-duty soldiers in their own communities where dissident republican sympathies might exist.

Sergeant Major Sanchez explains to me that the US military conceals names, unit and rank markings so as to avoid 'retribution in the field'. He tells me that there is a proliferation of media images of the camp available online. The US authorities are aware that groups such as Al Qaeda and other Islamist jihadi organisations constantly monitor these images in order to ascertain what US military units are involved in the detention and interrogation of detainees. Sanchez tells me, 'If they were able to abduct or kill one of our soldiers or marines in Afghanistan or Iraq, they'd have a major propaganda coup on their hands.' The sergeant major looks at me and smiles. 'I'm already all over the internet, so you can use my name. I don't care. But please don't identify any of my young soldiers or marines.'

At this point, the temperature has risen to around forty degrees centigrade. Sergeant Major Sanchez opens his backpack and gives me a two-litre bottle of water. 'Sir, I advise you to keep drinkin' water while you're here. If you don't, you're gonna' get dehydrated and you're not gonna be able to get good media product.'

We are joined at this point by a middle-aged lady who introduces herself as 'Helen'. She and Sheila seem to know each other well. Sheila informs me that Helen is just going to 'tag along' and that I'm not to address any questions to her. 'Just pretend she's not here.' So Helen is the lady who was 'not there' or barely there at all. A ghost. I think the Americans call them 'spooks'.

Sergeant Major Sanchez tells me that his priority for the detainees is their physical and mental well-being. He boasts that most of the detainees were illiterate on arrival, but that they have since been taught how to read and write in 'English, Arabic, Urdu, Pashtu, Farsi and Uzbek.' He tells me that the detainees are allowed to correspond with their families back home. 'We have a graduation ceremony for detainees when they write their first letter home.' Sanchez seems genuinely proud of this achievement. I detect no sense of irony. No cynicism.

As we speak, a convoy of quad bikes approach. They are driven by marines in sunglasses and digitised-pattern combat uniforms. Perched on the back of the first quad bike is a tall man in an orange jumpsuit. He is bearded and is sitting cross legged. He is the epitome of the iconic image of a Guantanamo prisoner. He is handcuffed and manacled at the ankles. His handcuffs are connected to his foot manacles by means of a chain, which forces him into a slightly stooped position. He stares at me as the quad bikes drive past. His eyes are intense and I am embarrassed by his direct gaze. It is not a hostile look. It is a fixed look. Defiant. It is a look I will not forget. I watch as he is transported deeper into the camp. The sergeant major turns to me. 'He's on his way to the medical centre. We like to take care of our detainees. They get the best medical attention available.'

The sergeant major explains the camp system to me. 'There are four camps here. Camps 1 and 4 are for compliant detainees. These are detainees who we deem not to be a threat to the guards or each other. These, sir, are detainees who are in dialogue with the United States of America. Camps 2 and 3 are for non-compliant detainees. These, sir, are detainees who are a danger to themselves and others. They are recidivist.' Captain Jim chimes in. 'Hell, yeah. They throw faeces, urine, anything they can get their hands on at our guards. Can't turn your back on them for a second.'

We move on into Camp 1. I'm shown into a concrete and steel detention block. Built by Halliburton, the squat detention block consists of a simple, straight central corridor running right through the middle of forty-eight cells. Twenty-four cells line either side of the corridor. Each cell, roughly the size of a small bedroom, contains a stainless steel sink unit, a stainless steel flush toilet in the floor, a metal-framed bed and a shelf for the Koran and other materials. I am struck by a number of things. First of all, the detainees have flush toilets. Unlike prisoners in Irish jails, there is no slopping out here. Secondly, the cells are simple, but stark. Painted green and black, there is little visual stimulus. They are spartan. What strikes me as extraordinary, however, is the fact that each cell is divided not by a wall, but by metal grilles. In other words, at all times prisoners can see each other clearly and can communicate with one another. They could even touch each other. Whilst there is no privacy in such a situation, the construction of the cells allows for full communication between prisoners and the possibility of collective action. This would never be tolerated in Portlaoise Prison. In Ireland, we like to keep our political prisoners incommunicado.

There are contradictions in GTMO. The handcuffing and manacling of prisoners seems excessive to me and not consistent with the threat posed by detainees. Especially in the context of their confinement within a maximum security facility monitored by electronic surveillance and armed guards. On the other hand, the prisoners are housed in such a manner as to promote free association and unrestricted communication with one another.

At the end of each corridor there is an exit to an exercise cage. This is literally a large metal cage in which detainees are allowed access for periods of exercise and recreation. There is a football lying in the corner of the cage. Captain Jim leans over to me. 'You should see those guys, in their beards and orange jumpsuits and all that. They just love soccer and basketball. Some of 'em are really good too. It is a sight, I can tell you.'

There is also a shower block at the end of the corridor. There are a half dozen showers for forty-eight men. Each one resembles a metal phone box. The steel-grille door is bolted and locked whilst the prisoner showers. It is an effective sanitary device but of minimalist, brutal construction. I try to imagine being incarcerated here. So many thousands of miles from home and family. It is a chilling thought.

As we pass back through the cell block, I spy what looks like a traffic cone set to one side. It has a large capital P stencilled on it. Sanchez anticipates my question. 'That's for when the detainees are praying. When they are at prayer, the guard puts that in the centre aisle. That way, we know not to interrupt their prayer session.' Sergeant Major Sanchez takes the opportunity to point out another 'humanitarian' feature of the cell block. On the floor, at regular intervals, the word 'Makkah' is stamped into the concrete. Makkah is accompanied by an arrow which points in the direction of Mecca. 'That's to help 'em pray right,' according to the sergeant major. 'They pray a lot,' adds Captain Jim.

We move out of the cell block and back into the heat. I drink a litre of water in one go. Sanchez nods approvingly. Sheila tells me that we are now going to visit the camp hospital, or medical centre. Sheila calls it the 'Camp Delta Medical and Outpatients Unit'.

This building is different from the cell blocks. It is newly built and fully air-conditioned. It is a state of the art building, not unlike any civilian hospital outpatients facility. The centre is run by US Navy Captain and surgeon, John Edmondson. One of the first things that Edmondson does is to reveal his name and rank to me. He tells me that he prefers to be identified and to go on the record. Sheila nods her assent. I decide to go for the most pressing question. 'How many prisoners are on hunger strike?' One of Captain Edmondson's aides corrects me. 'You mean, voluntary fasting?' Captain Edmondson cuts in. He sighs wearily. 'You are from Ireland. You're familiar with hunger strikes as a tactic. Yeah, it's a hunger strike. Call it what you will.' He informs me that the number on hunger strike fluctuates but that at the moment it is around fifty detainees. I ask him if they will be force-fed. 'Yes,' he replies. 'I'm a doctor, this is my hospital and I'm not in the business of letting people die.' I ask him how he force-feeds the detainees. 'Nasally, through a tube, some we have to restrain initially, but when they register their disagreement, they all accept the feeding. We've had a few take out the drip from time to time, but on the whole, they accept it.'

I ask if I can take some pictures. They go into a huddle and have a conversation among themselves. I take some shots of individual hospital rooms which resemble prison cells. I notice that there are restraints on the beds. Leather and metal wrist and ankle straps. I believe these pictures give a rare insight into the manner in which prisoners on GTMO are force-fed.

I then ask Captain Edmondson about prisoner abuse. He assures me that it 'doesn't happen at Guantanamo.' He states that he has never treated a patient at Guantanamo with injuries consistent with a beating or any other maltreatment. He also assures me that his predecessor found no evidence of maltreatment or beatings. Citing general concerns about privacy and consistent with 'the principles of the Third Geneva Convention', which 'prohibits the display of detainees for public curiosity', I am refused permission to see Guantanamo's hunger strikers.

The mysterious Helen comes to the conclusion that we have 'seen enough for one day'. The sergeant major escorts us out and back to the Sally Port. He brings us through Camp 4 on the way. 'This is where we allow full freedom of association for compliant detainees.' I see a number of prisoners in white clothing, including some traditional garb, wandering around a large sandy exercise area. There are basketball hoops at each end of the sand and dirt patch. There are also shaded areas with benches where groups of prisoners sit and chat and read books. They are listless-looking in the afternoon heat. They look at me languidly through the wire. I find it almost impossible not to wave at them or call out to them.

To me, this is a peculiarly white, Anglo-Saxon, Protestant view of crime and punishment. There is an Old Testament choreography to GTMO. The prisoners are carefully presented to the onlooker as manacled and chain-ganged. Images from the camp usually contain the iconic visual imagery of handcuffs and leg irons. I feel there is an expectation that such imagery will provoke feelings of approbation and disapproval in the viewer. That, somehow, audiences will respond to these visual images with feelings of antipathy towards the person in chains. I imagine that Irish people, for historical and cultural reasons, will respond differently. I find myself instinctively feeling sorry for the inmates. I abhor the manner in which they are shackled and chained. I feel that this is not preventative, but rather that it is overkill and punitive in nature.

But then I ask myself if I ever felt any sympathy for republican or other political prisoners in Portlaoise when I was a serving army officer myself. I have to answer truthfully that I didn't feel any sympathy for them. Nor do I feel any sympathy today for dissident republicans. I now feel conflicted. It is easy for me to stand in judgment of my American hosts. Far less easy to judge my own standards. Witnessing these scenes leaves me feeling deeply uneasy.

Sheila and Captain Jim bring me back over to the CBQ that afternoon. I spend a few hours writing my notes and emailing home. Darach is enjoying school. Eoghan has a runny nose. Ailbhe has migrated into our bed while I'm away. It is a world away.

At seven o'clock, Captain Jim knocks at my door. 'C'mon, little guy, the barbecue is waiting.' I go out and a much larger group of soldiers has congregated at the barbecue. I get a cheer from last night's group who tell me that I am 'master of ceremonies' for lighting the grill. I'm introduced to countless young male and female soldiers, many of whom tell me they are Irish. As we talk, I pour a bottle and a half of barbecue lighting fluid onto the charcoal. Unbeknownst to me, it seeps down past the coals and pools in the concrete cavity blocks. In the intense heat of Guantanamo, the fluid in turn begins to evaporate inside the concrete blocks. I light a match and toss it nonchalantly onto the grill. There is an enormous bang and a sudden flash. A tongue of flame licks out from the coals and takes my fringe with it. It also takes off most of my eyebrows. I am blinded temporarily and pushed aside as the troops leap back from the grill. I open my eyes tentatively and smell burnt hair. Apart from that I'm fine. The grill is well lit, that's for sure. A unanimous verdict is reached about my barbecue lighting skills. 'Awesome.' For all the wrong reasons.

Chapter 29

Camp Echo

'Because, believe it or not, some of our young soldiers and sailors here build up an affinity with the detainees. So it would be bad for morale to shoot them. That's why it'll probably be by lethal injection. The way we do it stateside.'

Camp Echo, Guantanamo Bay, Cuba
October 2005

The following morning, as per our now familiar routine, Sheila and Captain Jim escort me over to the other side of Guantanamo Bay. Jim has skipped breakfast and insists we pop into McDonald's for an Egg McMuffin. I settle for a coffee and rub my singed eyebrows. Sheila looks at me quizzically. 'Did you do something with your hair?'

Today we are going to Camp 5 or Camp Echo – 'Echo' being the phonetic name for E, the fifth letter of the alphabet. We drive over the ridgeline and descend to the camp.

As we dismount from the Humvee to meet up with Helen, I hear the Muezzin's call to prayer. The plaintive tones of the cry come from speakers somewhere in Camp Delta. It sounds incongruous as the rising sun bears down on the massive stars and stripes flying next to the steel ring-fence that surrounds Camp Echo. Camp Echo is markedly different from the single-storey steel and concrete cell blocks of Camp Delta. Architecturally, the newly built facility is ultra modern. Sheila tells me that it is modelled on Miami County Prison, Indiana. It is a fully automated, fully air-conditioned, all bells and whistles, state-of-the-art maximum-security prison. 'It incorporates,' Jim proudly announces, 'the very best features of the most secure lock-down facilities in the United States.' It is a frightening, forbidding building and is alien in almost every respect. It is space-age for certain. Like something out of a science fiction nightmare.

Sheila tells me that Echo holds around 16 percent of Guantanamo's prison population. She tells me that there is a mix of compliant and non-compliant detainees. What marks them out from their peers in the rest of the camp is their perceived intelligence value. Jim pipes up that some of them are on suicide watch. Sheila and Helen glower at him. He fails to notice and jabs at bits of Egg McMuffin with his toothpick. I'm taking notes as we go.

A marine opens the Sally Port in the perimeter fence and we approach the brooding building. The prison looks permanent. It does not have the transitional 'internment camp' feel that Camp Delta possesses. Camp Echo has been built with the medium- to long-term future in mind. We are met by a young lieutenant who shows us around. The front entrance is monitored electronically and opens automatically. There are four wings within the prison, each capable of holding twenty-four prisoners. Each cell is painted white and has its own slit window permitting natural light to enter. They are each equipped with a bed, stainless steel sink and toilet. Camp 5 has an eerie feel to it – a sterile, sanitised building with security doors that crash shut. At the centre of the building behind one-way plate glass windows, a central control room monitors each cell remotely. The prisoners are under surveillance constantly, 24/7. There are multiple microphones in each room. The stillness within the airless chambers of the prison give it a tomb-like quality. The prisoners detained within it, for an indeterminate period, seem to me like the living dead. As a tropical thunderstorm rages outside Camp 5, the thunder is barely audible.

Camp Echo has been suitably named; our footsteps reverberate around the artificial space. The entire complex has an air of permanency about it that fills me with foreboding as to the future of Guantanamo Bay. The massive investment in this facility along with the fact that it is, as yet, only half-full of prisoners deemed to be of high intelligence value to the USA seem to indicate that Guantanamo will be in operation for some years to come.

The marine lieutenant is keen to show me an interview room. 'I believe you asked Captain Edmondson about our interrogation techniques yesterday?' he enquires. 'Let me show you a typical interrogation suite. Note, there is no bare light bulb or two-way glass wall, like in the TV cop shows.' He laughs as a door buzzes open before us. The room, like the cells is painted white. It is carpeted. Sitting in the middle of the room – somewhat unexpectedly in this mausoleum-like structure – is a regular couch, of the type I have at home in my own living room. It is even the same colour. 'See?' says Jim. 'Real home comforts. Don't think I'd be sitting on something like that if Al Qaeda ever got me.'

I ask if I can take photographs. Helen and Sheila tell me that it is better if they take the shots so as not to inadvertently include any detail that is prohibited. While Sheila takes some shots of the couch, I notice a stainless steel ring on the floor. I squat down and pull at it. It is firmly anchored to the reinforced concrete floor underneath. The lieutenant explains. 'That's where we shackle the detainees.' He roots around under the couch and pulls out a stainless steel chain and a set of leg irons and handcuffs. 'See, this is how we restrain 'em.' I've seen enough. My blood runs cold at the sight of these restraints in this room. Next to that couch. On that carpet. It seems obscene to me.

We leave this sad room and continue down the hall. I look to my left and notice a room that is being worked on by some plumbers and electricians. It looks like an operating theatre. 'Oh, that's a sick bay,' the lieutenant tells me. I stop and everyone comes to a halt. I ask Sheila if they will execute any of the detainees. Sheila tells me that it is impossible to answer that question in advance of the deliberations of their court martial system, which is underway despite legal appeals in the US civil courts. 'So, you're not ruling it out then?' I ask. Sheila looks exasperated, and Captain Jim decides to help her out.

'Y'see Tom, this isn't Nuremberg. We're not going to hang people here, for like, war crimes and such.' I remark that I'm relieved to hear it. Jim is undaunted. 'Y'see Tom, believe it or not, the American people believe that hanging is a cruel and unusual punishment.' Helen and Sheila look anxious to move on. Sheila looks at her watch. Jim keeps going. 'And we can't shoot 'em either.' 'Why not?' I ask him. 'Because, believe it or not, some of our young soldiers and sailors here build up an affinity with the detainees. So it would be bad for morale to shoot them.' Captain Jim is ready for his finale. He inclines his head at the sick bay and announces, 'That's why it'll probably be by lethal injection. The way we do it stateside.' I am writing furiously. In a rare moment, Helen speaks. 'I think it's time we went over to see the general.'

I've been promised an on-the-record interview with the general in charge of the facility. We drive – in silence – over to his headquarters building. We are shown into the major general's office by a Colonel Stack. Colonel Stack is a tall black man who looks not unlike Sidney Poitier. He grips my hand firmly and tells me, in a very soft-spoken voice, that he has something he wants to discuss with me after my interview with the general.

The general enters the room. Major General Jay Hood. Everyone stands. Myself included. An old military habit I suppose. The general seems pleased and invites me to sit. I ask him, given the investment in Guantanamo, and given the negative public profile it attracts, on a cost-benefit analysis, how the US military is benefitting from the existence of the camp. The general lets out a long sigh. 'Twofold. One. Some very dangerous men associated with Al Qaeda and other related terrorist organisations are not free to come back at us on the battlefield. So, first off, this is the safe detention of detainees focused on preventing attack, preventing terrorist action by some of the men we're holding, against the United States.'

The general continues. 'The second thing is the gathering of intelligence. There are still significant pieces of information that we continue to learn about Al Qaeda and some of its key operatives. We know now how they recruit, train and compartmentalise its command and control. We also know how it funds and finances itself. We're still filling in all sorts of small pieces of intelligence into a giant, international mosaic and we're making progress. The intelligence value is less tactical and more strategic in nature.'

I ask him about the other agencies present on Guantanamo. I notice he keeps looking at my eyebrow and fringe. 'All of the major intelligence players in the United States have an interest here and have either had people here or sent people here to visit. For example the FBI.' I ask him if the CIA are present on the naval station. 'Tom, you know I'm not gonna talk about many of the agencies who may have had some time here.'

I ask the general if he has full oversight of all agencies and their treatment of detainees. 'Absolutely. Every single detainee here at GTMO Bay is under my control and any actions involving them are in accordance with DOD Directives at all times.' I ask him if he can guarantee that. 'Absolutely. Unequivocally.' I ask him then if the fact that the prisoners have no exit date and no release date does not constitute a cruel and unusual punishment. The general is less clear. 'You're asking me to speculate what's in their minds . . . I don't think I'm qualified to do that. What I would point out though . . . It's not clear when the Global War on Terror will end.'

I ask him then if the incarceration of the prisoners could be indefinite. The general is preparing now to leave. He has a busy schedule. 'That's a matter very much for the policy makers. What I can tell you is that I've asked my young soldiers and sailors to focus on their jobs as well as they possibly can and in a professional manner. That's what will lead us to success and over time we will be able to show folks in the US and in fact around the world in the international community that we intend to do this job properly. For as long as it takes.'

The general stands up and shakes my hand. He almost pulls my arm out of its socket. He retains his grip and looks me in the eye. 'Tom. While you are here on Guantanamo, you're my guest. If you have any doubts about the program or the dignity or safety of the detainees, call me. Colonel Stack will give you my cellphone. Call me if you have any questions. Even if it's at 4 AM. And if you want me to open any door on this facility. I mean, literally, any door. Call me and I'll come open it.'

And with that, the general is gone.

Colonel Stack invites me outside onto the porch for an orange juice. 'You were in the service I hear.' I nod. Colonel Stack nods gravely. He looks at my eyebrows. 'Did that happen when you were on active service?' He looks concerned. 'Er, no. It happened outside the CBQ last night.' 'Oh,' he replies. He looks like he's going to ask me something else, but he decides not to. He points to his name tag. 'Stack,' he says aloud. He smiles and looks at me. 'I'm Irish, Tom. And proud of it.' He tells me that he is close to retirement and that he has taken up genealogy as a hobby. 'I wanted to know a little of my family history. So I checked out my great, great, great whatever grandfather. He was Robert Stack from Gorey, in the County of Wexford. He came to the United States to escape the famine and I expect that's where he met my great, great, great, whatever grandmother.' He smiles again. 'The colloquial phrase at the time was, 'They went out back together.' And that's how this line of the Stacks got started. He tells me that he has traced his cousins online and has made email contact. 'I'm going home to Wexford next year, Tom, for a visit.' I wish him well and he tells me. 'Look, the general is a good man. What he really means is that he is determined that what we do here saves lives on the battle-field. No one wants another 9/11 Tom. You've gotta understand that.' I make a note.

Sheila and Jim are a little remote on the way back to the CBQ. That night there is another barbecue in my honour. I let Jim light it this time. I ask Sheila if I can see the non-compliant prisoners and their conditions of incarceration. She looks doubtful. I remind her of the general's promise to me. 'I don't want to call him this late,' I remark. Sheila says, 'Leave it with me.'

I check my emails. Darach's school is looking for photographs of us all, when we were babies, for a class project. Aideen wants to know if I can think of where they might be in the house. Eoghan's runny nose has turned into an ear infection. I've a text from Pauline. She tells me she feels great. She tells me that the boys are great. She says that she is already excited about Christmas. Ailbhe is sleeping well.

The next morning, over a coffee, Sheila tells me that she has swung it for me to attend an 'Administrative Review Board' or ARB. This is a quasi-legal process conducted by the US military in order to ascertain if a detainee should be sent forward for court martial. A sort of pretrial hearing. The prisoner in question is 'compliant' but believed to be personally very close to Osama Bin Laden.

We cross over to Camp Delta and are led through the Sally Port once more. Sergeant Major Sanchez seems surprised to see me again. 'You still here?' he asks me. Sheila, Jim and Helen lead me to a large, single-storey building at the centre of the camp complex. They introduce me to another sailor.

This time it is US Navy Captain John Salsman. He gives me a background legal briefing into the status of the Administrative Review Board and the process that I am about to witness. He explains that as Guantanamo is located outside of the continental United States, the legal status of its detainees remains a contested issue. At least forty *habeas corpus* civilian lawsuits are being fought in the US courts on behalf of detainees on Guantanamo. These legal challenges to the lawfulness of their detention in Camp Delta are slowly working their way towards the US Supreme Court. As such, many of the detainees receive regular visits from lawyers from all over the United States and as far afield as London and other EU states. I think of the travel involved and yet again I am impressed by the legal profession. I think of the captain and the big copilot and shudder inwardly.

Whilst the detainees remain in legal limbo, the US military remains the sole and final arbiter as to the continued detention or otherwise of Guantanamo's inmates. In the air-conditioned briefing room, Captain Salsman informs me that the deliberations of OARDEC – Guantanamo's Office for the Administrative Review of the Detention of Enemy Combatants – will decide the fate of the remaining 505 detainees in Guantanamo.

The primary means by which OARDEC works is through annual ARBs for each detainee. Captain Salsman insists that 'this is not a legal process, simply an administrative process that helps us determine whether or not a detainee remains a threat to the United States or its allies.' Captain Salsman confirms that I may attend the ARB of a detainee suspected to have very close links to Osama Bin Laden. As we head out of the briefing room, I ask the captain if all of the military officers involved in the process have legal qualifications. He looks at me. 'None of them do. Actually, none of them are lawyers.' I'm not inspired.

I am advised that I must remain silent throughout the ARB and that, along with the detainee, I will not be permitted to hear any of the classified intelligence or 'evidence against' the detainee. Captain Salsman informs me that 'on average, 80 percent of the information upon which the ARB will deliberate is classified.' According to Captain Salsman, for 'security reasons and in order to protect valuable intelligence sources', detainees at Guantanamo, on average, only get to hear around 20 percent of the charges or allegations made against them. Again, I'm not inspired. I'm not in awe of this procedure whereby you don't get to hear the charges laid against you. I'm also not enamoured of the idea of the executive – in the form of the military – being the arresting authority, detaining authority and judge, jury and, potentially, executioner of these prisoners. There is no separation of powers. No oversight. Whilst the processes might appear 'legal' because of choreography and so on, I'm coming to the conclusion that the fundamental underpinnings of Guantanamo are seriously flawed. Bogus.

Before the ARB convenes, I meet the panel of officers who will adjudicate. The panel consists of five US army and air force colonels. I introduce myself. Two of them state that they are Irish American, but that 'apart from a brief stopover at Shannon,' they've not yet had a chance to visit Ireland. I ask them if any have studied law. They smile and finish their coffee. I ask again. They each, one by one, confirm that they have no legal qualifications or training.

We enter the room where the ARB is to be held. 'Hassan' – the detainee in question – is seated beside an interpreter. He is a 'compliant' prisoner dressed in a tan uniform. Hassan is not his real name. I am directed by Sheila and Helen to use the alias 'Hassan' when writing about this detainee. Though aged thirty-one, Hassan looks to be in his mid-twenties. He is of average height and of slight build. He is bearded with braided hair and is shackled at the ankles and wrists. He is attached by a chain to a metal ring that has been embedded in the floor. As we enter he tries to stand. The chain, however, is too short to allow him to stand fully upright. He loses his balance and, unable to move his arms or legs, falls heavily to one side.

An air force colonel seated next to him embraces him in an attempt to break his fall. He holds him in a bear-hug and lifts him back into his seat. It is an uncomfortable moment. Enemies held in an intimate embrace. The colonel in charge of the ARB asks him through the interpreter if he is OK and reassures him that it is not necessary to stand up. The officers take an oath in English to discharge their duties to the best of their abilities. The detainee takes an Islamic oath in Arabic. The detainee is then asked through the interpreter if it is true that he attended a Saudi training camp in Pakistan where he learned to fire a Kalashnikov AK-47 assault rifle. Hassan answers the panel in English and, looking directly at me, says, 'Yes, I did – do I look like Rambo to you?' Everyone, including the detainee, breaks into laughter.

Hassan is then asked about his movements and activities in Bosnia during the civil war in the former Yugoslavia. He denies that he fought there and states that, 'I went there to get a wife, a blonde one, in a safe city.' There is more laughter. Hassan becomes agitated, however, at what he states are inconsistencies and inaccuracies in the summary statement. 'I have told my interrogators time and time again, maybe six hundred times these things are not true.' The chairman of the ARB assures the detainee that his observations will be noted 'for the record'.

Hassan continues to look in my direction from time to time. He asks the chairman of the ARB through his interpreter that he wishes to discuss some matters with the board in private. The ARB adjourns and I am escorted out of the room. Approximately fifteen minutes later I am escorted back into the room. The mood in the room has changed considerably.

Hassan is asked to make an oral submission to the board as to why he should be released. Addressing the Irish-American colonel who is chairing the ARB, he states in English, 'You are a very senior officer and an educated man, you can see that I am not a threat to the USA, I am not a threat to anyone.' Looking around at everyone in the room then and in a barely audible voice, Hassan states, 'I just want to go home and see my daughter. I want to make a new life, a new start, be with my family.' The board concludes its business.

I am informed by Captain Salsman that under OARDEC's rules I am not permitted to enquire as to Hassan's fate or the outcome of the ARB at any point in the future. As he is led in chains back into the suffocating heat of Camp Delta, I am told that Hassan will learn of his fate 'in a number of months'.

On my last evening in GTMO, Sheila, Jim and Helen conduct the Security Review Panel. They scan my laptop and camera. All is acceptable it seems.

That night, I attend my final barbecue on Guantanamo. A band of storms and hurricanes is approaching the Cuban coast. We have to fly out tomorrow. We are accompanied at our final barbecue by our pilot captain and the big guy. Despite the heat and the humidity, the dapper captain is wearing his pilot's uniform. I get the impression he likes uniforms. He gets a few beers under his belt and then does his party piece. He dips his finger into the brazier and paints a moustache on his upper lip. He rips open his shirt and jumps up on a table to wild applause. He sings 'In The Navy,' á la YMCA. It is a bizarre ending to a bizarre trip.

The following morning, I am weighed again by the big guy. I'm still 11kg. Our bags are weighed and a group of tight-lipped civilian 'contractors' join us for the flight out. One of them is an attorney representing one of the prisoners. He introduces himself and produces a flask of whiskey from his inside pocket. 'In-flight service,' he winks. The captain and the big guy crank up the engines and we whine down the runway and are suddenly airborne. We bank steeply out of the Windward Passage and for a moment I can see the Caribbean on one side and the Atlantic on the other. As we bank away, Guantanamo Bay recedes into the distance. I can make out the rows of cell blocks on Camp Delta quite clearly. I think of them down there. Hassan included. I share the whiskey with my fellow traveller. As we land in Florida, I remark how bumpy the flight was. He answers, 'Which would you prefer? Four hours in a bone-shaker like this, or four hours in a holding cell?' I see his point. 'We've got to get these guys out, Tom,' he tells me. 'Not just for them and their families. But for the US. Time is passing too slowly on this.' I wonder how many of them are still incarcerated there today.

For my part, the least I can do for the detainees is to publish the on-the-record intention of the United States to execute prisoners. I am the first journalist to wring this admission from GTMO officials. I am also the first journalist to get the US military to admit openly to the force-feeding of detainees on hunger strike. I hope and trust that these admissions will hasten the demise of Camps Delta and Echo on Guantanamo Bay.

Chapter 30

Landstuhl

'Imagine, Thomas. I'd be buried in on top of mammy. And then
he'd be buried in on top of me. I'd be stuck between them for all eternity.
Imagine the rows!'

Dublin

Christmas 2005

The return trip to Ireland is uneventful. I manage to get a lot of the material
written on my laptop on an Aer Lingus direct flight from Orlando, Florida to
Dublin. The plane is full of Irish families returning from holidays in
Disneyland. There are Mickey and Minnie Mouses all over the aircraft.
American icons that jar with my experience in GTMO. I write about the
force-feeding of hunger strikers and plans to execute prisoners in
Guantanamo.

When I get home, it is around 5 AM local time. I manage to get a taxi in
time for breakfast with the kids. I walk Darach to school. His hand in mine,
his fingers warm and tiny. The traffic on the Rock Road is heavy as usual. We
look at the drivers, mobile phones up to their ears, coffee cups perched on
dashboards. After the madness that is GTMO, it is a reassuring scenario.

Eoghan continues to make progress with the physiotherapy. Viktoria has
returned to Hungary after the latest six-week session. I tidy out the spare
room and drop the empty Unicum bottles into the green bin. I catch up with
my workload in DIT. Ailbhe is no longer breastfeeding. Aideen is back at
work and I'm able to bottle-feed little Ailbhe. I cradle her in my arms as she
sucks hungrily on the bottle. Little red kiss-curls across her forehead. Her big

green eyes locked on mine as she feeds. Her pupils dilate and suddenly she is asleep.

We bring Eoghan to the CRC. He is assessed regularly and we are coming to the inevitable conclusion, slowly but surely, that despite his progress at crawling and dressing and so on, he is not going to be able to walk independently. We try out various forward and rear-facing walkers. Eoghan enjoys being in the standing position. For a while he makes progress on the walking frames.

Eventually though, we arrive at the point where it is clear that Eoghan will need a wheelchair. He is going to be a wheelchair user. The physiotherapists in the CRC ask him what colour chair he would like. Eoghan says, 'Blue.' They show him pictures of spoke-guards to decorate his chair. There is *Sponge Bob Square Pants*, *Spider-Man*, concentric circles, abstract designs, all sorts. Eoghan picks out a blue spoke-guard decorated with black bats. 'Bats,' he says. It is Halloween after all. His little finger points at them, hovering a little in free space with his intention tremor. 'My bats.'

The *Irish Times* runs my Guantanamo Bay series over a weekend and into the following week. I do the usual round of RTÉ, Newstalk and TV3. I even supply audio. Audio of my interview with General Hood and the haunting 'call to prayer' over Guantanamo. A broadcasting assistant asks me if General Hood is his real name. 'Any relation to Robin?' Just before we go on air, a voice in the headphones asks me if General Hood's men were merry. When the red light goes on, the presenter works his way through the piece in his usual, professionally consummate manner.

The war in Iraq rages on. An average of one hundred US soldiers are killed in action each month in 2005. Many hundreds more are seriously injured. I am curious about the wounded and their injuries. Many of them suffer from multiple catastrophic injuries and yet survive, due to the latest innovations in battlefield medicine. The range of injuries inflicted by roadside bombs and IEDs or Improvised Explosive Devices is termed 'polytrauma'. I call on X once more in the US Embassy.

I'm a little nervous about X's reaction to the features in the *Irish Times* on GTMO. Particularly the admission that there was an intention or a contingency plan to execute prisoners there. I also felt that X would be uncomfortable with Captain Edmondson's on-the-record statements about the force-feeding of prisoners. But X is his usual breezy self. I ask him about polytrauma. He tells me that he'll see what he can do. A few weeks later, X calls me and tells me that he can get me to Landstuhl, the US military hospital near Ramstein in Germany. This is the hospital to which all those injured on the battlefield in Iraq and Afghanistan are medically evacuated. It is their first port of call on being airlifted out of theatre.

Pauline calls me just before Christmas. She is upset. She tells me that she is no longer in remission. The cancer is back.

The new year starts with further tests and test results for Eoghan. The suggested classification of Pelizaeus-Merzbacher disease remains the closest we have to a confirmed diagnosis. The paediatric neurologist books us into Temple Street Children's Hospital for another MRI scan. We need to continue to track and assess the status of the myelin sheath in Eoghan's neuromuscular system. We get Darach to school and make the frantic dash into the city centre. There is the usual stressful search for a parking space. Again, we'll need to feed the parking meter during the day – otherwise we'll get clamped. This is the usual and ongoing situation that parents with sick children attending the city-centre hospital must face. A taxi driver shakes his fist at us and shouts obscenities as we reverse into a spot around a half a mile from the hospital. We race to the MRI department with Eoghan in his buggy.

When we get Eoghan checked in and he is ready for the scan, we discuss his sedation with the medical team. We decide to try and do the scan with no sedation. Eoghan is only three years old. It is a big ask to expect him to lie still in the chamber of the MRI scanner for the half-hour or so that it will take to complete the scan. We talk to Eoghan about it. He looks at us with his still blue eyes and tells us that he is 'not afraid'. The nurses give us a little set of headphones so that Eoghan can listen to nursery rhymes when he is inside the bore of the scanner. In he goes. His little socks stick out at the end of the stretcher. His blonde curls just barely visible deep inside the machine. The scan begins with the usual deafening series of clicks, bangs and cracking sounds. It goes on for what seems like an eternity. Eoghan remains focused and unmoving. We hear him humming inside the machine.

When the scan is over, we hold him tightly. He is thrilled with himself. Even more thrilled with the lollipop he gets from the technicians. As we navigate our way around Temple Street, I am conscious of all the other children that are here. And their parents. White faces. Some tiny little bundles, barely moving. We thank our lucky stars for Eoghan's continued health and his progress against all the odds.

I meet up with Pauline. She is paler now. She is losing her hair once more and is resigned to wearing the blonde bob. Pauline tells me that the wig is very hot. She prefers to wear a scarf when she can. She tells me about her goals. 'I definitely want to see Christmas. I want to spend it with the boys. And I'd love to see the springtime. That's what we're concentrating on now.' Pauline knows that she is going to die. She has thought the unthinkable. Spoken the unspeakable. She tells me that she has spoken to dad about her illness. She tells me that at first he didn't seem to understand that it was terminal. It is impossible, I suppose, for my dad to accept that his little girl is dying. I think of Liadain and I think of Ailbhe. It is heartbreaking. I look across the table at Pauline. She smiles at me.

She tells me that a hospital chaplain spoke to her about her illness. 'He said that everyone has a cross to bear. And he said that if God sat us all down around a big table and told us to put our crosses down in front of us, and then gave us the opportunity to look at all the crosses and choose a different one, we'd probably choose our own cross anyway.' Pauline looks at me and tears come to her eyes. 'Only, I don't want this cross, Thomas. I really don't want it.'

I take Pauline's hand and she composes herself quickly. 'You'll never guess what daddy said to me after I told him I was going to die.' Pauline looks at me, smiling again and starts to giggle. 'When I told him I wasn't going to make it. When the penny dropped, we had a little cry together. He even hugged me.' I try to visualise my dad having a little cry. I try hard to visualise him hugging. Pauline continues. 'Anyway, he wipes his eyes in his hankie, and says that there's room in the family plot for me. Imagine, Thomas. I'd be buried in on top of mammy. And then he'd be buried in on top of me. I'd be stuck between them for all eternity. Imagine the rows!' Pauline is laughing now and gripping my hand tightly. 'I told him I'd think about it, Thomas.'

Landstuhl, Germany

March 2006

I've filled the freezer again with dinners for the week. Myself and Aideen cross-check our diaries and figure out how to juggle work and the nippers for the next few days. I've got to be back in Dublin on Thursday on the late flight from Frankfurt so that I can take Eoghan to his physiotherapy appointment in the CRC first thing Friday morning. I get up at the usual ungodly hour and in the dark, and get a taxi to Dublin Airport for the flight to Germany. I'm going to have the opportunity to meet some of the wounded soldiers from the ongoing wars in Iraq and Afghanistan. I'll see for myself, at first hand, where some of the soldiers who transit through Shannon end up.

The Aer Lingus flight from Dublin rolls down the runway in darkness. Another morning. Another plane journey. As Dublin drops below, out of sight, I think of Pauline. Maybe she'll make it. Maybe there will be a miracle. At 36,000 feet, I feel a little closer to God. I ask my mother to do something for her. Have a word with someone. I hear no answers. Just silence. And the hum of the engines at 36,000 feet.

At Frankfurt, I go to the car rental desk. I'm in luck, they tell me. They've upgraded me to a BMW. I glide out of the underground car park in a big black BMW and head for the Autobahn. Blue sky overhead. Frost in the neat, square fields that stretch in an orderly fashion for miles in every direction. Unlike Ireland, the terrain is flat. I see mountains on the horizon. It is all very Teutonic.

An hour's drive south of Frankfurt, the A6 Autobahn crosses the Rhine and enters the picturesque German Rhine-Pfalz region. The terrain changes from flat plain to mountains. Minutes later, south of Kaiserslautern, the pretty picture-postcard town of Landstuhl appears in the distance. It is nestled among hills lined with snow-covered firs and spruces. I follow the road signs. Eventually, I round a bend and see the red-tiled rooftops of the town before me. Landstuhl, with its myriad church steeples and quaint central square has its own Irish bar, the 'Blarney Stone' on Haupstrasse. I make a mental note of it. I'll go there for a drink later. Landstuhl itself is an unusually pretty German town. As it is home to the US military's Landstuhl Regional Medical Centre, there are lots of signs in English.

Perched on top of Landstuhl's Kirchberg Hill, the US military hospital was built in the immediate aftermath of World War II amid the ruins of the infamous Landstuhl Adolf Hitler School, a leadership academy for top Nazis. Throughout the Cold War, Landstuhl serviced the needs of the 50,000 or so US troops stationed in Germany. It still does so today and has evolved into a state-of-the-art hospital specialising across all the most significant medical disciplines from obstetrics and gynaecology to general surgery and of late, trauma surgery and critical care. In addition to the one thousand or so US citizens that are born in Landstuhl's maternity ward each year, the hospital's trauma centre annually treats up to ten thousand battle injuries sustained during Operation Iraqi Freedom and Operation Enduring Freedom in Afghanistan. The Regional Medical Centre, originally designed as a battlefield hospital in the event of a clash between US and Soviet armoured divisions in central Europe, is now playing its part in the Global War on Terror.

Just five hours by air from the heat and dust of Baghdad, the rural idyll of Landstuhl has now found itself on the front line in the United States's war in Iraq. Located just 6km from neighbouring Ramstein US Air Force Base, Landstuhl has become the key central stepping stone in the US military's medical air evacuation route from Iraq all the way to the United States. This is an air-bridge consisting of combat helicopters and C-17 jet aircraft which stretches from the remotest US Marine Corps forward operating posts in Iraq to Andrew's US Air Force Base just outside Washington in the United States. As I approach the hospital, security is tight and the perimeter fences and environs of the hospital are patrolled by armed German security personnel. I notice that the Germans are armed with heavy automatic pistols. They operate the outer perimeter of the hospital. A blue-uniformed German guard takes in the rental car and points me away from the entrance towards what looks like a small overflow car park.

I swing the BMW into a parking space reserved for *Gast*. As I gather up my laptop and phone, I notice a group of US troops patrolling just inside the perimeter fence. Their insignia indicate that they are part of a military police unit. They move slowly along the fence, sidestepping mounds of frozen snow that have lodged there. They are accompanied by three working dogs. Two are Alsatians. The other looks like a Doberman. They lope alongside and ahead of the troops, stopping now and again to sniff and root at tree stumps and clumps of grass. One of the Alsatians stops in his tracks and spots me through the fence. Its breath comes in short exhalations of steam in the frosty air. Dogs and men stare at me from among the trees. I wave at them. One of the soldiers nods back. They continue to stare as I make my way to the entrance area.

The German guards inspect my passport and letter of invitation. They process me through an airport-style security scanner. There is another working dog in the search area beyond. His handler, a US soldier, asks me to leave my laptop case and coat on the conveyor belt next to the scanner. The dog, a Golden Retriever, hops up and sniffs around my belongings. His handler encourages him with short commands. The dog returns to his feet and is rewarded with a small treat from the soldier's hand.

I'm then handed over to a military police corporal. He checks my name off a clipboard and walks me over towards the hospital. Once inside, I am introduced to Colonel John Sweeney, the medical head of the Deployed Warrior Medical Management Centre (DWMMC) in Landstuhl. Colonel Sweeney greets me warmly. He gives me a firm handshake and tells me that his family come from Donegal. '*Céad míle fáilte romhat.*' Sweeney greets me in faultless Irish, albeit with an American accent. Colonel Sweeney tells me that he began his military career with combat experience in a helicopter unit in Vietnam in the late 1960s. He later qualified as a medical doctor and specialises in psychiatry. He is responsible for coordinating the care of the daily planeloads of critically injured soldiers arriving directly from the battlefield. Colonel Sweeney's office in Landstuhl ensures continuity of care for US soldiers – from the site of injury in Iraq through to the trauma and intensive care unit in Landstuhl and on to the final destination of the wounded in the US Naval Hospital, Bethesda Maryland or at the US Army Hospital at Walter Reed.

Colonel Sweeney produces a box of Barry's Green Label tea bags, purchased during a recent stopover in Ireland. Over a cup of tea for his 'Irish guest', he explains the unique manner in which the war in Iraq is producing injuries of a type not previously survived in combat. Unlike Vietnam, where only 3 percent of casualties were caused by bomb and blast injuries, approximately 75 to 80 percent of the injured arriving at Landstuhl are wounded by the blast effects and shrapnel injuries sustained from IEDs, the weapon of choice in Iraq.

This has led to a situation where wounded US troops are not presenting at Landstuhl with 'simple' gunshot wounds, but complex blast and burn injuries combined with profound brain and spinal injuries. IEDs have killed almost 1,200 US troops thus far in Iraq. Troops who survive insurgent IED attacks are presenting to Landstuhl with multiple catastrophic injuries. Hence the newly coined term 'polytrauma'. Colonel Sweeney explains to me that polytrauma consists of multiple serious injuries caused by blast and shrapnel to those parts of the body least protected by body armour, especially the head – with brain and spinal injuries. These are usually combined with penetrating and rupturing injuries to internal organs along with massive orthopaedic injuries to arms and legs. In previous wars, troops injured in this way would simply not have survived.

According to Colonel Sweeney, 'The enemy is getting very good at these IEDs and the blast injuries are getting more serious. But we've got some very talented surgeons down-range [in combat] who do the initial life-saving procedures in the Combat Support Hospitals. Then, they send them to here where we can do what's necessary, surgically, for them to survive the nine and a half hour flight from Landstuhl to the US.'

As Colonel Sweeney explains, a soldier wounded in Iraq can be repatriated to a hospital in the United States in less than seventy-two hours. As a consequence, he tells me, 'morbidity rates among the wounded have decreased.' The colonel elaborates. 'To put the US military's current medical air evacuation route into perspective, Tom, it is worth bearing in mind that during World War II, it took an average of one hundred and twenty days to get a US soldier from the site where he was injured, whether it be in Europe, Africa or Asia, to a hospital in the United States. Approximately one-third of US soldiers wounded in such circumstances died of their injuries. During the 1960s, it took an average of forty-five days to evacuate a wounded US soldier from Vietnam to a hospital in the United States. Approximately one-quarter of these troops died of their injuries during this period. We are able to get the wounded from Baghdad to Ramstein literally within hours of them being hit. The flight time from Baghdad to Ramstein is just four and a half hours.'

As a consequence, in Iraq and Afghanistan today the mortality rate among wounded US troops has fallen dramatically to around 10 percent of the total wounded. Landstuhl is seen as crucial to the survival of these critically wounded troops. According to Colonel Sweeney, 'These kids just couldn't withstand the fourteen-and-a-half-hour flight direct from Baghdad to Washington. So we fly them here and it's saving hundreds if not thousands of lives.' So much so that there is a saying among US troops serving in Iraq to the effect that, when injured, 'If you make it to Landstuhl, you're good to go,' meaning that safe arrival at Landstuhl is almost a guarantee of survival.

Chapter 31

Polytrauma

'Her face has been blown off.'

Landstuhl Regional Medical Centre, Ramstein, Germany

March 2006

Shortly after I arrive at Landstuhl, a C-17 jet lands at the nearby Ramstein Air Base. The US air base is just a short distance from Landstuhl on the opposite side of the A6 Autobahn. Along with Colonel Sweeney's triage team of trauma surgeons and nurses, I await the arrival of the latest batch of wounded US troops. We wait at the hospital's main entrance. The air is extremely cold and I blow on my hands to keep them from going numb. Colonel Sweeney tells me that there are fourteen wounded soldiers en route.

They arrive within minutes aboard a large converted air force coach. Of the fourteen, nine are borne from the coach on stretchers. As they are gently lowered from the vehicle, some are still intubated with drips and oxygen masks attached; a team of US military chaplains including a rabbi and a Presbyterian minister whisper gentle words of encouragement to each one.

The chaplains carry well-thumbed copies of US Army Field Manual 16-100 'The Unit Ministry Team Handbook'. I ask to look at the handbook. It is dog-eared on a page headed, 'Words to a Dying Soldier'. For the 'Dying Christian soldier,' it recommends Psalm 23. For the 'Dying Jewish soldier' the manual recommends the Jewish prayer for the dying, the *Shema*. For the 'Dying Muslim soldier,' it recommends the prayer to Allah, the *Shahada*.

All of the injured are very young men and women. Many are still wearing the combat fatigues that they were wearing when they were injured, in some cases only hours earlier. The first soldier to be stretchered into the hospital has shrapnel injuries all over his face. His throat, cheeks and forehead are peppered with black marks from the blast and his face has swollen to the extent that one eye is squeezed tightly shut. The other eye is obscured by a dressing. He is completely immobile. I notice his combat boots are worn from patrolling – still dusty from the battlefield in Iraq.

The second patient is very pale. He appears disoriented, perhaps partially sedated. One of his legs appears to have been shattered by a blast and a large sponge-like bandage is seeping blood from under his right ankle. The next patient has a nasal tube inserted. He stares silently at the triage nurses and clutches a colostomy bag to his abdomen. The remaining soldiers, black, white, hispanic, male and female – all so young – are stretchered by in a blur.

Four of the wounded are 'ambulatory' and walk into the hospital reception area. They are still wearing their flak jackets and one carries his helmet. They shiver from the cold of this near-freezing morning in Landstuhl. Apart from the cold, they appear shocked and traumatised from their injuries. They glance anxiously around the room – scanning the phalanx of medical specialists and nurses for a familiar or friendly face as they enter.

One of the injured arrives in a separate ambulance and is wheeled directly to the intensive care unit. The injured soldier is a young black woman, aged just twenty-one. Her head and neck are swaddled in bandages, stained dark with blood. One of her arms is visible and I see goose pimples form on her skin as she is briefly exposed to the cold air during the transfer from the ambulance. One of the orderlies tells me that she is a 'very sad case among the wounded'. He looks at his clipboard. She has 'catastrophic facial injuries and the loss of one eye'. 'Basically,' he tells me, 'her face has been blown off.'

One of the chaplains, Major David Bowermann, explains to me that at this point, the soldiers will be keen to talk. 'Once they adjust to the reality of their admission to Landstuhl. Once they overcome the initial shock and trauma of their injuries, they'll want to talk about the experience. They need to talk it out of their system so to speak.' The chaplains have seen it all before. Morning after morning. Soldiers in shock who are very anxious to retell their stories – anxious to describe how they got 'hit up'. They'll also nervously enquire about other soldiers killed or injured in the same incident. The chaplain explains to me that the soldiers are often quite conflicted in their retelling of traumatic incidents, particularly if they have killed an enemy combatant.

Major Bowermann explains that the chaplaincy deals directly with the question of killing in combat and the manner in which they reconcile that with the fifth commandment, 'Thou shalt not kill.' He is at pains to point out that US troops do not receive any simplistic answers to this ethical dilemma and that each soldier has to work out their own individual route to salvation or inner reconciliation from the savagery of combat in the context of a forgiving God. The rabbi at the entrance asks me if I go to church. I tell him that I was brought up as a Catholic. 'An Irish Catholic?' the rabbi asks, eyebrows raised in mock surprise. 'That's original.'

I follow the wounded troops through to the emergency room and on to the trauma surgery centre and the intensive care unit. In the intensive care unit, I'm introduced to an army trauma surgeon, Dr Tim Woods. The doctor is a graduate of Notre Dame University – known as 'the Fighting Irish' he tells me with a grin. Dr Woods has been up for over thirty-six hours operating in the trauma room. The previous night, the trauma team lost the battle to save the life of a critically injured soldier.

Despite his fatigue, Dr Woods is upbeat about the work of the trauma team in Landstuhl and states that, 'there's no doubt that this war is going to teach us a lot about how we treat injuries in the civilian world.' Dr Woods refers specifically to brain injuries. 'We are continuing to learn about brain injury. One thing we are doing is deploying neurosurgeons to the front line. When troops sustain a brain injury, we immediately remove the skull, often near the scene, to allow the brain to swell. That way you don't get compression of the vessels and further damage. This has saved significant numbers of lives and has allowed significant improvements in the recovery prospects of wounded soldiers.'

Dr Woods goes on to describe the manner in which US army trauma surgeons are operating on leg injuries to try and avoid amputation. He describes the significant swelling associated with blast injuries to legs which can cause 'compartment syndrome', involving the compression and loss of further tissues and muscle mass in the leg often requiring amputation. According to Dr Woods, US army surgeons are now 'routinely cutting through the fascia or binding tissue of the leg to allow the injured muscle mass and tissue to swell unhindered during the recovery phase, thus saving the limb.'

He also describes the manner in which abdominal injuries are now being treated. In the past, penetrating injuries to the abdomen from shrapnel or bullets normally proved fatal. Now, according to Dr Woods, 'We're actually leaving the abdominal injuries open. Called an "open abdomen". That allows them to swell as the body needs. At a later date we can close the abdomen. So we can allow a patient to go through the significant injury phase in a sterile environment such as here and they survive to recover fully.'

Dr Woods also comments that US surgeons are seeing fewer injuries to the genitalia of soldiers due to the simple addition of a 'groin plate' to their Kevlar body armour. Despite these advances and the various high-tech and low-tech responses to the conflict, there are still large numbers of amputees processed through Landstuhl. Approximately four hundred amputees have passed through the facility; almost a quarter of these are double and triple amputees.

The medical staff are very excited about the improving survival rates for those with head injuries. One of Dr Woods's assistants tells me that she wants to specialise in neurosurgery once she has worked through her commitment to the army. She walks me through the intensive care area and down the corridor to the MRI suite. And there it is. A General Electric MRI scanner. I pause and look through the glass into the suite. There is a patient inside the bore of the scanner. I see a pair of feet protruding from the chamber. I think of Eoghan and his tiny feet. In his little Tigger socks. I can hear the bangs and clicks of the scanner out here in the corridor. That, and the all-too-familiar hospital smell of disinfectant makes me feel a little bit dizzy. The young female doctor looks at me quizzically. 'Don't worry,' she tells me. 'He can't hear a thing. He's out of it.' I ask her, foolishly, If they have learned anything about myelin loss. Or demyelination. She thinks for a moment and shakes her head. 'Not as such. But we are aware of the development of stem cell therapies to help regenerate some vital tissues. But not here. That stem cell research is real Frankenstein territory. That's for the real med-school nerds.' We laugh.

She has broken the tension and taken me out of my reverie about Eoghan. But I ponder the Frankenstein remark. Ironic to reference a horror story in the middle of such horror. Black humour. A survival mechanism. I say a silent prayer for all the wounded. I pray for Eoghan. And I pray for med-school nerds.

Colonel Sweeney arrives with the rabbi. 'There you are, Tom. Rabbi Silverman will introduce you to some of our recovering wounded.' Rabbi Silverman takes me down the corridor to the recovery ward. The ward is full. Most of the patients seem to be sleeping. One or two stare at me. They look disengaged, listless. The rabbi introduces me to Sergeant Frank Cuevas, aged twenty-seven, in the recovery ward. Based with the US 101st Airborne Division in Ramadi, Frank agrees to do an interview with me despite his injuries. At the beginning, when we start to talk, it is clear that Frank is in pain and slightly disoriented. He is unable to remember his unit initially. With some gentle prompting, he tells his story.

He describes being on a cordon and search operation in Ramadi. As they dismounted from their armoured vehicle to proceed on foot, their patrol was fired upon by a sniper. Frank describes the first shots: 'A shot rang out and one of the guys to my rear was hit in the buttocks area. I got out of the truck to run around and try to drag him back and then another shot rang out. It hit me in the leg and went through and hit my intestines and my colon. It just didn't hurt at first. I just crawled up under the axle of the vehicle and waited for them to come get me. They airlifted me to Camp Ramadi and they did surgery and then they got me here.'

Suffering from wounds that in recent conflicts might have proved fatal, Sergeant Cuevas is confident that he will return to the US and recover fully. At the only point in the interview when he manages to smile, he mentions Shannon Airport. 'On our way to Iraq, we stopped at Shannon. We got out and we were allowed to walk around the airport. It was pretty much the last time we were not actually locked down in combat – the last transition stage. I was wondering about the castles around there. When I'm back on my feet I'll go back there.'

Lieutenant Parker Hahn, the trauma nurse in charge of the ward, also mentions Shannon. After a discussion in which he describes 'removing the femur of a suicide bomber from the chest cavity of a guy in Iraq', he goes on to describe the stopover in Shannon. 'They let us off the plane to stretch our legs which was great. I remember it being very foggy and I think even rainy – go figure! It was different. Like where, before, you were always worried about mortars and rockets and someone shooting at you. To get off a plane and walk into a terminal a building without any of your weapons and gear was nice. To be just able to breathe.' Lieutenant Hahn, who has no Irish connections, goes on to say how the Shannon experience had prompted him to return to Ireland as a tourist, where he found the driving to be 'a nerve-wracking experience, even compared to Iraq, but the best country I've ever been in. The people and the countryside are beautiful.'

Rabbi Silverman and I move through the ward. Some of the troops have placed jars on the window sills with little pieces of metal inside them. 'That's their shrapnel jars,' the rabbi tells me. 'We've found it therapeutic to let the guys see some of the shrapnel that has been surgically removed from their bodies. They see what hit them. What was inside them. It gives them a focus and, believe it or not, they heal quicker,' he adds. 'I saw you looking in at neurology back there.' He looks at me questioningly. 'Er, I'm interested in the brain,' I explain. The rabbi strokes his chin thoughtfully. 'You know the brain is an amazing organ. We're learning about it all the time here. Did you know, if we get a guy or a girl in here, with what we call a 'through and through' – where the shrapnel has passed right through the body, then the victim remembers everything that happened, right up to the moment when they got hit.' The rabbi continues, enthusiastically now, 'But, if there's some shrapnel left in the body, inside the skull or anywhere else, the victim has no recall of what happened to them. It's like the brain is saying, I don't need to remember this traumatic stuff. I just need to get this crap out of my body. I just need to concentrate on survival. I don't need to be burdened with a traumatic memory. Isn't that something?' I agree it is quite something.

When we exit out on to the corridor, there are two young marines on crutches at the other end of the passageway. They are hobbling along, supporting each other awkwardly on their crutches. Each of the soldiers has lost a leg. The girl has lost her right leg. The guy has lost his left leg. They are leaning in on each other for mutual support. I can hear their laughter as we approach. 'How's the practising coming along?' asks Rabbi Silverman. The young female soldier answers him breezily, 'Oh, we're getting there. We're limping along.' They both laugh again. The young guy takes me in. He asks me what I'm doing in Landstuhl. I tell him I'm from Ireland. He leans heavily on his crutch and whistles. 'I was in Ireland once. On my way to Iraq. I had a pint of Guinness there. A pint of Guinness in Shannon and a wake-up call in Fallujah.' They both laugh again. As his female comrade supports him, Dwayne, the young guy, reaches over and strains to hold the swing door open for us. I try to take the door from him, to help. There are beads of sweat forming on his forehead from the effort. 'No man, just go. Please. After you.'

As I leave Landstuhl, Colonel John Sweeney tells me that the strain of dealing with so many critically injured young troops can take its toll on his surgical staff. He talks of the phenomenon of 'empathy fatigue' among doctors and nurses at the facility. As a psychiatrist, he tells me that he tries to ensure that everyone keeps in tune with their emotional workload as well as their medical caseload when they are posted to Landstuhl.

Colonel Sweeney also reminds me that the US medical staff at Landstuhl treat not just US troops but soldiers and civilians from thirty-seven different countries. He also tells me that they treat Iraqi and Afghan civilians also. 'Some of them are enemy combatants.' He goes on to inform me that he is responsible for the medical evacuation and care in Landstuhl of all of the Irish Defence Forces personnel that are currently serving with the KFOR NATO battle group in Kosovo and the Irish troops serving in Kabul, Afghanistan with the International Security Assistance Force (ISAF). I had not been aware of this link with the Irish army.

Colonel Sweeney shakes hands with me and Rabbi Silverman accompanies me to the gate. The rabbi asks me if I have any plans for the evening. I tell him that I'll probably get something to eat in the Blarney Stone. 'You could do worse,' he tells me. The Rabbi tells me that he'll meet me there at around 10 PM for a Guinness.

It is already dark when I get back to the BMW. I run the engine for a few minutes to de-ice the windscreen and think about the day's events. I'm haunted by the memory of the feet sticking out of the MRI scanner. I'm haunted by the memory of the two one-legged soldiers in the corridor. I check in to my hotel and scan my emails. Darach has a parent-teacher meeting on Friday morning. Can I make it before I get to the CRC? I email Aideen and confirm that I can come along to meet Darach's teacher on Friday morning.

The Blarney Stone is a welcome respite from the day's visit to the medical centre. As I had suspected, it is packed with US troops. They are drinking at the bar and noisily jostling for the pool table. None of the staff in the bar are Irish. I order the Hasenpfeffer from the menu. Whatever that is. I order a pilsener and the dish arrives a few minutes later. It is a hearty stew. As I eat the stew, I notice that the bowl is covered in pictures of rabbits in various traditional German costumes. Rabbits going hunting. Rabbits drinking beer. I'm thinking the kids would love these bowls when I realise that I'm probably eating a rabbit. I won't tell the kids that bit.

At ten bells the rabbi appears at my elbow. He has brought a friend. A local Catholic priest. At first, I think the priest is a young guy dressed up in a fancy dress outfit. But then I realise that he actually is a priest. It's just that as an Irish person, I'm not used to seeing young priests. I haven't seen a young priest since about 1972. All of the Irish priests I know are ancient. Fr Biermann looks to be about twenty-eight or so. He orders drinks and introduces himself to me as 'Ralf, Ralf Biermann.' I give the two holy men my card. Avi – Rabbi Silverman – asks me what my PhD was all about. I give him a potted history of my doctoral research into female soldiers, the findings in relation to sexual harassment and the subsequent fall-out with the military authorities. Avi laughs. 'Dr Popular, I presume.' I see Fr Ralf working out the joke. He eventually laughs also.

Avi looks at me thoughtfully. 'Your story has a ring to it. In the Bible, the Jews traditionally sacrificed two goats on the Day of Atonement. One goat, the Lord's goat, was sacrificed to atone for our sins. The other goat, the Azazel goat, was banished into the wilderness carrying the secret knowledge of our collective sins. This goat, known as the scapegoat, was banished and shunned, expected to die in ignomy. The scapegoat's secret knowledge of our sins would die and our sins would die with it.' Fr Ralf and I look at Avi for a while, in silence. Avi prompts us, 'You are the scapegoat, Thomas. You were told the secret sins of the army. And you were then banished, to hopefully die in the wilderness.' Fr Ralf proposes a toast. 'To Thomas, the scapegoat.' It feels oddly healing. Two holy men, in a pub in Germany, hinting at general absolution.

Chapter 32

Bessbrook Mill

'I will not be seeing this patient again.'

St James's Hospital, Dublin

Easter 2006

As I fly back from Frankfurt, I manage to write some of the feature on Landstuhl. The Aer Lingus hostess gives me a free gin and tonic as it is St Patrick's Day. Someone is in good humour. We descend gradually over the Irish Sea, Howth to the right, the sweep of Dublin Bay to the left. The flight touches down just before midnight. I race through the baggage hall to get to the taxi rank. It is a cold moonlit night. As the taxi crawls through the city centre, St Patrick's Day drunks stagger out onto the road. It's like a zombie movie. Drinking themselves into a stupor. Two drunks hold each other up at the side of the road. I get a flashback to the two one-legged marines in Landstuhl.

I tiptoe into the house and slip into bed. Everyone is sleeping. At around 5 AM, Darach appears in the doorway and asks me if I've brought him a present from Germany. The day begins a little earlier than intended.

The morning is a rush. I walk Darach to school earlier than usual. He holds my hand as far as the school gate and then relinquishes it. It is another little change. The schoolyard is full of little boys pursuing a football. They sweep past like a flock of sparrows and then wheel about and change direction. Darach is gone and disappears into the throng. I cannot pick him out in the crowd of boys.

Darach's teacher tells me that he is settling in well. Not a care in the world.

I race back to the house and get Eoghan ready for the CRC. His physiotherapy appointment is at 9.30 AM. Amazingly, I make it across town and get there in time. Eoghan's physiotherapist is beaming. 'Look what we have for you, Eoghan. It's a surprise.'

Eoghan's first wheelchair sits gleaming in the gym. As promised, it is blue. Shiny blue. And it has blue spoke-guards decorated with black bats. Eoghan wriggles with delight and the physiotherapist teaches me how to transfer Eoghan into the chair. We spend the session monitoring Eoghan's posture in the chair. I see him slowly, carefully, push himself away from me and wheel to the doorway. He looks hesitantly back at me and then disappears out into the corridor. Out of view. It is a morning of changes, big and small.

Eoghan's physiotherapist and his occupational therapist will review Eoghan's progress in the chair. He develops expertise surprisingly quickly and navigates our crowded family home with ease. Hopefully, he'll have no problem in the school environment. I say a silent prayer to whomever that he might successfully navigate the classroom and continue his journey in life.

I meet with Pauline. She has lost all of her hair now. My beautiful sister has lost all of her blonde curls. She is tired and drawn from her treatment. There is a catch in her breathing. Within a few weeks she is admitted to St James's Hospital for more intensive management of her symptoms. She attends St Luke's Hospital for radiotherapy. On Pauline's last visit to St Luke's, the doctor asks her if she wouldn't mind taking her chart with her on the short trip back to St James's. On the way back into the city centre, Pauline tells me that she opened the chart. 'There was a letter from the consultant in St Luke's to my team in St James's. It was a short note, Thomas. One line jumped out at me. "I will not be seeing this patient again."'

Pauline is in and out of St James's on a more regular basis now. I bring Eoghan in to see her. Pauline gets out of bed and pushes him around the long corridors in his wheelchair. Pauline's shoulders are slightly stooped. They make an odd couple as they wheel along the polished floors. Eoghan is delighted. Pauline is smiling.

Bessbrook Mill, Northern Ireland
June 2006

After the *Irish Times* has run the Landstuhl feature, I make repeated requests to visit the UK equivalent at the Selly Oak and Queen Elizabeth Hospitals in Birmingham. Night and day, for every day of the wars in Iraq and Afghanistan, RAF Aeromedical teams fly wounded and dying British soldiers from the battlefield to Birmingham Airport onboard specially converted Boeing C-17 jets. The British soldiers who arrive in Birmingham are suffering from the same catastrophic injuries as their US counterparts in Landstuhl. Polytrauma, brain injury, limb separation and multiple amputation are the order of the day. The Ministry of Defence in London gives me the run-around. Dozens of emails and phone calls end in frustration. The British don't seem as keen as the Americans to give me access to their medical operation in Birmingham.

I complain about this to my contacts in the UK Embassy in Dublin. They are apologetic and seem puzzled by the foot-dragging in London. There are, after all, hundreds of Irish citizens fighting in Iraq and Afghanistan in British army uniforms. They ask me to leave it with them. A few days later I get a call from my principal contact in the British Embassy. She apologises to me over the phone and tells me that she has had no luck with access to Selly Oak and the Queen Elizabeth Hospitals. She does, however, have an alternative. The opportunity is not directly related to the wars in Afghanistan and Iraq. It is related to a war much closer to home. The British invite me to witness the dismantling of the last of the iconic fortified watchtowers and observation posts in south Armagh, along the border between Northern Ireland and the Republic.

In an historic development, Operation Banner, the British army's military campaign in Northern Ireland, is coming to an end. Within less than a year, the British army will have handed primary responsibility for Northern Ireland's security over to the fledgling Police Service of Northern Ireland. Operation Banner is the British army's longest military campaign to date. It started in August 1969. In the Summer of 2006, thirty-seven years later, it is being wound down and dismantled, bit by bit. I'm especially interested in the controversial observation posts and fortified towers. They have dominated the landscape of south Armagh for most of my life. They were an ever-present feature of my own service on the border when I was a young army officer in the early 1990s. Part of the scenery. Unnatural structures on the brooding landscape of the border region. For many, they are symbols of British occupation. For me, as a soldier, as an academic and journalist, they are harbingers of the surveillance society. They were a nod to the future in terms of the militarisation of security in the post-9/11 world.

I'm invited to meet Colonel Harber in Bessbrook Mill – the last British army outpost near the border in south Armagh, not far from Crossmaglen. I drive up on a sunny day in June. The journey from Dublin takes just over an hour.

A few miles north of the border, I follow the signs for Bessbrook. The village itself, with its neat stone cottages and carefully tended gardens, is nestled snugly among the drumlins and hills not far from the Republic. It is surprisingly picturesque. Surreal to think that it was at the epicentre of the Troubles. Its dominant feature is Bessbrook Mill. It houses what remains of the British army garrison in south Armagh.

Historical records trace the ownership of Bessbrook Mill to Sir Toby Caulfield as far back as 1620. In 1845, it was purchased by John Cribb Richardson, a Quaker who built the town of Bessbrook around the mill as the first 'model' village in Ireland or Britain – predating by thirty years the famous Bourneville model village built by the Cadbury family near Birmingham. Richardson's ideal for Bessbrook was to revolve around the concept of the Three Ps – no public house, no pawn shop and no police.

Ironically, tragically, a century later Bessbrook would find itself at the centre of Northern Ireland's so-called 'murder triangle' in south Armagh – a far cry from Richardson's original utopian vision for the village. Between 1969 and 1998, fifty-three police constables from the RUC were killed in south Armagh by republicans. In addition, 119 soldiers from the British army were killed in the county during the same period – almost exactly the same number killed in action in Iraq and Afghanistan to date. A total of 172 members of the

British security forces were killed in the small villages, leafy back roads and fields of south Armagh during the Troubles.

In 1970, Bessbrook Mill was requisitioned by the British army as a base for its operations in south Armagh. At the height of the Troubles, there were almost three thousand British troops based between Bessbrook, Crossmaglen and Newtownhamilton. With a population of just twenty-three thousand, this made south Armagh one of the most heavily militarised zones in the world with an astonishing ratio of over one armed soldier per eight civilians. This presence, however, failed to prevent further killing and sectarian outrages, such as the murder of five Protestants in Newtownhamilton Orange Lodge in September 1975 and the infamous Kingsmill Massacre of January 1976 in which ten Protestant textile workers were shot dead by republican elements near Bessbrook. Based on these experiences, I wonder how the British army and US military might realistically expect to pacify the insurgencies in Afghanistan and Iraq.

In 1986, the British army attempted to further frustrate the activities of the Provisional IRA's South Armagh Brigade by erecting a series of hilltop observation posts (OPs) on the hills and drumlins straddling the border with the Republic. This series of OPs, equipped with night-vision equipment, long-range cameras and listening devices, was designed to finally tame the so-called 'bandit country' of south Armagh.

The OPs had some impact, albeit minimal, on the IRA campaign in the area. However, as the wider political situation began to alter, the towers themselves became symbols of what republicans regarded as a heavy-handed, oppressive and intrusive military occupation of the area. For want of any other useful purpose, they became targets. The same could be said of the permanent vehicle checkpoints that the British army operated throughout the border area. Like the towers, they ultimately served no useful tactical purpose and simply became static targets for a mobile enemy relying on terror tactics. On 12 February 1997, Lance Bombardier Stephen Restorick was shot in the head by an IRA sniper team as he manned the vehicle checkpoint outside Bessbrook Mill. He was the last British soldier to die in Operation Banner.

Following the announcement of the IRA's final ceasefire in July 1997 and the signing of the Good Friday Agreement in April 1998, the British army began to dismantle its thirteen OPs in the south Armagh area in December 1999. The last five towers, on Camlough Mountain, Jonesborough Hill and Croslieve Hill, are in the final phases of demolition and removal. Within weeks, the physical and political topography of south Armagh will have changed utterly. The coming months there will be an acid test of the process of security 'normalisation' for Northern Ireland. Bessbrook Mill will close as a British army base and along with it will close a salutary chapter in British military history. I have mixed feelings about this visit. It is history in the making. In the context of the British army's involvement in Iraq and Afghanistan, however, it begs questions of the logic of Britain and Ireland's military involvement there.

Bessbrook Mill is currently home to C Company, the Second Battalion, Princess of Wales's Royal Regiment (PWRR). Once the British army's main base in south Armagh, at the height of the troubles Troubles Bessbrook Mill was the busiest heliport in the world, with British army helicopter flights in and out of the base every fifteen minutes or so, twenty-four hours a day, seven days a week. As we discuss the current security environment, Colonel Harber recalls previous service in Northern Ireland in 1988 when he was based in south Armagh as a junior officer. 'At certain points then,' he says, 'we would have had as many as, say, 2,500 troops here in south Armagh.' The total numbers of British troops now stationed in the area, between Crossmaglen, Newtownhamilton and Bessbrook, is less than one hundred.

In addition to this dramatic reduction in troop numbers, the British army is hoping to completely remove all traces of their once-significant military infrastructure in the south Armagh area. According to the colonel, 'That epitomises our plan for south Armagh – to get rid of all of the concrete, the towers and the wire. We want to restore it to its former status as countryside. Beautiful countryside – plain and simple.'

Chapter 33

Pauline

'11811, Mary speaking. I'm going to connect you to the Lebanese Embassy in London. They should be able to put you through to Hizbullah's parliamentary group in Beirut. Hold the line please.'

Crossmaglen, Northern Ireland

June 2006

Colonel Barber introduces me to Captain John Baxter of the 25 Royal Engineer Regiment (25 RER), who is responsible for returning the sites of the former watchtowers to their original state as 'green grass' locations. He outlines in detail to me the ongoing process of consultation between the British army and the landowners – mostly farmers – as to the restoration and reclamation of the remaining OP sites. He also describes the level of environmental oversight provided by independent civilian contractors who carry out compulsory land quality assessments to ensure there is no residual contamination or pollution of the former military sites.

I ask Captain Baxter if there is any chemical or radioactive contamination of the sites from surveillance equipment that may have been housed in the observation posts located there. He replies, 'No, there is no radioactive contamination at the sites. That's a bit of a myth and besides, with health and safety for our own troops and the community being our primary concern, we wouldn't contemplate such a scenario.'

The main logistics problem confronting Captain Baxter and the engineers of 25 RER is the 'no-drive' line that separates this part of south Armagh from the remainder of Northern Ireland. Colonel Harber explains to me that, for ongoing security reasons and other sensitivities, British troops do not travel by road in south Armagh, south of the A25 running west to east from Newtownhamilton to Newry. 'Therefore,' he says, 'the only way to get to the observation posts is by air. We've got to airlift our engineer crews in and airlift everything out, every Portakabin, every nail, screw, piece of concrete – every pebble of gravel has got to be airlifted out.' I'm amazed at the no-drive policy in south Armagh. I wonder why the British army do not have a no-drive policy in Iraq and Afghanistan where the threat from roadside bombs is considerably higher.

It seems this fundamental lesson of Operation Banner is being ignored in Afghanistan and Iraq, with fatal consequences for ordinary British and US troops. One of the officers later confides in me that he feels it is due to a lack of resources in the British army. Following years of cuts, despite increased operational demands in the Global War on Terror, the British army simply does not have enough armoured vehicles and helicopters to protect their frontline troops against IEDs and sniper attacks.

Some of this precious helicopter fleet is still in use in Northern Ireland. Captain Baxter states that they have resorted to using specialised RAF Chinook helicopters with under-slung 8- to 10-ton containers to remove the remaining OPs. He states, '25 RER have so far supervised over one thousand such flights from the various sites and have removed over four and half thousand tons of material.' In a general discussion about their service in Northern Ireland, Colonel Harber, Major Bedford and Captain Baxter describe the manner in which their troops, many of whom are just home from a six-month tour of duty in Basra and Baghdad in Iraq, find Northern Ireland to be a busy, but peaceful and uneventful posting.

According to Major Bedford, 'A lot of the troops here go surfing along the coast. The amenities here are second to none.' Colonel Harber makes the point that such activities would have been unthinkable in the 1990s or 1980s due to the security situation. He concludes, 'The security situation here, like the landscape, has been transformed.' Colonel Harber points to the large three-dimensional cloth model of south Armagh that dominates Bessbrook Mill's briefing room. Once used for planning military operations, the detailed scale model shows every building, outhouse and unapproved road or laneway in the south Armagh area. 'This will be going to a museum soon,' he says.

It is an extraordinary installation. I've never seen anything quite like it myself. At first glance it looks like an enormous model railway set. It is only when you spot the military symbols on the buildings and checkpoints that one realises the significance of the model. In a digitised world and in the era of Google Earth, the British army's scale model of south Armagh looks suddenly redundant. Changes in technology and political change have made it an historical artefact.

Colonel Harber brings me out to the heliport and we board a British Air Corps Lynx helicopter to view the observation towers from the air. I notice that the pilots are armed and carry small HK assault rifles strapped to the rear of their seats. The 7.62 machine gun mounted at the door of the helicopter is fully loaded with the conventional mix of standard and tracer ammunition. The threat assessment is deemed low in south Armagh, however and throughout the flight, the door gunner keeps the side door of the aircraft closed.

Passing between the drumlins, the pilots do a 360-degree sweep of the observation tower sites. They are indistinguishable from the surrounding hills. Colonel Harber later explains to me that they had considered using natural yoghurt, dumped in giant drums on the sites 'to promote the growth of *verdi gris*, moss and lichen to help return the sites to nature.' However, such action has proven unnecessary due to the wet climate and rapid natural growth of grass, furze and heather.

Minutes later we descend to 'Golf Four Zero', (G40) the observation post at Croslieve Hill. Dismounting the helicopter, I am immediately struck by the commanding fields of vision afforded by the position. I'm also struck by the beauty of south Armagh and the spectacular views south and east towards County Louth and the Irish Sea. All of the British army officers I speak to remark on the tourism potential of the area and the opportunities for hill-walking 'once the army packs up and leaves.'

The engineers on the top of the windswept and wet post G40 explain to me how they are disassembling the observation post, piece by piece, and loading everything into metal containers for airlift off the site. Staff Sergeant

Chris Button of 25 RER explains to me how they are now engaged in the unpleasant task of having to remove the sewage system from the base and decant and bottle, in large plastic containers, their own waste for airlift off the hilltop. The engineers are also in the process of removing, by hand, every pebble and piece of gravel off the hilltop – literally leaving no stone unturned.

I watch as an RAF Chinook helicopter hovers precariously, buffeted by strong winds, over the hilltop as the engineers hook the large metal bins filled with debris to the underside of the aircraft. I am later informed that the Chinooks cross the Irish Sea every morning from Odiham RAF base in Hampshire to conduct the airlifts. 'Most of our Chinooks are in Iraq and Afghanistan,' observes Colonel Harber. The troops on G40 and at Bessbrook Mill are a mixture of young soldiers from England, Scotland, Wales, Ireland, Fiji, South Africa and Ghana. Most would have been in primary school when the IRA declared its ceasefire in 1997. When I ask them about what they think of Ireland, most of them express a keen interest in going to Dublin to visit Temple Bar. An unthinkable scenario in the grim decades of the 1970s and 1980s.

As I leave Bessbrook Mill, Colonel Harber gives me to understand that the British army now regards its role in Northern Ireland as very much reduced and secondary to that of the PSNI. 'It's up to them now, they need to get out and about amongst the neighbourhoods in their jam sandwiches – just like community police forces everywhere else.' With uncharacteristic understatement, he adds, 'The British army has a lot of interests globally now.' The colonel's description of the British army's exit strategy from Ireland places their aspirations for Iraq and Afghanistan in sharp relief. Northern Ireland is a functioning democracy with all of the critical infrastructure necessary for peace building. Iraq and Afghanistan have been practically destroyed by 'shock and awe' tactics. Both countries are now armed along ethnic lines and are on the brink of civil war. As the British army finally ends its military campaign in Ireland, I cannot summon up the suspension of disbelief necessary to imagine their campaigns in Iraq and Afghanistan will succeed.

The pilots have the last laugh with me as we fly off G40. Colonel Harber squeezes into the back of the chopper and holds on to the overhead bars. He's obviously seen this before. I'm perched on a bench seat overlooking the sliding door. The pilots tell me over the intercom that they are going to give me a tour. This consists of corkscrewing the helicopter down the hillside towards the Ravensdale hotel. The Hotel rushes up towards us through the open sliding door. I lose all sense of balance and feel like my stomach is going to somersault over my head. The chopper is then thrown violently sideways and we cannon over the fields and ditches just feet above the ground. I know this because the helicopter is now flying sideways. I've gripped the bench seat in a bear hug and imagine I'm going to fall out onto the ground flashing green all around us. The pilots then right the chopper and we return to Bessbrook in a sedate fashion. My legs have turned to jelly. I wobble a bit getting off the helicopter. The pilots smile at me from their caged-in cockpit. 'Thought you'd enjoy a bit of evasive flying – just like the good old days.' Colonel Harber grins at me as he waves goodbye.

After a day of briefings, I come away with the distinct impression that the two groups most anxious to see the British army leave south Armagh are Sinn Féin – and the British army itself. When that happens, Observation Posts Romeo One Three through to Romeo Two One and Golf Four Zero will return to the more poetic appellations of Camlough, Glassdrumman, Cloch Og, Tievecrom, Sugarloaf Hill, Creevekeeran, Drummuckavall and Croslieve Hill. That such serenity might be reflected in the political landscape in Northern Ireland remains to be seen.

Summer War

August 2006

In July, Hizbullah and the Israeli army recommence hostilities in south Lebanon. It is a depressing development. I had hoped, that after the Israeli withdrawal from Lebanon, the two countries might improve relations. Israel needs friends in the region, not enemies, and I had thought, naively, that Lebanon had the potential to be a great friend and exemplar for Israel. Sadly not. Hizbullah's indiscriminate attacks on Israel kill innocent civilians and the

Knesset authorises retaliation. In the cycle of violence that follows, over one thousand Lebanese men, women and children are killed. The Israelis repeat the tactics of Operation Grapes of Wrath in 1996 and bombard south Lebanon, the coastal cities of Tyre, Sidon and Beirut. They target the command and control centres of Hizbullah and, in the process, knock out Lebanon's mobile phone networks.

Four UN peacekeepers are killed in an observation post at Khiyam in late July. I try to reach my old contacts in Lebanon to find out what is happening on the ground. It is nigh on impossible without the mobile networks. I provide analysis as usual to the *Irish Times* and do follow-up interviews on RTÉ radio and television. On 30 July, the Israelis shell an apartment block in Qana and kill twenty-eight innocent civilians, many of whom are women and young children. It is history repeating itself. Ten years after standing in the rubble of Qana – as a UN peacekeeper – during the 1996 massacre of over a hundred men, women and children, I am commenting as a journalist on another massacre in the same village. It is deeply troubling. I do interviews on BBC's *Newsnight* and *Lateline* on Australia's ABC network.

One of the principal features of the 2006 war is the manner in which Hizbullah's combat performance has improved almost beyond recognition. Around three thousand Hizbullah fighters manage to force tens of thousands of Israeli troops to a stalemate and a complete standstill; inflicting heavy casualties in hand-to-hand fighting in Lebanese border villages. It is a worrying development for Israel and dents the IDF's military prestige somewhat. My Israeli contacts are deeply concerned about Hizbullah's actions along the border and justifiably suspect the influence of Iran in the conflict.

My contact in the Israeli Embassy in Dublin reacts angrily to my analysis of the slaughter of Lebanese civilians in Qana. I meet him in the Westbury Hotel off Grafton Street. He tells me that I am 'anti-Israeli'. He glares at me over coffee and biscuits. I glare back. Meanwhile, I'm excoriated in various online blogs and discussion boards as an Israeli 'lackey'. I even get an email from a Palestinian support group in Ireland which warns its members to keep an eye out for my 'militarist, pro-Israeli' analysis.

Peter Murtagh, my editor in the *Irish Times*, encourages me to seek out my old Hizbullah contacts to try and get a sense of their intentions and morale during the heavy fighting. I dial all of my old contact numbers to no avail. I keep getting a bleeping error code and a message in Arabic and in French telling me that the network is unavailable. I'm wracking my brains and idly dial 11811. Before I even have time to think, my call is answered. '11811, Mary speaking.' I fumble with the phone and mumble to Mary that I'm trying to contact Hizbullah. She replies without hesitation. 'Is that Hizbullah in Lebanon, caller?' I reply in the affirmative. Mary points out to me that I should have dialled 'International Directory Enquiries'. I hear her sigh in annoyance. She continues however. 'I'll make an exception this time, caller, can you hold the line, I'm going to connect you to the Lebanese Embassy in London. They should be able to put you through to Hizbullah's parliamentary group in Beirut. Hold the line please.' I'm surprised by Mary. The phone rings twice and a voice on the other end answers in slightly accented but perfect English. 'Hello, Embassy of Lebanon, London.' I'm very impressed with 11811.

I ask the Lebanese Embassy official if he can connect me to a Hizbullah spokesperson in the Lebanese Parliament. It seems like a long shot. The embassy official tells me to hold the line. Miraculously, I hear the continuous beep of a Lebanese ring tone in Beirut. The phone is answered. I introduce myself and ask if it would be possible to speak to someone from Hizbullah. The woman at the other end asks me to wait. She puts me through to Hizbullah's Dr Ali Mokdad. Mokdad is a Hizbullah member of parliament. Originally from Baalbek, Mokdad is a medical doctor, a neurologist. He speaks English perfectly. Dr Mokdad agrees to be interviewed on the record for the *Irish Times*.

I ask Dr Mokdad about the safety of Irish troops in Lebanon given the ongoing hostilities between Hizbullah and the Israelis. Mokdad tells me over the phone that the Irish are very welcome in Lebanon, and 'as long as the Irish don't interfere with our social work south of the Litani river, they should not have a problem.' Dr Mokdad does warn me, however, that any attempt on the part of the UN to 'interfere' with Hizbullah's combat operations would be considered a 'hostile act'. He explains, 'In these circumstances, let me be explicit. There should be no searches, no confiscation of weapons, or interference. If the UN did these things, it would help the Israelis and that would be a different story, with a different outcome for UN soldiers.' I take this to be a thinly veiled threat against Irish troops attempting to execute a UN mandate.

I press Dr Mokdad on this issue and ask him what precisely Irish UN soldiers might be permitted to do to prevent loss of life in their capacity as UN peacekeepers. Dr Mokdad's reply might be considered slightly amusing, were he not in deadly earnest: 'Hizbullah and the Lebanese resistance, the people of Lebanon, would invite the Irish to join them in the fight against the aggressor and to fight the Israelis for peace in Lebanon.' The birds outside my attic in Booterstown are chirping away as Dr Mokdad continues. Darach appears at the top of the stairs. I put my fingers to my lips and whisper a 'Sshh' to him. 'Who are you talking to, dad?' he asks me. 'The doctor,' I reply. 'Dr Who?' says Darach. He is excited at the idea that I might be talking to the space-hopping Time Lord. He scrambles over and climbs up on my lap, cocking his ear to the phone.

Meanwhile, Dr Mokdad continues. 'The Irish people have nothing to fear from Hizbullah. Orient your fear towards Israel and its intentions in Lebanon.' As I scribble down notes of the conversation and as Darach strains to hear the doctor, Mokdad moves on to the subject of US troops at Shannon Airport in County Clare. He pronounces 'County Clare' with great emphasis.

'There is no humanity when you allow your airports to be used to move soldiers or weapons from one side to another. It is not fair. It is not good. I am not glad to say it about the Irish, but it is true. I know that you have a special relationship with America, but it should be used for peace, not moving weapons and soldiers. These weapons hurt us and our children . . . the Irish should not cooperate with the movement of war materials and forces.'

I thank Dr Mokdad for his time and his comments. Darach says goodbye down the phone. Dr Mokdad calls him *habibi* or darling. It is the first time I have heard a major Islamic resistance group condemn the use of Shannon by US troops. The *Irish Times* includes excerpts from the interview the following day.

September 2006

Eoghan starts school in St Mary's National School in Booterstown. He is very proud of himself in his little grey trousers. He is welcomed into the school community with open arms. At lunchtime a few days later, I see him in his small blue wheelchair in the schoolyard. He is gripping the two ends of a scarf, tightly, his knuckles white, his face intense. The scarf is being used as a sort of harness by two older boys who are pulling him around the perimeter of the playground in a sort of wild chariot race. Eoghan's cheeks are pink from the fresh air. He is screaming enthusiastically. I come to the happy conclusion that Eoghan has been successfully 'integrated' into the mainstream school environment.

October 2006

Pauline is back at home with her husband and the boys. I call over to see her on Tuesday, 17 October. Pauline is tired but manages a smile or two during our brief conversation. When I go to leave, Pauline tries to get up to walk me to the door. She makes a huge effort to stand up. I put my hand on her shoulder and kiss her on the forehead. I tell her to take it easy. I'll see myself out.

The following evening, Pauline texts me to say that she loves me. She calls me 'little brother'.

On the morning of Thursday, 19 October, Pauline says goodbye to her two precious boys as they go off to school. After they leave, she goes upstairs to shower. She feels a little dizzy and asks her husband to sit with her for a little while on the bed. They sit on the bed and he holds her. Pauline shifts a little from the sitting position and lies down. She sighs gently. As the traffic passes by outside and as the morning rush-hour reaches its crescendo, Pauline passes away peacefully.

Pauline is buried in the family plot, next to my mother. I think of her laughter on the day that my dad had suggested it to her as a final resting place. I miss her. May she rest in peace.

Chapter 34

Shannon

'I intend to take Moqtada al Sadr down, Tom. Dead. Or alive.'

Shannon Airport, County Clare, Ireland
November 2006

Pauline's passing hits my dad very hard. He becomes frailer. Thinner and almost housebound. He looks skeletal. He still chain-smokes. Surrounded in a blue-smoke haze when I visit him at home. He has also had a series of mini-strokes and I suspect he is a little cognitively impaired. One of the results of this is that he has become quite disinhibited and has a tendency to tell me exactly what is on his mind at any given moment. When I call to see him, I turn my key in the door and walk down the hallway, turning right into the living room. When I open the door to the smoke-filled room, he looks at me, disappointed. With cigarette dangling from his lower lip, his habitual greeting now consists of, 'Ah, shite. It's only you. I thought it was one of your sisters.' I have to laugh. 'And good morning to you too, dad. I'll put on the kettle.'

He calls out to me as I disappear into the kitchen. 'Don't make a balls of it, Thomas, like you make a balls of everything else.' We exchange other pleasantries for an hour or so and then, as is his habit, he walks me to the front door. He wheezes as he walks beside me. Painfully, slowly. When I sit into the car, he waves at me with his hanky and – as is his habit – he sticks his dentures out at me. The same dentures that Darach discovered in the dishwasher the previous week. My dad looked at me defensively when I challenged him about the dentures in the dishwasher. 'They've never been cleaner. That dishwasher does a great job.'

But I'll never forget his face when the undertakers came to close the coffin at Pauline's funeral. He wept. Across the room from him, I watched him weeping as I said goodbye to Pauline. I would like to have tried to hug him then. But I thought the better of it. I resolve to try and hug him on one of the days I call to visit.

The US and its allies are now completely and hopelessly bogged down in the wars in Iraq and Afghanistan. The Sunni insurgency in Iraq intensifies. The Taliban continue to fight a guerrilla insurgency that resembles that fought by the mujahideen against the Soviet occupation during the 1980s. In December of 2006, the US government publishes 'The Iraq Study Group Report'. This major report describes the military and political situation in Iraq as 'grave and deteriorating'. The report concludes that there are insufficient US and coalition troops within Iraq to properly secure and rebuild the country. The report also concludes that the US military need to confront, head-on, the Sunni insurgency and growing Shia unrest. The Iraq Study Group recommends a troop 'surge' to tackle the unending cycle of violence. The report also recommends that the surge be followed by the rapid transition of all security and military operations to Iraqi forces in order to facilitate a US withdrawal.

The numbers of US troops passing through Shannon to fight in Iraq and Afghanistan continues apace. Eventually, over a million US troops will transit through the County Clare airport. Cumulatively, it is the largest foreign army of invasion on Irish soil in all of our troubled history. There is much mention of the US troops in the Irish media. However, no Irish journalist has interviewed the troops on their last stop before combat in the Global War on Terror. I approach X, my contact at the US Embassy and we discuss the matter. X tells me that it will be tricky, as he'll have to go through a lot of people in the US in order to get me the required permission. 'You can't just walk up to US soldiers in Shannon and start asking them questions. We've got to organise access on a strictly unit-by-unit basis.' He explains to me that permission to interview troops from specific units will have to be coordinated with the exact time and date of their rotation through Shannon. As usual, X asks me to leave it with him.

Within days, X calls to tell me he has it sorted. I can interview a selection of US troops passing through Shannon the following weekend. X gives me the mobile phone number of what he describes as the 'US-Europe Command liaison officer' at Shannon Airport.

Based full-time at Shannon airport, Major Chris Sabatini acts as liaison officer between the US military's European Command (EUCOM) in Stuttgart, Germany and the Shannon Airport authorities. When I talk to Major Sabatini on the phone, he is extremely helpful. He is anxious that I get to speak to as many soldiers as possible. 'So much is written about us here,' he tells me. 'But, I'm kind of surprised that no one has bothered to actually talk to us before.'

I drive to Shannon from Dublin early on Saturday morning. I crawl out of the house at 3 AM and try not to wake up Aideen and the children. The weather is wild. I get to Shannon at around 5 AM. The weather has deteriorated en route. I park in the car park and make a mad dash to the airport entrance. Atlantic storm-force winds and rain whip across the airport's runways and terminal buildings. Christmas trees and ribbons of festive lights sway crazily in the maelstrom. The illuminated 'Shannon Airport' sign blinks on and off. Major Sabatini is waiting for me inside the entrance. He greets me with a cappuccino. Over coffee, he tells me he is from Boston, Massachusetts. Despite the atrocious December weather, he assures me that all of the American military flights due at Shannon are on schedule for today.

Major Sabatini's job is to ensure the smooth passage of hundreds of US troops through Shannon's arrival gates and duty-free areas on a daily basis. According to him, 'An average of three thousand US personnel pass through here on a weekly basis. At busy times, like Christmas, that average goes up to five thousand soldiers per week.'

Most of the troops are bound for service in Iraq and Afghanistan. An occasional aircraft brings US troops to Germany and elsewhere in Europe. Once a week, the US navy operates a 'Weekly Rotation' flight through Shannon to its naval installations in the Mediterranean. Most of the Iraq-bound US troops in Shannon arrive on chartered civilian passenger jets operated by American Trans Air (ATA), North America Airlines and World Airways.

Having passed through Shannon's security search and screening system, the major points in the direction of the duty-free area. Approximately two hundred US troops, in distinctive and well-worn desert fatigues, are browsing the myriad souvenir stands and perfume counters in the main foyer. According to Major Sabatini, these troops are 'mostly from the US 82nd Airborne Division, returning to the United States after a tour of duty in Iraq. This group arrived on an ATA flight from Kuwait City this morning and are due to fly stateside to McGuire Air Force Base, New Jersey.'

The returning American soldiers are visibly relaxed with a large number queuing for drinks at the Joe Sheridan Bar in the open-plan duty-free area. The first soldier I approach, at random, is Staff Sergeant Debbie Ochsner who has been serving with the 82nd Airborne Division in Baghdad. Deployed to Iraq in April of this year, Ochsner tells me that she is returning to her home town Fayetteville, North Carolina to be with her two sons, Ryan, aged eight and Robert, aged fourteen. She shows me the Irish souvenir T-shirts she has bought them. She has also bought a 'worry stone' in the duty-free area. According to Ochsner, 'I'm carrying the worry stone as a reminder of my husband. Robert. He's still in Iraq, serving with the 82nd Airborne.' She also informs me that she is being sent home early to the US on compassionate grounds following the death of her husband's younger brother, James, aged thirty-six, who was recently killed in action in Afghanistan.

Ochsner then shows me a silver bracelet she is wearing with her brother-in-law's name engraved on it, along with the date, time and location of his death in action. 'We've all got them,' she says, 'to commemorate family members we've lost in the war.' Ochsner also adds that she was unable to see her husband during her tour of duty in Iraq, even though they were both serving 'in-country' at the same time. 'It's part of the sacrifice military families have to make,' she says. She plans to spend Christmas with her mother, who has been minding their two sons since she deployed to Baghdad eight months ago. I think of my own kids, safe and sound, asleep in Dublin. I don't think I could handle an eight-month separation. I cannot conceive of both parents deployed overseas at the same time. Debbie's kids seem very young to be without both parents for so long. And in such fraught circumstances.

The next soldier I meet in Sheridan's bar is Staff Sergeant Fran Smith, who was serving in Baghdad with the 263rd Air Missile Defence Unit. She states that she has been in Iraq since October 2005. She also explains that her daughter, Vicky, aged twenty-four, has just given birth to a baby girl called Audrey. Sergeant Smith goes on to say that arriving in Shannon is 'surreal. After all that time in the heat and dust of Baghdad, to see the green, green grass of Ireland is so strange to me.' She adds with a laugh, 'It's also strange to go home as a grandmother and not to have to carry a weapon – for now.'

Also in Sheridan's bar are Sergeant Major James McDowell and Sergeant First Class Steven Edmondson from Brooklyn, New York. They both claim Irish ancestry. Both are finishing a one-year tour of duty in Iraq with the newly configured Joint Improvised Explosive Device Defeat Organisation or JIEDDO based in Baghdad. Sergeant Major McDowell explains that 'So many of our guys and gals are getting taken out with IEDs in Iraq that we've started a whole program to wise them up to the threat.' He adds, 'We start stateside by briefing them in our training centres in Louisiana and California about the IED threat.' 'Then we tell 'em again in Kuwait just before they deploy to Iraq, but they don't really pay attention until they're in-country in Iraq. Then they see IEDs rolled up in foam rubber and dipped in cement to make the bombs look like rocks – then they pay attention real fast, because it's life or death. We've also come across hollowed-out kerbstones or dead dogs and cats stuffed with high explosives and detonated by remote control when our troops come by.'

McDowell and Edmondson describe at length the ingenuity of Iraqi insurgents in constantly devising new forms of IED to catch US forces off-guard. According to Edmondson, 'Our unit started to send out mobile teams to particular US positions to brief the troops locally about emerging IED threats, and how foxy they were. And then some of our own IED experts started to fall victim to these insurgent devices. Eventually we lost three guys, from this specialised IED unit, to IEDs.' McDowell points out that new medical advances being developed in the field in Iraq, such as powerful powdered coagulants designed to stem arterial bleeding, are saving lives among badly injured US troops.

An ATA announcement calls the US troops to board their return flight to New Jersey. Within minutes, the duty-free area empties of US troops. They file silently towards their departure gate, many carrying hastily wrapped gifts, soft toys, dolls and teddy bears for children they have not seen for over a year.

We follow them to the departure gate. However, I'm told that I'm not allowed to board the ATA flight. I am informed, somewhat apologetically by an ATA employee, that 'there are weapons and dogs on the flight and that it isn't very photogenic.' When I enquire about the weapons and dogs, I am informed that the troops sometimes carry their personal weapons, 'minus the ammunition' on board for ease of transport back to their home installations.

As for the dogs, a departing US soldier explains to me that 'we regularly get army dogs on the flights. Most of them are trained to sniff out bombs or drugs. They're not allowed off at Shannon to get air or exercise because of Irish Department of Agriculture rules about dogs. Which is a pity, because they get real excited in there when they smell the fresh Irish air and sometimes they pee on the carpet.' As he disappears into the air-bridge, the US soldier quips, 'Hey, make sure you tell your readers that it isn't just the troops that are enthusiastic about the Shannon stopover.'

Within forty-five minutes of the departure of the ATA flight to New Jersey, another ATA flight from the US Marine Corps' Camp Lejeune in North Carolina lands at Shannon. On board are members of the US Marine Corps Regimental Combat Team 2, 2nd Marine Regiment, bound for deployment to Al Anbar Province, Iraq.

As the ATA Boeing 757 aircraft taxies to the arrival gate, I haggle with the ATA ground staff and am given permission to board the plane. With the air-craft door just opened, the sight inside is a little unusual. There are no passengers crowding the aisles, reaching for hand luggage in the overhead cabins as is the norm among civilians prior to disembarking after a long flight. Instead, stretching right back to the rear of the aircraft, there are row upon row of crew-cut marines in identical combat fatigues, sitting in total silence. The ATA announcer on board the aircraft states, 'Folks, good morning, welcome to Shannon. You're going to be on the ground here for forty-five minutes. The bar and the duty-free are available and there is a smoking section just straight across from the bar. All weapons must remain on board the aircraft and that includes gun holsters. Thank you.' I scan the aircraft floor. Sure enough. There are weapons on board. Assault rifles and automatic pistols. So much for Irish government denials about the transit of armed troops through Shannon.

The marines leave the aircraft in near silence and head straight for the duty-free area – and Sheridan's bar. Their commanding officer, Lieutenant Colonel Andrew Smith, informs me that the marines are on their way to Al Anbar province for a year-long deployment. Lieutenant Colonel Smith, whose family are Irish-American, explains that he brought his family to Ireland to stay in Adare Manor this summer as a last family vacation prior to his deployment to Iraq. With a daughter named Shannon, Lieutenant Colonel Smith smiles as he describes the significance of the Shannon stop-over to the US Marine Corps. 'Shannon, for every US marine, is the highlight of any transit to Iraq. The people of Ireland are genuine and warm and it's always nice to land here. Plus, you get the benefit of a pint of Guinness. And, as you can see, there are lots of Irish marines and sailors, so it's always special to touch down here as you go in harm's way. For marines in transit, if they know they're landing in Shannon, it's a very big deal for them.'

These sentiments are echoed by Captain Conlon Carabine of the 2nd Marine Regiment. 'If you were to poll the US Marine Corps, 99 percent of them would say that Shannon is the stop-over of choice when passing to or from Iraq or Afghanistan.' Captain Carabine describes the manner in which Shannon has entered the informal culture and vernacular of the US Marine Corps – with the airport becoming synonymous with service in Iraq for most US soldiers. 'I'll tell you this, leaving Kuwait, leaving Iraq to come back to the United States, you land in one of two places. Either Hahn in Germany or Shannon in Ireland. Everybody, without exception wants to land in Shannon and celebrate with a Guinness. It's not just the Guinness though – the Irish and the American populations are tied together at the hip. We're inextricably linked since the famine I guess. More than any other European country, especially since the 1840s.'

The mood among the marines departing for Iraq is noticeably far more sombre than that of those returning to the US. When asked about leaving his young family of four children at Christmas, Lieutenant Colonel Smith is philosophical about the sacrifice his family has had to make for military service. 'Of the last four Christmases, I've spent one at home. I spent last Christmas in Al Anbar Province, Iraq. Sure, my kids are curious as to why their dad leaves around the Christmas timeframe, but that's just how the cards play out. They're old enough to know the risk, and they do ask about Iraq and what's going on there.'

Captain Carabine describes the ferocity of combat experienced by the 2nd Marine Regiment in Al Anbar province in their previous deployment, where they sustained many losses in battles with insurgents in the city of Khaim, close to the Syrian border. 'These guys don't just stand and fight, some of them are prepared to stand and die in battle.' Captain Carabine, who married his fiancée in August, describes to me the difficulty of leaving family behind in the US, especially at Christmas. 'I'll tell you, I've been shot at multiple times and it takes more courage to say goodbye to loved ones going to a combat zone, than going away to war.'

Captain Carabine, who spent his summer holidays as a child with cousins in Foxford, County Mayo, is philosophical about the risks in Iraq. 'Fear isn't an issue for me. I would say there is some anxiety with losing some of the troops under one's command. As far as myself is concerned, dying or getting hurt, I'm not afraid. To be honest, I do not fear death or getting hurt. There's anxiety, but not fear.'

Captain Carabine and Lieutenant Colonel Smith barely have time to finish a pint of Guinness before they are called to the departure gate and their journey to Kuwait City and Iraq. As the steady stream of young marines board the Boeing for Iraq, their dun-coloured desert combats seem poignantly out of kilter with the howling wind, driving rain and green, green grass of Shannon.

Before I leave the duty-free area, Chris introduces me to a gaggle of staff officers. They are all senior officers and one, who asks not to be identified, thanks me for talking to the troops. He is a marine colonel involved in 'planning'. He shakes my hand and thanks me again. 'It's good for the young marines to see some media interest in who they are and what they're embarked upon,' he tells me. I give him my card. He looks at my details and notes that I'm an ex-serviceman. He hands the card around to the others. 'Captain Clonan,' remarks one. 'You got out early, man.' They laugh. The colonel asks me about my PhD. I tell him about my research into female soldiers in the Irish military. I tell him about the negative fallout from the research. He pauses briefly. 'Fuck 'em Tom. You did 'em a favour. They just don't know it yet.' He then reaches into his combat fatigues and hands me a silver Iraqi coin. 'Tom, this is my lucky charm. It's a Saddam Hussein coin. I want you to have it.' I turn the coin over in my hand. On one side, it is embossed with an elaborate decorative design. On the other is the unmistakeable profile of Saddam himself. I ask him if he is sure. 'I've got a daughter in Westpoint. I want her to go all the way. Just like her daddy. She'd approve of your work. I approve.'

I ask the colonel about the Iraq Study Group. I ask him how it will affect his planning for operations in Iraq when they deploy in the coming days and weeks. The colonel looks at me and pauses once more. He seems to reflect on the question at length. Eventually he answers me. 'OK. So, this is an exclusive, Tom. Just for you because you seem like a good guy. We have a new priority now. Up to now, we've been chasing the Sunni insurgency. But we've got some new ideas on that score now. We're gonna try and get some of the Sunni leadership on board with us. The local leaders don't like the foreign Jihadis and the Al Qaeda nut jobs any more than we do. In the meantime, I have been tasked with prioritising Shia violence in Kerbala and Najaf. My number one priority Tom, my number one target is Moqtada al Sadr.' Moqtada al Sadr is leader of a radical Shia militia in central Iraq. Al Sadr and his armed 'brigades' have been involved in open confrontation with US forces of late. The colonel drawls exaggeratedly, doing a John Wayne impression. 'I intend to take Moqtada al Sadr down, Tom. Dead. Or alive.' His fellow officers raise their pints of Guinness. 'We'll drink to that.' They drain the last of the Guinness and disappear down the airbridge and into the aircraft bound for Iraq.

I put the Saddam Hussein coin into my wallet. It is still there today.

VIP Lounge, Shannon Airport

In addition to the many hundreds of thousands of US troops that transit through Shannon in the last three years, many of the leading players in the drama that is contemporary US foreign policy on the Middle East, Iraq and Afghanistan have also passed through the County Clare airport. A cursory look at the visitor's book for the VIP lounge in Shannon reads like a *dramatis personae* of the Bush administration's current war on terror.

In July, Iraqi Prime Minister Iyad Allawi signed the visitor's book on his way to meet President Bush in the United States. On 13 September, Iraqi President Jalal Talabani passes through Shannon airport, also on his way to the United States. On Ireland, he writes in Arabic, 'As I look at this beautiful green country on this perfect summer's day, I think of the suffering of the Irish people – a people that have suffered as the Iraqi people have. I pray that one day, the Iraqi people will enjoy the peace and prosperity that have so recently come to the Irish people.'

On 17 September, Afghan President Hamid Karzai stops over in Shannon en route to Washington. He writes in the visitor's book, 'This is my second stop at Shannon Airport. On both occasions I found Ireland very beautiful and green. [Irish] Airport hospitality was great! See you on my (next) road trip.' Mahmoud Abbas, the Palestinian leader, signs the Shannon visitor's book in September also.

Flicking back through the VIP guestbook, I see that the high-ranking military visits begin in earnest in January of 2003, just two months prior to the invasion of Iraq. On 7 January, a senior US staff officer from the United States military's Central Command responsible for the invasion and occupation of Iraq, notes in the visitor's book, 'A wonderful FIRST. Thank You.' Other regular high-ranking military visitors who have frequented Shannon since the invasion of Iraq include Lieutenant General John Abizaid and his command staff, along with, more recently, Lieutenant General John Saller, Commanding General of the US 1st Marine Expeditionary Force to Iraq.

In recent weeks, the Iraq Study Group have sipped Irish coffees and

Guinness at Shannon on their way to and from Iraq. According to the guest-book, another well-known figure who transited through Shannon is Secretary for Defence Donald Rumsfeld. A regular through Shannon in recent years, Rumsfeld – unlike Condoleeza Rice, who apparently prefers to wait out the Shannon stopover in her US government jet – is noted by airport staff to be a fan of Irish coffees prepared in Sheridan's bar. Apparently, Sheridan was the inventor of the Irish coffee.

Unfortunately, the affairs of state of so many stakeholders are unlikely to be sorted out over an Irish coffee in Sheridan's bar. They are fought out, often to the death, by the less well-heeled and less fortunate foot soldiers queuing for souvenirs in duty free, just down the hall from the VIP lounge.

Chapter 35

Thunderbirds Are Go

'I managed to get back around to that spot and I fired everything I had at that motherfucker. Then, I made my way back to the airport.'

Dublin / Shannon Airport, County Clare
2007

Christmas comes and goes. Santa Claus fills the house with an increasing amount of Lego. Walking around in the dark is hazardous. Little bits of plastic underfoot. Darach gets a little blue bicycle which matches Eoghan's wheelchair. They race each other up and down on the frosty deck outside. Ailbhe trundles up and down after them on her little pink scooter.

When the kids are in bed, I look out through the glass wall at the tyre and wheelchair tracks criss-crossing the frost. Illuminated under moonlight, the tracks remind me of the many journeys the kids will make. Eoghan's double wheelchair tracks converge with Darach and Ailbhe's single tracks. Blurred lines in the frost.

January is exam time in DIT. I collect hundreds of exam scripts and printed essays for assessment, comment and grading. The weather is too cold for the bicycle, so I take the DART. On my return home, I board the DART in Tara Street on the quays. The southbound train is packed and I just manage to squeeze into the carriage. With my nose almost pressed up against the glass, I look out the window as we wind our way towards Pearse Street DART Station.

The train slows down and everyone in the carriage sways a little, leaning forward as we decelerate. A sudden lurch as we come to a halt. The doors of the carriage slide open with a loud beeping sound. A couple of commuters get off. A man squeezes on. He wriggles his way into the space next to me and we are almost eye to eye. He looks Middle Eastern. He is very well dressed. Suit and tie under an expensive woollen overcoat. He carries a brown leather briefcase. He stares at me. There is no way to avoid direct eye contact in the confined space.

Eventually, he speaks. 'Tom Clonan. You are writing in the *Irish Times*.' I look straight at him. He smiles and offers his hand. 'Al-Sadr. My name is al-Sadr. You may have heard of my first cousin, Moqtada al-Sadr.'

I have my hand in my pocket. I can feel the outline of the Saddam Hussein 'lucky charm' coin in my wallet. 'Yes, I know of Moqtada al-Sadr.'

Moqtada's cousin – who is very well spoken – explains to me that he and other al-Sadr family members had fled into exile from Iraq when Saddam first came to power. The family story is heartbreaking. Parents tortured and murdered. Children forced to watch. Al-Sadr's cousin tells me that after Saddam was toppled, he and his brother managed to visit their old family home. 'My cousin, Moqtada. Well, what a change. I used to play football with him in the garden of my grandparents' house. Now he is a big player in the power struggle in Iraq. He takes himself very seriously now. Not like when he was a little boy. We taught him a few lessons in the little lane behind my grandmother's house back then.' We both laugh.

Al-Sadr's cousin tells me that he has been working in Dublin for many years and intends to stay. He has no intention of returning to live in Iraq. We talk about the pros and cons of living in Ireland. He tells me that he does not want his Irish-born children to get caught up in Iraqi 'civil-war politics. I hope they get interested in Irish civil-war politics.' We laugh again. 'There is a future in that.'

I get off at Booterstown. I shake hands with Moqtada al-Sadr's Irish cousin. The doors glide shut. He smiles at me through the glass as the train pulls away. I feel the Saddam coin in my wallet once more. I think of the US colonel's words in County Clare just weeks ago. 'I intend to take Moqtada al-Sadr down, Tom. Dead. Or alive.'

In DIT, I compete for and receive funding for an OECD Media and Civil

Society Research-Themed Study on journalism practice and professional routines in times of war. The funding allows me to travel to London and New York to interview high-profile foreign and war correspondents about their experiences of working in hostile environments.

I interview Nir Rosen of the *New York Times* in New York. He tells me of near-death experiences in Baghdad. In London, I interview Maggie O'Kane of the *Guardian*, Alex Thompson, Channel 4's Chief News Correspondent and Martin Bell, formerly of the BBC. I also interview Orla Guerin, BBC's Africa Correspondent and Patrick Cockburn of the *London Independent*. I interview each of them in depth about their route into journalism and their reasons for choosing foreign or war reporting. Certain similar patterns emerge. They are all graduates and a surprisingly high number are Irish passport holders.

They all agree that having an Irish passport, when travelling in a hostile environment, is a good thing. Patrick Cockburn tells me an extraordinary story about a lucky escape in Iraq. 'We were on our way to Najaf. We went through some pretty tough Shia towns, like Latifiyah and Kufa. All of a sudden, we came upon a Shia checkpoint. It was a Mahdi army checkpoint. I was wearing a Kefiya and got dragged out of the car by the guys on the checkpoint who were shouting "American spy." There was no discipline on the checkpoint and some of the guys wanted to kill us – myself and the driver. Some wanted to take us to the Mosque to their bosses and perhaps kill us thereabouts. Possibly film our execution. I showed them my Irish passport. The Irish passport definitely saved me.'

Cockburn adds that on another occasion, his Irish citizenship was acknowledged by hardline Sunni elements in Iraq. 'For example in Fallujah, on the day the insurgents brought down a US Chinook helicopter, some of the locals were asking me about Michael Collins. You know, they'd seen the film. They read a lot. They know a bit of Irish history. So the Irish passport – while it is increasingly dangerous for all western journalists – it is still a good thing to have.'

Many of the other journalists agree that having Irish citizenship is still of value when travelling through hostile environments caught up in the Global

War on Terror. However, they are all of the view that the situation is changing and that Islamist resistance groups are becoming less sensitive to issues of nationality.

Maggie O'Kane tells me of the particular challenges that face men and women in this unforgiving environment. She tells me of her ultimate decision to quit the field and pursue work with the *Guardian* in London that was more family friendly. 'Five miscarriages Tom. I had those miscarriages after I came back from the field. And it's a funny thing actually. Looking back at the first one that I had. The first one was at three months. But that's quite late for a miscarriage. It's not an early one. I'd been to Kosovo. It was after a hugely traumatic story about a whole family being assassinated and the mother trying to protect her kids with her own body and it was really, really upsetting. I don't know if there was any linkage with the miscarriage. I've really no idea. But it was my perspective afterwards. Losing a three-month-old foetus. Having just interviewed a woman who has just talked about using her body to protect her two-year-old child. And not succeeding. It certainly helped me psychologically to deal with it. It gave me perspective. It really did. And the others were quite early on. So I felt I was pushing my body too hard reporting in the field. Because it is a very unhealthy environment. You sort of live on cigarettes and adrenaline.'

I ask each of the foreign correspondents to tell me about a specific moment in their careers as war reporters in which they thought they were about to die. Their closest encounter with death, so to speak. They all tell me different hair-raising stories. Interestingly, however, for me as a researcher, almost all of the stories begin with getting into the wrong taxi. As one of the journalists put it to me, 'In the rush to get the story, especially a breaking-news story, the temptation is to run out of the hotel and grab the first taxi. That's your big mistake. It can be a fatal error. No taxi driver in the world is going to tell you they don't know the way. Especially when you've got dollars or sterling or whatever. And inevitably, they take a wrong turn and you end up at the wrong checkpoint, or in the middle of the wrong angry mob, pleading for your life.'

The lesson seems to be: always order a taxi from reception in the hotel.

The hotel, it seems, 'wants you back alive to pay your bill.' Most experienced journalists use drivers and fixers provided by their media organisations. Young freelance journalists are more vulnerable. Patrick Cockburn offers one piece of salutary advice for aspiring foreign and war correspondents: 'The trick is to stay alive.'

After interviewing Nir Rosen in New York, I get yet another text from Aideen. I'm in the departure lounge of JFK. We are pregnant again. The baby is due in November. I fortify myself once more at 39,000 feet, somewhere over the north Atlantic, with a double gin and tonic.

Shannon Airport
June 2007

In May of 2007, I learn that the US Air Force Thunderbirds Squadron – the aerobatic display team of the US air force – is due to perform at the Salthill Air Show. There is some controversy about the arrival of the team to Galway. The Irish Anti-War Movement and other protest groups are unhappy at the display team's participation given the role that the USAF is playing in the wars in Afghanistan and Iraq. X is still working in the US Embassy. He organises it for me to interview the Thunderbirds when they arrive in Ireland. They will be touching down in Shannon Airport a couple of days before the show.

I do my research into the aerobatic display team. Otherwise known as the United States Air Force Air Demonstration Squadron, the USAF Thunderbirds Squadron has performed aerobatic manoeuvres worldwide since its inception in 1953. The Thunderbird's performance at Salthill will be its first ever in Ireland and the unit's first deployment to Europe since the 9/11 attacks in 2001 and the subsequent invasions of Afghanistan and Iraq. It is a very significant visit for the Thunderbirds pilots and support team.

The squadron consists of six F-16 C fighter jets flown by experienced combat pilots chosen from among the US air force's top operational combat squadrons. Speaking to me over the phone from their home base at Nellis Air Force Base in the Nevada desert outside Las Vegas, Captain Elizabeth Kreft tells me that that the core mission of the Thunderbirds is to 'perform precision aerial manoeuvres that demonstrate the combat capabilities of the aircraft of the United States air force.' I know that the protestors will be delighted to hear this particular nugget of information.

Captain Kreft goes on to say that the pilots and support crews of the Thunderbirds are particularly excited about the upcoming Irish visit given that many have strong Irish family connections. Most of the unit's members have also passed through Shannon Airport in recent years on their way to operational assignments in the Middle East and Afghanistan. She also states that the squadron is especially proud to visit Ireland and to 'spread the good will of the United States air force amongst our allies, and particularly among our sister countries who have shown their preparedness over the last number of years to make a stand for freedom throughout the world.'

I arrive at Shannon Airport to await the arrival of the display team. Unlike my December visit, Shannon is bathed in sunshine. Perfect weather for flying. I get out onto the apron of the runway and join some US air force ground crew who are anxiously scanning the horizon. After a while, squinting into the bright sunlight over the Atlantic, we spy small specks in the sky. The F-16s look incredibly small as they come in to land at Shannon. The aircraft look like toys as they land, one by one and then taxi towards us.

The squadron's public affairs officer introduces me to the pilots as they dismount from their aircraft. They have flown non-stop across the Atlantic, with in-flight refuelling along the way. They all need a coffee.

For the squadron's lead solo pilot, Major Ed Casey from Sparta, New Jersey, the Thunderbirds' visit to Ireland is a homecoming of sorts. His mother, Ailish Casey from Schull in County Cork, emigrated to the US in 1974. His father, Maurice and grandmother Margaret Casey are still living in Ireland. Major Casey echoes Captain Kreft's views on the Irish trip and tells me that the unit plans to put the Irish Tricolour on the flag panels of its aircraft during and after the Irish visit. Many of the squadron's top combat pilots are women, including Major Nicole Malachowski, whose grandparents come from Mallow in County Cork.

According to Major Casey, 'All of our pilots have combat experience over

Iraq and many have been operational in Afghanistan.' He goes on to describe the logistics involved in getting the Squadron's F-16s from Las Vegas to Shannon Airport. 'We fly direct from Pittsburgh, Pennsylvania to Shannon, crossing the North Atlantic with an escort of two KC 10 Extender refuelling jets.' These large aircraft refuel each of the team's F-16s with approximately four thousand litres of aviation fuel at least three times during the transatlantic flight. According to Major Casey, the squadron's support team of approximately eighty personnel are travelling to Ireland in 'greater comfort' aboard two US Air Force C-17 transport aircraft.

Major Casey describes three previous trips through Shannon Airport whilst serving as a combat pilot in various operational units of the US air force on his way to deployments in Iraq and elsewhere. As has become customary among US military personnel who have served in Iraq or Afghanistan and who have 'been lucky enough to transit via Shannon', Major Casey emphasises the 'incredible hospitality and the warm welcome of the Irish' in County Clare. He also describes the almost legendary reputation of the pint of Guinness. It is the last drink of choice sought out by most young US soldiers on their final stopover prior to combat overseas.

According to Major Casey, 'The transatlantic flight from Pittsburgh to Shannon, including refuelling periods, is approximately six and a half hours. We could exploit the aircraft's capabilities and get there a lot faster, but we've got to shadow the big, heavy refuelling jets.' One of the more uncomfortable outcomes of such a lengthy transit is not lost on the squadron's pilots. Unfortunately for the Thunderbirds combat pilots, the spartan cockpit of the F-16 has no toilet – or indeed much room for manoeuvre. In terms of the delicate subject of relieving themselves en route to Ireland, Major Casey, combat veteran and 'Top Gun' in the US air force, states diplomatically, 'There are ways to do it – but it ain't easy.'

I get to interview some of the female pilots after they have had a chance to chill out after the transatlantic flight. The women pilots are exceptionally high achievers. They each have extensive combat experience in Iraq and Afghanistan. Having originally graduated from the US Air Force Academy in Colorado Springs, they've since done postgraduate degrees in various disciplines. One of the women has a PhD in physiology and anatomy – her research specific to the impact of high-altitude flying and G-forces on physical endurance and cardiovascular function. She asks me about my PhD. When I tell them about the findings of my research and the subsequent reaction of the military authorities, they laugh out loud. 'No shit. Who'd have guessed?' One of them tells me that the only way to persuade sexist men about equality issues for women is to 'kick butt. Kick their asses in exams, in the air and in combat. They get the message then.'

As one of the pilots is a mother, I ask her about separation from her children during combat deployments to Iraq and Afghanistan. She tells me that during her operational deployments, her children were living on a US air base in Germany, 'So that I could visit them as often as possible.' She tells me that the US air force provides accommodation for spouses, partners and children in Germany as it is a short four-and-a-half-hour flight from Baghdad. 'The air force thinks of everything.'

I ask another about her most serious challenge in combat. She tells me that she was providing close air support to a US armoured unit during the initial invasion of Iraq. When ground forces entered Baghdad, she tells me that her squadron was the first air force unit to occupy and use Baghdad International Airport. 'It was hairy, Tom. We came under fire every day. On the ground and during take-off and landing.'

She tells me that during one combat air patrol, her aircraft was hit by a shoulder-launched missile. 'I'm flying and I see the flare of the missile coming at me. I do the countermeasures and evasion but, next thing, wham, something hits the airframe. The plane is juddering and vibrating and it is all I can do to just stay airborne. I struggle with the controls, because all of the flying characteristics have changed. Then I climb a little and start to regain control. And that's when I had this thought.' She pauses and looks at me directly. 'I realised that I had enough fuel to do a go-around and kill that asshole with the surface to air missile. So that's what I did. I managed to get back around to that spot and I fired everything I had at that motherfucker. Then I made my way back to the airport.'

The Coombe
November 2007

In November, Rossa is born. He is a perfect little boy. As he is delivered, we harvest stem cells from the umbilical cord. We hope that they might someday be used to help Eoghan. If stem cell treatments are developed to treat neuro-muscular diseases. Rossa's new-born cries are the soundtrack to the harvesting of the stem cells.

When we have drawn out the stem cells and as they are being sealed in a container, I take Rossa from the midwife. He is swaddled in a pink cellular blanket. I talk to him. Soothing him. He eventually relaxes and his cries stop. He is like a kitten. I can hear his breathing. The nurses hand me the package of stem cells and I leave Aideen and Rossa in the delivery suite. I make my way as quickly as I can to DHL's offices in the south inner city. They take the precious package and it is couriered to a laboratory in Holland for storage in deep freeze. There is no facility to do this in Ireland. The service costs us thousands of euro. We think it is worth every cent.

My dad congratulates us on Rossa's birth. He is very, very frail now. Aideen's parents are delighted and Aideen's mum holds him in her arms. Singing him to sleep.

Two weeks later, Aideen's mum is knocked down in a tragic road traffic accident. She is on her way home from the shops when she is struck by a car. She was almost home. She suffers serious head injuries and slips into a coma. She passes away just before Christmas. My own mum's death, like Pauline's, was a long goodbye. This is completely different. A sudden and violent parting.

As we say our night-time prayers, Darach comments that we now have a very long list of guardian angels in heaven. 'Nana, Nanny, Liadain, Pauline.' I pray that they are watching over us.

Chapter 36

Missile Shield

'Yes, space detectors, put into orbit by the United States Air Force Space Command. You see Tom, we've identified the earth's near-orbit as a critical battle space.'

NATO Headquarters, Brussels, Belgium

Spring 2008

Over the winter of 2007 and the spring of 2008, tension grows between the United States and Russia over President Bush's plans for what is termed the European Interceptor Site or EIS. In short, President Bush is keen to extend the US ballistic missile capability from the continental United States and the Pacific to mainland Europe. The US – without consultation with the European Union or indeed NATO – want to site ballistic missiles in Poland and an anti-missile radar system in the Czech Republic. President Bush hints that this new missile system will act as a shield to protect Europe from a possible future nuclear strike by a 'rogue state' such as Iran or Korea. Russia sees the presence of US ballistic missiles along its border as provocative – as provocative as Soviet missiles in Cuba back in the 1960s. The war of words between Vladimir Putin and President Bush escalates.

I make enquiries at the US Embassy in Dublin and negotiate access to the US delegation to NATO Headquarters in Brussels. They in turn agree to give me access to personnel from the US Missile Defence Agency in order to explain precisely the nature and rationale of the proposed, and highly controversial, missile project.

Juggling the busy routine at home, I do some initial research. It seems the

US Missile Defence Agency (MDA) – without recourse to NATO – is engaged in bilateral negotiations with Poland and the Czech Republic to site missile-shield silos and X-Band radar facilities in central Europe. The US intends to site ten long-range interceptor missiles at one weapon silo – approximately the size of a football pitch – in Poland by 2011. They also intend to forward-deploy an X-Band radar station from the Marshall Islands in the Pacific to the Czech Republic in the same time period.

The Russians continue to react angrily to this development. Russian Defence Minister Anatoly Serdyukov states in advance of NATO's 2008 Barcelona summit that 'the deployment of the missile defence system in Eastern Europe will create conditions for higher tensions, violate strategic balance in the world and pose a threat to our national security.' The United States, by virtue of its exclusive bilateral negotiations with the Polish and Czech governments on this issue, has also generated considerable unease among its NATO partners.

Once more, I cook and freeze a week's worth of dinners and make sure that we have enough milk in the fridge for a few days. I pack my bag and yet again tiptoe out of the house at the crack of dawn to catch the early-morning flight from Dublin to Brussels. The Aer Lingus flight is full of Irish MEPs, their staff and Irish EU civil servants on their way back to Brussels after the weekend. I meet some of my former students on the flight. As the Celtic Tiger begins to unravel and as Taoiseach Bertie Ahern's government shows poor leadership – and even poorer communication skills – my ex-students tell me that Brussels is where their futures lay. They express serious misgivings about Ireland's political and economic future. One tells me that, in Brussels, the Irish government is seen as a 'cowboy outfit'.

I get a taxi from Charleroi Airport and head straight for NATO Headquarters. I walk past the distinctive sculpture at the front entrance to the NATO complex. The massive riveted steel monstrosity towers over me. Designed to resemble NATO's emblem, it looks like a giant gyroscope. On closer inspection, it looks like a bomblet of the type I have seen scattered from cluster munitions. It is ugly. I go through the usual security scrutiny. My mobile phone is retained at the entrance in a small locker.

I'm met at the US delegation to NATO by their press officers. They are – similar to the US Embassy staff I've met elsewhere – young, articulate, and scarily passionate about the proposed European missile shield. They explain the historical context of the United States's latest ballistic missile initiative.

One of the staffers explains to me that the US has been steadily building up its missile defence shield since the advent of Ronald Reagan's 'Star Wars' initiative in the 1980s. Through extensive, and very expensive, research and development programmes, the US military have developed viable, anti-ballistic long-range interceptor missile silos at Fort Greely in Alaska and at Vandenberg Air Force Base in California. They have also developed and deployed so-called X-Band anti-ballistic missile radar stations in Hawaii and at other locations throughout the Pacific and Asia. According to the young guys and girls at the US delegation to NATO, this gives the US a 'fool-proof all-round defence' against intercontinental ballistic missile attacks. After 9/11, this is an important psychological as well as strategic concept.

I am then ushered into another room to meet some 'missile experts' who will explain to me exactly how the US missile shield will work. The room is darkened and there is a large screen on one wall. The American missile expert emerges out of the shadows to greet me. He is straight out of central casting in Hollywood. He is wearing a white, short-sleeved shirt with a row of pens in the shirt pocket. His hair is neatly combed in a side parting. He is wearing dark-framed glasses. He looks like he ought to be at mission control for one of the moon landings.

He introduces himself as 'Hank' or 'Frank' or some such and gets straight down to business. He hits a computer key and a disembodied voice announces, newsreader style, that 'the US has been attacked by Islamic militants in Iran.' A blow-dried and tanned news anchor appears on the screen. The 'newsreader', who resembles Kent Brockman from *The Simpsons*, continues dramatically. 'At 5 AM today, Eastern Standard Time, the Iranian regime in Teheran, without provocation, launched an intercontinental ballistic missile at the United States of America. We are pleased to report that the missile has been intercepted.'

At this point, the theme music from *Rocky* strikes up and the screen is filled with images of US military personnel responding to an incoming missile alert. The president is awoken on the short film and he gives the thumbs up for the 'rogue missile' to be 'taken out'.

I'm enjoying this briefing. I wonder if there will be popcorn. To the strains of the *Rocky* theme tune, a US missile – in dramatic slow motion – erupts from a concrete silo somewhere in the US and heads skyward. As the music reaches a crescendo, the US missile – the good missile, because it is white with the Stars and Stripes on the fuselage – hits the rogue missile in outer space. The rogue missile is black. When it is hit, there is a massive flare and explosion. Job done. The video then does a cutaway to some Iranian guys shaking their fists in defiance and pulling at their beards in impotent rage. The next cutaway shows lots of 'Hanks' and 'Franks' high-fiving each other in their short-sleeved shirts somewhere in a command bunker in the US. I'm convinced. Ireland should buy some of these missiles – immediately.

When the music concludes, the credits roll and the missile expert pushes his glasses a little higher up on the bridge of his nose. He explains how the European system would work. 'Tom, the X-Band radar, which we, uh, would put in the Czech Republic, is designed to lock on to the flight paths of ballistic missiles headed towards targets in the United States.' He takes out a metal pointer from his shirt pocket and extends it. He points to the Czech Republic on a world map hanging on the wall.

He continues summarising how the system works. 'The launching of rogue missiles, from potentially hostile states such as North Korea or Iran, would be detected by a network of satellite-borne 'space detectors' that have been placed in orbit by the US.' I interrupt him. 'Space detectors?' He replies, 'Yes, space detectors, put into orbit by the United States Air Force Space Command. You see Tom, we've identified the earth's near-orbit as a critical battle space.' I am now expecting Captain Kirk of the Starship Enterprise to appear on screen. But he doesn't. And Hank continues explaining. This is not a joke. I've got to focus.

'So, Tom, in order to counter an attack from Iran for example, upon detection of missile launch, the US X-Band radar located in the Czech Republic would guide the long-range interceptor missiles based in Poland towards

Iranian missiles over Central European airspace. On the interceptor missile's final approach towards an Iranian projectile, an 'exo-atmospheric kill vehicle' or EKV would be released, which is designed to collide with and destroy by kinetic energy the enemy warhead.' Hank hits another key on the laptop. Up on screen, I see what I initially take to be a sequence from a James Bond movie, *Moonraker* perhaps. A white missile is approaching a black missile. The exo-atmospheric kill vehicle pops out of the white missile and hits the black one. Flash, bang, whallop, the rogue missile is destroyed. It reminds me of Roy Lichtenstein's Warhol-like comic-book depiction of a missile strike. I almost see the word 'Whaam' on the overhead screen.

Hank is oblivious to my musings and continues. 'The detection, interception and destruction phases of the US missile defence shield would take place within minutes of an Iranian launch – and crucially, the warhead of a rogue-state missile would be destroyed over European airspace.' Again, in my mind's eye, I see the Lichtenstein graphic, 'I pressed the fire control and ahead of me . . . rockets blazed through the sky.' I glance around the room nervously. No one is laughing. This is not science fiction. There is no over-the-top James Bond villain stroking a white cat. Just me, and Hank and George Bush's US Air Force Space Command Vision for 2020.

I learn more and more as the briefing extends up to lunchtime. According to the US Missile Defence Agency, the American military have developed a range of such interceptor missiles – and even airborne lasers – designed to intercept and destroy the ballistic warheads of rogue states in their midcourse and terminal flight path stages. For the US, the interception and destruction of rogue warheads in the midcourse range – far from US airspace – represents the optimum scenario for the neutralisation of what they consider to be an emerging missile threat. The US currently lists the proliferation of ballistic missiles capable of carrying warheads to US cities as a growing imminent threat to US security – second only to the Global War on Terror.

At the end of the briefing, I shake hands with Hank and thank my American hosts for their sobering brief. On the one hand, I can see the attraction for the American people of such a missile shield. Especially if it works. I cannot help thinking about the time and effort and ingenuity invested in weapon systems. I wonder if they are conducting similar research into neuro-muscular diseases. I think of the neurological unit in the US Regional Medical Centre in Landstuhl. Maybe the US military industrial complex is also exploring new medical frontiers. Hopefully.

The Americans treat me with great hospitality. I argue with them over lunch about the missile system. They hold their own and propose all sorts of counterarguments. And, similar to what I've seen elsewhere with US diplomatic and military people, diverging opinions emerge. Some of the military attachés criticise the approach. Some others endorse it. The Americans, reassuringly somehow, are not all 'on message'. There seems to be room for debate and disagreement. This is the customary 'frank exchange of views' that I have come to associate with the Americans I have met. It seems to me to be an intellectual tradition that is worth emulating.

After the lunch I go on to meet some NATO missile experts. One of them is English. He tells me that many of the United States's partners at NATO have serious concerns about the location of its proposed European missile shield. My newfound English NATO source tells me that the interception of ballistic warheads in European airspace would inevitably lead to 'collateral damage' and 'contamination' over European territory – particularly if such missiles were fitted with nuclear, biological or chemical warheads.

A German colleague agrees and tells me that the interception of nuclear warheads by Polish-launched American EKVs would carry with it 'the risk of a sub-atmospheric nuclear detonation over Europe'. The electromagnetic pulse or EMP of such a detonation alone would in theory result in the immediate loss of hundreds of passenger jet aircraft within European airspace. In the medium to long term, in such circumstances there would also be the potential for catastrophic environmental damage and the prospect of serious radioactive contamination as permanent pollution.

It seems to me that the Russians are not the only ones who are uneasy about the proposed US missile shield. Some of the other European NATO members are less sceptical, however.

On reflection, when I look at the global footprint of the proposed international US missile shield myself, it looks more like a system designed to protect the US from potential missile strikes from emerging nuclear powers in Asia than an attempt to counter a local and emerging missile threat from Iran.

After a couple of days of intensive briefings and research, I fly back to Dublin. Darach and Eoghan ask me about Brussels. 'Were they nice people? Did I get chocolate?'

With Darach and Eoghan in school, our daily routine has changed a little and has settled down somewhat. I get up every morning at around 6.15 AM. After sorting out the breakfast and the school lunches and uniforms, I go into Eoghan's room and gently wake him up. He is always very warm after his night's sleep and it is a good time to do some gentle stretches and some physiotherapy exercises with him. We do this most mornings for about half an hour. Working quietly in the dark before the rest of the house wakes up.

In April, Taoiseach Bertie Ahern resigns from office. His next public appearance is scheduled for McKee Barracks in Dublin where he will review Irish troops bound for Chad in Africa. As Ahern has effectively disappeared from public view after making his unexpected and sudden announcement, almost every journalist in the city converges on McKee Barracks for the press and photo opportunity it affords. It will be the first chance for many journalists to ask questions of the taoiseach about his resignation. My editor Peter Murtagh calls me and asks me to go along, to see if I can get a line from the taoiseach about sending Irish troops to Africa and potentially into harm's way.

I call the Defence Forces Press Office, my old workplace, and ask them what is the best time to arrive in McKee for what is going to be a hectic press opportunity. The officer at the other end pauses before he answers. 'You cannot come to McKee Barracks, Tom. You know that.' I am taken aback. To say the least. 'Why not?' I ask. 'Come on, Tom. You know the reason why.' I tell him that I don't know the reason and ask him to tell me the reason, as he sees it. He replies with a one-liner. 'Look, Tom, we couldn't guarantee your personal safety if you turned up in McKee Barracks on Friday.' His response silences me completely. I am also taken aback by the casual and dismissive nature of the remark.

I put down the phone and reflect on matters. Should I leave it be? Put up and shut up? I'm sick and tired of confrontation and adversarial encounters. I think carefully about my media work over the last number of years. I think over any contributions in media I've made that are specific to the work of the Irish Defence Forces. I've been almost universally positive and constructive, going out of my way where possible to praise the work of the army. I have also publicly praised their progress in dealing with the bullying and harassment issue. It doesn't seem to be enough, however. I still seem to be persona non grata.

I call a few journalist friends and run the scenario by them. None of them have ever been barred from a press conference or a photo opportunity. They advise me to contact the NUJ. With a heavy heart, I call Seamus Dooley, the Secretary General of the NUJ. Seamus meets me in the city centre and I go over the issue with him. Seamus is sympathetic. 'This is unacceptable, Tom.' I am relieved. 'This is Dublin. Not Beijing. It doesn't matter what your differences were with the Defence Forces, you cannot be blacklisted in this manner. Imagine if the government were to blacklist a journalist like Geraldine Kennedy [former editor of the *Irish Times*] because of court cases arising from state-sponsored phone-tapping and eavesdropping?'

Seamus asks me to leave the matter with him. As it happens, Seamus is acquainted with the army's new chief of staff, Lieutenant General Dermot Earley. Apparently, Seamus had once worked with a local newspaper in Roscommon and had got to know General Earley in his younger days. A few days later, Seamus calls me to tell me that the matter has been resolved. He tells me that Dermot Earley was horrified to hear what had happened. As chief of staff, he knew nothing about any residual ill-feeling towards me. He was disappointed to hear of the encounter and determined to ensure there was no such further behaviour from any quarter in the Defence Forces.

A few months later, I am invited by Dermot Earley to a reunion of Defence Forces press officers in McKee Barracks in Dublin. It is the first time I have stepped inside McKee Barracks in almost a decade. When I go into the officer's mess, there is a large group of my former colleagues at the bar. I have not seen most of them in years. There is a sudden silence as I enter the room. Time stands still. All eyes on me. Then a spontaneous welcome. Handshakes all round. The war, it seems, is finally over.

During the meal afterwards, Dermot Earley, as chief of staff and our host, gets up from the head of the table and approaches me, hand extended in greeting, to welcome me back. We have not seen each other since we last worked together at Defence Forces Headquarters. I congratulate him on his promotions and appointment as chief of staff. He congratulates me on my family and my subsequent career. It is a special moment. A moment of reconciliation. A homecoming of sorts.

Tragically, within months of this meeting, Lieutenant General Dermot Earley is struck down with a degenerative neurological disease. He passes away in June 2010. Eoghan's neurological condition continues to plateau. Thankfully, he is stable.

In August, Russia invades Georgia. Based on the speed of the intervention, the numbers of troops involved and the rate of advance, it is clear to me that the operation has been carefully preplanned. It is premeditated. I write a series of articles in the *Irish Times* reflecting this view.

After a few days, I get a call from Dimitri. I have not heard from him since the Beslan School siege. He invites me to London to meet Russian Embassy staff in order to 'discuss the Georgia situation'. I duly fly to London and meet my Russian contacts in Langan's Brasserie. I finally get to meet Dimitri. He introduces me to his 'friends' in the Russian Embassy including a 'specialist' on Georgia, Andrei, who grins at me. 'Before we start about Georgia, tell me Thomas, what do you think of our English hosts?' Andrei's question provokes belly laughs all round and a toast 'To Ireland and the Irish.' The evening is very enjoyable, but after three hours of questions and answers, I come away with absolutely nothing of value. Nothing to add to what I had already suspected or known about the Russian intervention in Georgia.

November 2008

In November, in an historic win, Barak Obama is elected President of the United States of America. A week or so later, I am invited by the University Philosophical Society, Trinity College, Dublin to conduct a public interview with US Assistant Secretary of State, Ambassador John Negroponte. The theme of the public interview is timely. I am to conduct a question and answer session with Negroponte on 'Eight years of foreign policy under President George W. Bush – A Retrospective and discussion of the foreign policy challenges confronting President Obama.'

Negroponte was appointed by President Bush as US Ambassador to the United Nations from 2001 until 2004 – during which period he played a pivotal role in attempts to garner international support for the invasion of Iraq in 2003. Subsequently, he succeeded Paul Bremer as the US Ambassador to Iraq from 2004 to 2005. Thereafter, he served as US Director of National Intelligence for two years from 2005 to 2007. As a high-profile Washington insider, throughout both terms of the Bush administration, Deputy Secretary Negroponte played a key role in determining the shape and nature of the Bush administration's responses to 9/11 and its subsequent robust military and foreign policy interventions in Iraq and Afghanistan.

The hall is packed with students and Negroponte faces a lively question and answer session at the Philosophical Society. Negroponte is asked many questions about the strategy behind the invasion of Iraq. Responding to observations that the US invasion force was relatively small, at less than 250,000, barely one-quarter of the total coalition force of over one million troops assembled for Operations Desert Storm and Desert Shield during the first Gulf War – he admits that the downsized US occupation force was not strong enough to provide security or the prospect of reconstruction for the Iraqi people. He observes that the Bush administration, after the initial success in toppling Saddam's regime, thought 'the rest would be easy'. He also observes that when he arrived as ambassador to Iraq in 2004, he expected to oversee the reconstruction of the country. However, he stated it was evident that reconstruction was simply not possible and that the country was in the throes of a 'widespread insurgency' – an insurgency that the Bush administration 'didn't foresee'.

This admission, and the assertion that the US did not anticipate a widespread insurgency within Iraq, although such an insurgency had been predicted at the time by the US general staff – along with most international intelligence and security analysts – leaves the Bush administration open to the charge of having recklessly failed in its duty of care to the newly 'liberated' citizens of Iraq. The fourth Geneva Convention explicitly sets out the obligations and duties of an occupying force with regard to the physical security, food security, health and welfare of its protected citizens. Deputy Secretary Negroponte's remarks at the Philosophical Society, coupled with the suffering endured by the Iraqi people in the immediate aftermath of the invasion and the uncontrolled destruction of the country's key infrastructure, suggest that the Bush administration were in clear breach of their obligations towards ordinary Iraqi citizens under the Geneva Conventions.

With President-elect Obama expected to step up the number of US troops deployed to an increasingly restive Afghanistan, Negroponte makes the insightful – and worrying – observation that the Taliban's theory of victory was simply to 'undermine the Afghan government and ultimately to simply outlast the NATO alliance presence in Afghanistan.' Based on the US experience in Iraq, as described by one of its chief proponents, a decisive victory in Afghanistan for NATO and its ISAF partners, including Ireland, appears to be as remote as it was for the Soviets during their occupation of the country.

Deputy Secretary Negroponte refers to some of ISAF's successes in Afghanistan including a reduction by 26 percent in the infant mortality rate there along with the considerable achievement of providing education for over 6.5 million Afghan children – including 1.5 million girls who were previously denied education under the Taliban regime. He acknowledges the significant challenges that lie ahead for the new administration in Afghanistan.

After the public Q and A, Negroponte continues to discuss with me the challenges that lie ahead for Obama. He identifies the interlinked issues of the insurgency within Afghanistan and an increasingly unstable and radicalised Pakistan as significant challenges for the incoming administration. Confronted with such seemingly intractable difficulties, in a significant statement, Negroponte also indicates that, on principle, he would not rule out talks or negotiations with the Taliban and other resistance groups if certain conditions were met and if there appeared to be some constructive political engagement possible.

As our conversation draws to a close, a member of the Philosophical Society approaches Negroponte and asks which one of the forty-three presidents of the United States he admires the most. Somewhat prophetically – and without hesitation – he replies, 'President Roosevelt, for getting us through a crisis.' As Ireland heads towards economic and social melt-down, it is interesting to note a high-profile, neoconservative cite Roosevelt and his citizen-focused New Deal politics as best practice for crisis management. Unfortunately, for Irish citizens, there is no 'new deal' in the wake of the economic crisis wrought by neoliberal, neoconservative foreign policy and banking policies. Instead, the Irish people get austerity.

Chapter 37

Syria

'Each year, dear, we pick a country on Ethel's atlas and we go there on a visit. This year we picked Syria.'

January 2009

Eoghan is called into the CRC for a review appointment. The physiotherapist and occupational therapist feel that Eoghan is progressing well with his manual wheelchair. He is navigating the classroom and home environment very successfully. His posture is good and he is coping well. However, they feel that as a consequence of Eoghan's neuromuscular condition, he would be better served by a power chair for longer distances. We discuss the options with the therapists and Eoghan's paediatrician at a team meeting. We agree that as Eoghan gets older, he will need to become more independent. We reach the conclusion that a power chair will facilitate this growing independence and Eoghan's expanding curiosity about the world beyond our home. Like any other child of his age, Eoghan needs to have the ability to roam wide and free. To experience the wider world and to broaden his social interactions. We realise that Eoghan needs his own space. He needs to be master of his own destiny. Eoghan is assessed for a power chair so that, in his own words, he can be 'out and about'. His most earnest desire is to get to the shops on his own, without parental supervision, to buy sweets.

At the end of January, I get confirmation from the European Journalism Centre in Brussels that I have been selected to participate in a European Union-sponsored visit to Damascus in Syria. I have not been in Syria since 1996. The last time I was there, I was still in the army. I remember Damascus as a city of contrasts. On the surface, I remember it as a fast-moving, cosmopolitan city. I also remember it for the massive prison that overlooked the city and the portraits of President Assad – Hafez al-Assad. The brutal dictator's portrait was displayed in any and all available public spaces, in shop windows and in the entrances and foyers of every building I entered. His face even hung from the rear-view mirrors of taxis. Everywhere you looked, through the traffic fumes and in the smoky dark of night clubs and bars, Assad looked back at you from some vantage point.

Getting a visa for Syria is a quirky undertaking. I call the embassy in London and they advise me how to fill in the application forms. They strongly recommend that I not declare I have been to Israel. 'Ever,' as the lady in the embassy puts it. They also advise me not to bother with a sterling bank draft or an international money order in order to pay the visa fee. 'Just send a fifty-pound note along with your passport.' It is with some trepidation that I send £50 and my passport off to an address in London. Lo and behold, as good as their word, the passport returns a week or so later with a short-term visa for entry at Damascus.

March 2009

Another daybreak, another journey. In the pre-dawn darkness, as per my ritual, I slip out of the house as Aideen and the children sleep. I look in on the four children before I leave. Listen to their gentle breathing. I kiss each of them and quietly click the front door behind me. The taxi driver asks me where I'm going. 'Damascus,' I reply. 'For a conversion?' he answers. Not bad for four in the morning.

I fly to London and connect with a British Midland flight to Damascus at Heathrow. It is an unusual journey. The cabin crew speak in singsong London accents. One could be forgiven for thinking that you were simply connecting to a regional airport in the UK. The cheery tones of the onboard announcements jar with the reputation of our destination as a central hub on the so-called 'Axis of Evil'. 'Welcome on board this BMI International flight to

Damascus. We ask you to relax, enjoy our free in-flight bar service and to please browse our extensive duty-free brochure.' The plane is almost empty. A large group of elderly English ladies board after me. Shortly after take-off, the cabin crew invite us all to sit a little closer to the front of the aircraft. The English ladies are drinking prodigious amounts of gin and tonic and getting louder and louder as we exit central Europe and enter Turkish airspace.

I ask them where they are from. They tell me that they are from Windsor. They are all in the same book club. One of the well-spoken, though slightly tipsy, ladies tells me that they go on a 'magical mystery tour' once a year. 'Each year, dear, we pick a country on Ethel's atlas and we go there on a visit. This year we picked Syria.' She grins a little lopsidedly at me. I'm wondering if she knows that Syria has been designated a 'rogue state' and is considered by both Britain and the United States as an evil dictatorship. I ask them if they had trouble with visas. 'Visas?' asks Ethel. 'No one said anything about visas.' They laugh it off and tell me to relax.

Eventually we cross the Mediterranean coastline over Lebanon. Buffeted by updrafts from the Chouf Mountains and Bekaa Valley, the aircraft gradually descends into Syrian airspace and towards Damascus International Airport. I look out over the city below with its Muslim, Jewish and Christian communities cohabiting in relative harmony. Despite its surface veneer of cosmopolitan harmony, Damascus is a city under constant surveillance. Under President Assad's watchful eyes – his portrait staring intently from every shop window, bar and Souk in the city – ordinary citizens go about their business.

As the wheels thump onto the runway, I wonder how Syria has changed after eight years of economic sanctions and political isolation during the Bush administration's Global War on Terror. I wonder how much it has changed since I was last here in 1996. The first thing I notice is that the ubiquitous portraits of President Hafez al-Assad have been replaced by portraits of President Bashar al-Assad, the late president's son. The elderly English ladies, sitting next to me on the plane, waltz over towards passport control. Ethel takes charge of the group and there is a heated exchange with the moustachioed men on the passport desk. Things look a bit precarious for a few minutes.

Another man with a moustache is called. He speaks some English. After a remarkably short conversation, the man gives Ethel a formal bow, almost a curtsey, and ushers the women through passport control to his office at the rear. As I join the lengthening queue, shuffling towards the immigration and customs booths, I see the ladies up ahead, having their passports stamped with much ceremony by their newfound friend. I am envious. They shake hands and teeter out of his office. Oblivious to the armed police that throng the airport, the English ladies hail two taxis and disappear into downtown Damascus.

I am eventually processed through passport control. A minibus takes me along roads lined with palm trees into the historical centre of Damascus. The city itself is as vibrant as ever, but fraying at the edges. My hotel is in the Christian quarter of Bab Touma, or 'Thomas Gate'. The hotel is a classic Arab construction. It is surrounded by a thick, impenetrable, dun-coloured wall. Set into the wall is a heavy wooden door mounted on dark iron hinges and studded with steel bolts. The taxi driver hammers on the door. A black metal grille in the door opens briefly and then a heavy lock is disengaged. The door creaks open onto a beautiful courtyard and garden where fountains and fragrant blossoms abound. Songbirds chirp and cheep among the climbing plants and trees. The owner greets me under the obligatory portrait of Assad. He tells me that business is slow. He also tells me that there are regular power cuts. As he does so, as if on cue, the lights go out, then flicker back into life as a diesel generators kicks in to take up the slack.

The owner tells me that life in Damascus has become harder over the years. There are many thousands of refugees from Iraq. Many Iraqi Christians have fled to Bab Touma. He tells me he knows of a Catholic priest from Baghdad who is so traumatised by his experiences there that he carries a gun under his vestments when celebrating mass. Despite the hardships arising from international sanctions and the brutal regime, the Syrians I meet are as friendly as ever. Everyone, without exception responds warmly to the Arabic greeting, '*Ahlan wa-Sahlan*.' The welcome for the Irish is particularly pronounced.

Many faces, however, are strained and one gets a sense from ordinary

Syrians of a feeling of foreboding; fears for the future of Syria as a rogue state, a fear of the unknown. I also notice an increase on the streets since my last visit of the numbers of women wearing religious headscarves. The Syrians acknowledge that there has been an increase in 'religiosity' in the region since the 'Anglo-American invasion' of neighbouring Iraq.

On this visit to Damascus I am one of a number of European journalists who have been invited to Syria by the European Union in order to witness at first hand the EU's emerging foreign policy or 'Neighbourhood Policy' in the Middle East. The next few days are an endless blur of daily briefings and visits to Syrian ministries, educational institutes and businesses including the fledgling, and eerily quiet, Syrian Stock Exchange.

As I recall from my last visit to Damascus, the food is spectacular, but not for the faint-hearted. Outside almost every butcher shop, the heads, with spines attached of course, of camels, calves, sheep and goats announce freshly slaughtered meat for the barbecue. At one venue, these heads are displayed to remind us of just how fresh our *shish-taouk* and other local delicacies are. One meal takes place in the revolving roof-top restaurant of the multi-storey Cham Palace Hotel in downtown Damascus. As the rotating dining room creaks, groans and grinds, in a most alarming fashion, around the precipice of the building, the views of Damascus are stunning and terrifying at the same time. Two groups are oblivious: the gin-drinking English ladies whom I spot in the restaurant and our Syrian hosts. The Syrians are used to living on the edge and, unruffled by the view, speak frankly of their real fears; fears that range from the spread of religious fundamentalism in the region to terrorism and above all to what they term 'Israeli and US aggression' in the Middle East.

It is clear to me that Syria is a country in flux with significant domestic, regional and international political and security challenges. Over bread and hummus, one of our Syrian hosts, Reem Haddad, tells me that Arabs and Europeans have 'much more in common than that which sets us apart'. Perched on the mountains high over the city, where Adam met Eve, she reminds us that Damascus was for many centuries a vital mid-way point in the silk route which stretched between China and Europe. Today, she tells us, 'Syria has the potential to play a vital role in the axis of communication between Europe, Iran and the emergent Chinese Tiger.'

Reem Haddad has red hair and speaks with a cut-glass English accent. An unusual look for a Syrian. She tells me that she spent part of her childhood in London. Over dinner she talks passionately about equality issues for women in Syria. She tells me that if Syrian stability is undermined, that religious fundamentalism will set Syrian society back hundreds of years. She expresses the view, forcefully and repeatedly, that 'if Syria is destabilised by Sunni extremists fleeing the war in Iraq, Damascus will become a mediaeval place governed by Sharia law.'

The Syrian information minister, Mohsen Bilal, joins us for dinner. He is accompanied by Bouthaina Shaaban. She, like Reem, speaks perfect English. She tells me that she holds a PhD in English literature from Warwick University. I tell her about my own doctoral research. Reem and Bouthaina express a particular interest in my research into the status and role of women in the Irish army. They are especially concerned by the findings in relation to the bullying, harassment and the phenomenon of sexual assaults against female soldiers. They exchange glances. Bouthaina shakes her head. 'Sexual violence against women is a major problem in the Arab world.' Reem and Bouthaina give me to understand that this is a red-line issue for them both.

I ask them repeatedly about the use of sexual violence by the Syrian regime in general and the Mokhabarat, or Syrian secret police, in particular against critics of Assad. They shrug off the questions. According to Reem, these are just rumours. Reem and Bouthaina, it seems to me, are part of an attempt to provide an 'acceptable face' for Assad's regime to western journalists like myself. They give passionate voice to opinions and concerns about equality issues and violence against women in the Middle East. They are both strangely cold and unresponsive to questions about sexual violence perpetrated by the regime for whom they are spokespersons and advisors. As key members of Assad's regime, I can only conclude they have entered into some sort of Faustian contract with evil.

Mohsen Bilal, the information minister, is all charm. He has a carefully cultivated air of bonhomie. From my own perspective, I find Bilal's presence to be deeply unsettling. Whilst he smiles at us, he barks and snaps at his subordinates, including Reem and Bouthaina. He has overheard some of our conversation as he approaches us. 'Ah, women's talk. Don't mind these women and their small talk.' He waves his hands in a gesture of dismissal. He asks me where I am from. When I tell him I am from Dublin, he tells me that he had an Irish girlfriend when he was a medical student in Italy. 'She taught me "Molly Malone".' He then clamps his hand on my shoulder and launches in: 'In Dublin's fair city, where the girls are so pretty . . .' He winks at all and sundry and sweeps outside when his mobile phone rings. He throws his eyes to heaven. 'It's the boss.' I'm assuming he means Bashar al-Assad – not his wife.

Reem relaxes visibly when Bilal exits the restaurant. She promises to introduce me to some other key players within Bashar al-Assad's regime. She is as good as her word. The next day she organises a visit to the offices of the Deputy Prime Minister, Abdullah Dardari. Unlike the other male apparatchiks of Assad's regime, Dardari is relatively youthful. In his mid-forties, Dardari has studied in London and California. His English is impeccable. He manages to appear relatively non-threatening. A former journalist, he affects affability and is comfortable in the company of foreign media. Another 'acceptable face' of the regime.

Dardari is a close ally and hard-line supporter of Assad. He tells me about the internal challenges facing Syria. 'On the domestic front, Syria faces a number of serious economic, political and security challenges. Economy-wise, Syria is moving from a centrally planned Soviet-style economy to a free-market model.' Dardari elaborates, 'We never had a fully socialist economy like Eastern Europe. Syrians have always been very entrepreneurial with approximately 40 percent of our economy in the private informal sector of barter and trade – a vibrant black market of sorts.'

With 60 percent of Syria's population of twenty million under the age of twenty-five, the successful transition to a competitive free-market economy will be crucial to the country's future prosperity, internal security and political stability. Dardari tells me that if there is insufficient employment and economic prospects for the twelve million or so young Syrians in the country, there may well be unrest and 'perhaps even violent unrest'.

Externally, the Syrians acknowledge that the invasion of neighbouring Iraq along with eight years – under the Bush administration – of political and economic isolation has undermined Syria's stability as a secular Arab state. I put it to Dardari, as forcefully as I can, that much of Syria's stability resides within the iron grip that President Assad holds over the state. Assad is a dictator who rules by force. Through fear. Dardari appears frustrated at this point. He tells me that the Syrian regime is 'conscious of the west's scepticism and criticism of the nature of the Assad regime.' However, he claims that he, along with President Assad and his other ministers are genuinely committed to reform, 'We know that economic reform will bring political reform. But we want to design, shape and implement that change ourselves.' He adds, 'You must understand. With the war in Iraq, the potential for civil war in Syria has never been stronger. We are trying to do this reform in very difficult regional circumstances.'

When our meeting is over, Dardari walks with me to the elevators. He takes my elbow and tells me again that Assad is 'genuinely committed to reform'. He tells me that things have improved for journalists. 'Journalists can openly criticise the regime now. They can do it freely. They can comment on our actions and pronounce judgement on our policies.' He presses the button to summon the lift. 'Of course there are still some old hang-ups. For example, it is not permitted to disrespect the image of Bashar al-Assad. Cartoons of Assad are forbidden as they are considered offensive and disrespectful.' He smiles at me. 'In time though, it will be possible to poke some fun at the president. He has a sense of humour, after all.' The bell for the lift pings and we take our leave of the Deputy Prime Minister.

Reem has also made arrangements for a meeting with Syria's Deputy Foreign Minister, Abdel Fatah Amoura. Amoura is not unlike Bilal. He possesses the superficial charm of the information minister, but is impatient and petulant with his Syrian staff. A rather severe man, he bangs the table now and then for emphasis. Amoura echoes many of Dardari's concerns about the external threats to Syria's stability.

He elaborates on what he terms these 'difficult regional circumstances'. He tells me that with the invasion of Iraq and the recent cyclical series of confrontations between Israel and the Palestinians and neighbouring Lebanon, the Syrians have observed a move towards religious fundamentalism throughout many Arab states – including Syria itself. Amoura claims that whilst Syria's notorious Mokhabarat closely monitor state and private sector media for any evidence of Islamic fundamentalism or direct criticism of Bashar al Assad's personal leadership, they do not have the capacity to monitor such religious or political discourse within the growing amount – numbering many thousands – of mosques scattered throughout the state.

Amoura observes: 'Extremism is not just an Islamic phenomenon. We've seen increases in ethnic and religious tensions wherever the west has sought to interfere or impose western-style democracy *á la mode Americain*. This is because Arabs are not consulted or involved in the change process. Iraq's Christians have fled to Syria. And the Americans have armed the Sunni militias and the Shia Badr and Mahdi armies, turning Iraq into an armed camp where religious intolerance is rife. The only way to defeat Islamic fundamentalism is to mobilise pan-Arabism and tolerance.'

I put it to Amoura that Syria is often accused in the international arena of facilitating the movement of iihadis or extremist mujahideen into neighbouring Iraq in order to attack US troops there. Amoura rejects this notion and elaborates on the attempts that Syria has made to secure its border with Iraq. 'We deployed ten thousand troops there and built trenches with electric fences. We put up over five hundred police observation centres and arrested over one thousand, four hundred foreign nationals, Saudis, Algerians, Tunisians and so on, engaged in criminal activities at the border. We secured our border better than the US secures its border with Mexico, but we got no help from the Americans or the British. We asked for night-vision equipment to help in the fight against terrorism and it was refused.' Amoura promises to arrange for me to visit the massive refugee camps where tens of thousands of Iraqis have fled to Syria along the border with Iraq's Al Anbar province.

After our conversation, Reem indicates that it will be possible to meet the Syrian Foreign Minister Walid al-Moallem. We navigate the Damascus crosstown traffic and are eventually ushered into another Syrian ministry building. I am told that al-Moallem can take a brief question from me. He enters the room. White-haired and overweight, al-Moallem looks a lot older than his sixty-eight years. I ask him about Assad's reputation as a dictator and whether or not the Syrian regime will do business with Senator George Mitchell, Obama's newly appointed Special Envoy for Middle East Peace. I also ask him if Mitchell's experience of the Irish peace process might help in talks with Syria.

Al-Moallem fires off his answers in a peremptory fashion. 'I don't know Senator Mitchell, so I cannot judge him, but in order to succeed in this process, all parties must have the will or desire for peace. As an honest broker also, Senator Mitchell must talk to all parties to the process, not just one.' Minister Moallem concludes his remarks to me by saying, 'Any regime in the Middle East that is not committed to peace will eventually fail. Any regime in the Middle East that commits itself to violent action will descend into anarchy.' Al-Moallem's words will prove prophetic in the years immediately following our conversation.

Reem asks her driver to drop me at my hotel. On the way, she tells me, in her English-accented, received pronunciation, 'Just like us, you in Ireland know that any fool can make war. It takes real humanity to sit down with your enemies and to make peace.' Outside the hotel, as I gather up my briefcase, Reem asks me if I will appear on Syrian television. Apparently, Reem Haddad has her own current affairs program. I agree to talk on her program on the basis that we focus on the lessons of the Irish peace process and the requirement for talks and negotiation; consensus building as opposed to coercion, physical force and state terrorism in the search for peace and reconciliation. She agrees.

The next morning I am brought from my hotel to the Syrian state television station. The Syrian state broadcasting campus is remarkably similar in appearance and architectural style to RTÉ's studios in Donnybrook. Except in Damascus, there are soldiers with AK47s manning the gate. In addition, there are no women in evidence around the buildings or studios. Just men. And all of the men have moustaches. And almost all of them are smoking. Reem is nowhere to be seen. Instead, I am brought into a studio and interviewed by a male journalist. He reads the questions in halting English from printed sheets. The producer and director reassure me that Reem will be filmed later asking the questions. When the prerecorded program is broadcast, it will appear to the viewer that Reem and I are in studio together. Though, obviously, we never appear in the same shot.

A few months after the recording, the Syrians send me a DVD copy of the broadcast. They have not edited my answers in any way. They have, however, added dramatic music and pictures of the Northern Ireland conflict to accompany some of my responses. Throughout the entire bizarre interview, Reem Haddad appears to be in studio with me. At the other end of the couch, looking at times concerned, absorbed, even interested in my answers. I wonder if this is how they do all of their interviews. Reem later becomes spokesperson for the Assad regime during the 2012-2013 civil war. Her peculiar interview style and absolute denial of the growing civil war in Syria invite comparisons with Saddam Hussein's controversial spokesperson, Mohammad al-Sahaff, who became known as 'Comical Ali'. She becomes known among western journalists as 'Comical Sally' for her bizarre and often contradictory statements on the war in Syria.

After recording the show, I am driven to a military base at the edge of the city centre. True to his word, al-Moallem has arranged for me to visit the Syrian border with Al Anbar province. I am ushered on board a rickety Mi-17 Soviet-manufactured 'Hip' transport helicopter and with much groaning, heaving and clattering we take off and head east over Damascus towards the Iraqi border. After a two-and-a-half-hour flight, I am vibrating from head to toe and am almost deaf. At the Al Walid-Al Tanf border crossing with Iraq, the pilots circle over a refugee camp for Sunnis fleeing the mayhem and anarchy of the US army's Operation Iraqi Freedom. The Mi-17 then executes a lazy turn, descending rapidly towards a military checkpoint. We touch down in a plume of dust. The pilots keep the engine running as one of the crew walks me to the edge of the rotor wash. The refugee camp at the Al-Tanf border crossing is home to Palestinians and mostly Sunni Iraqis who have fled the conflict in Iraq. The plight of the refugees is pitiable. The Syrians seem to be doing as best they can with limited resources to assist them. The scene speaks for itself.

The border itself is thousands of miles long. On the other side of the dirt track outside the refugee camp is Iraqi territory. In the distance we see US military aircraft operating in support of ground troops somewhere in Al Anbar province.

The Syrian flight crew ask me in broken English if I want to see any other camps. I've seen enough. After a brief refuelling stop, we arrive in Damascus at sunset. There is a massive thunderstorm raging over the city. Bolt lightning dances across the rooftops and along the horizon. I manage a brief visit to the Al-Hamidiyah Souq to buy gifts for Darach, Eoghan, Ailbhe and Rossa. I walk there from the hotel and am soaked to the bone in the rain. I catch the early-morning flight to London and connect to Dublin. That afternoon, I collect the boys from school and walk them home along the Rock Road. One of my neighbours remarks that I look sunburned. I am a little. It is a world away from the Al-Tanf border crossing and the Syrian desert stretching into Al Anbar province.

Chapter 38

Death

'I'm in a dead man's bed.'

April 2009

The home routine continues as normal. Up at 6 AM for physiotherapy and stretches with Eoghan. We call it 'quality time'. Then the rush to get the kids to school. Afterwards, cycling into the city centre to DIT for lectures and research. Sometimes writing up an academic article. Sometimes writing about the wars in Iraq or Afghanistan. And after that, the mad dash on the bicycle to get home. Check the homework. Get the dinner on. Aideen's routine in the hospital gets more hectic as increasing austerity measures and cutbacks to the Irish health system erode public services. We have less 'quality time' with the kids – maybe a half an hour to catch up on their hectic lives in the evening. Then fall into bed, get up and do it all again.

I try to visit my dad at least once or twice a week. He is skin and bone. Still smoking furiously. He no longer walks to the front door to wave me off. I no longer see him standing in the doorway of the house waving his hanky.

On a Friday afternoon, one of my sisters finds him lying on the floor of the sitting room. He had stumbled and fallen earlier. He cannot get up. My brother tries to persuade him to go into a nursing home for a few days, for some respite care. My dad doesn't want to leave the house. Eventually, he relents.

We manage to get him a bed for the weekend in a nursing home in Glasnevin. They have a sudden vacancy. My dad makes colourful remarks to me about this when I visit him on Saturday afternoon. 'I'm in a dead man's bed.'

The sun is shining outside as my dad shifts uncomfortably in the bed. He is wearing a hospital gown and I can see his legs. They are stick-like, pitifully thin. He has no flesh whatsoever. White, and bruised in places. His arms are the same. I feel dizzy looking at him. He looks like a corpse. He watches me appraisingly from the bed with his glittering green eyes. They, at least, are still fully animated. 'You think I'm fucked, don't you?' he rasps.

I cannot answer him. My eyes well up. I think of him when we were kids. Coming home from duty in his uniform. Tall, black hair. Green eyes. Indestructible. I can hardly bear to look at him now in the bed. He tells me to, 'Go outside into the sunshine.' I don't know what to say to him. As I leave, he is coughing and fighting to regain his breath.

The nurse, a Nigerian guy, meets me in the corridor. He smiles at me. 'Is that your dad?' I nod. 'He asked me to get him twenty cigarettes from the Texaco across the road.' The nurse laughs. 'He is a character.'

On Sunday morning I call in to see him again. Aideen comes with me. We talk to the nurse outside in the corridor. He has been on a drip for twenty-four hours now and is significantly rehydrated. The nurse tells me that he is much better today. Indeed, I can hear him from the corridor. He is shouting out my name. His voice has returned. 'Thomas. THOMAS? COME. HERE. NOW.'

I walk in to the room. He looks better all right. He has the quilt pulled up to his waist and has his teeth back in. He glowers at me. 'I heard you talking about me in the corridor. If you have anything to say about me, say it here to my face.'

I cannot think of anything to say to him. I know what he'll say if I ask him how he is. He'll say, 'I'm fucking miserable.' I ask him anyway. 'I'm fucking miserable,' is his answer. He adds, 'I've had enough of this place. I won't spend another night in here. Mark my words.'

After a while, we leave him in peace. As I'm leaving the room, he closes his eyes, drifting off to sleep. He looks comfortable.

We take the kids to Dun Laoghaire and walk the pier. I make the lunches for school the following morning and am making the dinner when my phone rings. It is a nurse in accident and emergency in the Mater Hospital. 'Is this

Thomas?' she asks. I reply in the affirmative. 'Your dad has been taken to the Mater Hospital. He has a cardiac issue.' Aideen looks at me, eyebrows raised. I quote the nurse's diagnosis of a 'cardiac issue'. I add, 'She says I should come in to see him, straightaway.' Aideen looks at me sympathetically and gives me her own medical opinion. 'Oh, Thomas, I'm sorry. He's gone. He's passed away.'

And so it is. We call into A&E. The early evening drunks and drug addicts are fighting it out among themselves and the medical staff as we enter. Security men and nurses in turn trying to calm things down. A nurse directs us to the rear of the unit. To a trolley surrounded by a curtain. And there he is. He's dead alright. I've seen enough dead people to know immediately. There are some electrodes still attached to his chest. Some wrappers scattered around the floor underneath him.

My sisters arrive. One of them raises his eyelids, which are half-closed, to have 'one last look' into his eyes. I can't look and turn away. I'm half-afraid he'll shout at me, one last time. 'THOMAS.' But he doesn't say anything. He is eerily, uncharacteristically quiet. That's what I'm thinking of when the hospital chaplain enters. Like the nurse, he is also from Nigeria. He pauses dramatically in front of my dad and looks around at us. He counts us out loud, jabbing with his index finger. 'One, two, three, four, my goodness, five, six, my goodness.' Everyone gets counted, including sons- and daughters-in-law. 'Eight children. This man has brought eight children into the world.' He squints at the name tag on my dad's chart. 'Eugene. Clonan. What a man. What a father.' He looks at each of us. 'Don't be sad. Don't cry for Eugene. Let us celebrate his life. What a life.'

The priest then says a quick 'Our Father' and a few 'Hail Mary's. He then shepherds everyone into the back for a strong cup of tea. He emphasises the point. 'What we all need now is a good cup of tea.' He's right.

As the dust settles, two gardaí arrive. A young garda and an older garda. The older guy introduces himself. 'Sorry to disturb you. Deepest sympathy on your loss. I'm from Fitzgibbon Street Garda station and, I'm sorry about this, but, since your dad was brought here by ambulance, and since he wasn't admitted here, I need someone to formally identify the body.'

I've seen this in the movies so many times, I immediately volunteer for the job. 'Can you identify the body, sir?' Anyhow, the atmosphere in the tea room is becoming a bit too funereal. Too much weeping and gnashing of teeth. Aideen comes with me for 'some fresh air'. Even though we are going to the morgue.

The older garda tells me in a monotone that I need to prepare myself before I see my dad's body. 'Thomas, your dad may look a little different in death than he did in life.' I'm impressed. This is obviously something they are teaching in Templemore, the garda training college. My dad would probably be less impressed. He was the type of garda who was inclined towards bluntness. I'm enjoying this so much, I don't point out to the older garda that I've just seen my dad laid out in A&E, not thirty minutes ago, with my sisters keening over him. The young garda is watching and listening. Some on-the-job training going on here.

I mention to the gardaí that my dad was a member of the force also. They both stop dead in their tracks. The older man looks at me with renewed interest. 'Where did he serve?' 'Store Street, Pearse Street,' I answer him. 'He was always in Dublin.' The older guy repeats my dad's name over and over. 'Eugene Clonan, Eugene Clonan.' He then looks at me like he's been struck by lightning. 'Oh, you mean Gene Clonan! We all know Gene!' I get a sudden flash of insight into a man I never knew. 'Gene.' I feel a stab of unanticipated pain. I really feel sorry now that I never got to call him 'Gene'. I'll never get to recall him in this informal, familiar, affectionate way. Maybe 'Gene' was the kind of dad I could have hugged from time to time. For the first time in the whole sorry evening, I realise that my dad is dead. Gone forever. 'Gene.' Smoking somewhere, no doubt; out there in the great wherever.

We stop outside the morgue and the older garda recomposes himself. 'Remember, Thomas, take your time. He may look . . .' I finish the sentence, 'Different in death.' 'Yes, that's it. No rush, Thomas. Take your time.' We go into the morgue. There is a large woman laid out in front of us. The sheet is neatly folded over her chest to reveal her white face. Her hair parted in the middle. The morgue attendant looks at me expectantly. The older garda gains control of the situation immediately. 'Eugene Clonan. Male. Seventy, eh, seventy-seven.'

The attendant apologises immediately and covers up the woman's face. He fusses about a bit and checks under the sheet of another trolley. He clears his throat. I almost expect a drum roll as he lifts the sheet. It is 'Gene' alright. But, in the forty or so minutes since I've last seen him, he has changed colour. He is now green. A purple tinge also. Very odd. I hear a sigh behind me and turn around just in time to see the older garda catch the younger garda who is in the process of fainting.

We get the younger garda sitting down. Aideen tells him to put his head between his knees. He apologises over and over. We tell him not to worry. I know for a fact that my dad would have loved this. He would have had a lot to say about this little drama.

The younger garda recovers somewhat and looks at me. 'Do you mind me asking?' He looks directly at me, deliberately avoiding the temptation to have another look at the green corpse on the trolley that was once my dad. 'What did he die of?'

'Cigarettes,' is my answer. He was the colour of a box of twenty Major in the end.

June 2009

A few months after my dad's passing, I am in our old house tidying things away. We take turns in emptying our home of all of my mum and dad's possessions. They threw nothing out. It is like a time machine. I find my dad's swimming togs. His infamous orange togs. He thought he looked like Tarzan in them. We kids did too. They were the same swimming togs he wore throughout my childhood. And here they are, wrapped up in a towel, ready to go. For a swim. He was optimistic.

I go through his precious 'bureau.' This was his so-called office. In reality, it was a shelf unit with a drop-down door. I open the door and find his old cheque books and various receipts and bits and pieces. Some of the stubs and tickets date back to the 1970s. And then, in amongst all of the letters and forms, I find a stack of newspaper articles. They have been carefully cut out of the *Irish Times* and neatly kept in order. Some of the edges are ragged as his hands were crippled with rheumatoid arthritis. They are my articles. From the *Irish Times*. He has kept them together with a big paper clip.

My turn to cry. I wish I'd found them when he was alive. I'd like to have thanked him for keeping them. Maybe even hugged him – like Pauline did, before she shuffled off her mortal coil. Or something. Anything. It is the first time I've cried since my dad passed away. I think I can hear him, out there in the great, vast, nothing. 'THOMAS.'

Chapter 39

Postscript

'Will he eat my penguin?'

The Global War on Terror
Dublin, 2009

Beginnings and endings. On the day that I bury my mum, the United States invade Iraq. I imagine her at the gates of heaven, presumably in an orderly queue of elderly ladies, suddenly joined by thousands of Iraqis. All scratching their heads at the term 'Shock and Awe'. The day I bury my dad, President Obama declares an end to the Global War on Terror. After almost a decade of fighting and over one million dead – direct and indirect casualties of the war – the US rebrands the conflict.

On the day that my dad is buried, the US redesignates the Global War on Terror as 'The Overseas Contingency Operation'. In the vernacular of acronyms, so beloved of the US military, GWOT is replaced by OCO. I imagine Osama Bin Laden's text message to Ayman al Zawahiri. 'GWOT is over. OCO is begun. OMG. WTF?'

The fighting continues, however. The United States Central Command continues to oversee military operations in Operation Enduring Freedom, Afghanistan. In less well-publicised initiatives, the US military open more fronts in their global war. Africa Command or AfriCom oversees Operation Enduring Freedom, Horn of Africa and Operation Enduring Freedom Trans Sahara. US troops are also deployed on Operation Enduring Freedom, Philippines.

United States Europe Command or EuCom continues to coordinate the movement of US troops to these wars on multiple continents through Shannon Airport in County Clare. Ireland remains at the heart of the Global War on Terror.

In addition to these developments, the US military has identified the Asia Pacific region as the next major 'Theatre of Conflict'. The US has established permanent military bases on Australian territories for the first time since World War II. The US is now squaring up to the emerging military prowess of China in the competition for resources in the Asia Pacific region and in the South China Sea. Russia, India and other power blocs are also flexing their muscles. I suspect there will be plenty of work for security analysts in the international media for decades to come.

In parallel with the evolution of the Global War on Terror, there have been significant, groundbreaking medical and technological advances; many directly attributable to the conflict. Due to the proliferation of battlefield polytrauma and traumatic brain injury, there have been game-changing developments in the scanning and treatment of neuromuscular injuries. There have been similar significant developments in stem cell research and gene therapies for brain and nerve trauma. I hope and pray that Eoghan and others like him around the world might benefit in some way from this bleak decade of global asymmetrical warfare.

In September 2001, the United States military possessed a mere sixty Unmanned Aerial Vehicles, UAVs or 'drones'. As I write, the US military and security establishment operate over ten thousand drones worldwide. President Obama has personally endorsed and expanded the drone warfare programme. Extrajudicial killings and assassination by Drone are now routinely carried out in Afghanistan, Pakistan, Yemen and throughout trans-Saharan Africa. Conservative estimates put the international death toll from drone strikes at around 3,500. At least 15 percent of the dead are innocent men, women and children. The drone program is sowing dark seeds of hatred worldwide. The United States and its allies, Ireland included, will yield a bitter harvest from this form of warfare.

The Local War on Terror
'Man harnesses dog. For many purposes.'
Belfast, 1986

I remember a visit to Belfast in 1986. This is my first experience of a working dog. British soldiers are waiting at Great Victoria Street Station. The soldiers cradle rifles in the low-port position. One of them, rifle slung to the rear, handles a cocker spaniel. The dog, tail wagging furiously, sniffs our bags as we file past the British soldiers on the platform. Sniffing for explosives. Semtex, the explosive of choice for terrorists in the 1970s and 1980s. Over the years, working dogs are constantly in the background. I see them, in my peripheral vision, at airports and at ferry ports.

When I become a soldier myself, my working life intersects with dogs. Occasionally we shoot at wild dogs in Lebanon – Wadi-dogs, we call them. We fire at them when they get too close. They are feral, some rabid. They keep their distance.

Through binoculars, I see trained dogs. German shepherds working with Israeli soldiers on IDF patrols. I watch as black and tan Alsatians race ahead of the Israeli troops. Slowing to a trot as they enter the olive groves. Then halting. Sniffing the air for improvised explosive devices. Some are trained to sniff out people. Usually dead or dying at this point. Hizbullah fighters, or injured civilians. The dogs seek them out and point. The soldiers follow cautiously and call encouragement to the dogs.

I've seen Israeli dogs with missing limbs. Forepaw wrapped in a tight white bandage. Or the stump of a leg poised as they move ahead of an Israeli patrol. A Lebanese version of 'One man and his dog.' No sheep here though. No pens to corral them in. Just olive groves, scrub and bodies in the wadis.

On the return trip to the Israeli firebases, the long walk back up the slopes, the dogs are excited. They race forward in bounds. Ears back. Tails wagging as they skirt back and greet their handlers, over and over. The soldiers weave their way back into cover. Seeking out dead ground. Constantly moving. The dogs gambol alongside. Tongues lolling. Enjoying the game. Occasionally, a hand moves from weapon or trigger-guard to pat dog's head. Dog is delighted.

Crouches on hindquarters, licks hand, runs forward. Man and dog working together.

All through the Global War on Terror, I notice working dogs in the background. Attack dogs in Abu Ghraib. Dogs in Guantanamo. Dogs on the perimeter fence in Ramstein and at Landstuhl in Germany.

We are driving through the Jack Lynch tunnel in Cork when I see a van. 'Irish Dogs for the Disabled' is printed on the side. There is an image of a child on a wheelchair. Beside the child is a dog. A working dog. After all those years of looking at working dogs in airports and in conflict zones, it had never occurred to me that a dog might work with Eoghan.

We call the number on the side of the van. Jennie Dowler answers the phone. I describe Eoghan's neuromuscular disease. Jennie tells me he might benefit from an assistance dog. He'll need to be assessed. Later, we download an application form and email it to the charity. Irish Dogs for the Disabled receive no state funding whatsoever. We go on a waiting list.

Two years later, Eoghan and I go for the crucial assessment at the charity's offices, near Blarney in County Cork. It is December and there is snow on the ground. It is a long drive. Eoghan is lost in thought. 'Will he eat my penguin?' he asks. I reassure him that the dog won't eat him or his woollen penguin. Myself and Eoghan arrive at Fiddler's Brook as sleet begins to fall. I lift Eoghan out of the car and we are greeted by Duke. Duke is a Golden Retriever. His tail wags furiously. His ears go back. Duke ignores me. Tail and hind quarters wagging, Duke pushes his wet nose into Eoghan's face. Eoghan's arms reach out instinctively and grip Duke the dog in embrace. A partnership is born.

After an initial assessment, Jenny embarks on an intensive program of training with Duke that is tailored to Eoghan's specific needs. We return to Fiddler's Brook in June. In the summer sunshine, Eoghan learns how to handle Duke. Eoghan learns the commands, prompts and rewards that will cement his relationship with Duke. Eoghan's voice improves in pitch and volume. Eoghan's self-esteem swells. He is giddy with excitement in Duke's company. He literally trembles.

Physically, Duke completes a number of tasks with Eoghan. He is trained to help Eoghan with dressing and undressing. As Eoghan undresses, Duke grips the waistband or legs of his trousers and helps to pull them down over his knees. As Eoghan giggles, Duke grips the toes of Eoghan's socks and pulls them off. The sock trick is preceded by a little gentle gnawing as Duke's teeth work their way gently between cotton cloth and Eoghan's toes in order to get a grip. This is a tickly experience for Eoghan. Dog growls. Eoghan squeals. Socks are pulled clean off.

Eoghan can dress independently with Duke's help. Duke opens doors for Eoghan as he navigates his way around the house and other buildings. Duke is also a stability dog. As Eoghan levers and eases himself out of his wheelchair, Duke instinctively pushes in against him. Duke is 37kg of lean muscle. Eoghan grips his back and shoulders and eases down to the floor. He is rewarded with a series of licks and wet sniffs. It is natural physiotherapy.

Emotionally, there is alchemy between dog and boy. Eoghan sleeps downstairs in a converted bedroom. Duke sleeps on the floor beside him. Dog and small boy keep each other company during the long winter nights. Eoghan tells me that he prefers being on his own with Duke. Eoghan tells me that he cannot wait until his power chair arrives. He and Duke will go on 'adventures'. Far beyond our house and garden. Eoghan tells us that he and Duke will go on their own.

When Eoghan is out and about with Duke, people no longer see the wheelchair. They only see a boy and his dog. People approach Eoghan and engage him in conversation. Eoghan has hundreds of social interactions that he might otherwise not have had. For whilst people are very positive about disability – many are shy, afraid to say the wrong thing to a small boy in a wheelchair. Duke breaks down all those barriers. Duke opens the door to an infinite number of possibilities for Eoghan.

Eoghan's power chair arrives. It is bright red. Eoghan passes his 'driving test' and he and Duke head out the door. Aideen and I watch as he disappears out of the garden. Eoghan looks back once or twice. Duke is all ears and wagging tail as they move further up the street. They eventually disappear around the corner. Eoghan is gone. His journey begun. A small step for your average eleven-year-old boy and his dog, a giant leap for Eoghan and Duke.

My own journey over the last decade or so has taught me about the goodness in people. It has also taught me, sadly, about the propensity for evil among small, but vocal, self-selecting cohorts of individuals. The US military have a quaint term for such people. They call them 'assholes'. I like the term. These are the psychopaths and sociopaths who put personal status and ambition ahead of respect for others. These are the business, media and political leaders who allow the psychopaths and sociopaths among them to dominate and shape the political economy toward ego, power and self-aggrandisement. In such a false polity, wrong-doers are rewarded. Those who strive to do the right thing are punished. No nation or ethnic group seem to have a monopoly on this dynamic. The universal phenomena of greed and hatred underpins all economic strife and global conflict.

The Global War on Terror, with millions dead and displaced at a cost of trillions of dollars, is an abiding legacy of the neoconservative policies of George W. Bush and his cronies. The neocons also brought us light-touch regulation and unbridled global capitalism. These twin pillars of the neoconservative mindset have spawned human suffering on a global scale and financial collapse and austerity worldwide. Ireland has played a central role in exporting the former and has lost its financial and political sovereignty to the latter.

The so-called Celtic Tiger and the ensuing ideologically driven austerity program have made Ireland a divided, more brutal society. Sadly, many 'assholes' have been emboldened in the process. In this perfect storm, the disabled, the most vulnerable of our citizens, are the hardest hit. Eoghan will need all the luck, help and kindness that he can get as he comes of age in Ireland's battered and bruised republic.

However, Eoghan also has plenty of guardian angels as he embarks on his life's journey. Above all, he has Duke – the Superdog – on his side.